Children, the Law and the Welfare Principle

This book continues the themes addressed by its two predecessors in this mini-series by examining the role of the principle of the welfare interests of the child in the law of the U.S. and Canada. It provides a record of the key milestones in its development in each country and conducts a comparative analysis of the contemporary law relating to children in both. In doing so, it focuses also on the Indigenous communities – the AN/AI and the First Nations – of the U.S. and Canada respectively.

By identifying and analysing the functions of the principle in the public (care, protection and control, etc), private (matrimonial, adoption, etc) and hybrid (adoption from care, surrogacy, etc) sectors of family law, it builds a picture of the law relating to children in the two countries and reveals significant jurisdictional differences. By examining the legislation and related caselaw, it assesses the different effects of the same legal framework on the welfare of Indigenous and other children.

In addition to a digest of cases and legislation that identifies and tracks the role of this legal principle, lawyers, academics and other researchers will find a wealth of information on how it has evolved to reflect corresponding changes in social mores. For those interested in politics and social policy, there is much illuminating evidence of how the law has balanced this principle relative to others in both civil and criminal contexts.

Kerry O'Halloran – a professionally qualified lawyer, social worker and academic – has recently retired from 13 years as an adjunct professor at the Australian Centre for Philanthropy and Nonprofit Studies at QUT, Brisbane. In Northern Ireland, he served on the Social Care Tribunal and on an HSS Trust adoption panel, has advised the Irish government on law reform matters, and has served in a consultancy capacity on government bodies such as Courts Services (Northern Ireland) and to the Open University in England. Previously employed as Assistant Director (Research) at the Centre for Voluntary Action, University of Ulster in Northern Ireland, his 30 books and many other publications include *Conscientious Objection* (Springer, 2022), *The Politics of Adoption*, 4th ed. (Springer, 2021), *Adoption Law and Human Rights: International Perspectives* (Routledge, 2018), *Religion, Charity and Human Rights* (CUP, 2014) and *Child Care and Protection: The Law & Practice in Northern Ireland* (Thomson Reuters, 2003).

Children and the Law

The Principle of the Welfare of the Child
A History
Kerry O'Halloran

Children, the Law and the Welfare Principle
Perspectives from North America
Kerry O'Halloran

For more information about this series, please visit: Children and the Law: From Welfare to Rights – Book Series – Routledge & CRC Press

Children, the Law and the Welfare Principle

Perspectives from North America

Kerry O'Halloran

Routledge
Taylor & Francis Group
LONDON AND NEW YORK

First published 2023
by Routledge
4 Park Square, Milton Park, Abingdon, Oxon OX14 4RN

and by Routledge
605 Third Avenue, New York, NY 10158

Routledge is an imprint of the Taylor & Francis Group, an informa business

British Library Cataloguing-in-Publication Data
A catalogue record for this book is available from the British Library

ISBN: 978-1-032-21689-8 (hbk)
ISBN: 978-1-032-21690-4 (pbk)
ISBN: 978-1-003-26956-4 (ebk)

DOI: 10.4324/9781003269564

Typeset in Times New Roman
by Apex CoVantage, LLC

To
Elizabeth

Contents

Acknowledgements

This book owes much to the groundwork laid in earlier publications, including *The Welfare of the Child: the Principle and the Law*;[1] *The Politics of Adoption*,[2] *Child Care and Protection: The Law & Practice in Northern Ireland*;[3] and my earlier contributions[4] to this series.[5] Given the not-dissimilar subject matter and related caselaw, focused on many of the same jurisdictions, there is inevitably some degree of overlap, and I thank the publishers concerned for their understanding.

There were many who contributed along the way to making this a better book. Particular thanks are due to those who offered comment on draft chapters or related text, particularly Lori Chambers[6] (Canada), Diane Kunz[7] (U.S.) and Hadley Friedland[8] (Indigenous communities). Their encouragement, support and advice have meant a lot, and this book and its author would have suffered without them.

I am very thankful to Routledge, particularly Siobhán Poole,[9] for commissioning the book and the series. Responsibility for any mistakes, inconsistencies or other faults, and for all views expressed, must, unfortunately, rest wholly with me.

1 Aldershot, Arena/Ashgate Publications, (1999).

2 *The Politics of Adoption: International Perspectives on Law, Policy & Practice* (4th ed.), Springer, (2021).

3 Dublin, Thomson Round Hall, (2003).

4 *The Principle of the Welfare of the Child: A History*, Routledge 2022, and *Children & the Law: Shaping the Modern Welfare Principle in the British Isles*, Routledge, (2023).

5 Series, Children & the Law (forthcoming titles: *Children, the Law and the Welfare Principle: Perspectives from Australia and New Zealand*, (2023); *European Perspectives on Child Welfare and Rights*, (2025); and *Child Welfare and Rights: A Contemporary Family Law Analysis*, (2026), 2022–26.

6 Lori Chambers, Professor and Chair, Gender and Women's Studies, Department of Women's Studies, Lockhead University, Thunder Bay, Ontario, Canada.

7 Counsel to Rumbold & Seidelman and Executive Director of the Center for Adoption Policy, New York, U.S.A.

8 Associate Professor, Faculty of Law, Academic Director, Wahkohtowin Law and Governance Lodge, Edmonton, Canada.

9 Commissioning Editor, Routledge Law Research.

Introduction

The U.S. and Canada are at the forefront of developed Western nations. However, within their national boundaries – hiding in plain sight – are Indigenous communities living in 'third world' conditions that co-exist alongside and in an uneasy relationship with the prevailing Western culture: sharing time, territory and the necessities of life but often very little in the way of values, knowledge and social infrastructure.[1] This book – the third in a series – examines and differentiates between the U.S. and Canada and their respective Indigenous communities, in relation to the varying ways in which their laws address the welfare and rights of children.

The welfare of a child is not assured in either the U.S. or Canada. Both countries may be positioned as world leaders in terms of GDP,[2] but in terms of child well-being, the indicators suggest a ranking wholly at variance with their economic success. For example, in 2020, the U.S. infant mortality rate was 5.4 deaths per 1,000 live births, placing that country 30th out of 33 OECD countries, while in terms of maternal mortality, it came last with a rate (17 out of every 100,000 live births) which was double that of most other developed nations.[3] In Canada, the rate for 2020 was 4.25 deaths, ranking Canada as 16th out of 17 countries, while its maternal mortality rate (3.7 out of every 100,000 live births) was considerably higher than in most of Europe.[4] These figures are important because, arguably, there is no more seminal indicator of a nation's regard for the welfare of its children than the investment it makes to ensure they have a safe start in life. Given their national

1 See, further, U.N. Department of Economic and Social Affairs, State of the World's Indigenous Peoples: Indigenous Peoples' Access to Health Services, United Nations, (2016).

2 As of 2022, the U.S. was the world leader, accounting for almost 40% of total global GDP; Canada is ranked the world's tenth-largest economy. See, further, at https://worldpopulationreview.com/countries/countries-by-gdp.

3 See, further, Chen, A, Oster, E and Williams, H., Why is Infant Mortality Higher in the United States Than in Europe?, *Am Econ J Econ Policy*, (2016): 8(2), 89–124 and at www.commonwealthfund.org/publications/issue-brief-report/2020/dec/maternal-mortality-united-states-primer.

4 It may be that such death rates are linked to the fact that these countries have the lowest overall supply of midwives, obstetricians/gynecologists: 12 and 15 providers per 1,000 live births respectively. Other countries have a supply that is between two and six times greater. See, further, at www.ajmc.com/view/us-ranks-worst-in-maternal-care-mortality-compared-with-10-other-developed-nations.

DOI: 10.4324/9781003269564-1

wealth and obvious capacity to do better, it has to be asked – why do some of the richest countries on earth perform so much worse than many of the poorest in relation to matters of such fundamental importance to the welfare of children?

The answer may lie partly in political ideology. Both countries share a democratic liberalism, though this is more emphatic in the U.S., that draws a firmer line between public and private than would be the case in the U.K. and in many other European nations. As much as possible, the state leaves responsibility for matters affecting the personal life of its citizens to lie where it falls. In no area has this been clearer than in health and social care: 'user pays' has been the state's traditional approach to this and other aspects of public benefit service provision. Ensuring that basic social infrastructure is in place is state business; accessing it – subject to regulatory standards – is a matter for users to negotiate. In most free market of economies, it may be that there are not enough midwives, obstetricians or gynaecologists available where they are most needed – and where they would reduce infant and maternal mortality rates – because market forces dictate their distribution, and potential users simply cannot afford to access their services. State intervention in private family matters is at best hesitant, and their failure to invest in ensuring access to the services necessary to reduce those rates is perhaps symptomatic of prevailing political values.

The answer may lie partly in cultural context also. It is more than probable that the extreme mortality rates shared by both countries is, at least to some extent, attributable to the disproportionate contribution made by their Indigenous communities. This may, in turn, be due to an embedded cultural disconnect between Indigenous people and public service providers who live parallel lives, leaving the latter unable or unwilling to fully appreciate the many distinctive strengths of the former, including community connectedness, breadth of family relationships and their different interpretations of what constitutes child welfare. Moreover, the history of brutalising state intervention in the form of residential schools and enforced adoption must act as a constraint on the current willingness of those communities to seek and to receive assistance from public service providers.

Poverty, in either case, plays its own characteristic role of reducing coping capacity, leaving those afflicted more vulnerable and less able to access resources, and it ultimately causes most harm to the welfare of children. In both countries – but again, more so in the U.S. – the degree of wealth disparity between rich and poor has become much more acute in recent years, which in itself is now a factor that adds to the likelihood of perceived parental failure with consequent adverse effects on the welfare of many children, particularly those belonging to Indigenous communities where the levels of poverty are greatest.

Although the differences between the Indigenous and non-Indigenous sectors of the population in both countries are intriguing, as are the resulting implications for the welfare of their children, this should not distract from recognising that statutory domestic law and ratified international law are equally binding on the circumstances of all children. It is that legal framework and the accompanying caselaw – as it applies to the welfare of both Indigenous and non-Indigenous children – that remain the primary focus of this book.

Children, the Law and the Welfare Principle: Perspectives from North America is in five parts and continues the work of its two predecessors.[5] Its purpose is to explain how the law relates to children in both the U.S. and Canada, identify characteristic jurisdictional differences, and identify and assess the differences between the impact of the national legal system on Indigenous and non-Indigenous children and the Indigenous communities in both countries. It employs the template of themes previously identified to explore areas of difference and commonality in the relevant law and the role therein of the welfare principle, as applied to the U.S. and Canada.

Part 1 – Concepts, constructs and cultural context – begins the book with Chapter 1, under the same title, which considers concepts that have a crucial if varying application to both countries, such as 'sovereignty' and 'federalism.' It identifies and assesses the policies and organisations that, in the 19th century, prepared the ground for legislation which thereafter structured state intervention on child welfare grounds in Indigenous and non-Indigenous communities. In so doing, it provides an explanatory preamble to the following core section of the book.

Part II – The United States of America – is in three chapters. Chapter 2, Policy, principles, legislation and courts, outlines the framework of legislation, courts, and regulatory bodies, both domestic and international, which define the role and functions of the principle of the welfare interests of the child. Chapter 3, The welfare principle in contemporary practice: Public family law, civil and criminal jurisdictions– profiles the contemporary application of the law in that country as it relates to public family law, both civil (child protection, etc) and criminal (juvenile justice, etc). Chapter 4, The welfare principle in contemporary practice: Private family law and hybrid provisions, deals in the same way with private family law (adoption, divorce, etc) and with an emerging hybrid public/private sector (adoption from the public care system, surrogacy, restraining orders, etc).

Part III – Canada – again in three chapters (5, 6 and 7) repeats the Part II template in an examination of the law as it relates to the welfare of Canadian children. The same chapter structure focuses the material into similar blocks to facilitate a comparative jurisdictional analysis through the use of a fixed menu of welfare indicators.

Part IV – The Indigenous children of North America – is in one chapter. Chapter 8, Americans/Indians[6] and the First Nations/Inuit, begins with an outline of the legal framework specific to Indigenous people and continues by identifying the characteristics that differentiate the Indigenous and non-Indigenous populations

5 O'Halloran, K., *The Principle of the Welfare of the Child: A History*, Routledge, (2022), and *Children & the Law: Shaping the Modern Welfare Principle in the British Isles*, Routledge, (2023).

6 'American Indian' is used throughout in preference to 'Native American' as it is the author's understanding that it is more respectful. Sincere apologies are offered in the event of this causing any inadvertent offence.

that co-exist on the main landmass of North America: in the U.S., the American Indian/Alaskan Native (AI/AN) communities and in Canada, the First Nations, Métis and Inuit communities. It then applies much the same template as used in previous chapters to identify the differences between the functions and effects of the legal system on Indigenous and non-Indigenous communities and to consider their significance for the welfare/rights of children in terms of law, policy and practice.

Part V – Themes and a comparative jurisdictional analysis – again in one chapter and under the same title identifies jurisdictional differences in the law and the functions of the welfare principle as applied generally to child welfare issues in the U.S. and Canada, particularly to those issues in an Indigenous context. It conducts a comparative analysis of the significance of such jurisdictional differences.

The conclusion closes the book, as did its predecessor, by benchmarking the distinctive characteristics and primary jurisdictional differences against the principles established by the Convention on the Rights of the Child 1989.

Part I

Background

1 Concepts, constructs and cultural context

Introduction

This introductory chapter begins by considering some concepts and social constructs common to both the U.S. and Canada which are critical to an understanding of jurisdictional differences. It identifies the religious organisations, charities and other voluntary organisations, existing before the introduction of public services for children, which contributed towards building local and national safety nets for those in need of care and protection. It reflects on the policies that initiated care arrangements for children abandoned, neglected, or abused by their parents in North America: policies that laid the foundations for the contemporary mix of public and private arrangements and, in particular, structured a differentiated approach to the well-being of Indigenous and non-Indigenous children.

From the outset, the links between Great Britain and its North American colonies did much to shape subsequent developments. The colonial power did not just transfer cultural hallmarks, including language, the common law, Christianity with its denominational organisations and a legislative/judicial model of governance.[1] It also transferred an administrative system, formed during the Poor Laws era, for responding to the needs of the poor and destitute and to the welfare of the many abandoned children who burdened its cities and taxes. Not least, it transferred tens of thousands of its own children.

The chapter concludes with an examination of the residential schooling and enforced adoption policies that were common to the experience of Indigenous children in both the U.S. and Canada. It closes with a brief summation of the broad impact that the colonial cultural heritage has had on the evolving approach to child welfare in North America.

Concepts and constructs

The U.S. and Canada have much in common, but perhaps nothing is more significant than their shared history as colonies of the British Empire. Other empires – the Spanish and French – also left their mark, but it was primarily the enduring

1 See O'Halloran, K., *The Principle of the Welfare of the Child: A History*, Routledge, (2022).

DOI: 10.4324/9781003269564-3

influence of British legal, institutional and administrative systems that laid the foundations for the development of two very similar but distinctively different nations.

Colonialism

Unlike other former colonies – India, Pakistan, Ireland, etc – with established cultures imparting a unifying sense of identity that remained relatively intact, if suppressed, under an imposed veneer of imperial authority, the experience of colonisation in North America was more of a holistic transplant of British culture and institutional infrastructure. In North America, as in Australia and, to a lesser extent, New Zealand, the disparate and mainly nomadic tribes had no national institutional structures to organise their societies. There was, therefore, nothing to stop the colonial power from filling that space with its own well-developed cultural, legal and political institutions. In short, colonial penetration – and with it, a body of family law including the law relating to children – became much more deeply rooted in those countries than elsewhere.

Colonialism in North America

When the British Empire imposed control over most of North America, it also imposed its laws (common law and a great deal of statute law), modes of governance, and administrative machinery and a dense culture that included language, religion, religiously based values and many other facets of what, at that time, constituted civilised British life.[2] Other nations also competed for territorial control and cultural input, including Spain and France, the latter of which succeeded in stamping its language, culture and civil law enduringly on a large section of Canada.

The natural affinity between the North American colonies and between each of them and Great Britain was never very deep and has, arguably, grown less so over time. This is due partly to differences in the accommodations the colonies reached with their respective Indigenous populations, with rival colonial powers and with successive waves of immigrants. They also, on gaining independence, developed into societies that differed in important respects from each other and from the former imperial power: the U.S. having a degree of federal over-reach, becoming a competitive 'free-market' economy with minimum state regulatory intervention, scaled-back welfare and public benefit provision, a 'melting pot' approach to cultural assimilation, and ever-hardening religion-based 'class war' divisions, while Canada, with its weaker federal authority, espoused multiculturalism and some government commitment to public benefit provision, in health care anyway, and continued its bilingual and bijural administrative systems; the law in both countries became increasingly human rights oriented and subject to ongoing testing for constitutional compliance.

2 Ibid at Chapter 1.

EFFECTS OF COLONISATION

Oppression and subjugation of the tribes, suppression of their culture, and ownership or despoiling of their lands (mainly through mining, forestry and farming), social marginalisation and high levels of poverty, have been among the common consequences of colonialism for Indigenous people.

Indigenous

Indigenous people have been defined by the U.N. as the 'inheritors and practitioners of unique cultures and ways of relating to people and the environment' who 'have retained social, cultural, economic and political characteristics that are distinct from those of the dominant societies in which they live'[3] and in the ILO Convention as:

> peoples in independent countries who are regarded as Indigenous on account of their descent from the populations which inhabited the country, or a geographical region to which the country belongs, at the time of conquest or colonisation or the establishment of present state boundaries and who, irrespective of their legal status, retain some or all of their own social, economic, cultural and political institutions.[4]

In practice, there is a continuing degree of uncertainty surrounding the definition of an Indigenous tribe or person in North America. For most legal purposes, a community of Indigenous persons constitute a tribe if registered as such with the federal authorities: in the U.S., 574 are so registered; in Canada, there are at least 630. Some are not registered federally but are registered or known to state/provincial authorities, and many communities are, in fact, 'bands' rather than tribes. Again, for most legal purposes, an Indigenous person is someone who self-identifies as such and who is accepted by a tribe or community as a member. However, in many cases, a person will not be accepted as a member unless they can prove they have a reasonably direct blood relationship – the quantum varies – to an already-accepted member (see, further, Chapter 4).

Sovereignty

The supreme and autonomous authority of any entity, and the extent of that sovereignty, can only be verified through challenge as wars have demonstrated and as many despots and nation-states have discovered. An assertion of sovereignty or a conferring of that status requires reciprocal recognition. It may be tightly

3 See Indigenous Peoples at the United Nations: https://www.un.org/development/desa/indigenouspeoples/about-us.html.

4 See the ILO Convention concerning Indigenous and Tribal Peoples in Independent Countries 1989, Article 1b.

circumscribed, but, if validated internally and externally by the acceptance and compliance of others, then an entity may be taken to be vested with sovereignty within its chosen terms of reference. On the other hand, an entity may believe it has sovereignty, and relevant others may provide assurance that that is the case, but in practice, some aspects of its treatment by those others may indicate that sovereignty is little more than a chimera.

Tribal sovereignty: Canada

Initial governmental efforts to legislate the relationship between the state and the Indigenous people – the Royal Proclamation 1763 – were chiefly concerned with establishing colonial authority: the state would assume a protective paternalistic role towards the tribes; the latter would surrender much of their land and would become 'one people' with the white Caucasian settlers. The 1763 provisions were essentially endorsed two centuries later in section 25 of the Constitution Act 1982, which stated that the charter should not be construed so as to abrogate or derogate from previous treaties.[5] In *R. v. Sparrow*,[6] the SCC examined the extent of the rights of Indigenous people and concluded that they comprised a range of cultural, social, political and economic rights, including land rights, hunting and fishing rights, and the right to practise one's own culture but could not include any rights that had been extinguished by the federal government prior to 1982. This '*Sparrow* test' indicates that Canada's federal government may infringe upon any protected right so long as the infringement serves a 'valid legislative objective' and is tailored to serve that objective, and both fair compensation and notice are provided. Then, in *R. v. Pamajewon*,[7] the SCC noted that Canada's Constitution Act of 1982 recognises certain Indigenous rights tied to the traditions and customs of First Nations and that, in order to qualify as an Indigenous right, an activity must be 'a defining feature of the culture in question.'

Tribal sovereignty: U.S.

Tribal sovereignty refers to the right of American Indians and Alaskan Natives to self-government. In the early decades of the 19th century, the U.S. Constitution recognised Indian tribes as distinct governments and established that they had, with a few exceptions, the same powers as federal and state governments to regulate their internal affairs. More than a century was to pass before, in *Fisher v. District Court of Rosebud County*,[8] it extended recognition to tribal authority in child placement cases in which all parties were members of the tribe and resided on the tribe's reservation. A decade later, in the landmark case of *California v. Cabazon Band of Mission Indians*,[9] the USSC stated: 'the Court has consistently recognized

5 *Tsilhqot'in Nation v. British Columbia* [2014] S.C.J. No. 44, [2014] 2 S.C.R. 257 (S.C.C.) and *Delgamuukw v. British Columbia* [1997] S.C.J. No. 108, [1997] 3 S.C.R. 1010 (S.C.C.).

6 [1990] 1 S.C.R. 1075.

7 [1996] 2 S.C.R. 821.

8 424 U.S. 383 (1976).

9 480 U.S. 202 (1987).

that Indian tribes retain 'attributes of sovereignty over both their members and their territory,' and 'tribal sovereignty is dependent on, and subordinate to, only the Federal Government, not the States.'[10] Sovereignty for tribes was held to include the right to establish their own form of government, determine membership requirements, enact legislation and establish law enforcement and court systems.[11]

Nonetheless, in the intervening years, Congress has modified tribal sovereignty: Public Law 280, 1953, permitted certain specified states to assume a general criminal and some civil jurisdiction over Indian reservations within those states while allowing tribes to retain limited powers, and the Indian Child Welfare Act (ICWA) 1978 recognised limited tribal sovereignty in relation to the upbringing and welfare interests of children, and, by establishing mandatory protocols for state agencies and courts when dealing with Indian child custody matters, effectively created dual state/tribe jurisdictions. The fact that Congress is vested with plenary power to legislate in the field of Indian affairs was demonstrated in *Cotton Petrol. Corp. v. New Mexico*,[12] and indeed, Congress has exercised its authority to enact a multitude of federal statutes governing American Indian tribes and people.

TRIBAL SOVEREIGNTY: ITS SIGNIFICANCE

The Constitutions of Canada and the U.S.[13] make declarations regarding the sovereignty of their nations: indeed, a justification for the U.S. not accepting the jurisdiction of the International Criminal Court has been that to do so would be to compromise U.S. sovereignty; these same nations have, from time to time, made treaties with their respective Indigenous tribes grounded in each party's declaration of respect for the other's sovereignty. The sovereignty of the Indigenous tribes is, however, sourced differently: that of the AI/AN derives from treaties, the Constitution and federal recognition; that of their Canadian counterparts derives from those 'traditions' that have acquired the status of being a 'defining feature of the culture.' This would seem to place the AI/AN in a stronger position, but in both cases, federal actions indicate that the concept of 'tribal sovereignty' has been interpreted loosely by the authorities (and mainly interpreted in relation to land ownership). Arguably, as the federal government retains the power to abrogate Indigenous rights, neither the AI/AN nor their Canadian counterparts[14] have genuine sovereignty.

10 Ibid, citing *United States v. Mazurie*, 419 U.S. 544 (1975) and *Washington v. Confederated Tribes of Colville Indian Reservation*, 447 U.S. 134 (1980).

11 See: *Johnson v. McIntosh*, 21 U.S. (7 Wheat.) 543 (1823); *Cherokee Nation v. Georgia*, 30 U.S. (5 Pet.) 1 (1831); and *Worcester v. Georgia*, 31 U.S. 515. Also, much later, see, *Alaska v. Native Village of Venetie Tribal Gov't*, 101 F.3d 1286 (9th Cir. 1996).

12 490 U.S. 163, 192 (1989).

13 The Tenth Amendment states, 'The powers not delegated to the United States by the Constitution, nor prohibited by it to the States, are reserved to the States respectively, or to the people' while the Declaration of Independence sought to establish a government 'for the people, by the people' and thereby to vest sovereignty in them.

14 The Constitution Act of 1867, s 91(24), states: '[I]t is hereby declared that . . . the exclusive Legislative Authority of the Parliament of Canada extends to all Matters coming within the Classes of Subjects next hereinafter enumerated; that is to say, . . . Indians, and Lands reserved for the Indians.'

For present purposes, the reality or otherwise of tribal sovereignty has important implications for determining the welfare interests of Indigenous children: do tribal courts and processes automatically have jurisdiction for determining civil and criminal issues affecting those interests? If not, when and why does tribal jurisdiction give way to that of state/provincial courts, and, in practice, does this result in any meaningful difference between the U.S. and Canada as regards the way in which the law relates to Indigenous children?

Federalism

Federation is when a number of regional governments are loosely bound together into a democratic political system in which there is an agreed division of authority.[15] Both the main countries of North America are federalist states, with constitutions that govern their respective interpretations of 'federalism.' In the U.S., all powers not specifically granted to the federal government are retained by the states (Tenth Amendment), whereas the reverse is the case in Canada: powers not explicitly granted to the provincial governments are retained by the federal government. The differences in interpretation are important, with consequences that include an impact on the welfare of Indigenous children (see, further, Chapter 8).

The U.S.

This country has a propensity towards a strong centralised federal power, but that potential is mitigated by a bicameral division of political authority in which a pretty even balance between two strong rival political parties prevents either from securing a sufficient majority to control Congress and exercise federal authority to define the areas in which states may legislate. Federal government determines matters of national importance and interstate significance. States have jurisdiction in relation to family law, public health,[16] and criminal law matters. Any tendency towards developing a more unitary federal entity has been dissipated in recent years as some states demonstrate an increasing political willingness and capacity to steer legislative initiatives either towards or away from liberal social programmes centred around a nexus of issues that include those generated by the LGBT community and access to abortion. This has been reinforced by judicial rulings that the federal government cannot require states or state officials to adopt or enforce federal law,[17] and consequently states may – and increasingly do – legislate in noncompliance with federal laws,[18] though there is an argument that such initiatives violate the

15 See, for example Ziblatt, D., *Structuring the State: The Formation of Italy and Germany and the Puzzle of Federalism*, Princeton University Press, (2006).

16 *Jacobson v. Massachusetts*, 197 U.S. 11 (1905).

17 See *New York v. United States*, 505 U.S. 144 (1992) and *Murphy v. National Collegiate Athletic Association*, 504 U.S. _ (2018).

18 See *Gonzales v. Raich,* 545 U.S. 1 (2005); *Gonzales v. Carhart*, 550 U.S. 124 (2007); and *United States v. Lopez*, 514 U.S. 549 (1995).

'Supremacy Clause' in Article VI of the Constitution, which requires state law to give way to federal law when a conflict arises.[19] The more basic fact that states are free to legislate and interpret the meaning of that legislation – subject to it being constitutionally compliant – has been recognised for almost 150 years.[20]

Canada

Unlike the U.S., Canada is not a republic, and although the country became a sovereign state in 1931,[21] and the role of the Privy Council ceased in 1949, that of the Governor General continues, and the Regent of England retains their titular position as head of state. The Constitution Act 1867 is of central importance: s 91 lists the major federal parliament powers while s 92 lists those of the provincial governments. Matters reserved to the federal government include the power to determine criminal, marriage and divorce laws. Reserved to the provinces are such matters as the administration of justice, including organising the criminal courts and the police force, and the solemnisation of marriages. The Supreme Court of Canada (SCC) does not defer to province law in the same way that the USSC does to state law. Canada has more centralised judicial control of provincial law, and provincial courts have less of a separate sphere of authority than provincial legislatures do or than the state judicial system in the United States does. Moreover, the federal government 'may reject unsatisfactory provincial laws through its powers of reservation and disallowance . . . the provinces seem less supreme than the U.S. states.'[22]

The beginnings of organised care for abandoned, neglected and abused children

Professional residential care for children in need is of relatively recent origin. Up until the mid-20th century, unless they were taken in by relatives, fostered, or informally adopted, orphaned or abandoned children and those suffering from physical or mental disability could expect little more than 'warehousing' in institutions. Many children entered such facilities following the successful criminal prosecution of a parent for cruelty.[23]

19 As Justice Marshall put it in *McCulloch v. Maryland*, 17 U.S. (4 Wheat.) 316 (1819): 'States have no power, by taxation or otherwise, to retard, impede, burden, or in any manner control the operations of the Constitutional laws enacted by Congress to carry into execution the powers vested in the Federal Government.'

20 *Memphis v. Murdock*, 87 U.S. (20 Wallace) 590 (1875).

21 The Statute of Westminster 1931 reset the relationship between Great Britain and the commonwealth dominions. It granted Canada the freedom to pass, amend, and repeal laws within an autonomous legal system and full independence in relation to governing its foreign affairs.

22 See Field, M.A., The Differing Federalisms of Canada and the United States, *Law and Contemporary Problems*, (1992): 55(1), 107–120, at pp 119–120.

23 See, for example, *People v. Benson*, 6 Cal. 221, (1856). See, further, Myers, J., A Short History of Child Protection in America, at: https://us.sagepub.com/sites/default/files/upm-binaries/35363_Chapter1.pdf.

Service provision by religious organisations

From the mid-18th century to the middle of the 19th, children in need were dependent on the traditional but discretionary service provision of religious organisations (e.g. foundling hospitals) and on the very basic forms of institutional care provided by public authorities (shelters, orphanages, asylums, industrial schools and reformatories, etc). Whether orphaned, abandoned or with special needs, children were accommodated together, often sharing residential facilities with adults. Not until well into the 20th century did responsibility for basic health care generally pass to the state. In many instances, religious organisations continued their involvement in national health and social care and in providing a basic safety net for the destitute. Roman Catholic nuns – including the Sisters of Mercy and the Sisters of Saint Francis – founded, staffed and still continue to provide mother and baby units, hospitals and other facilities in the U.S., Canada, and elsewhere.

Foundling hospitals

Adopting the model first established in London in 1741,[24] foundling hospitals – providing care for abandoned infants often relinquished by impoverished unmarried mothers – were eventually introduced in the U.S. and Canada.

THE U.S.

A century after the founding of the Coram Foundling Hospital in London, such facilities were launched by Roman Catholic nuns in the U.S. The first was probably St. Vincent's Infant Asylum in Baltimore, opening in 1856, followed by the New York Foundling Hospital, established in 1869 by the Sisters of Charity. Over the past 150 years, the latter has evolved from a foundling hospital for abandoned children to a provider of comprehensive community support services, and it continues in the 21st century to serve its initial purpose of supporting the children and families of New York. In due course, similar hospitals, founded mostly by the Catholic Church or by private charities, spread across the U.S. These facilities were supported by a parish-based network of priests who identified suitable foster and adoptive homes across the country. From 1875 to 1914, foundling children were sent to such homes; by 1910, approximately 1,000 infants a year were being so placed.

CANADA

The history of foundling hospitals in Canada is somewhat obscure, partly because convents discreetly served that function under the auspices of what was then a powerful Catholic Church. This, for example, was the case with the convents of

24 Established in Bloomsbury, London, by the philanthropist Thomas Coram and continued under the auspices of the Coram Foundation which, three centuries later, is still funding the organisation's work with children.

Montreal and Québec, which, from the early 17th century, also functioned as the foundling hospitals for those cities. In 1875, the first large children's hospital was founded in Toronto, followed by the Montreal Children's Hospital in 1903 and the Winnipeg Children's Hospital in 1909.

Orphanages

Given the prevalence of diseases such as tuberculosis, smallpox and cholera, it is unsurprising that children were often bereft of parents. In such cases, and in the absence of extended family, the rudimentary care provided by an orphanage, almost always located in a city or urban area, was the only care option available. However, in fact, not all children so housed were orphans; many had one if not two live parents but were abandoned or relinquished due to poverty.

THE U.S.

Reputedly, the first orphanage in the United States was established in 1729 in Natchez, Mississippi, to care for the children of settlers orphaned as a result of the Indian Wars. Thereafter, such provision by philanthropists, charities, and religious organisations spread across the country: between 1830 and 1850, it is estimated that collectively, they established 56 orphanages in the U.S. alone.[25] The use of orphanages peaked during the years of the Great Depression and the two world wars, declining as the government and child-care workers adopted a policy favouring family-based rather than institution-based care for children.

The term 'orphanage' is a bit of a misnomer. For example, it was noted that:

> from 1847 to 1869, a review of the Protestant Orphan Asylum in St. Louis, Missouri, revealed that only twenty-seven percent of the children were full orphans. Sixty-nine per cent of the children had one parent, the other parent being deceased or absent.[26]

Moreover, the purpose of these facilities was not exclusively to provide a safe refuge for children in need. By the end of the 19th century, they were also being used by the authorities to further the assimilation policy: some of the many thousands of Indigenous children removed from parental care were housed in the orphanages, from which they were often adopted into non-Indigenous families.

25 See Bremner, R., *Children and Youth in America: A Documentary History*, Harvard University Press, (1970).

26 Family and Children's Services Division, Minnesota, Orphanages: An Historical Overview, (1995), p 3, at: https://www.leg.mn.gov/docs/pre2003/other/950265.pdf.

CANADA

During the 18th and most of the 19th century, such institutional care as existed was provided by religious organisations, charities and philanthropists. Not until the Charity Act 1874 did legislation encourage voluntary organisations to establish and support orphanages based on the British system. Initially, these orphanages sought apprenticeships for most of their children, but gradually, they moved towards implementing long-term care programmes. One of the more traditional orphanages was the Mount Cashel Orphanage in St. John's Newfoundland run by the Christian Brothers, which was eventually closed and demolished in 1992 following prosecutions of several staff for historical child abuse. As Brookfield points out, formal adoptions were rare then; instead, recourse was had to industrial schools, apprenticeships, farm placements and domestic service positions.[27] The last Canadian orphanage closed in 1994.

Service provision by secular voluntary organisations

By the 1850s, a new type of organisation began to appear: charities and nonprofits established by philanthropists, their founders often religiously motivated but with goals focused more on providing for the practical necessities of everyday life and the welfare of children than on saving souls.

The U.S.

In the absence of any government body with a brief for child welfare, voluntary organisations were free to develop the type of services appropriate to meet child welfare needs and were also best placed and most informed to credibly lobby government to introduce child protection legislation, but they were necessarily restricted to city locations. In 1909, federal government initiated a Conference on Children, which brought together representatives of the various voluntary child-care organisations in order to assist their coordination and promote best practice and so that they could place on record the type and scale of the issues then threatening the welfare of children. The consensus of this conference was that 'home life is the highest and finest product of civilization. Children should not be deprived of it except for urgent and compelling reasons. . . . [T]his consensus has formed the basis of child welfare theory ever since.'[28] Indeed, that view presaged the decline of orphanages and the beginnings of their replacement by foster care. Thereafter, the push to put in place protective legislation and to initiate appropriate services came from voluntary organisations, which paved the way for eventual, more geographically evenly spread government provision. The first step in that direction came with the establishing of

27 See Brookfield, T., *History of Adoption and Fostering in Canada*, Oxford University Press, (2015).
28 See, Jones, M.B., *Decline of the American Orphanage 1941–1980*, University of Chicago Press, (1993).

the Children's Bureau in 1912, and a second followed in 1935, with the introduction of the Social Security Act, making it possible for children who would otherwise have been placed in orphanages to be supported in their own homes.

By the mid-20th century, in the U.S. as in the U.K., the era of child protection dominated by voluntary organisations was drawing to a close. Government bodies, in compliance with federal and state legislation, had subsumed the responsibilities, the work and many of the staff of the pioneering nonprofits, leaving only a small remnant of the latter. However, unlike in the U.K., where Lord Beaverbrook oversaw the nationalisation of health and social services, bringing the relevant charities and their staff and facilities into the public sector, the handover was far from smooth, with many voluntary organisations disappearing before government services were in place, leaving a rudimentary child protection service provided by the juvenile courts or none at all. As Myers puts it, '[F]or the first 6 decades of the 20th century, protective services in most communities were inadequate and in some places nonexistent.'[29]

CHILDREN'S AID SOCIETY (CAS)

Founded in New York in 1853 by Charles Loring Brace, this nonprofit organisation was established specifically in order to provide emergency housing and permanent homes for orphaned, abandoned or impoverished children and to assist thereafter with their education and employment. This initiative was both a practical response to the plight of the many thousands of destitute children in New York and a deliberate choice not to resort to orphanages and other forms of institutional care, which the founder believed to be counterproductive to the primary goal of assisting youths to become independent in life. In making that choice and setting up a network of facilities to operationalise it, CAS was far ahead of its time and created a model for intervention that would later be viewed as a trailblazing initiative. In 1854, CAS opened the nation's first sheltered accommodation for youths, the Newsboys' Lodging House, and at much the same time, it launched the 'orphan train' movement, which transported many thousands of children from a dangerous street life of begging in New York and other Eastern cities to family life in foster homes and with adopters in the rural Midwest (see further, later in this chapter). In due course, CAS established branches across the country and diversified its services to provide community-based schools and health centres delivering dental care, mental health counselling, employment advice, infant day care for working parents, and other services that enabled children and families to build independent lives.

Currently, with an annual budget of over $100 million, a presence in 45 cities, and over 1,200 full-time employees, Children's Aid is one of America's oldest and largest children's nonprofits.

29 See Myers, J., *A Short History of Child Protection in America*, op cit at p 8.

CHARITY ORGANISATION SOCIETY (COS)

Established in 1857 in New York, the society emulated the approach taken by the Charity Organisation Society in the U.K. It similarly sought to coordinate the work of all agencies involved in catering for the needs of those socially disadvantaged for reasons of poverty, disability or disease. COS eventually had a hundred branches spread across the country.

By the 1870s, poverty had become endemic in the Eastern U.S. cities. The records of the New York Society for Improving the Condition of the Poor, for example, show an increase from 5,000 families on relief in 1873 to 24,000 in 1874 and to an average of more than 20,000 families during the later 1870s. It was a time which saw a corresponding increase in voluntary organisations engaged in poverty relief and provision for abandoned children.

Professional methodology COS – a precursor of contemporary social work intervention – employed a scientific methodology to cope with the expanding problems of urban dependency and the proliferation of social welfare agencies and to prevent multiple organisations from involvement with the same family. It introduced methods of investigation, registration, and supervision of applicants for charity and of designating and monitoring the work of a specified organisation with a specified family. It targeted intervention towards 'worthy' families, assigning a 'friendly visitor' to supervise and support each family, requiring profiles of the family to be drawn up and an assessment made of the member's strengths and weaknesses. It mentored and monitored standards of parenting. It set up centralised records and administrative services and emphasised objective investigations and professional training, all of which prepared the ground for professional child-care social workers.

The New York Society for the Prevention of Cruelty to Children

This, the world's first organisation of its kind, was founded in 1875 following public outrage over the abuse suffered by eight-year-old Mary Ellen at the hands of her foster parents. At that time, the only organisation dealing with cruel treatment was the Society for the Prevention of Cruelty to Animals. The NYPCC is credited with establishing the fundamental principles of contemporary U.S. child-protection legislation.[30] Such was the success of this initiative that by 1922, there were some 300 child protection societies in the U.S. Ten years later, the society was joined in its child-protection mission by Save the Children.

30 See, further, Katz, S.N., McGrath, M., and Howe, R.-A., *Child Neglect Laws in America*, American Bar Association, (1975) and Myers, J.E.B., *Child Protection in America: Past, Present and Future*, Oxford University Press, (2006).

The Settlement Movement

The example set by Toynbee Hall, established in London in 1884 to provide supportive community life for destitute families, was transferred to the U.S. in 1886 when the Neighbourhood Guild of New York City was founded, followed by the prestigious Hull House in Chicago in 1889. This political experiment relied on sociological methods to induce families to support each other under the guidance of 'experts' who lived in and became part of a disadvantaged community.[31] While this form of intervention was not specifically oriented towards child welfare, it did demonstrate that improvements in the quality of life for families and communities enabled better parenting and thereby increased the probability of achieving the same end result. When, in 1911, the National Federation of Settlements was instituted, there were some 440 settlements throughout the U.S.

Canada

Public concern for the welfare of Canadian children became apparent at an early stage. In 1799, town wardens were empowered to bind orphans to apprenticeships. In 1827, local courts were authorised to appoint legal guardians for children without families. In the mid-1800s, legislation was passed stipulating that any city or town could bind, as an apprentice, any minor whose parents were in jail or dependent on public charity.[32]

Children's Aid Society (CAS)

In 1887, the Toronto Humane Society was founded. This voluntary organisation was committed to the protection of women, children and animals. It became the first Children's Aid Society in 1891, modelled on its U.S. predecessor, in response to the numbers of abandoned and orphaned children who roamed the streets, sleeping in doorways and begging for food. It quickly came to the forefront of the lobbying that resulted in Canada's first child protection statute, the Act for the Prevention of Cruelty to and Better Protection of Children 1893, which made child abuse an indictable offence. This legislation made provision for the setting up of a network of CAS branches throughout Ontario; it promoted foster care and authorised local CAS organisations to apprehend and provide guardianship for neglected children. It also required every town of 10,000 people or more to establish a receiving home or shelter for the temporary care of children apprehended by CAS until homes could be found. By 1930, there were over 800 children residing in shelters throughout the province, but by the end of World War Two, the shelters had been phased out and replaced by small group or receiving homes.

31 See, further, Berry, M.E., *The Settlement Movement: 1886–1986*, published by the United Neighborhood Centers of America, (1986).

32 As stated on the CAS website; see https://www.casott.on.ca/en/about-us/history/.

By the turn of the century, CAS had become a powerful advocacy agency, lobbying government for measures to protect children. More than 200 children had by then been brought into its care: 130 were in foster homes; 20 returned to their natural parents; and the remaining 35 were in various institutions, orphanages and asylums. Significantly, as CAS states on its website, from an early stage, the organisation embraced the view that 'children should be in their own homes rather than putting into effect the extreme measure of forceful separation. In situations where the child could never be returned to its parents, the Society favoured adoption.'

Historical, state-sanctioned child abuse

Any book setting out to explore the principle of the welfare of the child has to take into account the capacity of the state not just to promote but also to violate that principle. In the latter case, as was mentioned in Book I of this series,[33] Great Britain demonstrated considerable aptitude in this respect when, one day in 1814, its courts condemned five children aged between eight and twelve to be hanged for petty larceny.[34] In the latter half of that century and continuing well into the first half of the 20th, it added to its negative record by implementing a policy of consigning tens of thousands of pauper children to be transported – or 'trafficked' – to its colonies.

State relocation policy and 'orphans'

The policy of allowing private citizens to bear what would otherwise be the public cost of caring for children whose birth parents are unavailable or unwilling to do so was probably first formulated in Great Britain before being subsequently embraced with some enthusiasm by the U.S.

Child transports from Great Britain

The Poor Laws[35] in Great Britain provided a basic framework of state care for children and others unable to care for themselves. The overcrowded poorhouses and workhouses became the source from which the state transferred to its colonies the children unwanted in their homeland.[36] In the latter half of the 19th century and continuing well into the first half of the 20th, this imperial nation shipped tens of thousands of children to be adopted or otherwise taken in by families in its colonies in Australia, New Zealand, South Africa, North America, the West Indies, Canada

33 See O'Halloran, K., *The Principle of the Welfare of the Child: A History*, op cit.

34 See Morris, A., and Giller, H., *Understanding Juvenile Justice*, Croom Helm, (1987), at p 6.

35 In England, these were first codified in 1597–98, followed by a series of Poor Laws, including the Poor Law Amendment Act 1834, until the Poor Law system was abolished in 1948. See, further, Book 1, chapter 1, in this series.

36 See, for example, Bean, P., and Melville, J., *Lost Children of the Empire*, Unwin Hyman Ltd., (1989).

and elsewhere[37] where, it was felt, they would have opportunities to lead useful lives.[38] It was also candidly admitted that this would ease the burden on English ratepayers by avoiding the necessity of having to provide housing, education and health-care facilities, etc. It has been estimated that approximately 100,000 such children aged five years and older were received in Canada alone between 1826 and 1939, the peak period being from 1870 to 1920.[39]

The children were sometimes orphans, but more often, they were the abandoned offspring of parents who had migrated from Ireland or from rural parts of England into industrial cities such as London, Manchester, Liverpool and Glasgow seeking employment. Others were children admitted to state care due to abusive or neglectful parents, and some were young offenders, having been convicted of petty theft or of being a 'vagabond.' This transportation policy was very much supported by the government, through local government funding, successive government schemes and boards such as the Overseas Migration Board. Reputable English child-care organisations such as Barnardos were also involved in arranging the safe passage of children who were orphaned, homeless, or otherwise uncared for to overseas adopters only too happy to welcome into their family an extra pair of hands to share the work on farms, etc. Indeed, a damning report by Andrew Doyle in 1874 on the policy of child migration to Canada was particularly critical of the use of such children as cheap labour.[40]

The 'orphan train' movement

This 'movement' occurred largely during between 1854 and 1929 when approximately 250,000 'orphans' were transported by rail from cities in the East of the U.S. to anonymous homes, mainly in the rural Midwest.[41] It was a response to the conditions of city life on the Eastern seaboard in the early decades of the 19th century. By 1850, there were an estimated 10,000 to 30,000 homeless children in New York City alone, where the total population was only 500,000. In 1853, the Children's Aid Society was founded to help the many children in that city who lived in poverty with parents who abused alcohol, engaged in criminal activity or were otherwise unfit parents. These children, who were begging and selling newspapers and matches, were often referred to as 'street Arabs.' While some may well have been orphans – their parents having died from cholera or other illnesses – they were

37 Some estimate that the policy began as early as early as 1618 and continued until 1967; see, further, at: https://media.nationalarchives.gov.uk/index.php/child-emigration-to-canada/.

38 See, for example, Tizard, B., *Adoption: A Second Chance*, Open Books, (1977).

39 See, for example, Kohli, M.P., *The Golden Bridge: Young Immigrants to Canada, 1833–1939*, Natural Heritage Press, (2003). Also, see Parker, R., *Uprooted: The Shipment of Poor Children to Canada, 1867–1919*, Policy Press, (2008).

40 See British Home Child Group International at http://britishhomechild.com/the-doyle-report/.

41 See, further, National Orphan Train Complex, Orphan Train Rider Stories, at https://orphantraindepot.org/history/orphan-train-rider-stories/.

mostly poor and neglected children or those being cared for in orphanages, having probably been abandoned by destitute immigrant families.

The movement was largely organised by the society with the intention of rescuing children from the dangers of exploitation and abuse in overcrowded cities – including New York, Boston, Chicago and Philadelphia – where they were not wanted. It offered them a new life on the farms of the Midwest, where labour was in short supply. Children were selected and accompanied on the trains by members of the society and were met at designated stops by members of local committees who had organised lodgings for the children, notified prospective adopters, and arranged the adoptions. The committees liaised with the society regarding the suitability of adopters, matching them with available children, and annual monitoring visits. The children were expected to write letters reporting on their progress to the society twice a year.

The Children's Aid Society's sent an average of 3,000 children by train each year from 1855 to 1875. During the early years, Indiana received the largest number of children. Orphan trains were sent to 45 states, as well as to Canada and Mexico, though most went to upper New York state, Connecticut, New Jersey and Pennsylvania. By the 1870s, the New York Foundling Hospital and the New England Home for Little Wanderers in Boston each had its own orphan train programme.

In 1910, a survey conducted by the society concluded that 87% of the children sent by orphan trains to country homes had 'done well.'

RELOCATION AND DISRUPTED IDENTITY

From the archives of material collated over decades of academic research, it is clear that many of those who experienced state-induced relocation came to suffer uncertainty as to their personal and cultural identity: a compromised sense of 'belonging,' often with accompanying attachment issues. For some, this was a direct result of experiencing separation from siblings, enforced name changes, and repeated moves to different 'homes.' For others, it was a natural consequence of being uprooted from kith and kin, from a familiar cultural context, and being immersed instead in a wholly different one, with no connection to the people or the place they found themselves in. It was an experience presaging the more acute disruption of identity that came to be suffered by Indigenous children.

State assimilation policy and Indigenous children

Across both the U.S. and Canada, the assimilationist policy was probably driven primarily by government determination to undo the effects of earlier treaties with the Indigenous tribes: treaties that had ostensibly recognised Indigenous land rights. Instead of continuing to maintain a largely fictional stance that purported to acknowledge tribal sovereignty, accompanied by respect for traditional land ownership, governments sought to confine tribes to reservations as a means of paving the way for licensing mining and railway companies to extend their activities onto ancient tribal lands. Consequently, in the early 19th century, Canada introduced such assimilationist legislation as the Crown Lands Protection Act 1839 and the Act to Encourage the Gradual Civilization of the Indian Tribes of the Canadas 1857 while in the U.S., this was represented by such legislation as the Indian Civilization Act 1819. One strategy for furthering this policy was the cynical removal of children from their birth families and tribes, to be shriven of their cultural identity and tribal loyalty and indoctrinated instead in the cultural norms of non-Indigenous society.

Residential/industrial schools

As in other common-law countries – including Australia and Ireland – the use of residential/industrial schools to implement a wholly misguided government assimilationist policy left children alienated from their communities, often abused, with a compromised sense of cultural identity and resulted in a lengthy period of intergenerational trauma that Indigenous people in many countries are still trying to work through. These residential schools were established ostensibly to teach children the rudiments of a trade so as to equip them to be useful members of society.

IN THE U.S.

The abusive use of residential schools in the U.S. as a means of severing Indigenous children from their cultural roots and immersing them in Christian cultural norms began in 1879 with the opening of the Carlisle Indian Industrial School[42] and ended around 1970. Between 1879 and 1918, a total of over 10,000 children from over 142 Indian nations attended the Carlisle School. By 1900, the number of schools had grown from 150 to 307, and the number of child residents had increased from 3,598 to 21,568. According to a departmental enquiry, the federal government operated more than 400 boarding schools across the country and provided support for more than 1,000 others during the period from 1819 to 1969. The schools programme represented a key component in the federal policy of dealing with the marginalisation of Native Americans by assimilating them into mainstream American society, starting with the removal, cultural reeducation and absorption of their children. Many tens of thousands of Indian children spent years away from their families and tribes, being exposed to cultural indoctrination designed to immerse them in the language, basic numeracy/skills, and Christian morality of their white Caucasian teachers. The brutalising regime operated within such schools, and their effects on the cultural identity of pupils and on the cultural integrity of the tribes involved has been well documented.[43]

42 Lee, A.A., An empirical examination of the Indian Child Welfare Act and its impact on cultural and familial preservation for American Indian children, *Child Abuse & Neglect*, (2005): 28(12), 1279–1289.

43 See, for example, Adams, D.W., *Education for Extinction: American Indians and the Boarding School Experience, 1875–1928*, University of Kansas, (1995), (reprinted 1997).

In 1928, the Meriam Report disclosed that the conditions suffered by the children included physical punishment for practising their religion, speaking languages specific to their tribe, using their birth names, and wearing long hair; Indigenous clothing was burned, and AI/AN children were given European names.[44] The report resulted in policy changes in education, health care, and land rights for AI/AN people.[45] In 1934, the U.S. Congress passed the Johnson-O'Malley Act in response to the report's disclosures, providing federal funds to subsidise state provision of education, medical attention, financial relief, and social welfare for each enrolled child and giving AI/AN people the right to choose where their children went to school.

IN CANADA

The first residential or boarding school for Indigenous children was established in 1620, before they spread all over Canada (excepting New Brunswick and Prince Edward Island) and the last – Kivallik Hall – closed in 1997.[46] This assimilationist policy came to be embodied in the Gradual Civilization Act 1857 and the Gradual Enfranchisement Act 1869, collectively known as the Indian Act 1876. This act, as amended, provided authority for the removal of some 150,000 children – First Nations, Metis and Inuit – from their homes, communities and culture to residential educational institutions, triggering what is now recognised as 'the beginning of an intergenerational cycle of neglect and abuse.'[47] It was a federal policy funded by the Department of Indian Affairs, implemented by the Christian churches, and reinforced by government measures, including compulsory attendance in 1894, and by further legislation in 1920.

The objective of the residential/industrial schools[48] was, as infamously declared, 'to kill the Indian in the child'[49] or, as Duncan Campbell Scott (the Superintendent of Indian Education) explained in 1920:

> I want to get rid of the Indian problem. I do not think as a matter of fact, that the country ought to continuously protect a class of people who are able to

44 The Meriam Report, *The Problem of Indian Administration*, (1928), at https://narf.org/nill/resources/meriam.html.

45 See, for example, Woolford, A., *Colonial Genocide in Indigenous North America*, 1971, Duke University Press, (2014).

46 Initially, boarding schools and industrial schools were different entities, but by the turn of the century, they had become indistinguishable, and in 1923, they formally merged to become 'residential schools.'

47 See Saskatchewan Child Welfare Review Panel Report, For the Good of our Children and Youth: A New Vision, A New Direction, at p 18. See, further, at http://saskchildwelfarereview.ca/CWR-panel-report.pdf.

48 See, further, Iozzo, A., In the Best Interests of the Child?: The Industrial School System in late Nineteenth and Early Twentieth Century Ontario, MA thesis, Carleton University Ottawa, (2000), at https://www.collectionscanada.gc.ca/obj/s4/f2/dsk2/ftp03/MQ57663.pdf.

49 In 2021, more than 1,000 bodies of children were discovered in unmarked graves on the sites of former residential schools.

> stand alone. . . . Our objective is to continue until there is not a single Indian in Canada that has not been absorbed into the body politic and there is no Indian question.[50]

This approach was accompanied by other government strategies similarly directed towards racial assimilation. Across the centuries, the collaboration between government and church saw residential school provision gradually extended across Canada. As has been noted:[51]

> What distinguishes the residential schools for Aboriginal children is that they were part of a policy of assimilation that was sustained for many decades.

The findings of the Truth and Reconciliation Commission, established in 2008, concluded that the residential school system constituted cultural genocide.[52] Recently, there have been reports of thousands of unmarked graves on the grounds of former residential schools.[53] The Indian Residential Schools Settlement Agreement Act 2006 provided for a comprehensive settlement of numerous individual and class actions related to the residential school system.

Enforced adoption

For some decades, the federal government gave effect to its assimilationist policy by a strategy of removing Indigenous children from their birth families – usually on a pretext of neglectful parenting or poor school attendance – and placing them with Christian non-Indigenous couples for adoption.

IN THE U.S.

Adoption as a formal statutory procedure was first introduced in the U.S. by the Massachusetts Adoption of Children's Act 1851 – preceding the introduction of similar legislation in England and Wales by 70 years – and set out for the first time some of the more basic functions of the law relating to adoption. By 1929, all states had followed the example of Massachusetts and enacted some form of adoption legislation. Some few decades later, the federal government contrived to use adoption to further its assimilationist policy.

50 See National Archives of Canada, Record Group 10, vol. 6810, file 470–2–3 and vol. 7, 55(L-3) and 63 (N-3).

51 See The Law Commission of Canada, *Restoring Dignity: Responding to Child Abuse in Canadian Institutions*, The Law Commission of Canada, (2000), at p 51.

52 See the Truth and Reconciliation Commission of Canada, Indigenous and Northern Affairs Canada, (2015) at https://www.rcaanc-cirnac.gc.ca/eng/1450124405592/1529106060525#chp2.

53 See the Truth and Reconciliation Commission of Canada, The Missing Children Project, https://www.rcaanc-cirnac.gc.ca/eng/1524504992259/1557512149981.

In the mid-to-late 20th century, as the abusive residential school era drew to a close, it was replaced by the Indian Adoption Project. Traditionally, the responsibility to ensure the proper care of Indian children fell to the tribe as a whole, as monitored and enforced by the tribal chief. Customary adoption, whereby a child would be placed with a member of the extended family without any legal process to terminate or transfer parental rights, was a traditional practice, sanctioned by elders and the tribe chief. However, the Indian Adoption Project, driven by a conviction that 'no Indian child who can benefit from adoption should be deprived of that option,' was responsible for the removal of thousands of children for that purpose. This federal programme, a joint enterprise between the Bureau of Indian Affairs and the Child Welfare League of America, funded the prestigious Child Welfare League of America and its successor, the Adoption Resource Exchange of North America, to work with religious organisations to place Indian children for adoption in white Caucasian families.[54] These adoptions bypassed tribal authorities and ignored the tribal practice of customary adoption to take children from their families and tribes in 16 Western states and transfer them to white Caucasian adopters in the Midwest and Eastern states. It is estimated that as many as one-third of all Indian children were separated from their families between 1941 and 1967, of whom 85% were fostered or adopted by non-Indian families or placed in institutions. The programme contributed to the degrading of Indian culture and has corroded relations between native Americans and the U.S. government ever since.[55]

IN CANADA

During the period 1960 to the mid-1980s, in keeping with similar cultural assimilation programmes in the U.S. and Australia, some thousands of Indigenous children were forcibly separated from their birth families by government social workers and religious organisations and placed for adoption with non-Indigenous families in Canada and elsewhere, a practice that continued until condemned by a government inquiry in the late 1980s.[56] The fact that adoption was utilised by the state in furtherance of its assimilationist policy was forensically corroborated by the Stolen Generations project. Statistics from the Department of Indian Affairs reveal that a total of 11,132 children with 'Indian' status were adopted between 1960 and 1990, 70% by non-Indian adopters, pejoratively referred to as 'the 60s scoop' following the 1965 agreement between the Federal Crown and Child Welfare Services which allowed a 'well intentioned but profoundly uninformed child protection

54 See, for example, Mannes, M., Factors and events leading to the passage of the Indian Child Welfare Act, *Child Welfare*, (1995): 74(1), 264–282.

55 Fanshel, D., *Far From the Reservation: The Transracial Adoption of American Indian Children*, The Scarecrow Press, (1972).

56 See Nichols, R. L., From the Sixties Scoop to Baby Veronica: Transracial Adoption of Indigenous Children in the USA and Canada, in Shackleton, M., (ed.), *International Adoption in North American Literature and Culture: Transnational, Transracial, and Transcultural Narratives*, Palgrave Macmillan, (2017).

bureaucracy to 'scoop' thousands of Indian children that were found to be in need of protection off Indian reserves and place them in non-Indigenous homes.'[57] As noted in the report by the Aboriginal Justice Inquiry:[58]

> [B]etween 1971 and 1981 alone, over 3,400 Aboriginal children were shipped away to adoptive parents in other societies, and sometimes in other countries.

It has been estimated that:

> around 16,000 Indigenous children were taken from their families and communities and put up for fostering or adoption by mostly non-Indigenous families across Canada and the United States – often without the consent of their parents. Some were sent as far away as New Zealand and Australia.[59]

State failure to protect children

In both the U.S. and Canada, there have been strong and repeated claims of endemic racist attitudes and policies among state/provincial authorities in their approach to Indigenous people and their children. Most, usually those making such claims, point to the gross overrepresentation of Indigenous children in the child welfare and juvenile justice systems as evidence of prejudicial intervention by the relevant authorities. The same claims are also made as an explanation for the decades of inactivity by officials in relation to the many Indigenous women and girls murdered or going missing every year, most notably in British Columbia and Nunavut in Canada[60] but also in the U.S. Additionally, there are now the well-documented and heavily litigated cases of clerical child abuse, which persisted throughout the latter half of the 20th century across all of Canada, though particularly in Newfoundland, and in many states of the U.S. Again, this would seem to indicate an unwillingness on the part of the state – specifically, officials such as the police and social workers – to intervene to protect children when that would mean confronting embedded cultural values.

57 *Brown v. Canada* (Attorney General), 2013 ONSC 5637, (2014).

58 See Aboriginal Justice Inquiry, 1999 at Chapter 14. The report also notes that 'between 1971 and 1981, 70–80% of Manitoba's Aboriginal adoptions were in non-Aboriginal homes' at Chapter 14. See, also, the Law Commission report, op cit, and Miller, J.R., *Shingwauk's Vision: A History of Native Residential Schools*, University of Toronto Press, (1996).

59 See *The Guardian* report, Indigenous Canadians Taken from Homes as Children Get Day in Court, (2016), https://www.theguardian.com/world/2016/aug/22/indigenous-canadians-children-sixties-scoop-court.

60 The preamble to the 'National Inquiry into Missing and Murdered Indigenous Women and Girls' (2016) states that in the period 1980–2012, Indigenous women and girls represented 16% of all female homicides in Canada while constituting only 4% of its female population.

The missing and murdered Indigenous women and girls enquiries

The Canadian National Inquiry into the Missing and Murdered Indigenous Women and Girls[61] was established in September 2016 and published its final report, entitled *Reclaiming Power and Place*, on 3 June 2019. In the U.S. 'MMIW: Understanding the Missing and Murdered Indigenous Women Crisis in the United States,' published in October 2020, focuses on the MMIW crisis and its causes in the United States specifically. In both countries, the research findings document the lack of attention paid by the authorities over recent decades to the alarming numbers of Indigenous women and girls who have been found murdered or not found at all. While under-recording has been a systemic problem in both countries, the slippage is typified in the disclosure by the National Crime Information Center that, in 2016, there were 5,712 reports of missing American Indian and Alaska Native women and girls, though the U.S. Department of Justice's federal missing person database, NamUs, only logged 116 cases. The intensive though belated research has called for child-care workers, among others, to be more aware of vulnerable Indigenous girls.

Clerical child abuse

Revelations of clerical child abuse in Canada began with the disclosures at an orphanage in Newfoundland that led to the Canadian Conference of Catholic Bishops publishing the 1992 report *From Pain to Hope*, which acknowledged the harm done, expressed sorrow for the child victims, and sought to empathise evenly with the 'survivors': meaning both the families of the victims and the many blameless clergy who had been tarnished by the actions of a few.[62] The Newfoundland disclosures were followed by a great many others including from Alberta, Manitoba, New Brunswick, Vancouver and Toronto, revealing a scale and duration of abuse that had grown virtually untroubled by police intervention for many decades. Prosecutions did not begin until the turn of the century, and when they did, they revealed that the Catholic Church had often known about specific paedophile priests and the offences perpetrated by them for many years and had responded to disclosures with internal transfers of the perpetrators. Not until 2007 did the conference issue a series of protocols advising diocesan personnel to make disclosures to the police a priority, rather than attempting to address matters internally, and not until 2021 was the Vatican's Code of Canon Law amended to explicitly decree that sexual abuse of minors by clergy, or by laypeople working with minors, should be punished. The early decades of the 21st century saw a litany of successful prosecutions and financial reparations made by the Catholic Church with respect to

61 See, *Reclaiming Power and Place: The Final Report of the National Inquiry into Missing and Murdered Indigenous Women and Girls*, (2019), https://www.mmiwg-ffada.ca.

62 The Canadian Conference of Catholic Bishops, Ad Hoc Committee on Child Sexual Abuse, *From Pain to Hope*, see further at https://www.cccb.ca/wp-content/uploads/2017/11/From_Pain_To_Hope.pdf.

criminal child abuse that had frequently occurred many decades previously, some involving perpetrators who had long since died.[63]

Beginning in the last decade of the 20th century, the pattern in the U.S. followed much the same as that established in Canada: public disclosures, internal Church reshuffling of priests to move paedophiles to other locations, successful prosecutions, Church reports of acknowledgement and contrition,[64] and extensive settlements out of court and reparation payments. The Jay Report found that during the period 1950–2002, there had been a total of 10,667 claims of child sexual abuse in the U.S. involving some 4,392 clergy of the Catholic Church. Again, it was established that diocesan officials had often known about paedophile clergy, had dealt with the issue by moving the perpetrator to another location, and had not made any disclosure to the police but instead had deliberately sought to cover up incidents, and, again, many of the perpetrators had died before prosecutions were completed.

This record of criminal activity against children – both the Indigenous missing or murdered and the non-Indigenous victims of sexual abuse – is, of course, dreadful in itself, but the fact that it continued for so long on such a scale is particularly troubling. Something obstructed or obscured the responsibility to make the necessary inquiries, to sound the alarm. Speculation regarding the nature of the crimes would suggest that the answer lies in the cultural context: a set of values prejudicial towards Indigenous people, females in particular, and another set that protected the social standing of Catholic priests. Both had the effect of preventing the effective state intervention necessary to safeguard the welfare of many children.

Conclusion

The present legislative and organisational framework for safeguarding the welfare of children in both the U.S. and Canada clearly owes a great deal to their shared 19th-century experiences, which, in turn, drew heavily from models of care established in Great Britain. The North American foundling hospitals, orphanages, etc all had British antecedents, and in both the U.S. and Canada, it was the same Catholic orders of nuns that initially provided the only available form of child-care services. Since secular service providers began their work with children, it has often been the same voluntary organisations, most notably CAS, that began the professionalising of those services. Given that level of jurisdictional commonality,

63 See, also, the Office of the High Commissioner for Human Rights (OHCHR) report to the Vatican expressing 'utmost concern about the numerous allegations around the world of sexual abuse and violence committed by members of the Catholic Church against children, and about the measures adopted by the Catholic Church to protect alleged abusers, cover up crimes, obstruct accountability of alleged abusers, and evade reparations due to victims,' (2021), https://www.ohchr.org/en/press-releases/2021/06/un-experts-urge-catholic-church-act-against-sexual-abuse-provide-reparations?LangID=E&NewsID=27184.

64 See the U.S. Conference of Catholic Bishops, *The Nature and Scope of the Problem of Sexual Abuse of Minors by Catholic Priests and Deacons in the United States* (the 'John Jay report'), published by the John Jay College of Criminal Justice, (2004).

it is unsurprising that both countries went on to share the same misguided assimilation policy and an approach of deference to the proclivities of the Catholic Church, which combined to traumatise the Indigenous communities. This has left a legacy of profound mistrust that now obstructs the building of a working relationship with state public services and results in the current gross overrepresentation of Indigenous children in the child welfare and juvenile justice systems.

This brief introductory chapter reveals not just the historical links between both countries and Great Britain but also the extent to which a Eurocentric culture sought to impose its values on the Indigenous people with consequences that can be seen in an ongoing cultural dissonance and in the relatively much worse prospects for the well-being of Indigenous children.

Part II

United States of America

2 Policy, principles, legislation and courts

Introduction

The United States of America is a federation of 50 states and the District of Columbia, each of which is a separate jurisdiction with independent responsibility for enacting legislation, providing a judicial system and managing programmes of related service provision. Federal government provides an overarching framework of law that sets out the parameters for state legislation and a judicial system that considers issues with a constitutional or federal dimension. Family law, a matter constitutionally reserved to the states, includes issues and administrative systems relating to children. However, federal powers and responsibilities are relatively constrained. Indeed, policy making and legislative initiatives are largely reversed in a manner very different to the U.K. model, with primary jurisdictional authority vested in the states rather than in the national government.

In practice, the autonomy of individual states in matters relating to the welfare of children, as in so many other areas, is balanced to some degree by constitutional, judicial and budgetary constraints. The federal government has responsibilities in relation to funding service programmes across all states (though often only partially) and an accompanying oversight role monitoring their effectiveness. This power, exercised under the Spending Clause, provides it with some authority to shape state policy: by tying federal funds to specified processes, services and outcomes, states may be nudged towards compliance with federal policy, but states value their ability to act independently and have habitually done just that, asserting their leadership on family matters and accepting supplementary federal input only when fiscally prudent to do so. In a sense, this was illustrated by the recent *Dobbs*[1] decision: once the USSC ruled that *Roe v. Wade*[2] did not establish a constitutional right, then abortion was no longer a matter that fell within federal jurisdiction. There was no incentive for states to continue to follow federal leadership; each state was free to abandon that leadership and assert its own legislative policy, which many promptly did.

1 *Dobbs v. Jackson Women's Health Organization*, No. 19-1392, 597 U.S. ___ (2022).
2 *Roe v. Wade*, 410 U.S. 113 (1973).

DOI: 10.4324/9781003269564-5

The autonomy of the U.S. within the framework of international law also gives rise to problems. When it comes to engaging with international law, the U.S. proceeds with caution, adroitly guarding its sovereignty in a manner not unlike a reverse image of the federal/state relationship. Concerns regarding U.S. sovereignty were cited as reasons for not accepting the International Criminal Court, for withdrawing from UNESCO and the U.N. Human Rights Council (in 2017 and 2018 respectively), and for repeatedly failing to ratify the U.N. Convention on the Rights of the Child. For some, U.S. hesitancy in engaging with international law was demonstrably justified by the consequences that ensued from becoming a signatory state to the Hague Convention on Protection of Children and Co-operation in Respect of Intercountry Adoption (signed in 1994 with effect from 2008), which resulted in the termination of many intercountry adoption arrangements, causing a steep fall in subsequent annual ICA rates and resulting in tens of thousands of overseas children in need not being offered adoption with available, approved and highly motivated U.S. families.

All this indicates that federal and state law in relation to the welfare interests of children is unusually complex, quite different in many respects from the more centralised, linear application of policy, principles and law in the U.K. and Ireland as profiled in the previous book in this series.[3]

This chapter begins with a brief overview of the policy that laid the foundations for the law relating to children in the U.S. It sketches an outline of the basic divisions: public family law and the civil and criminal jurisdictions, followed by private family law and, finally, the emerging hybrid orders and proceedings that are neither exclusively public or private. It identifies the significance of some fundamental principles that shaped the evolving law. It then provides tables of the statutes and courts, both domestic and international, that now constitute the relevant contemporary legal framework. The chapter concludes by considering how the voice of the child is heard and their welfare and rights represented in court.

Policy, principles, legislation and courts

As has often been judicially emphasised, the right of a parent to maintain a relationship with their child is among the interests included in the constellation of liberties protected through the 14th Amendment. In practice, the policy, principles and legislation in relation to children are largely determined and adjudicated at state or county level and can vary considerably across the U.S. More perhaps than for any other developed nation, this must be also be seen in the broader social policy context of a patchy inclusiveness and pluralism, where wealth disparity and uneven access to a reasonable standard of health, housing and education services – compounded by problems associated with guns, drugs, racism and culture wars –

3 O'Halloran, K., *Children & the Law: Shaping the Modern Welfare Principle in the British Isles*, Routledge, (2023).

create what can be a particularly stressful environment for children and for other socially dependent groups.

Policy

The inherent jurisdiction of *parens patriae* – initially vested in the sovereign as protector of those subjects unable to care for themselves such as 'lunatics' and children – as exercised by the High Court in England, provided the foundations for U.S. child protection law and policy. Recognition of the need for associated services can, arguably, be dated from the founding of the world's first organisation dedicated solely to that objective: the New York Society for the Prevention of Cruelty to Children in 1875.[4] A nationwide government response probably commenced with the establishment of the Children's Bureau in 1912, which included a brief for children's welfare.

Public family law policy relating to children: civil jurisdiction

Between 1985 and 1995, the population of children removed from homes and placed in substitute public care almost doubled from 276,000 to 494,000. Since then, the numbers have steadily increased. From the 396,000 in care in 2012, there was an 11% increase to 442,995 in 2017, the rate of abuse reaching nine in a thousand. There was a further slight increase to 443,000 in 2019.[5]

THE PREVENTION/PROTECTION BALANCE

By 1967, every state and the District of Columbia had enacted laws requiring the mandatory reporting of suspected cases of child abuse or neglect to a public agency, reinforced by the landmark statute the Child Abuse Prevention and Treatment Act 1974 (CAPTA), which authorised the use of federal funds to improve state responses to child abuse and neglect.[6] (See, further, later in this chapter). It has had multiple amendments[7] and was completely rewritten in the Child Abuse Prevention, Adoption, and Family Services Act 1988.[8] As late as 1989, the USSC

4 See, further, Katz, S.N., McGrath, M., and Howe, R.-A., *Child Neglect Laws in America,* American Bar Association, (1975) and Myers, J.E.B., *Child Protection in America: Past, Present and Future*, Oxford University Press, (2006).

5 The AFCARS Report, Preliminary FY1 2017 Estimates as of 10 August 2018, No. 25. See, further, https://www.speakupnow.org/foster-care-statistics-resources/. Also, see https://www.childtrends.org/indicators/child-maltreatment.

6 See, further, Child Welfare Information Gateway at https://www.childwelfare.gov/pubs/issue-briefs/cm-prevention/.

7 Including by the Child Abuse Prevention and Treatment and Adoption Reform Act 1978, the Child Abuse Amendments 1984, and the Children's Justice and Assistance Act 1986.

8 Subsequently amended in 2015, 2016, and 2018 and then by the Victims of Child Abuse Act Reauthorization Act 2018.

in *DeShaney v. Winnebago County Social Services*[9] was able to make a finding that the government was not obligated to protect its citizens against harm inflicted by private individuals. This was a case concerning a mother's complaint that the public social services agency had failed to act to protect her four-year-old son from abuse – causing brain damage – inflicted upon him by her husband, the boy's father, from whom she was estranged. She maintained that by failing to intervene, the agency violated her son's 14th Amendment right not to be deprived of life or liberty without due process of the law. Rehnquist CJ took the view that such nonintervention was explicable and excusable as intervening officials are often charged with 'improperly intruding into the parent-child relationship.' Justice Brennan, joined by Justices Marshall and Blackmun, dissented and quite rightly warned that 'inaction can be every bit as abusive of power as action, [and] oppression can result when a State undertakes a vital duty and then ignores it.'

In 1990, a new section – Certain Preventive Services Regarding Children of Homeless Families or Families at Risk of Homelessness – was added to the 1988 Act. In 1991, the National Commission on Children presented its report *Beyond Rhetoric: A New American Agenda for Children and Families* to Congress, providing a body of evidence substantiating the commission's concern regarding the vulnerability of children's welfare interests in the U.S., particularly those being reared by single mothers.

By the turn of the century, preventative state intervention to assist vulnerable families had become defined as a public health matter, was centred on the Maternal, Infant, and Early Childhood Home Visiting programme located within the HHS Health Resources and Services Administration, and was being delivered across most states.[10] At much the same time, a separate policy focus on child protection took shape, which included several amendments to CAPTA specifying grounds for coercive state intervention in family affairs.[11] These included the Keeping Children and Families Safe Act 2003. In 2005, the Office on Child Abuse and Neglect (OCAN) within the Children's Bureau began to incorporate protective factors into its programmes. A decade later, CAPTA was further amended by the Justice for Victims of Trafficking Act 2015, which focused on child victims of sex trafficking and expanded the federal definition of 'child abuse and neglect' and 'sexual abuse' to include such children. Further amendments were made by the Comprehensive Addiction and Recovery Act 2016 to provide protection for infants identified as being affected by maternal substance use or withdrawal symptoms or foetal alcohol disorders and subsequently by the self-explanatory Substance Use-Disorder Prevention That Promotes Opioid Recovery and Treatment for Patients and Communities Act 2018. Most recently, CAPTA was amended by the Victims of Child Abuse Act Reauthorization Act of 2018, which provides immunity from civil and

9 489 U.S. 189 (1989).

10 See Information Gateway at https://www. childwelfare.gov/topics/preventing/prevention-programs/homevisit/homevisitprog/.

11 Including the Child Abuse, Domestic Violence, Adoption, and Family Services Act 1992.

criminal liability for those who, in good faith, report allegations of suspected child abuse or neglect.[12]

This synoptic overview of legislative developments reveals a very functionally oriented federal policy regarding coercive state intervention on child protection grounds: by channelling the flow of funding streams towards designated aspects of child abuse and neglect, the federal government sought to steer states into implementing a national strategy focusing on prioritising the protection of specified aspects of children's welfare interests. Consensual intervention on preventative grounds fell more within the states' discretionary remit to be delivered by doctors, nurses and midwives as part of general public health-care provision. This difference in approach to coercive and consensual intervention very much reflected constitutional provisions governing the state/family relationship.

The Constitution, as interpreted by the USSC, requires a state to show compelling reason for infringing rights of family privacy and for overriding parental autonomy, as these fundamental liberties are protected by the 14th Amendment and its guarantee of due process.[13] *Santosky v. Kramer*,[14] a benchmark case in this context, raised the bar for state intervention in child protection by replacing the 'preponderance of the evidence' standard that had been widely accepted as sufficient to challenge parental custody rights with the more stringent 'clear and convincing evidence,' which strengthened the presumption of parents' rights to the care and custody of their children. This decision set the direction of public policy regarding state intervention in family matters on child protection grounds until 2019, when the Family First legislation was introduced. (See, further, later in this chapter.)

Safe havens This is the U.S. equivalent to the practice in parts of Europe and elsewhere of providing 'baby hatches' or designated safe places where a parent, usually a young unmarried mother, may abandon their child safely and anonymously, with confidence that it will be taken into state care and probably adopted. A federal study in 1993 found that at least 22,000 babies were left in hospitals each year by parents unwilling or unable to care for them.[15] The study, commissioned by the Department of Health and Human Services, found that the babies were clustered in six major urban areas, with Cook County (Chicago), Ill., New York City and Washington, D.C. having the highest numbers. Twenty years later, every state had introduced safe haven laws and facilities catering for a total of perhaps 200 or so infants abandoned annually in 'baby hatches,' most of whom, presumably, filter

12 See, further, Child Welfare Information Gateway, *About CAPTA: A legislative History*. Washington, DC: U.S. Department of Health and Human Services, Children's Bureau, (2019), at https://www.childwelfare.gov/pubPDFs/about.pdf.

13 *Meyer v. Nebraska* 262 U.S. 390 (1923), *Stanley v. Illinois* 405 U.S. 645 (1972), and *Wisconsin v. Yoder* 406 U.S. 205 (1972).

14 455 U.S. 745 (1982).

15 See, further, at https://www.latimes.com/archives/la-xpm-1993-11-10-mn-55141-story.html.

through into the U.S. adoption process. Diane Kuntz comments that the number of babies abandoned in safe havens is now very low.[16]

FOSTER CARE

This form of care for children began in 1869 in Massachusetts when the Board of State Charities initiated the practice of 'placing out,' whereby, instead of being admitted to orphanages, children orphaned or failed by parental care would be placed with approved families in the local community.

In September 2020, there were 407,493 children in foster care. The foster care population, which had plateaued for some years, would now seem to be on a downward trajectory, indicating the positive impact of the Family First initiative: 2019, 426,566; 2018, 435,031; 2017, 436, 656; 2016, 430,101; and 2015, 421,428.[17] The numbers in foster care following termination of parental rights increased from 62,230 in 2015 to 71,860 in 2019 but then dropped back to 63,815 in 2020.[18] In recent years, individual states have, to a varying extent, privatised their foster care services in what is seemingly like a return to the 19th-century practice of relying on religious organisations to arrange placements. For-profit agencies are also involved; the introduction of such entities to the protection of children in state care would seem to be a singular aspect of U.S. policy towards the welfare interests of children.[19]

KINSHIP CARE

For states to receive federal payments for foster care and adoption assistance, federal law, under Title IV-E of the Social Security Act, requires that they 'consider giving preference to an adult relative over a nonrelated caregiver when determining a placement for a child, provided that the relative caregiver meets all relevant state child protection standards'[20] and that they serve notice on parents, grandparents, and other adult relatives of the removal or planned removal of a child from parental custody and of the options available to a relative to participate in the care and placement of the child. In 2012, for example, 31% of adoptions from the care system were in favour of relatives.

16 See, further, at https://pubmed.ncbi.nlm.nih.gov/18174351/#:~:text=Of%2093%20infants%20%2853%25%20male%29%20identified%20during%20the,abandoned%20following%20passage%20of%20the%20Safe%20Haven%20law.

17 See the AFCARS Report at: https://www.acf.hhs.gov/sites/default/files/documents/cb/afcarsreport28.pdf.

18 Ibid.

19 See, for example, Schwartz, I.M. and White, T., Adoption and Foster Care: United States, in Smelser, N.J. and Baltes, P.B. (eds.), *International Encyclopedia of the Social and Behavioural Sciences*, Elsevier, (2001).

20 42 U.S.C. § 671(a)(19) (LexisNexis 2017).

ADOPTION FROM PUBLIC CARE

The amending of CAPTA by the Child Abuse Prevention and Treatment and Adoption Reform Act 1988 to incorporate the Adoption Opportunities Program marked the start of a federal policy to develop adoption as the preferred exit strategy for those children in the public care system who could not be safely discharged back to parental care. By the closing decades of the 20th century, there was an established policy of facilitating the adoption of such children, a policy driven in part by the inexorable logic that private adoption costs less than public foster care: the Brookings Institute has estimated that 'annual state and federal expenditures for foster care total more than $9 billion under Title IV-E of the Social Security Act alone.'[21] Where parents had shown no consistent interest in their child and there was no reasonable or foreseeable likelihood that they could, or would, resume care responsibility, legislative provisions enabled parental rights to be terminated. Adoption became the preferred alternative arrangement as, in addition to being cheaper, it was viewed as more conducive to promoting a child's welfare interests than foster care.

This policy was consolidated by the Adoption and Safe Families Act 1997 (ASFA), which represented a federal shift away from public service resource investment in long-term foster care when family reunification was not an option and towards the promotion of adoption as a private resource for the care of children, together with support for kinship care. As Woodhouse commented, 'In essence, ASFA shifts money and services from biological families and foster families to adoptive families.'[22]

Notwithstanding this policy and practice, however, the fact remains that every year, approximately half the children in the care system due to parental abuse or neglect were simply returned to their parents; the proportion adopted into alternative families, approved as being able and willing to further a child's welfare, has never in any year exceeded one-quarter of the children failed by their family of origin. More recently, perhaps having become a victim of its own success, adoption from public care was questioned, resulting in a change of policy towards family reunification, supported by foundations such as Annie E. Casey and the abolition movement,[23] a policy change given effect by the Trump administration's Family First Prevention Services Act 2018. (See, further, Chapter 3.)

21 See, Zill, N., Adoption from Foster Care: Aiding Children While Saving Public Money, the Brookings Institute, May 2011, at http://www.brookings.edu/research/reports/2011/05/adoption-foster-care-zill.

22 See, Woodhouse, B., The Adoption and Safe Families Act: A Major Shift in Child Welfare Law and Policy, op. cit. at p 383.

23 \See, further, at https://cssp.org/2020/06/what-does-it-mean-to-abolish-the-child-welfare-system-as-we-know-it/#:~:text=Ultimately%2C%20the%20upEND%20movement%20calls%20for%20the%20abolition,racism%20that%20can%20cause%20more%20trauma%20and%20harm.

RESIDENTIAL CARE

As a consequence of the history of abuse that characterised the use of residential schools and in common with other countries, the state has been hesitant to use residential facilities as a contemporary option for children admitted to the public child-care system.

Residential facilities – now termed 'congregate care' – are operated by public or private agencies and provide an array of specialist services which include therapeutic services for children and families and educational and medical services for children or youths. Placements in residential care facilities are reserved for those whose needs are such that family-based foster care is inappropriate, and community-based services have proven ineffective. The legislative intent underpinning the Family First Preventative Services Act 2018 is directed in part towards reducing reliance on institutional care or on large foster homes and instead encouraging the use of family-based care. There is a dearth of statistical information on annual admissions and on trends relating to the use of such facilities.

Public family law policy relating to children: criminal jurisdiction

In 1899, the world's first juvenile court was established in Chicago, and within 20 years, they were fixtures in all but three states. The incentive for these courts came from public concern regarding juvenile delinquency, but from the outset, their remit also included child abuse and neglect. They largely dealt with the needs and deeds of those children – then less than 16 years of age – out of parental control and/or alleged to have be in breach of the criminal law. They were preceded by the New York House of Refuge, founded in 1825 specifically to house juvenile delinquents.[24]

Currently, the governing federal legislation is the Juvenile Justice and Delinquency Prevention Act 1974 as amended by the Juvenile Justice Reform Act 2018.

THE WELFARE/JUSTICE BALANCE

The emphasis in the new juvenile courts was on welfare rather than justice: relying less on adjudication, more on mediation; on community-based services rather than prison; on treatment rather than punishment.[25] This approach sought to clearly differentiate between the criminal behaviour of adults and children, aiming to educate the latter to an understanding of the significance and consequences of their behaviour by providing vocational training, usually in an industrial school, or placing them on probation, thereby seeking to rehabilitate them to a useful and responsible role in society. It was an approach replicated by the network of juvenile courts that spread across the U.S. in the early decades of the 20th century. By the 1950s, a psychosocial interpretation of human behaviour was confidently labelling juvenile

24 See, further, Zimring, F.E., Tanenhaus, D.S., *Choosing the Future for American Juvenile Justice*, University Press, (2014).

25 See, *Ex parte Crouse*, 4 Whart. 9 (Pa.1839).

delinquent behaviour as symptomatic of the stresses in the family and poverty in the community.

From the 1960s, however, the USSC had the opportunity to examine this differentiation in a series of seminal cases that collectively directed state juvenile courts to respect and apply certain constitutionally protected standards of justice. In *Gideon v. Wainwright*,[26] the USSC held the proceedings to be deficient because no provision had been made for the juvenile to be represented in court as required under the Sixth Amendment. In *Kent v. United States*,[27] it ruled that arresting, questioning, and detaining a juvenile over a period of several days before charging them violated the 'due process' clause, as did confessions obtained under duress[28] or without a *Miranda*-type caution.[29] It found the clause to be similarly violated in *In re Gault*[30] as the conciliation approach adopted by the juvenile court deprived a child facing possible incarceration (in a reformatory or industrial school) of all the formal safeguards that such proceedings provide for an adult facing a possible prison sentence. It then affirmed four basic rights: the right to counsel, the right to be notified of the charges, the right to confront and cross-examine witnesses, and the privilege against self-incrimination. In *In re Winship*[31] the USSC held that proof beyond a reasonable doubt was as necessary to substantiate a guilty verdict on a criminal charge against a child as it was in relation to an adult, but in *McKiever v. Pennsylvania*,[32] it found a jury trial to be unnecessary in criminal proceedings against a juvenile defendant.

In the face of rising crime rates, spurred on by President Ronald Reagan's mantra of 'tough on crime and tough on the causes of crime,' juvenile courts leaned more towards retributive justice rather than welfare considerations throughout the 1970s and 80s.[33] As the Inter-American Commission on Human Rights (IACHR) noted:[34]

> [B]y the year 1990, many states across the U.S. had passed highly regressive changes to their legislation and policy with regard to youth involved in the justice system. The changes varied in the details of their implementation, but the broad theme was the denial of access to rehabilitative juvenile justice systems, and consequent mandatory processing of juveniles in the more punitive adult systems. . . . [H]undreds of thousands of children in the United States are denied their essential guarantees in adult criminal proceedings that do not respect or acknowledge their status as children.

26 372 U.S. 335 (1963).
27 383 U.S. 541 (1966).
28 *Gallegos v. Colorado*, 370 U.S. 49, 55–56 (1962).
29 *Miranda v. Arizona*, 384 U.S. 436 (1966).
30 387 U.S. 1 (1967).
31 397 U.S. 358, 361, 365 (1970).
32 403 U.S. 528 (1971).
33 See for example, Finley, L., *Juvenile Justice*, Greenwood Press, (2007).
34 See the Inter-American Commission on Human Rights, Children and Adolescents in the United States' Adult Criminal Justice System, (2018), at pp 26 and 63. See, further, at http://www.oas.org/en/iachr/reports/pdfs/Children-USA.pdf.

By the end of the 20th century, despite falling crime rates – which plateaued in 1998 – both legislation and judicial process were being applied with little differentiation between adults and juveniles, particularly as regards crimes relating to drugs, guns and violence; juvenile offenders being two or three times more likely to have non-white racial origins; and a policy of incarceration resulting in the system being saturated with offenders from socially marginalised groups convicted of low-level offences for whom no meaningful rehabilitation programme was available.

In recent years, however, the U.N. CRC[35] and the USSC have reaffirmed the importance of a policy that differentiates between child and adult offenders, the latter on the basis that the developmental process of childhood necessarily means they bear less culpability than adults in a criminal law context.[36]

School shootings Children who kill other children is neither a new phenomenon nor one that is exclusive to the U.S., but unquestionably, it is now a serious problem for this country.[37] The phenomenon is partly an aspect of an embedded gun culture in a country where guns far outnumber citizens and where gun killings are an everyday event: some 12 children die and a further 32 are injured on a daily basis in the U.S. mass shootings of children in schools, however, would seem to be something different. In almost half the cases, they have been carried out by children – perpetrator and victims being pupils at the same school[38] – and this has come to be recognised as a singular characteristic of modern U.S. society, which has experienced 2,032 school shootings since 1970.[39] In 2022 alone, by May, there had been 119.[40]

Private family law policy relating to children

The 'liberty' interests of parents – their *locus standi* as autonomous guardians of children and protectors of family boundaries – is a long-standing reference point in U.S. family law. This was inferred in cases such as *Wisconsin v. Yoder* when the court stressed that 'our holding today in no degree depends on the assertion of the religious interest of the child as contrasted with that of the parents.'[41]

35 Committee on the Rights of the Child, General Comment No. 10, Children's rights in juvenile justice, CRC/C/GC/10, 25 April 2007.

36 See: *Roper v. Simmons*, 543 U.S. 551; *J.D.B. v. North Carolina*, 564 U.S. 261; *Miller v. Alabama*, 567 U.S. 460; and *Graham v. Florida*, 560 U.S. 48.

37 In January 2023, a six-year-old boy in Newport, Virginia, was detained in custody after shooting his teacher on school premises.

38 See, further, at https://www.campussafetymagazine.com/safety/k-12-school-shooting-statistics-everyone-should-know/.

39 See, further, at https://www.sandyhookpromise.org/blog/gun-violence/16-facts-about-gun-violence-and-school-shootings/.

40 See, further, at https://www.statista.com/statistics/971473/number-k-12-school-shootings-us/.

41 406 U.S. 205 (1972) at 230.

MATRIMONIAL

The U.S. divorce rate peaked in 1980 at 7.9 (per 1,000 of the population aged 15–64) and has declined slowly but steadily ever since, dropping to 5.2 in 2008 and down to 2.9 in 2018,[42] though it is still among the highest in the world.[43]

The welfare interests of the child and their wishes regarding the parent best placed to be entrusted with furthering those interests have long been recognised in matrimonial proceedings. Under the Uniform Marriage and Divorce Act 1973 – commonly referred to as UMDA – when determining child care arrangements in the context of divorce proceedings, 'the court shall determine custody in accordance with the best interest of the child [and] . . . shall consider . . . the wishes of the child as to his custodian.'

GUARDIANSHIP AND WARDSHIP

The Uniform Guardianship, Conservatorship and Other Protective Arrangements Act 2017 is a model federal statute developed by the Uniform Law Commission. It uses the term 'guardian' for a person appointed by a court to manage the care and well-being of another person, 'conservator' for a person appointed by the court to manage the property of another person, and 'other protective arrangements' to describe a less-restrictive alternative to guardianship or conservatorship, an arrangement that is limited to addressing a specific need. In practice, the appointment of a guardian is most often made for an elderly person who has been assessed as incapable of making decisions regarding their well-being and financial affairs. When a parent or the court makes an appointment for a child, the effect is to vest, in a named person, custody and the authority to make decisions concerning their protection, education, care, discipline, etc. Such appointments are often made for a child who has been placed in out-of-home care or in favour of stepparents and kinship placements. The parents' legal rights are not terminated; they remain entitled to play a role in their children's lives.

Wardship, on the other hand, is not a statutory power but an inherent jurisdiction of the High Court, enabling it to take important decisions regarding the upbringing of any child made a 'ward of court.'[44] Any child subject to a court order vesting parental rights in the state can be defined as a 'ward of the state.'

ADOPTION

In Massachusetts, the Adoption of Children Act 1851 launched adoption as a statutory process in the U.S. Significantly, it required the court to be satisfied that the adoption was 'fit and proper,' thereby embedding the welfare of the child as a

42 See, further, at https://www.statista.com/statistics/195955/divorce-rate-in-the-united-states-since-1990/.

43 See, further, the Heritage Foundation, The Divorce Rate Is Declining but Still High, at http://www.familyfacts.org/charts/120/the-divorce-rate-is-declining-but-still-high.

44 *State v. Weidner*, 6 Ore. App. 317, 321 (Or. Ct. App. 1971).

necessary requirement for an adoption order, though how that test was to be interpreted was a matter left entirely to judicial discretion.

Thereafter, it was primarily married or divorced 'working-class' women who relinquished their usually older children for adoption, which they did most often for economic reasons. After WWII, it became common for younger, white, more broadly middle-class unmarried women to do so with children in infancy. From the late 1950s until the mid-1970s, the social stigma and financial hardship accompanying the role of single parent made adoption a likely option for many unmarried mothers of babies, in this country as elsewhere. More recently, as pregnancy rates have fallen,[45] the stigma reversed and attached to relinquishment rather than to single parenthood, but poverty or relative poverty has continued to significantly influence the decisions of unmarried mothers. Indeed, Patricia Strowbridge of Adoption Professionals has claimed:[46]

> Take Florida, which has 5,000 to 7,000 adoptions a year. Over 80% of them are private and most of these involve young women. In many cases they simply can't afford to keep their babies because income is so low and welfare is so poor. So they get in touch with an adoption agency.

However, a sense of perspective is needed. It has been estimated that from the early 1970s to the late 1990s, the voluntary relinquishment for adoption of children born 'out of wedlock' in the United States decreased from 8.7% to 1%.[47] The rates of births to unmarried women, however, have been increasing: from an estimated 18.4% of all live births in 1980 to 40.6% in 2008, dipping slightly to 39.6% in 2018,[48] with the U.S. having the highest teen pregnancy rate of the Western industrialised world. Moreover, statistically, most 'private' adoptions are, in fact, those made in favour of stepparents and relatives. This is also the form of adoption that attracts the least professional scrutiny. Hollinger has noted that 'perhaps half or more of all adoptions are by step-parents; many others are by grandparents or other relatives, who like step-parents, have long been the de-facto parents of the children they adopt.'[49]

45 See statistics collated at the Centers for Disease Control and Prevention, which reveal that fewer women in the United States are having children. Between 2000 and 2009, pregnancy rates for U.S. women fell by 12%, or nearly 6.4 million pregnancies. The pregnancy rate in 2013 was the lowest it had been in 12 years. See, further, at www.cdc.gov/nchs/data/databriefs/db136.htm.

46 See, *The Independent Review*, 5 January 2005, as cited by Hilpern, K., in her feature article 'The Daddy of All Game Shows' at p 3.

47 See, for example, Jones, J., Adoption Experiences of Women and Men and the Demand for Children to Adopt by Women 18–44 years of age in the United States, 2002, National Centre for Health Statistics, *Vital and Health Statistics*. (2008): 23(27); Chandra, A. et al., Adoption, Adoption Seeking, and Relinquishment for Adoption in the United States, National Centre for Health Statistics, Advance Data No. 306, 11 May 1999.

48 See, further, at https://www.statista.com/statistics/276025/us-percentage-of-births-to-unmarried-women/.

49 Hollinger, J.H., *Adoption Law and Practice* (vol. 1), Matthew Bender/Lexis-Nexis, New York, 2005 update. Note that, unusually among the common-law jurisdictions, adoptees in the U.S. may be adults.

INTERCOUNTRY ADOPTION: HISTORICAL

A characteristic feature of adoption in this country is the extent to which it has accommodated children born elsewhere: from at least the era of the Korean War, intercountry adoption has played a prominent role, subsequently growing to constitute a significant proportion of annual adoptions. The collapse of the Soviet Union in 1991 triggered a flow of some 60,000 children from Russia to the U.S. In 2004, the peak year for intercountry adoptions, the number of ICAs reached 22,884 before entering into its current period of decline, which saw the number drop to 4,059 in 2018 (down 655 from the previous year).[50] The continuing fall in intercountry adoptions masks what Hollinger sees as an interesting trend: the decline is largely limited to young babies.[51] Since 2004, the number of international adoptees aged between five and twelve fell only slightly while the number of children under age one plummeted by 90%. While the children are now older, they are also more likely to have been institutionalised (with resulting attachment disorders), possibly have 'special needs,' and probably have significant health or social care problems.[52]

After acceding to the Hague Convention, the U.S. ended its former practice of approving adoptions from countries where fraud and corruption surrounded the availability of children. In so doing, the U.S. demonstrated the ironic reality that meeting Hague standards, imposed to safeguard children, can result in denying many their best opportunity for a safer life. In a reverse dynamic, for the past 50 years, the U.S. has become a 'sending' country, with 26 agencies in the U.S. now accredited by the State Department to process outgoing adoptions.

FAMILY PLANNING, ABORTION, SURROGACY, IVF, ETC

Family planning or 'women's reproductive rights' has had a contentious political and legal history. All along the continuum from the availability of contraceptives[53]

50 See, FY2018 Intercountry Adoption Statistics at https://travel.state.gov/content/dam/NEWadoption-assets/pdfs/Tab%201%20Annual%20Report%20on%20Intercountry%20Adoptions.pdf.

51 Note that Hayes compared domestic placements by public agencies and by ICA in the U.S. in 2006 and discovered that intercountry adoptees were much younger than domestic adoptees: 42% under one year and 84% under four years, as opposed to 46% from public agencies (citing statistics from the U.S. Department of Homeland Security 2007 and the U.S. Department of Health and Human Services 2008).

52 See the Donaldson Adoption Institute, *A Changing World: Shaping Best Practices through Understanding of the New Realities of Intercountry Adoption*, (2013).

53 See, for example, *Griswold v. Connecticut*, 381 U.S. 479 (1965) (a state may not prohibit distribution of contraceptive devices to married couples); *Eisenstadt v. Baird*, 405 U.S. 438 (1972) (single persons cannot be denied contraceptives); and *Carey v. Population Services International*, 431 U.S. 678, (1977) (a statute prohibiting the sale of contraceptives to minors under the age of 16 was unconstitutional).

to abortion services[54] to IVF and now to commercial surrogacy and gene editing, there has been a constant stream of caselaw which has entrenched the associated deep social divisions. From the perspective of the welfare interests of children, the central concern of this book, the current constraints introduced in states such as Arizona on what had been previously been understood under the rubric of *Roe v. Wade*[55] as a woman's right to choose can sadly only result in unwanted births. The welfare of many of those conceived as a consequence of rape or born with congenital defects or following anticipated obstetric issues that compromised the health or life of their mother will inevitably be at risk from the outset. Moreover, at this point, it is difficult to predict what ramifications may flow from the *Dobbs* decision: the rationale grounded on the 14th Amendment, as construed in its original social context, may logically be extended to include matters such as access to contraceptives, surrogacy, and other associated developments that have since come to redefine 'the family.'

The contemporary availability of improved fertility treatment (AID, GIFT, etc.), including donor embryo implantation, is having a growing impact on the extent to which adoption is the preferred choice for infertile heterosexual couples, while surrogacy arrangements – particularly commercial arrangements contracted overseas – are now increasingly used instead of adoption, or in conjunction with it, by those in same-sex relationships.

Surrogacy In some states, most notably California, surrogacy is legal whether undertaken on a commercial or altruistic basis. Whatever the sexual orientation of the commissioning parents, parentage may be legally safeguarded without recourse to adoption, and surrogacy contracts are regularly enforced by the courts.

Principles

As Justice Stevens has pointed out:

> [T]he constitutional protection against arbitrary state interference with parental rights should not be extended to prevent the states from protecting children against the arbitrary exercise of parental authority that is not in fact motivated by an interest in the welfare of the child.[56]

54 See: *Roe v. Wade,* 410 U.S. 113 (1973), which legalized abortion nationwide, as subsequently endorsed in *Planned Parenthood of S.E. Pa. v. Casey*, 112 S. Ct. 2791 (1992); *Planned Parenthood v. Danforth*, 428 U.S. 52 (1976) and *Bellotti v. Baird,* 443 U.S. 622 (1979) (state laws requiring teenagers to have parental permission for abortion nullified).

55 410 U.S. 113 (1973), overturned by the ruling in *Dobbs v. Jackson Women's Health Organization*, No. 19–1392, 597 U.S. ___ (2022).

56 *Santosky v. Kramer*, 455 U.S. 745 (1982).

Paramountcy principle

The 'welfare interests of a child' is an amorphous concept,[57] only capable of acquiring functionality when applied to the circumstances of a particular child. When so applied, it becomes critically important in any judicial determination of issues relating to that child's upbringing. However, it cannot be said that it is then given a paramount weighting in law. Indeed, the main reason the U.S. has declined to become a signatory state to the U.N. CROC and why the paramountcy principle cannot be said to function in child care law as it does in most other developed Western countries is because of the constitutional protection singled out for the rights of parents[58] as established by the USSC in cases such as *Santosky v. Kramer*[59] and emphatically declared by Thomas J in *Troxel*: 'Parents have a fundamental constitutional right to rear their children, including the right to determine who shall educate and socialize them.'[60] This has been noted by the Inter-American Commission on Human Rights, which points out that, although the U.S. has ratified the Optional Protocols to the U.N. CROC on the Sale of Children, Child Prostitution and Child Pornography and the Involvement of Children in Armed Conflict, its domestic laws do not adequately or consistently reflect the principle of the primacy of the best interests of the child.[61] It is of the view that there is no comprehensive system required under international law to protect and promote the rights of children. While there are established government agencies and institutions that address specific issues involving children – such as child welfare, abuse and neglect, and education, as well as juvenile justice – there is no overall mechanism in place that can serve to coordinate and implement one unified system throughout and across federal, state and local levels so as to ensure a consistent and comprehensive approach to policies, strategies and services aimed at the promotion of child welfare.[62]

PARAMOUNTCY: CHILD'S CONSENT

As might be expected, given this legal presumption, the right of a minor to refuse treatment would seem to be dependent on parental endorsement. In *Zoski v. Gaines*,[63] for example, a physician was found liable for damages resulting from removal of the tonsils of a fourth-grade boy because it was clear that his parents would have refused treatment had they been present. Again, in *In re E.G.*,[64] the

57 See, for example, Weinstein, J., And never the twain shall meet: The best interest of children and the adversary system, *University of Miami Law Review*, (1997): 79, 108.

58 See Volokh, E., Parent-child speech and child custody speech restrictions, *New York University Law Review* (2006): 81, 631 (2006).

59 *Santosky v. Kramer*, op cit.

60 *Troxel v. Granville*, 530 U.S. 57 (2000).

61 See The Inter-American Commission on Human Rights, Children and Adolescents in the United States' Adult Criminal Justice System, op cit at p 134.

62 Ibid, at p 138.

63 260 N.W. 99, 102–03 (Mich. 1935).

64 549 N.E. 2d 322, 328 (Ill. 1989).

Illinois Supreme Court recognised the importance of parental authority and asserted that if a parent were to oppose a child's refusal of life-saving treatment, 'This opposition would weigh heavily against the minor's right to refuse.' Only in the absence of conflict with parental authority are the U.S. courts willing to permit minors to make such decisions.[65]

Parental rights again determine whether or not a child with a mental health disability will be committed to institutional care, with or without the consent of the minor concerned. An extreme example of this occurred in *Parham v. J.R.*,[66] a case in which the court acknowledged that commitment to an institution placed the child's liberty interest at stake but found that the interest was subsumed by the parents' interest in caring for the child. It deferred to the parents' decision to commit their child and found that a minor was entitled only to a 'neutral fact finder' (such as a mental health practitioner), not a full judicial hearing to challenge the parents' decision. This case stands as an indicator of the weak weighting given in U.S. law to the capacity of a child to determine their welfare interests relative to the capacity of parents and others to do so on their behalf.

However, under the common law, an 'emancipated minor' has long been held to be exempt from the normal requirement that their medical treatment be authorised by parental consent.[67] So, most notably, it had been judicially recognised that some minors possess the maturity to make certain specific constitutionally protected decisions, such as the decision to have an abortion,[68] although, as such a decision is no longer constitutionally protected, probably neither is the accompanying right of a mature minor.[69] In *Bellotti, Attorney General of Massachusetts v. Baird*,[70] the court indicated that adolescents' constitutional rights could not 'be equated with those of adults' due to 'the particular vulnerability of children; their inability to make critical decisions in an informed, mature manner; and the importance of the parental role in child rearing.' This opinion was echoed at much the same time by the Supreme Court comment that 'Most children, even in adolescence, simply are not able to make sound judgments concerning many decisions, including their need for medical care or treatment.'[71]

It would seem that in the U.S., the concept of an 'emancipated minor' requires evidence of a good deal more independence than is necessary under the '*Gillick*

65 See, *Bakker v. Welsh*, 108 N.W. 94, 96 (Mich. 1906) and *Younts v. St. Francis Hospital and School of Nursing*, 469 P.2d 330, 333 (Kan. 1970).

66 141 442 U.S. 584, 606 (1979).

67 See, for example: *State ex. rel. Scott* v. *Lowell,* 78 Minn. 166, 80 N.W. 877 (1899) and *Smith* v. *Seibly* 72 Wash.2d 66, 431 P.2d 719 (1967).

68 *Planned Parenthood of Central Missouri v. Danforth, Attorney General of Missouri*, 428 U.S. 52 (1976).

69 The USSC decision in *Dobbs v. Jackson Women's Health Organisation et al., No. 19–1392*, 597 U.S. ___ (2022), to the effect that there was no constitutional right to an abortion, overturned *Roe v. Wade*.

70 443 U.S. 622 (1979) at p 634.

71 See *Parham, Commissioner, Department of Human Resources of Georgia v. J. R.*, 442 U.S. 584 (1979) at p 603.

test'[72] in the U.K. Some statutes stipulate that the concept needs to be substantiated by the minor living and supporting themselves away from their parents. There is also caselaw providing an equivalent to the *Gillick* test: an unemancipated mature minor may give a valid consent to medical treatment where the procedure is for the benefit of the minor, and, in the judgment of the treating physician, the minor has sufficient intelligence to understand its nature and consequences.[73] In addition, allowances may always be made for medical practitioners who act in good faith on the basis of a child's consent in an emergency.[74] It would seem that welfare interests, if not paramount, are at least sufficiently weighty to overcome rules regarding the competency of minors.

APPLICATION TO ADOPTION AND OTHER MATTERS

The presumption of a parental right to custody can only be vitiated by voluntary relinquishment or by 'clear and convincing' evidence that the birth parents are unfit to care for their child.[75] This was established at an early stage in the aforementioned *Sanotsky* case, when the court commented that 'the fundamental liberty interest of natural parents in the care, custody and management of their child does not evaporate simply because they have not been model parents.'[76] In short, the presumption favouring parental care is paramount in law, and not until that is negated can welfare assume primacy.

Principle of parental rights

Unlike in the U.K. and elsewhere, family law in the U.S. has not exchanged the language of a patriarchal era for that used by the U.N. CROC: the concept of 'parental responsibilities' has yet to displace 'parental rights.'

The presumption that birth parents have a legal right to the custody of their children is well established[77] and probably originates in the constitutionally protected fundamental 'right' of parents with respect to their children.[78] Indeed, the courts have often commented that 'natural bonds of affection lead parents to act in the best interests of their children,'[79] that 'there is a presumption that fit parents

72 *Gillick v. West Norfolk and Wisbech Area Health Authority* (1985) 2 A11 ER 402.

73 *Bishop* v. *Shurley*, 237 Mich. 76, 211 N.W. 75 (1926); *Lacey* v. *Laird,* 166 Ohio St. 12, 139 N.E.2d 25 (1956); and *Younts v. St. Francis Hospital,* 205 Kan. 292, 469 P.2d 330 (1970).

74 *Jacko-vach v. Yocum*, 212 Iowa 914, 237 N.W. 444 (1931) and *Luka v. Lowrie*, 171 Mich.122,136 N.W. 1106 (1912).

75 *Custody of a Minor*. 389 N.E.2d 68 (Mass. 1979).

76 *Santosky v. Kramer*, op cit.

77 See, for example, *Ellerbe v. Hooks*, 416 A.2d 512, 514 (Pa. 1980).

78 The parental right to custody has been deemed a fundamental right by the USSC: *Santosky v. Kramer*, ibid.

79 See, for example, *Parham v. J. R.,* 442 U.S. 584, 602 (1979); *Casey*, 505 U.S., at 895; and *Santosky v. Kramer*, ibid at 759.

act in the best interests of their children,'[80] and that the law respects 'the liberty of parents and guardians to direct the upbringing and education of children under their control.'[81] As the court declared in *Pierce*: 'The child is not the mere creature of the State; those who nurture him and direct his destiny have the right, coupled with the high duty, to recognize and prepare him for additional obligations.'[82]

It continues to be largely the case, though not always,[83] that 'so long as a parent adequately cares for his or her children (i.e., is fit), there will normally be no reason for the state to inject itself into the private realm of the family.'[84] The aforementioned *DeShaney v. Winnebago Social Services*[85] was a milestone in judicial pronouncements to that effect, and the ruling in *Pletcher v. People*[86] that 'if the parent commits wanton and needless cruelty upon his child, either by imprisonment of this character or by inhuman beating, the law will punish him' is a judicial reminder that parental rights must be exercised responsibly.

PARENTAL RESPONSIBILITY AND CORPORAL PUNISHMENT

The Child Abuse Prevention and Treatment Act (CAPTA) 2003[87] sets the threshold for child abuse which will be breached by any parental chastisement that leaves bruises or breaks a child's skin. As of May 2022, parental 'spanking' is legal in all states, but many prohibit corporal punishment in schools.[88]

SHARING PARENTAL RESPONSIBILITIES

The concept of parents and the state sharing responsibility for broadly ensuring a safe environment for the welfare interests of children has, arguably, been largely absent in the U.S. As memorably enunciated by the court almost a century ago, in *Pierce v. Society of Sisters*, 'The child is not the mere creature of the state; those who nurture him and direct his destiny have the right, coupled with the high duty, to recognise and prepare him for future obligations.'[89] However, a few short years later as the Depression took hold, President Franklin Roosevelt launched the New Deal programme, part of which included the Social Security Act 1935, which had a section that channelled federal funds to states for the support of disadvantaged families and authorising the Children's Bureau 'to cooperate with State public-welfare agencies in establishing, extending and strengthening, especially in

80 *Troxel v. Granville*, 530 U.S. 57, 68 (2000) at 68.
81 See *Pierce v. Society of Sisters*, 268 U.S. 510 (1925) and *Meyer v. Nebraska*, 262 U.S. 390 (1923).
82 Ibid.
83 In *Routten v. Routten*, 843 S.E.2d 154, 159 (2020), the court found the purported right of a fit parent to the custody of her child to be irrelevant.
84 *Troxel v. Granville*, op cit.
85 489 U.S. 189 (1989).
86 52 Ill. 395 (1869).
87 Originally enacted in 1974, and amended by the CAPTA Reauthorization Act of 2021.
88 See, further, at https://worldpopulationreview.com/state-rankings/child-discipline-laws-by-state.
89 268 U.S. 510, 535, (1926).

predominantly rural areas, [child welfare services] for the protection and care of homeless, dependent, and neglected children, and children in danger of becoming delinquent.' It was an initiative signalling that the state would not leave parenting wholly to parents: it had a duty of care to ensure the protection of children, which could and would extend to supporting disadvantaged parents.

However, since then, a focus on constitutional privacy rights, rigorously policed by the USSC, perhaps combined to some degree with a culture of private insurance–based health provision, has resulted in the state role in relation to parenting being either one of negative monitoring – intervening only after being put on notice of a breach of parental duty – or one of providing support services as a constituent part of its general responsibility for public health-care standards.

Family First legislation, clearly proclaiming its purpose as preventing children from entering foster family care, is a landmark statute in that it is anchored in a shared parent/state responsibility for the welfare interests of children. It gives legal recognition to both the importance of parental care and an accompanying parental entitlement for the state support necessary to maintain it. (See, further, later in this chapter.) However, while it may well be that the welfare principle dictates that the state should emphasise consensual rather than coercive intervention – to keep children in their birth families – the policy might have been driven more than a little by fiscal concerns; the cost to the public purse of foster care greatly outweighs the cost of supporting private family care.

Consanguinity principle

The fact that, at any one time, approximately a quarter of all children in state care due to parental fault or default are placed by the state with blood relatives testifies to the strength of a presumption that, in the U.S., the blood link is viewed as a positive indicator for furthering a child's welfare interests.[90] It would certainly seem to have guided judicial decisions in custody cases in which the choice lies between a birth parent and a third party.[91] However, the presumption has not always been borne out by judicial rulings.

NO PRESUMPTION FAVOURING CONSANGUINITY

In *Lehr v. Robertson*,[92] the USSC reiterated comments made in an earlier case that a parent's liberty interests 'do not spring full-blown from the biological connection between parent and child. They require relationships more enduring.'[93] More

90 See, for example, Child Welfare Information Gateway, Partnering With Relatives to Promote Reunification, (2020), at https://www.childwelfare.gov/pubs/factsheets-families-partner-relatives/.

91 See, for example, *Bancroft v. Bancroft*, 578 A.2d 114 (Vt. 1990); *In re D.G.*, 583 A.2d 160, 164 (D.C. 1990); and *P.G. v. W.M.T. (In re D.B.G.)*, 590 So.2d 329 (Ala. Civ. App. 1991).

92 463 U.S. 248 (1983).

93 Ibid at p 260, citing *Caban v. Mohammed*, 441 U.S. 380, 397 (1979).

recently, in *Adoptive Couple v. Baby Girl*,[94] the court dismissed a noncustodial parent's claim that he had an innate right to intervene in his unmarried partner's decision to place their child for adoption. The court found that the father had never lived with the unmarried mother, nor had he ever had any direct care responsibility for the child. He had never contributed financially to the maintenance of mother or child, and he had earlier declared that he would relinquish his parental rights.

Proportionality principle

The principle that state intervention in family affairs, on the grounds of protecting the welfare interests of a child, should be proportionate to the risk involved to those interests – a benchmark principle, frequently applied and reviewed by the ECtHR – has not received nearly as much judicial attention in the U.S.

Liberty principle

The principle that an individual enjoys the right to be free, independent and autonomous, relatively unconstrained by the state, is written into the country's founding documents,[95] draws support from frontiersman folk history, and has been something of a cultural benchmark since independence from colonial rule. The principle lies at the heart of the recent *Dobbs* decision. As explained in the syllabus:[96]

> *Roe* held that the abortion right is part of a right to privacy that springs from the First, Fourth, Fifth, Ninth, and Fourteenth Amendments. See 410 U. S., at 152–153. The *Casey* Court grounded its decision solely on the theory that the right to obtain an abortion is part of the 'liberty' protected by the Fourteenth Amendment's Due Process Clause.

The Court then, memorably, went on to find that *Roe* was 'egregiously wrong and on a collision course with the Constitution from the day it was decided.'[97]

The *Dobbs* decision, being clearly rooted in original constitutional principles, has significant implications for the law relating to children (as well as many other areas of law) because it indicates that the USSC, in its consideration of the balance between state interventionist powers and the citizen's right to autonomy, will look to ground its determination in those principles as originally stated in the 14th Amendment rather than reinterpreting them in light of changing contemporary social circumstances. If the law relating to abortion is to be understood as being anchored in constitutional principles reflecting the social circumstances prevailing in

94 12–399 (2013); 398 S.C. 625, 731 S.E.2d 550 (2012). See 2013 U.S. LEXIS 4916, 2013 WL 3184627.

95 See the Preamble to the Constitution and the Declaration of Independence 1776, paras 1–2.

96 *Dobbs v. Jackson Women's Health Organization,* op cit, at p 2. See, further, at https://www.supremecourt.gov/opinions/21pdf/19–1392_6j37.pdf.

97 Ibid, at p 5.

the pre-*Roe* era (when it was largely a criminal offence), it may well be that when child welfare/rights issues arise that engage the Constitution, the *locus standi* of the child relative to parents and to family unity must also be similarly subject to a traditional interpretation (i.e. as prevailed at the time of the 14th Amendment). The parameters of such an approach are difficult to discern but could logically extend to include same-sex relationships and marriage. The body of federal caselaw, accrued over many decades tracking the developing social mores that have redefined 'the family,' may be found to have little if any precedent value. Whether such revisionism will be maintained by the USSC or accepted and followed by state legislatures and judiciary is open to question.

FAMILY LIFE

The deference shown by the state and the law to the constitutionally protected individual liberty of a parent to exercise care and control over their children has been affirmed by the USSC.[98] This is centred on the right to custody but extends to determining education (including homeschooling) and religious upbringing and has included reasonable chastisement.[99] It has been evident in cases such as *Eisenstadt v. Baird*,[100] in which the USSC extended the protection of privacy, initially confined to the marital family unit, to the individual.[101]

Legal system: legislation, courts, welfare/rights and representation

As there is no national legal system focused on the law relating to children, law and regulatory matters are determined separately by each of the 50 states and the District of Columbia.

Legislative framework

All domestic law – whether state or federal, statute or administrative – can be and often is tested against the overarching principles of the Constitution, which provide federal recognition of and protection for human rights. The Bill of Rights, in conjunction with the 13th, 14th and 15th Amendments, may be considered to provide a body of provisions with particular relevance for family matters. The American Declaration of the Rights of Man, especially Article 6, concerning the right to a family and to the protection necessary to enjoy that right, and Article 7, which recognises a child's right to protection, is clearly also relevant.

98 *Pierce v. Soc'y of Sisters*, 268 U.S. 510 (1925) and *Meyer v. Nebraska*, 262 U.S. 390, 399 (1923).

99 *Pierce v. Soc'y of Sisters*, ibid, at 534–35.

100 405 U.S. 438 (1972).

101 See *Stenberg v. Carhart*, 530 U.S. 914, 921 (2000); *Planned Parenthood of Se. Pa. v. Casey*, 505 U.S. 833, 847 (1992); and *Griswold v. Connecticut*, 381 U.S. 479, 485–86 (1965).

INTERNATIONAL LAW

The U.S. has been a member of the Organization of American States since 1951 and is therefore subject to the obligations derived from the OAS Charter. Although a founding member of the United Nations and signatory state to the UDHR, the U.S. has been cautious in its approach to international law, being wary of obligations that may compromise its sovereignty.[102] For that reason and others, unlike some 200 other countries, it has failed to ratify the U.N. Convention on the Rights of the Child (U.N. CROC), with its unequivocal Article 3 declaration that the best interests of the child must be the primary consideration in all decisions affecting their welfare. This declaration is viewed as problematic as it may conflict with constitutional provisions regarding the parent/child relationship and the concept of 'family.' The fact that the U.S. is now the sole U.N. member state not to have ratified this international instrument – crucially important for children's welfare interests and rights – is a matter of some significance for this chapter and, indeed, for the book.

The Hague Convention on Protection of Children and Co-operation in Respect of Intercountry Adoption came into effect for all intercountry adoptions (ICAs) between the United States and other Hague Convention countries in 2008.[103] The U.S. has also ratified the Convention on the Civil Aspects of International Child Abduction 1980; signed and ratified the International Covenant on Civil and Political Rights (ICCPR); and signed but not yet ratified the Convention on the Elimination of All Forms of Discrimination against Women (CEDAW) and the International Convention on Economic, Social, and Cultural Rights (ICESCR). It has not signed either the U.N. CRC or the Rome Statute of the International Criminal Court. Similarly, as founding member of the American Convention on Human Rights, this nation has committed itself, in Articles 17 and 19, to defending the integrity of the family unit and ensuring the protection of children respectively. Other relevant legislation includes the Protocol of San Salvador and the Riyadh Guidelines.[104]

DOMESTIC LAW: THE CONSTITUTION AND FEDERAL LEGISLATION

The Constitution has been and continues to be of fundamental importance to the development of family law in the U.S. This product of the common law has, over many generations, been creatively interpreted by the USSC to meet the challenges presented by a constantly evolving society – challenges that could not possibly

102 See, *Roger v. Simmons*, 543 U.S. 551 at 622–628.

103 Intercountry Adoption Act of 2000, codified at 42 U.S.C. sec. 14901 *et seq*. The Child Protection Convention, signed by President Obama, has not yet been ratified by the U.S. Senate. Also note the Intercountry Adoption Universal Accreditation Act 2012, which requires adoption service providers working with prospective adoptive parents in non-Convention adoptions to comply with the same accreditation requirements and standards that apply in Convention adoption cases.

104 For further information on relevant international treaties, conventions, protocols, etc, see O'Halloran, K., *Children, the Law, and the Welfare Principle: Perspectives from Europe*, Routledge, (forthcoming).

have been foreseen by or within the intent of its founders. Same-sex marriage is only the most recent of a range of such instances in which that court has set aside previously established legal determinations and affirmed a more expansive interpretation of the law to accommodate a new form of social need. Arguably, that common law approach – reinterpreting by analogy the application of a principle to a meet the needs of a contiguous manifestation of much the same circumstance – is now in doubt following the USSC ruling in *Dobbs*. (See, further, Chapters 5 and 9.) Ultimately, however, the Constitution requires a state to show compelling reason for infringing rights of family privacy and overriding parental autonomy. As these fundamental liberties are protected by the 14th Amendment and its guarantee of due process, it is possible that the *Dobbs* decision may prove to be of limited effect as a constraint on personal freedoms.[105]

Increasingly, in recent years, model statutes have been drawn up to provide a template for that which the federal government, at any point in time, considers to be a body of core provisions for U.S.-wide legislation. States are free to enact such legislation in whole or in part or to ignore it. In addition, 'uniform' statutes (providing recommendations for removing obstructive inconsistencies between states in areas of similar legislative provision) are prepared within states which may then attract federal government endorsement, funds and pressure to adopt such legislation.

Family First Prevention Services Act 2018 This act enables states to use federal funds to provide enhanced support for children and families, thereby preventing the need to take children into the public care system. It supports states to establish an electronic interstate processing system for the placement of children in foster care, guardianship or adoption, and it supports the recruitment and retention of high-quality foster families. The 2018 act was reinforced by the Family First Transition Act 2019 and subsequently by the Further Consolidated Appropriations Act 2020, which provides financial relief for states to develop prevention-focused infrastructure for their child welfare systems. As of 2020, some 38 states had introduced bills modelled on the 2018 act.[106]

Juvenile Justice Reform Act 2018 Effective from 2020, this act changed the definition of terms used in the original 1974 statute, including 'adult inmate,' 'contact,' 'Indian Tribe,' and 'jail or lockup for adults.' It also made changes to annual reporting requirements, state allocations, state planning requirements and the distribution of federal funds.

Uniform Guardianship, Conservatorship and Other Protective Arrangements Act 2017 Comprising seven articles, this legislation establishes three different levels of responsibility –

105 See, for example, *Meyer v. Nebraska*, 262 U.S. 390 (1923); *Stanley v. Illinois*, 405 U.S. 645 (1972); and *Wisconsin v. Yoder*, 406 U.S. 205 (1972).

106 See, further, at https://www.ncsl.org/research/human-services/family-first-updates-and-new-legislation.aspx.

'guardianship,' 'conservatorship' and 'other protective arrangement'– that may be assigned to an appointed person or entity with respect to someone incapable of managing their affairs. The act modernises the law and protects the rights of individuals who are subject to guardianship and conservatorship. It encourages courts to impose the least-restrictive orders possible to adequately protect vulnerable minors and adults and to monitor the protective arrangement to continuously adapt to an individual's changing capabilities and needs.

Every Child Deserves a Family Act 2013 This legislation states that any organisation dealing with the foster and adoptive care of children which receives federal funding is prohibited from discriminating against prospective adopters in same-sex relationships or identifying as LGBT. However, the Trump administration, in a pushback on such measures, favoured instead a reinforcing of conservative religious values which has eroded the legislative intent and effect of this statute.[107]

Interstate Compact on the Placement of Children (revised 2008) Developed in 1974, the compact was designed to ensure protection and services to children placed across state lines. It imposes a number of procedural requirements on domestic adoptive placements that involve more than one state.

Children's Health Act 2000 This act reinforced the Adoption Incentives Programme, which provides for the payment of incentive funds to eligible states and territories to facilitate the recruitment of adoptive families for children with special needs and increase the number of children adopted from public foster care.

The safe haven laws Since 1999, most states have passed 'safe haven' laws in an attempt to prevent unsafe abandonment of babies and neonaticide. These tend to include provisions allowing parent(s) or those designated by the parent(s) to anonymously leave an 'unwanted infant' at a safe haven centre (hospital emergency room, fire station, police station): no questions are asked; no identification of parent(s) or social or medical history of baby is required. Note that such action – invariably by or directed by a birth mother – can constitute a peremptory strike against the human rights of a putative father and will compromise those of the child thereby deprived of their right to access origin information needed to develop an authentic identity.

Uniform Child-Custody Jurisdiction and Enforcement Act 1997 Designed to deter interstate parental kidnapping and to promote uniform jurisdiction and enforcement provisions in interstate child-custody and visitation cases, this act has been enacted by 25 states and the District of Columbia and introduced into legislatures in several other states.

107 See, further, at https://everychilddeservesafamily.com/no-adoption-discrimination.

Adoption and Safe Families Act 1997 The principal aim of this statute – commonly referred to as ASFA – was to promote the adoption of children in foster care. It amended but did not repeal the 1980 act and introduced two new concepts: the duty of a state to make reasonable efforts at 'permanency planning' once adoption or permanent guardianship becomes the goal and the concept of 'concurrent planning.'[108] It also introduced 'legal guardianship,' which provides authority for the transfer of parental rights to a relative, enabling them to assume permanent care responsibility for a child failed by parental care.[109] States are eligible to claim financial bonuses from federal funds if they exceed their set quota of annual adoptions.[110] To qualify for federal funds, a state scheme must show that 'in determining reasonable efforts . . . to be made with respect to a child, and in making such reasonable efforts, the child's health and safety shall be the paramount concern.'[111] This shifted the legal emphasis from family preservation to the priority of child safety. It requires a clear statement made in court when a care order is issued of the changes to be made by the parents within a 12-month period, after which the child will either be returned to parental care or placed for adoption; a permanency hearing to be held 12 months after the issue of a care order; and mandatory concurrent planning, and, after a child has been in care for 15 out of 24 months, good reason must be shown as to why a petition to terminate parental rights should not be filed. In effect, the 1997 act imposed a 15-month time limit on the use of financial resources to achieve family reunification, after which resource allocation switches to supporting permanency through adoption. This was seen by some as a worrying development:[112]

> This shift of resources into promoting adoption, as opposed to state-managed foster care, as a solution for children in 'dysfunctional' families can be seen as a form of 'privatising' child welfare.

There were also worries that adoption through the foster care system would be viewed by some as a low-cost and 'working class' alternative to intercountry adoption, which, at up to $50,000 or more for per child, is an option in practice only open to the more wealthy.

108 42 USC section 675 (E).

109 A 'legal guardianship' order bears a strong resemblance to the English 'special guardianship' order. Both offer a strategic halfway house between long-term foster care and adoption that does not require the extinguishing of birth parents' rights.

110 Federal funds were used as an incentive to encourage states to expedite the adoption of children in the public care system: states would receive $4,000 for every child adopted beyond their best year's total, an extra $4,000 for every child aged nine and older, $2,000 for every special-needs child adopted above the baseline year, and additional federal funds if they exceeded their prior number of completed adoptions.

111 42 USC section 671 section 15.

112 See Woodhouse, B., op. cit. at p 375.

The adoption incentives programme authorised by the 1997 act began the following year and has since been reauthorised twice: as part of the Adoption Promotion Act 2003 and the Fostering Connections to Success and Increasing Adoptions Act 2008. This approach has since been implemented through replicated state legislation across the U.S.[113] The 1997 act also established the Adoption and Foster Care Analysis and Reporting System (AFCARS), a mandatory data-collection system. This provides evidence that the policy drive to use adoption to secure permanency for children unable to return to their birth families is indeed working.

Multi-Ethnic Placement Act 1994 The legislative intent driving this federal statute was to reduce delays in finding foster and adoption homes for children admitted to the public care system by prohibiting any consideration of race, colour or national origin in identifying a permanent family home. It compelled states to make diligent efforts to recruit and retain foster and adoptive families that matched the ethnic diversity of 'waiting' children. Two years later, it was amended

Adoption Assistance and Child Welfare Act 1980 This federal legislation, which was a response to concerns that too many children were being removed from parental care only to disappear into the public care system, established the modern legal framework for child protection. It introduced and positioned within statute law the formative concepts of 'permanency' and 'reasonableness' and provided the basis for a generation of professional intervention focused on rehabilitating children within their families of origin. It authorised the channelling of federal funds to those states that implemented child welfare laws emphasising family preservation and reunification and made 'reasonable efforts' to prevent the removal of children from their families or to reunite them as appropriate. It also funded state initiatives to provide post-adoption support for adopters of hard-to-place children. The human rights dimension to this legislative initiative was reinforced by the decision of the Supreme Court in *Santosky v. Kramer*,[114] which ruled that states must have 'clear and convincing evidence' that parents would be unable to care for their child before terminating parental rights, or such action would be in breach of the 14th Amendment.

This legislation inaugurated an era characterised by public service investment in family reunification, but, as Woodhouse pointed out, it was a failing policy:[115]

> An over emphasis on 'reasonable efforts' was preventing children who would never realistically be reunited with their parents from moving on to find safe, permanent families through adoption.

113 See, further, U.S. Department of Health and Human Services, Children's Bureau, at http://www.acf.hhs.gov/programs/cb/focus-areas/adoption.

114 455 U.S. 755 (1982).

115 See Woodhouse, B., The Adoption and Safe Families Act: A Major Shift in Child Welfare Law and Policy, in Bainham, A. (ed.), *The International Survey of Family Law, 2000 Edition*, Family Law, Bristol, (2000) at p 380.

Accordingly, in 1997, Congress passed the Adoption and Safe Families Act in order 'to move abused and neglected kids into adoption or other permanent homes and to do it more quickly and more safely than ever before.'[116]

Indian Child Welfare Act 1978 This statute is commonly regarded as establishing the 'gold standard' for relationships between the state and Indigenous people. The legislative intent was to empower Indigenous communities by purposefully transferring to them legislative, administrative and judicial decision-making authority on certain matters. As was explained in *Adoptive Couple v. Baby Girl*,[117] this legislation was designed, in particular, to stop the unwarranted removal of Indian children from Indian families 'due to the cultural insensitivity and bias of social workers and state courts.' Consequently, as Diane Kunz notes, 'it has made it extremely difficult for potential adoptive parents to adopt children whose birth parents are members of federally registered Indian tribes.'[118] In practice, the provisions of the Indian Child Welfare Act often need to be considered in conjunction with those of the Interstate Compact on the Placement of Children.[119] (See, further, Chapter 8.)

Child Abuse Prevention and Treatment Act 1974 This is the foundation stone of modern U.S. child protection law. The 1974 act provides federal funding to states in support of their prevention, assessment, investigation, prosecution, and treatment activities relating to child abuse and neglect while also providing grants for the same purpose to public agencies and nonprofit organisations. It established the Office on Child Abuse and Neglect and has since been amended many times, most recently in 2021.

Juvenile Justice and Delinquency Act 1974 This federal statute established the Office of Juvenile Justice and Delinquency Prevention within the Justice Department to fund preventative juvenile crime programmes and research projects, coordinate statistics and generally act as a hub for resource distribution and policy development.

OTHER RELEVANT LEGISLATION

The Fostering Connections to Success and Increasing Adoptions Act 2008, as the title suggests, was intended to increase support for foster parents and improve incentives for adoption. The Adoption Promotion Act 2003 reauthorised the adoption incentive payments programme under part E of Title IV of the Social Security Act.

116 See Senator Rockefeller of West Virginia, 143 Cong. Rec. 12199.
117 *Adoptive Couple v. Baby Girl*, 12–399 (2013); 398 S.C. 625, 731 S.E.2d 550 (2012). See 2013 U.S. LEXIS 4916, 2013 WL 3184627.
118 Note to author (30 August 2020).
119 See, further, at http://law.capital.edu/adoption/#sthash.r0UHEGH0.dpuf.

The Intercountry Adoption Act 2000 gave effect to the Hague Convention. The Small Business and Job Protection Act 1996 prohibits:

> a state or other entity that receives federal assistance from denying any person the opportunity to become an adoptive or a foster parent on the basis of the race, color, or national origin of the persons or of the child involved to prohibit any denial or delay in placement on the basis of race, color, or national origin.

The Uniform Adoption Act 1994 attempted a complete codification of adoption law.

Courts and regulatory framework

Legal issues relating to the welfare interests and rights of children are adjudicated on an exclusively domestic basis and resolved in federal and state courts and administrative proceedings.

Courts and regulatory bodies

The U.S. continues to refute the jurisdiction of the International Criminal Court with respect to its citizens, on the grounds that it cannot accept any constraints on its sovereignty. A perceived threat to that sovereignty prompted U.S. withdrawal from the United Nations Educational, Scientific and Cultural Organisation (UNESCO) and United Nations Human Rights Council (U.N. HRC) in October 2017 and July 2018 respectively. The Human Rights Committee (HRC) is a body of international experts that monitors the progress of states parties, including the U.S., in implementing the provisions of the ICCPR. The U.S. submitted reports pursuant to the Universal Periodic Review process in 2010, 2014 and again in 2020.

FEDERAL COURTS AND REGULATORY BODIES

Each state has its own judicial and regulatory system, including a state Supreme Court.

United States Supreme Court (USSC) This is the ultimate court of appeal, to which appointments are made on the basis of nomination by the president and confirmation by the senate. The review jurisdiction of the USSC is discretionary and is exercisable, with respect to controversies, on a writ of certiorari under Rule 10 of the U.S. Supreme Court's rules of procedure.

Article III of the Constitution grants federal courts the authority to hear only 'cases' and 'controversies.'[120] The federal Circuit Court of Appeals hears cases on appeal from rulings issued by state district courts, and when sitting *en banc*, the court has authority to review and set aside its earlier precedents.

120 U.S. Const. Art. III, § 2, cl. 1.

SPECIALIST COURT SYSTEM

There is no national system of specialist courts to adjudicate matters affecting the welfare interests of children, but most cases dealing with children and youths under age 18 come before juvenile or family courts.[121]

Juvenile courts These deal with child abuse and neglect, delinquency and status offences; most also hear termination of parental rights (TPR) cases and adoption matters. They are supported as required by a high level of specialist input from CPS caseworkers, juvenile probation officers, psychologists, mental health professionals, physicians, domestic violence specialists, educators, child development specialists and others.

Family courts Introduced in several states, these provide a more holistic and co-ordinated professional response from a specialist team, on an ongoing basis, to all legal and service provision issues affecting a family. Drug courts, dealing with drug-related offences, are also utilised in many states. Tribal children are treated separately and come under the jurisdiction of the Indian Child Welfare Act, which empowers the child's tribe and family in decisions affecting the child.

Due process implies a requirement that all persons are served with notice of proceedings affecting them and that representation is provided to those (such as children) whose interests are being determined. It also implies that any delay in proceedings relating to children is prejudicial to their interests. Time is clearly an important factor: timely professional involvement, appropriate representation, prompt decision-making and expeditious legal proceedings all contribute in giving effect to due process. In *DeShaney v. Winnebago County Department of Social Services*,[122] the failure on all fronts was comprehensive, resulting in irreparable damage to the abused child's welfare interests. As the USSC noted:

> [I]nconsistent approaches taken by the lower courts in determining when, if ever, the failure of a state or local governmental entity or its agents to provide an individual with adequate protective services constitutes a violation of the individual's due process rights.[123]

Nonetheless, in this and other such cases it was held that the 14th Amendment did not provide an abused child failed by state child protection procedures with an enforceable claim under the due process clause.

In all probability, the current lengthy delays in proceedings to terminate parental rights with respect to abused children and the 'limbo' period that then ensues while they await the possibility of adoption also constitute failures of due process.

121 See, further, at https://www.childwelfare.gov/pubPDFs/courts.pdf.
122 489 U.S. 189 (1989).
123 Ibid.

Regulatory bodies Each state has its own set of regulatory bodies, but there are also some federal entities, such as the Equal Employment Opportunity Commission (EEOC), which administers and enforces civil rights laws and is the regulatory body for matters arising under Title VII and other titles of the Civil Rights Act 1964. It is responsible for enforcing federal laws that make it illegal to discriminate against a job applicant or an employee because of the person's race, colour, religion, sex (including pregnancy, gender identity and sexual orientation), national origin, age (40 or older), disability or genetic information. Many states have equivalent agencies with a right of appeal to the courts which adjudicate points of law and may grant leave of appeal to the state Supreme Court.

CHILDREN'S OMBUDSMAN

There is no national representative for children's issues; however many states have a Children's Ombudsman Office or Office of the Child Advocate. As of 2020, 22 states had a Children's Ombudsman/Office of the Child Advocate with duties and purposes specifically related to children's services. Another five states had a statewide ombudsman programme that addressed the concerns of all governmental agencies, including children's services. In general, such offices provide an independent agency for conducting enquiries, ensuring accountability and recommending improvements in aspects of service provision affecting children.[124]

SPECIAL RAPPORTEUR

The UN's special rapporteur on extreme poverty and human rights, in his 2017 report on the U.S., drew attention to the fact that some 40 million of its people are currently living in poverty. He noted that, in 2013, the U.S. had the highest infant mortality rate in the developed world and that the youth poverty rate is the highest across the OECD, with one-quarter of youth living in poverty compared to less than 14% across the OECD.

Representation for children

The right to due process, both 'procedural' and 'substantive,' is enshrined in the 5th and 14th Amendments and is exercisable by or on behalf of children. As has been judicially declared, '[N]either the 14th Amendment nor the Bill of Rights is for adults alone.'[125] Procedural due process implies a requirement that the legal system and its processes and protections are available to all. In practice, while the court is obligated to respect this right if a juvenile alleged offender insists, many do not insist, and so are not represented. Moreover, the right does not extend to representation in child protection cases; only 32 states make provision for a child to be represented in cases of alleged child abuse or neglect.

124 See, further, at https://www.ncsl.org/research/human-services/childrens-ombudsman-offices.aspx.
125 *In re Gault*, 387 U.S. 1, 13 (1967).

Although the general practice is to assign a guardian *ad litem* (GAL) to provide a report to the court which details all matters the GAL considers relevant to the welfare interests of the child, the guardian has no brief as advocate for the child, and while they will guide the child through the proceedings, this will not necessarily entail ensuring that their wishes are presented to the court. In most states an attorney – privately hired or appointed by the court – will represent and argue for those wishes, but there is no certainty that such representation will be available.[126] Moreover, as the Inter-American Commission on Human Rights have pointed out, '[M]any defense attorneys appointed to represent children accused of crimes are not sufficiently specialized, or often do not employ necessary diligence with respect to their more vulnerable clients, due to lack of training or resources.'[127]

THE CHILD IN COURT

While the 'due process' and 'equal protection' requirements of the 5th and 14th Amendments, respectively, necessitate legal representation for all parties in legal proceedings, due to their constitutional *locus standi*, parents have traditionally been recognised as appropriate representatives of the legal and welfare interests of their children. The constitutional protection singled out for the rights of parents conditions the right of a child to be heard in legal proceedings affecting their welfare interests.[128]

Douglas J, in *Wisconsin v. Yoder*,[129] con-tended that 'children should be entitled to be heard' on 'important and vital matter[s]' and criticised his colleagues on the bench (the majority) for having 'little regard for the views of the child' even though 'children them-selves have constitu-tionally protectable interests.' In what was, tellingly, a minority opinion, he suggested that 'the education of the child is a matter on which the child will often have decided views,' and if that child objects to his or her parent's wishes 'and is mature enough to have that desire respected, the state may . . . override the parents' [religious] . . . objections.'

CONSENT OF CHILD

In most states, a child may give a valid legal consent when they have reached 16 years of age, though in a minority, they must be at least 17 or 18. The informed consent of an older child is, for example, a precondition for their adoption in virtually all states.

126 In June 2020, President Trump signed an executive order which, among other things, authorised federal funding to further develop legal representation for parents and children.

127 The Inter-American Commission on Human Rights, Children and Adolescents in the United States' Adult Criminal Justice System, op cit at p 66.

128 See, further, Lee, S.J., A Child's Voice v. A Parent's Control: Resolving a Tension Between the Convention on the Rights of the Child and U.S. Law, *Columbia Law Review*, (2017): 117(3), at https://columbialawreview.org/content/a-childs-voice-vs-a-parents-control-resolving-a-tension-between-the-convention-on-the-rights-of-the-child-and-u-s-law/.

129 406 U.S. 205, 241–49 (1972), at 244–5.

In *Custody of Vaughn*,[130] the court noted the 11-year-old child's preference in having his custody awarded to the father and was of the view that such an expressed preference was enough to tip the balance in favour of the father, all else being equal, but ultimately remanded the hearing to allow for further enquiries.

Conclusion

The introduction of the Family First legislation in 2019 would seem to mark a significant turning point in the federal approach towards vulnerable families and failing parental care or, rather, a return to a policy represented 40 years ago by the Adoption Assistance and Child Welfare Act 1980. Such a policy change or reversal may indicate an acknowledgement that the welfare interests of children have not been best served by a system that now removes an unusually large number of children from parental care, only to return half of them to that care. Arguably, there is now a real tension, if not an outright conflict, between some of the principles that have been fundamental to the development of the law. In addition, this uncertainty has been further compounded by the *Dobbs* ruling. It is impossible to predict the future implications of the current revisionist approach of the USSC when applied to family matters; other landmark legal rulings – such as those relating to same sex marriage – may suffer the same fate as *Roe*. Until it becomes clearer which principles are to govern policy, more turmoil can be expected in the law relating to children and their welfare interests in the U.S.

130 664 N.E.2d 434, 438–40 & n.11 (Mass. 1996).

3 The welfare principle in contemporary practice

Public family law, civil and criminal jurisdictions

Introduction

In 2020, as the Trump administration drew to a close, governing policy and principles seemed to be coalescing more around traditional family values and the role they grant to the inherent rights of parents, rather than being based on maintaining a clear and distinct focus on the welfare interests of the child. As the Biden administration takes office in 2022, it is an interesting time to take stock of the values conflict in family law matters in the U.S.

This chapter considers contemporary law and practice in the civil jurisdiction as it relates to the welfare/rights of children in the U.S. Beginning with consensual state intervention in family affairs, it considers the strategies and the effectiveness of service provision aimed at preventing vulnerable families from breaching child care and protection standards. The bulk of the chapter then examines the civil law governing coercive state intervention: identifying the different routes into the public welfare system and the grounds for the associated orders, the forms of state care then provided, and the exit routes from that system. The chapter concludes with a consideration of criminal jurisdiction as it relates to children: the workings of the juvenile justice system, the role of the youth court, and the disposal options available to the court and reflects on how the balance between justice and welfare considerations is managed at federal and state levels.

Prevention

The Trump administration presided over a sea change in federal policy aimed at bolstering preventative and consensual state intervention in relation to vulnerable families. It deliberately set out to counter the policy direction indicated by the Adoption and Safe Families Act 1997 and the Every Child Deserves a Family Act 2013 by placing an emphasis on funding the family support services necessary to prevent entry into public care. In June 2020, President Trump signed an executive order aimed at strengthening child welfare programmes nationwide by lowering rates of child maltreatment, strengthening adoption programmes and boosting

DOI: 10.4324/9781003269564-6

supports for at-risk families, thereby reducing the number of children entering foster care.[1]

State duties to support families in need

As Luth has explained:[2]

> The preservation of the family is the highest priority of all child welfare services. The goal is for all children to remain with their parents or guardians. Family preservation programs may offer family counselling, substance use recovery, mental health services, domestic violence, sexual assault therapy, and food assistance. These programs include the Supplemental Nutrition Assistance Program (SNAP), food stamps, the Women, Infants and Children (WIC) program, the Temporary Assistance for Needy Families (TANF) program, housing assistance (Section 8 Housing Choice Voucher and Project-Based Rental Assistance), among others.

Until the introduction in 2019 of the Family First legislation, federal funds provided by way of Title IV-E of the Social Security Act could be used only to help with the costs of foster care maintenance for eligible children; for administrative expenses to manage the programme; for training for staff, foster parents and certain private agency staff; for adoption assistance; and for kinship guardianship assistance. It should be noted, however, that the costs of foster care are borne, at least to some degree, by the birth families: being billed by state authorities for foster care expenses has often been a serious obstacle to family reunification.[3]

SERVICE PROVISION

The Family First Prevention Services Act 2018,[4] as the title suggests, crystallised a new policy of focusing on consensual and preventative state intervention:

> to enable States to use Federal funds available under parts B and E of title IV of the Social Security Act 1980 to provide enhanced support to children and families and prevent foster care placements through the provision of mental

1 See, further, https://abcnews.go.com/Health/wireStory/trump-signs-order-strengthen-us-child-welfare-system-71433006.

2 Luth, R.J., The Intersection of American Indians/Alaskan Natives and the Child Welfare System: A Review of the Literature, in *McNair Scholars Research Journal*, (citing THE OFFICE OF FAMILY ASSISTANCE), (2016): 9, Article 8, at pp 89–90.

3 See, further, https://theconversation.com/us-child-welfare-system-is-falling-short-because-of-persistent-child-poverty-180543.

4 Part of Division E in the Bipartisan Budget Act of 2018 (H.R. 1892).

health and substance abuse prevention and treatment services, in-home parent skill-based programs, and kinship navigator services.[5]

Title IV-E funds can now be directed by states with federally approved family assistance plans towards the provision of preventative services that enable 'candidates for foster care' to stay with their parents or relatives.[6] The widespread take-up across the country of federal funding for family assistance plans indicates the extent of a resurgence in conservative values centred around strengthening legal protection for parental rights and state respect for the autonomy of birth families. Of course, it may also indicate both a policy to reduce unwanted state intrusion into family life and an awareness that its cheaper to offer early support than to later have to remove children in need.

State intervention: consensual

Consensual state service provision in support of vulnerable families has traditionally been delivered as part of local community public health programmes. National family support programmes such as Temporary Assistance for Needy Families (TANF) and Head Start (school preparation services for under-fives in disadvantaged families) have been in place for many years.

SPECIFIC SUPPORT SERVICES

As explained on the Children's Bureau website:[7]

> Family support programs may address the general population or target particular groups, such as ethnic and cultural minorities; adolescent parents; kinship caregivers; or families facing health, mental health, or substance use issues. They can be comprehensive or focus on a specific goal.

The Family First Prevention Services Act 2018 provides additional and targeted federal funding to enable the delivery of a broad range of services by states and tribes to give vulnerable families the support necessary to prevent their children from entering the public care system. Such federal funding may be accessed through the Title IV-E Prevention Services Clearinghouse, consisting of a continuously updated comprehensive list of evaluated and tested prevention services and programmes.[8] Preventative services take the form of home visiting by nurses

5 Family First Prevention Services Act 2018, TITLE VII – Subtitle A – Investing in Prevention and Supporting Families, s 50702.

6 See, further, www.ncsl.org/research/human-services/family-first-prevention-services-act-ffpsa.aspx#:~:text=The%20Family%20First%20Prevention%20Services%20Act%20also%20seeks%20to%20curtail,for%20more%20than%20two%20weeks.

7 See www.childwelfare.gov/topics/supporting/support-services/.

8 See, further, www.childwelfare.gov/topics/systemwide/laws-policies/federal/family-first/.

and social workers, parent education programmes, parent support groups, family resource centres and other services. The Strengthening Families National Network provides programmes and services in more than 20 states to support families and prevent child abuse and neglect. The fact that more funds are now available and specifically targeted towards such services must be conducive to improving the welfare interests of many children, as would seem to be borne out by the HHS announcement in 2020 that the preventative work of its Administration for Children and Families had helped reduce the number of children entering foster care in 2019 by about 9% since 2016, a trend that was maintained in 2020.

Children with disabilities The Individuals with Disabilities Education Act (IDEA) 2004 provides that all children with disabilities are entitled to a free appropriate public education to meet their unique needs and prepare them for further education, employment and independent living. Part C of the act recognises the need for identifying and reaching very young children with disabilities. It provides guidelines concerning the funding and services to be provides to children from birth through to two years of age. Part D describes national activities to be undertaken to improve the education of children with disabilities, including grants to improve the education and transitional services provided to students and resources to support programmes, projects and activities for children with disabilities.

PROMOTION

Service provision aimed at promoting children's welfare interests, rather than preventing their impairment, is hard to identify but would probably include grants aiding voluntary community-based family support organisations, financial and other support for adopters, and the new federally subsidised services to youth who have aged out of foster care.

Protection

The Family First legislation marks a change in policy by placing the onus on HSS to increase intervention aimed at supporting failing parental care rather than at peremptorily rescuing children at risk. It remains to be seen whether this will translate into legal change with the judiciary raising the bar on the standard of proof required to justify the removal of parental rights.

In most states, the Children's Bureau of the HSS is the agency designated to receive reports, conduct investigations and assessments, and provide intervention and treatment services to children and families. Statistics from the National Child Abuse and Neglect Data System (NCANDS) show that while nonconsensual state intervention in families is increasing, by far, the majority of interventions involve neglect rather than abuse.[9]

9 See U.S. Department of Health and Human Services [HHS], Administration for Children and Families [ACF], Children's Bureau, (2017).

State intervention: coercive

The rate of state intervention in families on child protection grounds would seem to be considerably higher in the U.S. than elsewhere: approximately 74 per 10,000 of children are in the public care system, compared, for example, with 47 per 10,000 in England.[10] Whether this is attributable to a lower U.S. legal threshold of tolerance for child abuse or to more effective detection and intervention strategies is perhaps debatable, but the onus on the court to ensure that state intervention is justified is unmistakable: 'due process requires that the state support its allegations by at least clear and convincing evidence' before it 'may sever completely and irrevocably the rights of parents in their natural child.'[11]

Vreeland, however, has more recently drawn attention to what she perceives to be a police policy of peremptorily arresting a parent believed to be abusing or, more frequently, neglecting their child.[12] She states that 'often the perpetrators arrested are parents who, because of poverty or poor judgment, have committed comparatively minor offences such as leaving children un-supervised, at home or on the street.' This 'criminalization of child welfare law,' she claims, 'is having a dramatic effect on the rights of children within the family.'[13] If she is right and the New York experience has been adopted in other states, then it may well be that this has become a contributory factor to the higher numbers of children now in the U.S. public care system.

MANDATORY REPORTING

Suspected child abuse or neglect is now a mandatory reporting matter in all states. Such allegations are reported to the local Child Protective Service (CPS), the headquarters of which is located within the Children's Bureau of the Administration for Children and Families in the U.S. Department of Health and Human Services (HSS).

Care proceedings

Proceedings concerning alleged child neglect, abuse, or abandonment or general parental failure to provide care and protection are most often brought by the state Child Protection Services on grounds specified in the relevant state child protection statute and are heard in the state juvenile court.

CARE PLAN

A child protection plan is required to be drawn up by the local CPS agency for any child it has reason to believe is suffering from significant harm or is at risk of doing so. It must specify the nature of the harm or the risks thereof, the plan of action, and

10 See, further, data published by the Performance and Innovation Unit (U.K.), (2000).

11 *Santosky v. Kramer*, 455 U.S. 745, 768 (1982).

12 Vreeland, A.B. 'The Criminalization of Child Welfare in New York City: Sparing the Child or Spoiling the Family?, *Fordham Urban Law Journal*. (2000): 27(3), 1053–1103.

13 Ibid, at p 1054.

the resources that will be needed to ensure protection for the child. Unlike its U.K. equivalent, a U.S. child protection plan would appear not to have the status of a court-endorsed document – in effect, a plan agreed between court and child protection agency – which commits the agency to proceed in an agreed direction and in accordance with specified objectives, which it can change once a care order is issued. Instead, it would seem to be an internal agency document to be agreed between agency, parents and child, detailing their respective areas of responsibilities and goals.

EMERGENCY PROTECTION ORDER

An EPO grants authority to the HSS for the temporary removal of a named child from the family home to a place of safety on the grounds that they have suffered harm or are at risk of doing so if not removed. State authorities will have jurisdiction to so intervene when the family is domiciled within and are citizens of that state and will also have authority with respect to an abandoned child or one who is judged to be at risk due to violence within the family or directed at it.

CARE ORDER

Following a CPS investigation, if the court determines the family home to be unsafe, at a 'dispositional hearing,' the custody of the child is vested in the CPS, which will organise a placement with family members, in foster care or elsewhere and agree on a child protection plan. After 12 to 18 months, the court will determine the child's permanent living situation, which will most usually be reunification with parent(s) and/or caregiver, guardianship, permanent placement with a relative, or the termination of parental rights (TPR) and adoption. Some 24 months later, if the child is still in CPS custody, an TPR court application is lodged, and if approved, the CPS proceeds with plans for adoption.

Public care

In 2015, the Annie E. Casey Foundation estimated that there were more than 400,000 children in the child welfare system on an average day in the United States.

It is salutary to note that while parental abuse or neglect is most usually responsible for children entering the system, many if not most of those exiting do so by returning to that same parental care. In 2020, of the 224,396 children who exited, 107,333 (48%) went back to their parents, and a further 6% went to other relatives; in 2015, the corresponding numbers were 243,060 and 123,894 (51%); and in both years, 6% went to other relatives.[14] This pattern, much the same for a decade or so, would seem to indicate that ultimately, the state considers the welfare interests of most children removed from failing parents to be best served by returning them to their families or extended families of origin.[15]

14 Ibid.

15 See AFCARS Report FY 2019, www.acf.hhs.gov/sites/default/files/documents/cb/afcarsreport27.pdf.

Foster care: partnership, rehabilitation and concurrent planning

The fact that nearly half a million children are currently in the public care system, together with the steadily rising trend in annual admissions, is attributed in large measure to the corresponding rise in rates of parental opioid addiction and overdoses.[16]

FOSTER CARE

As of 2020, there were approximately 430,000 children in the U.S. foster care system, including nearly 124,000 eligible for adoption.

In 2018, of the 63,100 exiting the public care system, some 51% were adopted by their foster parents.[17] The Family First Prevention Services Act 2018, reinforced by President Trump's 2020 executive order, aimed to accelerate this process by directing increased funding towards foster care to ensure that more of the children coming into public care system were placed with foster parents. Family First also provides federal funds for Kinship Navigator programmes to develop kinship foster care networks.

Laws relating to equality and nondiscrimination have impacted care arrangements for children in the U.S. as they have in the U.K. and elsewhere. For example, because Catholic Charities accepted public funds, state administrators required that organisation to ensure that its adoption agencies provided adoption and foster care services to same-sex couples in the same manner that they serviced different-sex couples. Rather than comply, Catholic Charities closed most of its Illinois affiliates, forcing the state to transfer more than 1,000 children from the charity's custody to secular agencies. The consequent disruption to the care arrangements for so many children, including the probability of losing the opportunity for adoption, clearly had a negative impact on their welfare interests.

Partnership and rehabilitation Following the court-authorised removal of a child from their family home and placement in foster care or elsewhere, federal law requires every child welfare agency to make reasonable efforts to achieve family reunification.[18] As was stressed in *Santosky*, 'when the State moves to destroy weakened familial bonds, it must provide the parents with fundamentally fair procedures.'[19] This sentiment is given effect through a case plan drawn up by the agency, in conjunction with the parents, which sets out a step-by-step programme of goals to be achieved by the latter, within a specified time frame and with the support of identified resources, if their child is to be returned. It should be noted that some research findings suggest that any such prospect of return is lessened in

16 See, further, https://familyfirstact.org/about-law.

17 See, further, http://s3.amazonaws.com/ccai-website/afcarsreport25.pdf.

18 See Reasonable Efforts to Preserve or Reunify Families and Achieve Permanency for Children' in Information Gateway's State Statutes series at www.childwelfare.gov/topics/systemwide/laws-policies/statutes/reunify/.

19 *Santosky v. Kramer*, 455 U.S. 745 (1982) at 753–54.

the case of Black American children. It has been asserted that 'in the United States, Black children spend more time in out-of-home placement than other children and are less likely to experience family reunification following involvement with child welfare services.'[20]

Termination of parental rights (TPR) Parental failure to meet the goals set in the case plan within the agreed time frame will lead to a court hearing. Then, if the state grounds for parental unfitness can be met (usually meaning evidence of severe or chronic abuse or neglect, sexual abuse, abuse or neglect of other children in the household, abandonment of the child, long-term parental incapacity due to mental illness or alcohol/drug dependency, or failure to support or maintain contact with the child) and 'clear and convincing evidence'[21] establishes parental inability to undertake safe care of their child, a TPR order will be issued. This order signifies the official and permanent termination of the parent-child relationship and of all parental rights with respect to the child. Following introduction of the Family First legislation, the court now requires stronger evidence than formerly that such a total severance of parental ties, though justified on statutory grounds, would necessarily be wholly compliant with such a child's welfare interests. The welfare test threshold has, arguably, been raised, and the outcome of contested proceedings is now more likely to be an order other than adoption, guardianship being a probable option.

The issue of a TPR order does not necessarily lead to the adoption of the child concerned, and many now remain in the public care system as 'legal orphans' with no legal ties to any family. In the period 2000–2005, while the number of children whose parental rights had been terminated ranged from 73,000 to 65,000, those adopted annually remained relatively constant in the low 50,000s. From 2010 to 2018, the corresponding figures were 66,000, 71,000, and the mid-50,000s.[22] It seems somewhat anomalous that a byproduct of adoption for children in public care should be the state creation of tens of thousands of 'legal orphans' whose welfare interests – and, very probably, their rights to an identity and private life – are severely compromised by what appears to be a failure of due process.

Approximately 22 states have provisions for reinstating the rights of a parent once they have been terminated; in 13, if a permanent placement has not been achieved within a specific time frame, a petition may be filed with the court requesting reinstatement of the parent's rights; in 10, the statutes specify that reinstatement is available only to older children who have not attained a permanent placement. In all cases, the court must determine if the parent has made substantial progress in correcting the conditions that led to the termination and

20 See, Boatswain-Kyte, A., Esposito, T., and Trocme, N., Impacts of race on family reunification etc, in *Child Abuse & Neglect*, (2022): 125. www.sciencedirect.com/science/article/abs/pii/S0145213422000023.

21 *Santosky v. Kramer*, op cit, set this as the standard of proof required in termination of parental rights proceedings.

22 See, further, www.acf.hhs.gov/sites/default/files/cb/trends_fostercare_adoption_09thru18.pdf.

is now able and willing to provide the child a safe home. Any such reinstatement of parental rights is conditional on the court finding that this would be conducive to furthering the welfare interests of the child and on the consent of both parent and child.

Concurrent placements Where there is good reason to believe there are grave risks in returning a child to their family home, CPS will formulate a case plan around the concept of 'concurrent planning,' which entails placing the child with foster carers approved as potential adopters.

Residential care

The legislative intent underpinning the Family First Preventative Services Act 2018 is directed in part towards reducing reliance on institutional care or large foster homes and instead encourages the use of family-based care. It limits the use of group and residential homes, which are facilities with specialist staffing for those such as pregnant adolescents and children and youth with mental health or behavioural problems, by reducing federal funding for placements that are not short-term residential treatment programmes.

SECURE ACCOMMODATION

Disruptive behaviour in children and adolescents would seem to attract a professional response that is more likely to use resources such as psychosocial treatment (treatment with a trained therapist) and/or medication than a secure residential facility. Behaviour modification programmes in a structured setting are preferable to confinement. Specific forms of professional intervention, compatible with the welfare interests of the child concerned, can be ordered by the court.

Adoption

Unlike in the U.K., the state does not have a significant role to play in consensual U.S. adoptions. Arguably, the fact that such a large proportion of all annual adoptions are completed without the benefit of an independent professional assessment of the welfare interests of the children concerned would seem to constitute a failure of due process.

DOMESTIC VOLUNTARY ADOPTION

Most of these are private family law proceedings which do not give rise to a need for state intervention: stepparent or kinship adoptions rarely require the welfare interests of the child to be the subject of an independent report from a guardian *ad litem* or representation by an attorney. Again, the decision to complete a voluntary TPR and/or to place a child for adoption is defined as a private matter, unless notice to the contrary is served on the local CPS.

ADOPTION FROM STATE CARE

This form of adoption – in which the need for parental consent has been judicially dispensed with – was possibly pioneered in the U.S. and has since become firmly established policy.

Racial discrimination has probably been a constraint in determining which children enter the adoption process. While African American children are overrepresented in the care system,[23] there is a scarcity of available African American foster parents, and adopter preference overall is for white children. Consequently, there is a stronger probability that Black children will be denied access to adoption. Some infants, most of whom are Black or Asian, leave the U.S. through outgoing adoption every year.[24]

Unaccompanied migrant minors

It has been estimated that, as of 2019, some six million children resident in the U.S. were unauthorised. Of those children who were properly documented citizens, 4.1 million were living with at least one parent who was not, and 5.9 million lived with an undocumented family member.[25] The government response is one largely driven by a policy of detention[26] and resettlement, pursued under s 67 of the Immigration Act 2016, as policed by the Immigration and Customs Enforcement (ICE) agency. Whether or not the children of illegal immigrants end up in the public welfare system – and many do – the threat or actuality of parent deportation by ICE (often by night raids on immigrant communities) clearly has a negative impact on their welfare interests, as is recognised in the ICE 2017 'Detained Parents Directive.' Concern has been expressed by various bodies regarding the welfare interests of the many children detained and separated from their parents.[27]

23 Stehno, S., The Elusive Continuum of Child Welfare Services: Implications for Minority Children and Youth, *Child Welfare*, (1990): 69, 551–562. Also, Tatara, T., *Characteristics of Children in Substitute and Adoptive Care: A Statistical Summary of the VCIS National Child-Welfare Database*, American Public Welfare Association, Washington, DC, (1993).

24 Buckwalter-Poza, R., America's Unseen Export: Children, Most of them Black, Pacific Standard, 24 June 2014. www.psmag.com/navigation/politics-and-law/outgoing-adoption-americas-unseen-export-children-black-84084/.
Also, see, Selman, P., The Rise and Fall of Intercountry Adoption in the 21st Century: Global Trends from 2001 to 2010, in Gibbons, J. and Rotabi, K. (eds.), *Intercountry Adoption: Policies, Practices, and Outcomes*, Farnham, Ashgate, (2012).

25 American Immigration Council statistics (see website).

26 See *AAM (A Child) v. Secretary of State for the Home Department* [2012] EWHC 2567 (QB).

27 See, further, American Bar Association website, including Chiamulera, C., Protecting Unaccompanied Immigrant Children' and Parker, P.K. 'Meeting the Citizenship and Immigration Needs of Foster Children.' www.americanbar.org/groups/public_interest/child_law/resources/child_law_practiceonline/article_collections0/immigrants/.

TRAFFICKING

The United States is ranked as one of the worst countries globally for human trafficking.[28] It is estimated that 199,000 incidents occur within the U.S. every year: one in five human trafficking victims are children, exploited for begging, child pornography or child labour. The 2020 UNODC report *Trafficking in Persons*,[29] which records the global experience of this prohibited trade,[30] notes that in North America, there are multiples more girl than boy child victims of trafficking for sexual exploitation.[31]

The Trafficking Victims Protection Act 2000 was introduced to combat trafficking, including the trafficking of children.[32]

The welfare principle in contemporary practice: public family law, criminal jurisdiction

The ability of the juvenile justice system to influence the welfare interests of juvenile offenders is constrained by the fact many children and adolescents in conflict with the law are tried in adult criminal courts each year; as many as 4,500 children are currently in adult prisons.[33] It is also constrained by the fact that such children are subject to the uniform application of rules such as 'three strikes and you're out,' the 'common enterprise' doctrine, plea bargaining, strict liability, and mandatory minimum sentences.

The system

The U.S. juvenile justice system is the responsibility of the Office of Juvenile Justice and Delinquency Prevention and is governed by the federal Juvenile Justice and Delinquency Prevention Act (reauthorised in 2002). The act defines a juvenile as 'a person who has not attained his eighteenth birthday, or for the purposes of proceedings and disposition under [the act] for an alleged act of juvenile delinquency, a person who has not attained his twenty-first birthday.'[34] The Violent Crime Control and Law Enforcement Act 1994, a federal statute, allows children as young as 13 to be tried as adults in federal courts when accused of felonies such as murder, attempted

28 See Human Trafficking Statistics by State 2022, https://worldpopulationreview.com/state-rankings/human-trafficking-statistics-by-state.

29 See, further, www.unodc.org/documents/data-and-analysis/tip/2021/GLOTiP_2020_15jan_web.pdf.

30 Prohibited by the Trafficking in Persons Protocol 2003, with 178 state signatories, mandated under the United Nations Convention Against Transnational Organized Crime.

31 Ibid at p 85.

32 This legislation called for the creation of the President's Interagency Task Force to Monitor and Combat Trafficking in Persons to coordinate anti-trafficking efforts among U.S. federal government agencies.

33 See, further, https://eji.org/issues/children-in-prison/.

34 United States Code, Title 18 – Crimes and Criminal Procedure, Part IV – Correction of Youthful Offenders, Chapter 403 – Juvenile Delinquency, § 5031. Definitions.

murder and bank robbery. In practice, however, many if not most children tried in adult courts are charged with nonviolent offences.[35] This legislation has added to the ongoing concern regarding the fact that states are not required to separate youths from adults in adult facilities and that 'a significant number of children are being consistently treated as adults in the U.S. criminal justice system. . . . In 2010, an estimated 139,000 children were housed in adult prisons and jails across the country.'[36] Of grave concern to the Inter-American Commission on Human Rights (IACHR) was the fact that:

> [A]ccording to research conducted in the U.S., children and adolescents confined in adult jails and prisons are at a higher risk of self-harm and have a much greater likelihood of committing suicide as opposed to those in juvenile facilities. . . . According to data from adult facilities nationwide, over 40 incarcerated adolescents committed suicide between 2000 and 2012, twice the rate of incarcerated adults.[37]

Children who pose a threat to the welfare of self or others

According to statistics reported by the U.S. Department of Justice, the rate of arrest of youths for violent crimes peaked in 1994 and since then has consistently declined. In 2012, the arrest rate for violent crime was at its lowest for three decades.[38] Between 2010 and 2019, the number of juvenile arrests fell by 58%; there are now approximately 423,000 cases heard in the juvenile courts annually. However, the fact that children of African American descent are so disproportionately represented in the number processed by the legal system is clearly a matter of concern in terms of their welfare: children of African American descent represent 16% of the total youth population in the U.S. but 28% of all youths arrested, 35% of youths transferred to adult courts, and 58% of youths sentenced to confinement in adult prisons.[39] According to the U.S. Department of Justice, African American youths are twice as likely as their Caucasian counterparts to be arrested.[40] A similar marked disparity can be seen in the treatment of Hispanic

35 See U.S. General Accounting Office, Report to Congressional Requesters, Juvenile Justice: Juveniles Processed in Criminal Court and Case Dispositions 1 (Aug. 1995).

36 See the Inter-American Commission on Human Rights, Children and Adolescents in the United States' Adult Criminal Justice System, (2018), at p 9 and p 32. See, further, www.oas.org/en/iachr/reports/pdfs/Children-USA.pdf.

37 Ibid, at pp 110–11.

38 Office of Juvenile Justice and Delinquency Prevention, U.S. Department of Justice, Statistical Briefing Book, 17 December 2012.

39 National Council on Crime and Delinquency, 'Justice for Some: Differential Treatment of Youth of Color in the Justice System,' 2007.

40 National Center for Juvenile Justice, Juvenile Arrest Rates by Offense, Sex, and Race (1980–2011), February 2014.

and Caucasian youths.[41] An inescapable conclusion is that there is racial bias in the application of the welfare principle to children entering the U.S. juvenile justice system and in their treatment until they exit from it.

AGE OF CRIMINAL RESPONSIBILITY

The age at which children can be held criminally liable for their actions is not federally determined, other than for federal crimes, for which the threshold is eleven years of age. Otherwise, it varies across the states. It is mostly set at seven years of age in 35 states.

The U.S. has the singular distinction among modern Western democracies of not only retaining the death penalty for certain crimes but also of executing those who were minors when they committed such crimes.[42] The justification offered by the USSC in *Stanford v. Kentucky*[43] was that '[W]e discern neither a historical nor modern societal consensus forbidding the imposition of capital punishment on any person who murders at 16 or 17 years of age.' Until the USSC decision in *Roper v. Simmons*,[44] children below the age of 18 could be eligible for state execution for certain crimes. Despite that ruling, the debate as to whether the use of capital punishment constitutes the infliction of 'cruel and unusual punishment' – prohibited under the Sixth Amendment – continues.

PREVENTION

The U.S. has some of the highest levels of youth violence and crime in the developed world, making it a leading cause of injury and death for young Americans aged 15 to 24 years.

The Juvenile Justice and Delinquency Prevention Act 1974, reauthorised most recently in 2018, is the governing federal legislation. Among its provisions are those that provide nationwide funding for delinquency prevention. Other relevant federal legislation is the Violent Crime Control and Law Enforcement Act of 1994, which also provides funding streams for state crime prevention schemes. The IACHR, in its 2018 report, details at length the many ways in which the juvenile justice system is currently failing youth who commit offences and has 'highlighted the need to prioritise prevention policies.'[45] Such policies would, however, require a step-change from the established punitive approach to one that developed violence prevention strategies in schools and neighbourhoods and promoted rehabilitation.

41 Note that the Youth Criminal Justice Act, s 38(2)(b), requires regional parity of sentencing for similar crimes.

42 A total of 38 states permit the use of the death penalty, of which 23 authorise its use on those who were juveniles when they committed their crimes.

43 492 U.S. 361, 378–80 (1989).

44 543 U.S. 551 (2005).

45 See the Inter-American Commission on Human Rights, Children and Adolescents in the United States' Adult Criminal Justice System, op cit at p 75.

Juvenile court

The jurisdiction of the juvenile court (commonly known as 'teen courts') is generally confined to children who commit offences before their 18th birthdays (though in some states, the upper age limit is 21). However, many child offenders are excluded from such courts for various reasons, one such being the 'once an adult, always an adult' rule, which prevails in 34 states. The rule requires the automatic transfer of a child with a previous conviction in an adult court to an adult court when charged with a further offence.[46] A child tried in an adult court will not be accompanied by their parent(s), which is mandatory in juvenile courts; the lack of any opportunity for that support must, in most cases, be noncompliant with their welfare interests.

ROLE OF THE WELFARE PRINCIPLE

The USSC has declared that:[47]

> the Juvenile Court is theoretically engaged in determining the needs of the child and of society rather than adjudicating criminal conduct. The objectives are to provide measures of guidance and rehabilitation for the child and protection for society, not to fix criminal responsibility, guilt and punishment.

In practice, there is considerable scepticism regarding the capacity of the juvenile justice system to achieve its declared objective. The IACHR, for example, was of the view that:[48]

> [T]he principle of the best interests of the child is restricted to certain areas of the law that are related to child welfare and the family. The principle has not been made effective in all federal and state legislation and policies involving children in particular with regard to the treatment of persons less than eighteen years of age in the criminal justice system.

It found the objective to be essentially punitive[49] and referred to the system's demeaning treatment of juveniles:[50]

> The Commission also noticed the consistent use of full restraints, including handcuffs and belly- and ankle-shackles on youth. This practice, known as 'shackling,' is uniformly applied to all youth in the justice system, regardless of whether they represent a risk of danger or escape. Its use is mandated for

46 The Comprehensive Youth Justice Amendment Act 2016 provides for the monitoring and, where appropriate, the reversal of such transfers.

47 *Kent v. United States*, 383 U.S. 541, 544 (1966).

48 Op cit, at p 136.

49 The Inter-American Commission on Human Rights, Children and Adolescents in the United States' Adult Criminal Justice System, op cit, at p 61.

50 Ibid, at p 105.

> all courtroom appearances, where youth are especially affected in their ability to participate in the hearing that involves them. Moreover, its use is not limited to these occasions. Youth interviewed by the IACHR affirmed being subjected to such degrading treatment even for dental care visits.

The IACHR draws attention to 'the absence of a holistic view of children and the protection of their rights' and notes that a systematic approach of this nature has neither been defined nor implemented in the national, state and local legislation and policies of the United States. It suggests that 'such an approach is needed in order to optimize State efforts and direct the required State resources toward the protection of children and the effective enjoyment of their rights.'[51]

The system's success in pursuing its declared objective may perhaps be best judged by its outcomes, i.e. in the court choice of disposition: a community or a custodial sentence. The former and most welfare compliant would seem to have become the preferred option: in contrast, use of custodial facilities, generally reserved for those presenting a threat to the public, has steadily decreased since the turn of the century. This trend towards accentuating welfare considerations was strengthened by the rulings of the USSC in *Graham v. Florida*[52] and *Miller v. Alabama*,[53] which prohibited both sentences of life imprisonment without parole for children convicted of non-homicide offences and sentences of mandatory life imprisonment without parole for children convicted of homicide offences respectively. It was also very much in evidence in the important ruling by that court in *Montgomery v. Louisiana*[54] to the effect that states and the federal government are required to consider the unique circumstances of each juvenile defendant when deciding the most appropriate sentence for them.

COMMUNITY SENTENCES

Youth courts, for example, which provide formal hearings for minor offences and first-time offenders before a court comprising youths, have been operational for several years in many states and seek to divert petty offenders from the statutory legal system by providing for accountability within the local community. This approach is reinforced by the restorative justice philosophy, which aims to bring victims and offenders together in approved schemes that allow the offender to make amends for their behaviour in local community-based projects. However, the IACHR has criticised the 'inadequate provision of age-appropriate probation and parole supervision and related services to ensure adequate rehabilitation of youth who commit crimes.'[55]

51 Ibid at p 139.
52 560 U.S. 48 (2010).
53 567 U.S. 460 (2012).
54 577 U.S. _(2016).
55 The Inter-American Commission on Human Rights, Children and Adolescents in the United States' Adult Criminal Justice System, op cit, at p 80.

CUSTODIAL SENTENCES

Those receiving a custodial sentence – a decreasing number in recent years – are sent to residential facilities such as youth detention centres, group homes, shelters, correctional facilities or reform schools. However, given that the U.S. has one of the world's highest rates of adult incarceration, coupled with the fact that so many juveniles are caught up in its adult legal system, there is a likelihood that any auditing of juvenile offenders might fail to take fully into account those who are swept into adult correctional facilities.

In short, the probability is that juvenile offenders in the U.S. incur a higher rate of custodial sentences – in which African American youth are overrepresented – than in other countries.[56] The sentencing tariff is also higher than in other countries,[57] causing the IACHR to comment that 'the United States continues to be the one of the few countries in the world to sentence children so severely, in some cases incarcerating them for life without the possibility of parole.'[58] Further, it adds that children sentenced to adult prisons have a 34% higher risk of recidivism than youth in the juvenile system.[59] The role of the welfare principle in the context of juvenile justice must, inevitably, be similarly correlated.

Solitary confinement It has been estimated that approximately 35,000 children are being held in solitary confinement in the juvenile system alone.[60] Such treatment is also imposed on children in custody in adult facilities. There is no federal or state legislation prohibiting such treatment of children, though in 2016, President Obama issued an executive order banning the use of solitary confinement for youths in federal prisons. There is a considerable weight of professional opinion condemning this practice as damaging to the welfare interests of children.[61]

56 The United States, with only 5% of the world's population, has almost 25% of the world's incarcerated population, representing a nationwide rate of imprisonment of approximately one out of every hundred persons. See 'The Solitary Confinement of Youth in New York: A Civil Rights Violation,' New York Advisory Committee to the U.S. Commission on Civil Rights, December 2014. See also 'The Pew Center on the States, One in 100: Behind Bars in America' (2008); International Centre For Prison Studies, World Prison Population List (10th ed. 2011).

57 The severity of possible punishments for juvenile offenders has attracted criticism from both the special rapporteur on torture and other cruel, inhuman, or degrading treatment or punishment (A/HRC/28/685 March 2015, Human Rights Council, 28th session, at para 78) and the U.N. CRC (Children's Rights in Juvenile Justice, General Comment No. 10, U.N. Doc. CRC/C/GC/10 (25 April 2007)).

58 The Inter-American Commission on Human Rights, op cit, at p 78.

59 Ibid, at p 125.

60 U.S. Department of Justice, Office of Juvenile Justice and Delinquency Prevention, Conditions of Confinement: Findings From the Survey of Youth In Residential Placement 9 (2010).

61 The American Academy of Child and Adolescent Psychiatry (AACAP) recommends that solitary confinement for youth be completely abolished. (Juvenile Justice Reform Committee, *Solitary Confinement of Juvenile Offender*, Approved by Council, April 2012). It has also been condemned by the Committee on the Rights of the Child, the Committee against Torture, and the special rapporteur on torture.

Conclusion

Arguably, the welfare interests of children have not been best served by a system that removed an unusually large number of children from parental care, only to return half of them to that care while arranging for the nonconsensual adoption of a small proportion and retaining the remainder at considerable expense to be shuttled between foster homes for the duration of their childhood. The reversal of that policy – if that's what it was – during the Trump administration, which saw a heavier federal emphasis on preventative strategies designed to shore up vulnerable families, might be interpreted as being prompted by an intent to make the child welfare system more effective. The issue being addressed by the policy change may simply have been the costs of public foster care. Whether the proportion of nonconsensual adoptions from the public welfare system increased or decreased was beside the point; reducing the overall number entering foster care was the objective.

On the other hand, such a development might have been expected. State policy towards the welfare interests/rights of children will always reflect the prevailing cultural context, and the Trump administration era was marked by a conservative pushback on the frontlines of this nation's entrenched culture wars. As Diane Kuntz comments, '[A]t the same time, the abolition movement, which views foster care as a racist institution and is a tenet of the Black Lives Matter movement, also seeks to end foster care.'[62] Parental rights and the autonomy of the nuclear family unit are traditional benchmarks of conservatism and are now, perhaps, being viewed as touchstones for its revival. This is very much in keeping with the legacy of the constitutional rights of birth parents as established by the ruling in *Santosky v. Kramer*[63] and also with the failure to ratify U.N. CROC and CEDAW. After the hubris that accompanied the equality rights achievements, there may now be a falling back to foundational principles: to the requirement that the state show a compelling reason if it is to infringe on family privacy and parental autonomy. The argument is that these fundamental liberties, protected by the 14th Amendment, strongly suggest that the welfare interests of children are best assured by the parental right to custody, and state intervention, if it is to further those interests, should focus on supporting the parents.

62 Note to author (23 September 2022).
63 455 U.S. 745 (1982).

4 The welfare principle in contemporary practice

Private family law and hybrid proceedings

Introduction

This chapter is concerned with the essentially private nature of a birth parent's right to take decisions – as to custody, place of residence, religious upbringing, education, etc – relating to the upbringing of their child. It is a right firmly established in *Troxel v. Granville*.[1] The courts look first to the proposed arrangements of fit parents, confining adjudication to specific issues of parental conflict. Whether or not the presumptive right to custody of a fit parent should then be subject to the welfare test has been contentious.[2]

The chapter examines the legislation, court orders, and caselaw associated with parenting decisions in the context of the forming of families (adoption, surrogacy, etc), in their dissolution (divorce, separation, annulment, etc), and in their reconstitution (stepparents, etc), in all of which contests can and often do arise regarding the welfare/rights of any children involved. The chapter also gives broad consideration to the effect of public services and to the emerging role of hybrid public/private court orders and proceedings.

Children and reconstituted families

Given the high national divorce rate, which affects some one million children annually, there are now many reconstituted families. The Pew Centre estimates that approximately 40% of all U.S. families now meet that definition, and, according to the Census Bureau statistics, some 60 to 70% of marriages involving children from a previous marriage fail.

Matrimonial

The Uniform Marriage and Divorce Act 1970, as extensively amended in 1973, although only adopted in a small minority of states (a total of eight), has greatly influenced most. Since then, the definition of marriage (and associated proceedings

1 530 U.S. 57 (2000).
2 *Routten v. Routten*, 843 S.E.2d 154, 159 (2020).

DOI: 10.4324/9781003269564-7

for divorce, separation, custody etc) has been extended to include same-sex couples, reinforced by the Defence of Marriage Act 1996 as conditioned by the ruling in *Windsor v. U.S.*[3]

The 1970 act introduced the requirement that '[T]he court shall determine custody in accordance with the best interest of the child [and] . . . shall consider . . . the wishes of the child as to his custodian.'[4] Some states have adopted an age-based rule or policy, wherein children at a specified age are granted a more substantial say in the outcome of such decisions.

DIVORCE, NULLITY, JUDICIAL SEPARATION AND RELOCATION

Generally, in all legal proceedings following family breakdown, the proceedings will be heard in a family court and will require parents to submit agreed care arrangements identifying the designated custodial parent (corroborating paternity when they are unmarried) and showing how the other parent – if they have a meaningful relationship with their child – proposes to maintain contact and sustain that relationship. Arrangements for child maintenance will also need to be confirmed by the court. In principle as in law, all else being equal, sexual orientation and gender identity (SOGI) considerations should not negatively impact the welfare test in determining parenting capacity or suitability. So, for example, the transexual status of a parent should not of itself be a determining factor in child custody cases.[5]

The welfare checklist While state courts hearing proceedings for divorce, nullity, and judicial separation will need to be satisfied as to the 'parenting plan' and child support arrangements, the completion of such proceedings is not conditional upon satisfying any general federally applicable welfare checklist.

Relocation Where an issue arises concerning the proposed relocation of a custodial parent – whether outside the jurisdiction of the state or to another country – it is required to be judicially determined in accordance with the welfare interests of the child(ren) involved. The provisions of the Uniform Child-Custody Jurisdiction and Enforcement Act 1997 may well be relevant. While a statutory 'welfare checklist' is not provided, the factors to be considered in Texas, for example, will include relationship with and presence of extended family; existence of a stable and supportive environment for the child; the relocating parent's improved financial or job situation and ability to provide a better standard of living; the reasons for and against the move; a comparison of the education, health and leisure opportunities; the child's age, community ties, preferences and health and educational needs; each

3 570 U.S. 744 (2013).

4 See, Vasterling, C.G., Child Custody Modification under the Uniform Marriage and Divorce Act: A Statute to End the Tug-of-War?' 67 *WASH. U. L. Q.* 923 (1989).

5 See *Mayfield v. Mayfield*, Case No. 96AP030032, 1996 Ohio App. LEXIS 3724 (Ohio Ct. App. Aug. 14, 1996).

parent's plans for the child; cooperation between the parents; and each parent's parenting skills.[6]

COURT ORDERS

Custody, conservatorship, and guardianship are the three procedures constituting the legal framework for the parent/child relationship following family breakdown.

Custody Issues regarding custody arrangements typically arise in proceedings for a dissolution of marriage or separation, as well as in paternity, annulment and other legal proceedings. Equality rights have swept aside earlier presumptions that might have favoured custody of young children with mothers, boys with fathers, etc. A custody order may either appoint both parents as joint custodians with equal rights in relation to parenting decisions and time-sharing arrangements with their child(ren); designate one spouse as the custodial parent, subject to specified visitation conditions for the other; or designate one spouse or other person as having exclusive custody and parental rights.

In a dispute between two 'fit' parents, 'the trial court must apply the "best interest of the child" standard to determine custody and visitation questions.'[7] Despite the presumptive rule that a fit parent has a right to custody of their child, when there is a contest between two equally entitled parents, then the rule must give way to the best interests principle. This will determine the child's place of residence and visitation rights for the noncustodial parent and possibly for such others as grandparents. In rare cases where a birth parent is dead, unavailable or disqualified, custody may be awarded to a relative or a third party who has assumed care responsibility. There is no equivalent to the menu of function-specific private family orders available in the U.K., such as child arrangements orders, 'prohibited steps,' etc.

When determining issues of child custody and contact arrangements, the court may appoint a guardian *ad litem* to advise the court on matters relating to the child's welfare interest and/or an attorney to act as advocate for the child's rights. Other experts such as a child psychologist may also be appointed if the court deems this necessary.

Guardianship In a small minority of proceedings for divorce, nullity or judicial separation – usually when the parents have been convicted of abusing their children – the court may terminate parental responsibility and instead issue a guardianship order or orders with respect to the children involved. (See, further, later in this chapter.)

Conservatorship A 'conservatorship' refers to the judicial appointment of a person to act as a guardian with respect to the finances/property and/or to manage the

6 See https://uk.practicallaw.thomsonreuters.com/5–616–4573?transitionType=Default&contextData=(sc.Default)&firstPage=true.

7 *Routten v. Routten*, op cit, at 159.

personal affairs of someone who lacks the capacity to do so for themselves. Essentially, it denotes a fiduciary relationship. The terms of the conservatorship are defined and confined by the specification of rights and duties as stated in the court order. While most often used in relation to elderly persons or adults with incapacitating health issues, it may also have application to children. In respect of the latter, a conservatorship order may vest certain parental responsibilities in the conservator: the right to make major decisions regarding the child and to have physical possession of them and a duty of maintenance. A conservator is required to act in the best interests of the conservatee.

Guardianship

There are two forms of guardianship: a permanent guardianship order and 'standby guardianship.' The former allows for a permanent transfer of parental rights and responsibilities to a named guardian and is most often made by court appointment following a ruling that the child concerned has been neglected, abused or abandoned or the parents are unable to provide a stable home environment. (See, further, later in this chapter.) It may also be made by a parent or by the court to safeguard the welfare interests of a child and to take effect after the death of that parent. The latter, which has no equivalent in the U.K., differs from the former in that it does not terminate parental rights but instead allows the parent to retain much of their authority over the child; it transfers custodial rights to a named guardian, leaving intact other legal rights such as those relating to inheritance; and, as the name suggests, it is often used to allow a guardian to 'step into the shoes of a parent' and take over child care responsibilities when the parent is ill or unavailable. Most often, the standby guardian and parent have a concurrent or shared authority. The parent determines commencement of the guardianship appointment and may vary or terminate it at their discretion. It is intended for use by relatives of the child and is seen as particularly appropriate in relation to older children.

COURT APPOINTMENT

Some 30 states have statutes permitting the appointment of a 'standby guardian': a minority of seven require this to be a court appointment; in others, it is accomplished by a formal legal document, signed and witnessed. When confirming the appointment of a guardian, approximately nine states require that at a certain age, the child must be notified of the hearing, and the court must consider the child's preferences. The age requirement varies by state; in most, the court must consider the wishes of a child aged 14 or older.[8]

8 See, further, www.childwelfare.gov/pubPDFs/guardianship.pdf.

Adoption

By far, the largest proportion of all children adopted annually in the U.S. are simply the subjects of a process intended to legally consolidate their positions within newly configured family arrangements.[9] While birth parents clearly determine those adoptions, they also, in fact, and unlike the law and practice in other developed countries, determine the arrangements for most U.S. adoptions. Any birth parent may apply for a voluntary termination of parental rights (TPR) order and then place or arrange the placement of their child for adoption.

The right of a birth mother to place her child for adoption with whomsoever she chooses or to authorise another person to do so on her behalf is embedded in the laws of most states; only four restrict placement to agencies in nonrelative adoptions.[10] Such placements are often conducted on a for-profit basis: 'accredited agencies' must be nonprofit, but in an ICA context, 'approved persons' or 'facilitators' – a category that may include large organisations as well as lawyers, social workers and independent consultants – are entitled to operate on a fee-for-service basis. The fact that some 45% of U.S. adoptions originate in private arrangements[11] and may be influenced by profit considerations would seem less likely to be in the best interests of the children concerned and, in some cases, may well be detrimental.[12]

ADOPTERS

While neither the Uniform Adoption Act nor state legislation modelled on it places any restrictions on adoption by unmarried applicants, there is still some ambivalence and an outright ban in some 12 states, including Louisiana.[13] In addition, some states disqualify those suffering from physical or mental disabilities or impose 'reputability requirements.' The Freedom to Serve Children Act, introduced by the Texas legislature in 2017,[14] proposed giving children's service providers, including adoption agencies, the right to decline services to individuals based on 'the provider's sincerely held religious beliefs.' By 2020, a succession of HSS rulings had granted similar exemptions to faith-based foster care and adoption

9 See, for example, Kreider, R.M., Adopted Children and Stepchildren: 2000' (U.S. Census Bureau, Census 2000 Special Reports, August 2003). The full report is available at www.census. gov/prod/2003pubs/censr-6.pdf.

10 Colorado, Connecticut, Delaware, and Massachusetts.

11 In 2000–01, it was estimated that 45% of adoptions were initiated by private arrangement. See, further, U.S. Child Welfare Information Gateway: 'How Many Children Were Adopted in 2000 and 2001?' www.childwelfare.gov/pubs/s_adopted/s_adopteda.cfm.

12 See, further, www.childwelfare.gov/pubPDFs/s_adopted.pdf#page=6&view=Findings:%20Children%20Adopted.

13 As identified by the Williams Institute of the UCLA School of Law in 2013, these states include Alaska, Iowa, Kansas, Kentucky, Maine, Nebraska, New Hampshire, North Dakota, Ohio, West Virginia, Wisconsin, and Utah.

14 HB 3859.

agencies from the requirements of equality and nondiscrimination legislation,[15] enabling them to refuse to engage with the LGBT community, including same-sex foster carers and adopters. Arguably, in addition to being discriminatory, such restrictions on adopter eligibility are prejudicial to furthering the welfare interests of children as they reduce the availability of potentially otherwise suitable and well-motivated adopters.

This development needs to be viewed against a backdrop which has seen adoption championed by religious organisations as a means of ensuring the salvation of the souls of children. An evangelical adoption culture has been developed by those with fundamentalist Christian beliefs, leading to thousands of Christians attending annual adoption conferences where denominations like the Southern Baptist Convention have fervently encouraged their members to adopt.[16] Arguably, when religion becomes the driving force – for or against adoption – then the welfare interests of children are at risk.

The practice known as 'rehoming' may perhaps also be seen against the background of the complexities and stresses of contemporary adoption, particularly as regards ICA. 'Rehomed' adopted children are those who are voluntarily transferred by their adopters to new families through a basic 'power of attorney' document – a notarised statement declaring the child to be in the care of another adult.[17] It would seem to be a practice confined to the U.S. and may involve between 1 and 5% of adoptions;[18] as it bypasses the adoption process and all relevant professional screening, it is little more than a form of 'trafficking' and, as such, seriously violates an adoptee's human rights and may well breach those of the birth parents.

Stepparent adoption The legal adoption of a child by the spouse of the child's birth parent has been the most common form of adoption in the U.S. and the one attracting minimum professional scrutiny. In recent years, this would seem to have changed: in 2018, 35% of all children adopted went to relatives, including stepparents. The fact that, for such a large proportion of annual adoptions in the U.S., there is judged to be no 'welfare factor' (and therefore, in some if not most states, no need for a home study report, the child concerned being seen as having no

15 For example, on 23 January 2019, the HHS ruled that, in South Carolina, the Miracle Hill Ministries and other taxpayer-funded faith-based foster care agencies could maintain their rejection of all foster parents other than those who subscribed to Miracle Hill's particular interpretation of Protestant Christianity.

16 See, for example, the Christian Alliance for Orphans, which, as stated on its website, 'unites more than 140 respected Christian organizations and a national network of churches. Working together, our joint initiatives *inspire* and *equip* Christians to reflect God's heart in caring for orphans in adoption' (www.christianalliancefororphans.org).
Also see Joyce, K., The Evangelical Orphan Boom, *New York Times*, 21 September 2013 and Joyce, K., *The Child Catchers: Rescue, Trafficking, and the New Gospel of Adoption*, Public Affairs, (2013).

17 See, Reuters, The Child Exchange: Inside America's Underground Market for Adopted Children, *Reuters*, 9 September 2013. www.reuters.com/investigates/adoption/#article/part1.

18 See, further, www.theatlantic.com/family/archive/2018/11/children-who-have-second-adoptions/575902/.

actual need which this procedure could remedy) does, perhaps, add to the questions regarding the mix of public and private interests now served by adoption in this jurisdiction.

Cultural/religious affinity Racial compatibility is a live issue in relation to the proportion of African American children in foster care who are adopted by white Caucasians. The converse is a factor in the proportion of such children for whom domestic adoption is unavailable and who consequently become the subject of ICA to be found homes in countries such as Canada and the U.K., which adds another layer of cultural dissonance.

The issue of cultural compatibility also arises in relation to children with Native American ancestry. The Indian Child Welfare Act 1978 requires that a court considering a fostering or adoption application for such a child must, in order of importance, give first priority to placement with a relative, then to another member of their tribe or band, and then to another Indian family. Only when those options have been exhausted can consideration be given to third-party unrelated non-Indian adopters. Although the ruling in *Adoptive Couple v. Baby Girl*[19] narrowed the constraints imposed by this cultural imperative, it remains a potent caveat to welfare interests where children with even a tenuous genetic ancestry traceable to a federally registered Indian tribe are involved.[20] (See, further, Chapter 8.)

POST-ADOPTION CONTACT, INFORMATION DISCLOSURE AND STATE SUPPORT SERVICES

Where all parties agree, including the child concerned (if aged 12 years or more), then an adoption order can be accompanied by an agreement for ongoing contact between the adoptee and members of their birth family.[21] Many states have enacted laws permitting the enforcement of such agreements.

A long-standing, continuing and very divisive feature of U.S. adoption law – which may have the status of a distinguishing jurisdictional characteristic – has been the proportion of adoption files that remain 'closed,' sealed by birth parent veto, preventing adoptees from accessing information regarding their origins, thereby precluding post-adoption contact. While the Uniform Adoption Act 1994 allows the release of non-identifying information and permits access to identifying information on the basis of mutual consent or in cases of medical need, it otherwise respects any birth parent veto on information disclosure. In some instances, the judiciary have ruled that an adoptee is entitled to access at least the names of their birth parents and may access related court records and documents with a court order on showing good cause (e.g. in New York, California, Michigan, Washington,

19 398 SC 625, 731 S.E. 2d 550.

20 *Carter, et al. v. Washburn, et al.*, No. 15-CV-1259, U.S. Dist. Ct. for the Dist. of Arizona. See, further, www.bu.edu/bulawreview/files/2013/11/EDITORS-FOREWORD1.pdf.

21 See Information Gateway's 'Postadoption Contact Agreements Between Birth and Adoptive Families,' www.childwelfare.gov/topics/systemwide/laws-policies/statutes/cooperative/.

Wyoming and New Jersey).[22] Nonetheless, the continued strong resistance to open access from organisations representing the interests of birth parents is another distinguishing feature of modern adoption practice in the U.S. and one that must compromise the welfare interests of many children.[23]

Ongoing post-adoption support services have been generally available since the introduction of the 1997 Act, and almost all child care adoptions automatically receive financial subsidies. Some states provide post-adoption support as a public service while many nonprofit and for-profit providers are available, some of which offer specialised services.[24] In addition, important tax credit benefits are available to intercountry as well as to all other adopters.[25] ICA and private domestic adoptions are now also more likely to receive support services on request.

INTERCOUNTRY ADOPTION: CONTEMPORARY

Although the U.S. was once the global leader in its recourse to ICA, as noted earlier, this has been severely scaled back in recent years. State intervention to safeguard the welfare interests of the children involved is very largely confined to registering and regulating the standards of practice of adoption agencies and responding to requests for post-adoption support from ICA families.

In 2019, under the terms of the Intercountry Adoption Act 2000, consular officers issued 2,971 immigrant visas to children adopted abroad or to be adopted in the United States by U.S. citizens, which represented a marked fall from the 4,059 adopted the previous year.[26] As in almost all cases, such adoptions can only promote the welfare interests of the children concerned, the dramatic fall in numbers from 22,884 in 2004, the peak year for intercountry adoptions, is a measure of the corresponding negative impact on those interests.

It is a matter of considerable irony that the continued downward trend in ICA is directly attributable to the U.S. having become a signatory state to the Hague Convention, the provisions of which were intended to raise standards of practice and safeguard the welfare of children in international adoption. Ratification of the convention in 2008 had the immediate negative effect of stalling many adoption processes, leaving children and their prospective adopters in limbo, often for years. In Guatemala, approximately 4,000 U.S. adoptions, some at an advanced stage, came to an abrupt halt when the standards of practice governing the legal availability of

22 See, for example, *In re J.N.H.*, 2009 Colo. App. LEXIS 569 (Colo. Ct. App. Apr. 16, 2009).

23 Nations currently facilitating access to records include the U.K., Sweden, the Netherlands, Germany, South Korea, Mexico, Argentina, and Venezuela.

24 See, further, Child Welfare Information Gateway, Finding and Using Postadoption Services, Department of Health and Human Services, Children's Bureau, Washington, DC, 2012.

25 See, further, www.irs.gov/Individuals/Adoption-Benefits-FAQs, www.adoption101.com/adoption_tax_credit.html.

26 See, further, https://travel.state.gov/content/dam/NEWadoptionassets/pdfs/Tab%201%20Annual%20Report%20on%20Intercountry%20Adoptions.pdf.

children were judged to be non–Hague compliant.[27] However, Hague ratification did bring the positive development of broadening the previous restrictive definition of 'orphan' to include children with both parents alive (married or unmarried), so long as the parent(s) or an entity with legal custody of a child 'have freely given their written irrevocable consent to the termination of their legal relationship with the child, and to the child's emigration and adoption.'[28] Adverse effects followed from the political decision in Russia to terminate ICA arrangements with the U.S.[29] and from the Chinese revision of its adopter eligibility criteria, resulting in the exclusion of many prospective U.S. adopters; consequently, many children were denied adoptive homes in the U.S.

Adverse consequences have also accompanied some of the aforementioned religiously motivated adoptions of children from countries such as those in sub-Saharan Africa. Attention was drawn to the particular risks involved in religiously sponsored ICA by the death in May 2011 of 13-year-old Hana Williams at the hands of her abusive adopters, three years after leaving Ethiopia. She was just one of dozens of adoptees alleged to have been killed by their U.S. adoptive parents in the previous 20 years.[30] Many of those deaths shared a common factor: they were children reared in large families (ranging from six to dozens of children) by adopters with fundamentalist Christian beliefs – beliefs that translated into a harsh disciplinary approach to childrearing centred on the importance of obedience. While court proceedings have revealed some of the tragic outcomes of this approach, it is probable that the lives of others, uprooted from their countries, culture, and kinfolk by devoutly religious adopters have been damaged and distorted by good intentions that, in some instances, proved wholly adverse to their welfare interests.

Surrogacy

There are no federal laws governing surrogacy. Most states have legislated for surrogacy contracts and tend to be broadly facilitative.[31] Others have either not passed laws or have passed laws expressly forbidding all or some forms of

27 See, further, Stalled Adoption Program in Guatemala Leaves Families in Limbo, *New York Times*, 8 December 2012.

28 See 8 U.S.C. § 1101(b)(1)(G).

29 Ostensibly this was in reaction to the ill treatment and deaths of several Russian adoptees in the U.S., but arguably, it was a response to the Magnitsky Act and had little to do with state concern for the welfare interests of children.

30 See, further, Joyce, K., The Tragic Death of Ethiopian Adoptee Hana Williams, and How It Could Happen Again,' www.slate.com/articles/double_x/doublex/2013/11/hana_williams_the_tragic_death_of_an_ethiopian_adoptee_and_how_it_could.html, posted 11 November 2013. Also see Washington's Department of Social and Health Services (Office of the Children's Ombudsman), which published a report on the 'Severe Abuse of Adopted Children' in September 2012: www.dshs.wa.gov/pdf/ca/SevereAbuseofAdoptedChildrenReport2012.pdf.

31 See, for example, Finkelstein, A., Mac Dougall, S., Kintominas, A., and Olsen, A., Surrogacy Law and Policy in the U.S., Columbia Law School, (2016), https://web.law.columbia.edu/sites/default/files/microsites/gender-sexuality/files/columbia_sexuality_and_gender_law_clinic_-_surrogacy_law_and_policy_report_-_june_2016.pdf.

surrogacy. Almost every state allows compensated surrogacy.[32] However, Michigan and Nebraska only allow uncompensated surrogacy, also known as compassionate or altruistic surrogacy. Model federal laws, intended to bring legal uniformity across the country, have had limited success.[33]

SURROGATE, CHILD AND THE COMMISSIONING PARENTS

Insofar as altruistic surrogacy – in which the services of a surrogate are not bought – can be considered to be a matter of private family law, the practice cannot be so defined in most of the U.S. Only in Louisiana and Michigan, where commercially based surrogacy arrangements continue to be prohibited, does surrogacy meet that definition. (See, further, later in this chapter.)

Abduction

The high level of parental abduction in the U.S.[34] was the primary reason for the introduction of the Parental Kidnapping Prevention Act 1980. Indeed, it has been estimated that some quarter of a million such alleged abductions are reported annually to the authorities, even though the parental removal of a child across state lines without the consent of the other parent is not a crime in many states.[35]

RETURNING AN ABDUCTED CHILD

The relevant federal law governing international child abduction is provided by the International Parental Kidnapping Crime Act 1993,[36] s 1738A of which declares the legislative intent as being to 'deter interstate abductions and other unilateral removals of children undertaken to obtain custody and visitation awards' while s 1204 criminalises the removal or retention of a child outwith the U.S., or the attempt to do so, with the intent to obstruct a parent's custodial rights.[37]

Abbott v. Abbott,[38] a leading U.S. child abduction case, concerned a mother's removal from Chile of her son, for whom she had been awarded legal custody, without permission from either the father or the court. The USSC found that the

32 See, further, www.modamily.com/blog/us-surrogacy-laws-by-state.

33 Storrow, R.F., Surrogacy American Style, in Gerber, P. & O'Byrne, K., (eds.), *Surrogacy, Law and Human Rights,* (2015).

34 See, for example, Fass, P., *Kidnapped: A History of Child Abduction in the United States*, OUP, (1997) and the U.S. Department of Justice, The Crime of Family Abduction, www.ojp.gov/pdffiles1/ojjdp/229933.pdf.

35 See, further, https://origins.osu.edu/article/child-kidnapping-america.

36 See also the Uniform Child Custody Jurisdiction Act, s 23, which requires the court to recognise and enforce foreign custody orders so long as reasonable notice and opportunity to be heard are given to all affected persons.

37 Giving effect to the Hague Convention on the Civil Aspects of International Child Abduction 1980, which requires a U.S. court to 'decide the case in accordance with the Convention.'

38 130 S.Ct. 1983 (2010).

father shared a right of custody with the mother, a U.S. citizen, and that as 'the Convention is based on the principle that the best interests of the child are well served when decisions regarding custody rights are made in the country of habitual residence,' ordering the return of the child 'does not alter the existing allocation of custody rights . . . but does allow the courts of the home country to decide what is in the child's best interests.' Noting that 'some child psychologists believe that the trauma children suffer from these abductions is one of the worst forms of child abuse,'[39] the court held that the father had a right to seek the return of his child. In 2020, the USSC considered the meaning given to 'habitual residence' in the Hague Convention (Child Abduction). It concluded the parents' intent that Italy was to be their child's habitual residence was sufficient and, on that basis, endorsed the trial court's determination that the child should be returned to the father in Italy.

Proportionality The *Abbott* case would seem to indicate a shift in judicial approach from simple verification of the facts constituting the pre-abduction status quo – sufficient to justify an order for expeditious return – to a broader consideration that takes into account the abductor's interpretation of facts, which may offer a potentially different understanding of that status quo. The straightforward linear Hague intent has perhaps been customised and realigned to fit with established U.S. custody law, a development not unlike that adopted in Ireland.

Child's wishes Being a signatory nation to the Hague Convention, the U.S. is bound to respect the Article 13 defence of an objection by the child to their proposed return to the jurisdiction (Hague compliant) and to the parent from whom they were removed. The judiciary have demonstrated an alertness to the possibility of those wishes being manipulated by the abducting parent: in *Sheikh v. Cahill*[40] and *Navarro v. Bullock*,[41] for example, the court was not persuaded by the children's wishes to remain with the abducting parent and ordered their return.

The welfare principle in contemporary practice: public/private family law

Caution regarding state intervention in personal and family matters is an inbuilt characteristic of U.S. society. Evident in many socio-economic aspects of life, it is also apparent in the relatively few hybrid procedures and orders that transect both public and private family law.

39 H. R. Rep. No. 103–390, p 2 (1993), citing in support Faulkner, N., Parental Child Abduction is Child Abuse (1999), www.prevent-abuse-now.com/unreport.htm.
40 145 Misc. 2d 171, 546 N.Y.S.2d 517 (Sup. Ct. Kings County 1989).
41 15 Fam. L. Rep. (BNA) 1576 (Super. Ct. Cal. 1989).

Public/private family law

It would be hard to overstate the impact of opioid addiction – particularly the ongoing fentanyl dependency crisis – on parenting arrangements in the U.S. Opioid deaths are estimated at half a million in the first two decades of this century, with millions incapacitated.[42] The full consequences, in terms of disrupted parental care and harm caused to the welfare interests of many children, are unfathomable. Inevitably, that crisis, followed by the COVID-19 pandemic with a death toll of more than one million, has generated an increase in both public and private family law proceedings as the courts respond to applications for care arrangements for many bereaved and often traumatised children.

Public service matters

The U.S. has yet to ratify either U.N. CROC or the International Covenant on Economic, Social and Cultural Rights. The former – in Articles 24, 28/29 and 32 – addresses rights to health, education and employment respectively. The latter has a specific focus on matters such as education and health. Both would require the U.S. to ensure that specific basic public services were available and accessible to safeguard and promote the rights/welfare of children.

The Census Bureau, however, reports that in 2020, there were 37.2 million people in poverty, and the official poverty rate was 11.4%, up 1.0 percentage point from the previous year, resulting in approximately 3.3 million more in poverty in 2020 than in 2019.[43] This indicates that present levels of public service provision are wholly insufficient to combat poverty, that the trend may be worsening, and that, despite being the richest nation on earth, the U.S. would currently be unable to meet the requirements of U.N. CROC and the ICESCR.

EMPLOYMENT

Federal legislative benchmarks for the employment of children were first established by the Fair Labor Standards Act 1938, which continues in effect. This sets out protective measures with respect to children aged 16 years or younger, to ensure that employment opportunities do not subvert their education and to prohibit forms of employment that would jeopardise their health and safety. It provides that children under 14 years of age may not be employed in nonagricultural jobs; between the ages of 14 and 16, they may be employed in certain occupations for limited periods; and between 16 and 17, they may be employed for unlimited hours in nonhazardous occupations with some exceptions, such as for newspaper delivery and child actors. In addition, each state has its own labour laws stipulating the terms and conditions for employing children. Moreover, the federal Child Labor

42 See, further, Keefe, P.R., *Empire of Pain*, Picador, (2021).

43 See U.S. Census Bureau, Income and Poverty in the United States: 2020, www.census.gov/library/publications/2021/demo/p60–273.html.

Law prohibits the interstate transportation of goods produced in establishments which use child labour.[44]

The findings in a recent Human Rights Watch report[45] include that 'child farmworkers as young as 12 years old often work for hire for 10 or more hours a day, five to seven days a week. . . . [S]ome start working part-time at age 6 or 7,' which suggests that the 1938 act is failing to protect the welfare interests of many children.

HEALTH

In 2022, a report warned that 'the U.S. child welfare system is falling short because of persistent child poverty.'[46] This problem is one that necessarily lowers the threshold for the welfare interests of U.S. children.

Access to adequate health care is unavailable for many children in poor families in the U.S. According to Children's Health Fund, at a minimum, 20.3 million children in the United States (28% of all children) faced barriers to accessing essential health care in 2016. That estimate included children who (a) were uninsured, (b) did not receive routine primary care, and (c) were publicly insured and connected to primary care but had unmet needs for paediatric subspecialty care when needed, such as paediatric cardiology or paediatric endocrinology. By 2020, according to a recent report, the situation may have improved: 4.3 million children under the age of 19 – 5.6% of all children – were then estimated to have been without health coverage for the entire calendar year; more children under the age of 19 in poverty were uninsured in 2020 than in 2018.[47] Further, the findings of a 2022 report show that:[48]

> [B]etween 2016 and 2020, there were significant increases in children's diagnosed anxiety and depression, decreases in physical activity, and decreases in caregiver mental and emotional well-being and coping with parenting demands. After the onset of the pandemic specifically, there were significant year-over-year increases in children's diagnosed behavioral or conduct problems, decreases in preventive medical care visits, increases in unmet health care needs, and increases in the proportion of young children whose parents quit, declined, or changed jobs because of child care problems.

44 *United States v. Darby,* 312 U.S. 100 (1941).

45 See Human Rights Watch, 'Fields of Peril: Child Labor in U.S. Agriculture' and 'US: Child Farmworkers Dangerous Lives' at www.hrw.org/news/2010/05/05/us-child-farmworkers-dangerous-lives.

46 See, further, https://theconversation.com/us-child-welfare-system-is-falling-short-because-of-persistent-child-poverty-180543.

47 Starkey, K.K. and Bunch, L.N., Health Insurance Coverage in the United States: 2020. www.census.gov/library/publications/2021/demo/p60–274.html.

48 See Lebrun-Harris, L.A., Ghandour, R.M. and Kogan, 'M.C., Five-Year Trends in US Children's Health and Well-being,' 2016–2020, *JAMA Pediatrics.* 2022; 176(7), https://jamanetwork.com/journals/jamapediatrics/fullarticle/2789946.

Establishing equity of health-care access for children and young persons with transgender issues has also been problematic but was eased by the Affordable Care Act, particularly s 1557 as amended by the 2016 HHS 'Final Rule.'[49] This, in effect, prohibits SOGI discrimination by government-funded health-care providers and the majority of related insurance companies.

EDUCATION

The relationship between parents, the state and the welfare of children in the context of education has perhaps attracted more judicial attention in the U.S. – with more weight being given to the rights of the former – than in any other common-law nation.[50] Despite the combined effect of the Establishment Clause[51] and the Free Exercise Clause[52] in the First Amendment being, as declared in *Everson v. Board of Education*,[53] to erect 'a wall of separation between Church and State. . . . [T]hat wall must be kept high and impregnable,' the reality has been pretty much a constant flow of litigation regarding religious influence on pupils in state-funded schools. So, for example, there have been decades of school prayer cases, which established that any activity sponsored or organised by a school that involved a prayer would compromise the neutrality of the public education system.[54]

Indeed, a considerable body of caselaw has accumulated which upholds the policy of insulating public schools from religious influence.[55] Essentially, the caselaw affirms the parental right to act as the representative of their child, in relation to what the parent perceives as being the latter's welfare interests, when negotiating provision of educational services with state authorities. So when, in *Wisconsin v. Yoder*,[56] the USSC ruled that Amish parents could not be compelled to send their children to high school when they had 'deep religious convictions' for not doing so,[57] it thereby set a legal precedent legitimating the homeschooling of children. In the second decade of the 21st century, this practice is escalating as parents,

49 See Department of Health and Human Services (HHS), *Final Rule: Nondiscrimination in Health Programs and Activities*, www.hhs.gov/sites/default/files/1557-summary-508.pdf.

50 See, for example, *Myer v. Nebraska*, 262 U.S. 390 at 399–400, (1923); *Pierce v. Society of Sisters*, 268 U.S. 510, at 534–35 (1925); and *Wisconsin v. Yoder*, U.S. 205, 214, 219 (1972).

51 See *Everson v. Board of Education of Ewing Township*, 330 U.S. 1 (1947): it cannot 'set up a church' or 'adopt . . . teach or practice religion' (at pp 15–16).

52 See, for example, *Sch. Dist. of Abington Twp., Pa. v. Schempp*, 374 U.S. 203, 305 (1963).

53 *Everson v. Board of Education*, op cit.

54 See, for example: *Santa Fe Indep. Sch. Dist. v. Doe*, 530 U.S. 290 (2000); *Lee v. Weisman*, 505 U.S. 577 (1992); *Wallace v. Jaffree*, 472 U.S. 38 (1985); *Sch. Dist. of Abington Twp., Pa. v. Schempp*, op. cit.; and *Engel v. Vitale*, 370 U.S. 421 (1962).

55 *Edwards* v. *Aguillard*, 482 U.S. 578 (1987), invalidating mandatory teaching of creationism; *Stone v. Graham*, 449 U.S. 39 (1980), invalidating mandatory display of the Ten Commandments; *Epperson v. Arkansas*, 393 U.S. 97 (1968), invalidating the prohibition on teaching evolution; *McCollum v. Board of Education*, 333 U.S. 203 (1948), prohibiting in-class sectarian religious instruction; and *Bd of Educ. of Kiryas Joel Village School District v. Grumet*, 512 U.S. 687, 705 (1994).

56 *Wisconsin v. Yoder*, op cit.

57 Ibid.

dissatisfied with the religious or SOGI awareness content of teaching in the public education system, now opt to teach some 3.5 million children at home. This, together with the contention over unisex bathrooms, contributes to creating stress and divisiveness among school-aged children.

Interestingly, although teaching in public schools while wearing religious clothing is impermissible, being taught while doing so is not: this distinction owes something to the absence of any public representative role on the part of the child pupil and also to the bearing of established caselaw precedents upholding a child's right to freedom of expression.[58] *Hearn and United States v. Muskogee Public School District*,[59] for example, concerned a Muslim girl who was suspended twice from school for wearing a hijab as required by her faith. The court ruled that she was entitled to do so; the school authorities, by singling her out because of her Islamic faith, had intentionally discriminated against her, and the court quoted from the ruling in *Lukumi* that 'at a minimum, the protections of the Free Exercise Clause pertain if the law at issue discriminates against some or all religious beliefs.'[60]

Many parents, in particular those with traditional or fundamental religious beliefs, such as evangelical Christians, Muslims and ultra-Orthodox Jews, are currently engaged in protests across the country. They challenge the content of sex and health education programmes for young children, claiming that material dealing with SOGI and LGBT awareness or trans issues exposes children to too much information and ideology too soon without effective opt-out opportunities.[61]

Legal proceedings

Given the constitutional protection afforded to family life, it is unsurprising that the law in the U.S., rather like Ireland and for the same reason, maintains a clear demarcation between its public and private sectors. Unlike Ireland, however, adoption from state care in the U.S. is a process which for decades has straddled both sectors.

ADOPTION FROM STATE CARE

The Adoption and Safe Families Act (ASFA) requires state agencies to file a petition to terminate parental rights, with certain exceptions, when a child has been in foster care for 15 of the most recent 22 months, and a court has determined that

58 See, for example, *Tinker v. Des Moines Indep. Cmty. Sch. Dist.*, 393 U.S. 503, 506 (1969), pupils wearing black armbands to signify disapproval of Vietnam war; *Chalifoux*, 976 F. Supp. 659 (1997), high school students wearing white rosary beads to signify their Catholicism; and *Alabama and Coushatta Tribes v. Big Sandy Schools District et al.*, 817 F. Supp. 1319 (1993), Native American school children with long hair to signify tribal identity.

59 020, No. Civ. 03 598-S (E.D. Ok., 2003).

60 *Church of Lukumi Babalu Aye, Inc. v. City of Hialeah*, 508 U.S. 520 (1993) at p 532.

61 See Morrar, S., 'Too Much, Too Soon: Families Rally at Capitol Against Sex Education and LGBT Curriculum,' *The Sacramento Bee*, 28 March 2019, at www.sacbee.com/news/local/education/article228532414.html (accessed 24 April 2019).

the child is an abandoned infant, or the parent committed/attempted murder or was otherwise involved in the murder/manslaughter/serious injury of another child of the parent.

As such adoptions usually concern a child in the custody of CPS for whom a TPR order has been issued, the proceedings are no longer open to being contested by the birth parent(s). Where an adoption application made with respect to a child in state care is contested, the court will require evidence that the grounds of child abuse or neglect, as set out within parameters established by the Adoption and Safe Families Act 1997, can be satisfied and will then accede to the application only if satisfied that this is compatible with the welfare interests of the child.[62] In 2020, adoption was the route taken by 25% of the children exiting the public care system.[63]

Post-adoption support Considerable financial support is available to those who adopt a child from the state care system.[64] Consequently, the number of children exiting the public care system by way of adoption following removal of parental rights has steadily increased. AFCARS reveals that they increased dramatically from 37,000 in 1998 to 51,000 in 2000, declined to 50,000 in 2001, then rose to 53,536 in 2015 and increased further to peak at 66,035 in 2019 but fell back to 57,881 a year later.[65] Most often, adoption is by the child's foster parents as research findings[66] discovered that children adopted by their foster parents did better than those who were not, with ongoing state financial support.[67] Interestingly, a further 35% of adoptions in 2020 were kinship adoptions.

WARDSHIP

The doctrine of *parens patriae* – allowing state interference to protect a child's welfare – is now far from being restricted to coercive state intervention in family matters where there are grounds for believing that a child is being or has been abandoned, abused or wilfully neglected. It is often also used by private parties when the life-saving treatment needed by a child is being refused by that child

62 See, *Curtis v. Curtis* 71 Mass (5 Gray) 535, 537 (1856), cited by Katz, S., Dual Systems of Adoption in the United States, op cit, at p 283.

63 See, AFCARS Report FY 2019, www.acf.hhs.gov/sites/default/files/documents/cb/afcarsreport28.pdf.

64 See, Child Welfare Information Gateway, (2020). *Adoption Assistance for Children Adopted from Foster Care*. Washington, D.C.: U.S. Department of Health and Human Services, Administration for Children and Families, Children's Bureau.

65 See AFCARS, annual reports, www.acf.hhs.gov/sites/default/files/documents/cb/afcarsreport28.pdf.

66 Cushing, G. and Greenblatt, S.B., Vulnerability to Foster Care Drift After the Termination of Parental Rights, in *Research on Social Work Practice*, 2009: 19(6), 694–704.

67 See AFCARS Report FY 2020, which records that 54% of all children adopted from foster care were adopted by their foster parents and that 94% of those received adoption subsidies. Note that some states have legislation that expressly prohibits same-sex couples or single applicants from adopting children in foster care.

and/or their parents. The principle established some 80 years ago in *Prince v. Massachusetts*[68] continues to govern such difficult matters:[69]

> Parents may be free to become martyrs themselves. But it does not follow that they are free, in identical circumstances, to make martyrs of their children.

Essentially, in circumstances of either public or private family law, where the welfare interests of a child are placed in grave and immediate danger, in the absence of alternative statutory authority, the court will exercise its *parens patriae* jurisdiction and assume all parental powers and responsibilities and direct such state intervention as is necessary to safeguard the welfare interests of the child concerned. While the wishes of the child will be sought and may be legally represented if appropriate, then taken into account and given such weighting as their age and discernment may merit, it will be the paramountcy principle as applied by the court which will override all other considerations and determine all issues relating to the child's upbringing for as long as the child remains a ward. Usually, in such cases, the duration of wardship is confined to resolving the presenting issue.

COMMERCIAL SURROGACY

The welfare interests of a child may well be negatively impacted by their realisation, as expressed in a U.S. court, that they were 'bought and paid for.'[70] An approach reinforced by a Vermont court that specifically pointed to the adverse consequences for such interests of a child born of artificial insemination if denied access to its second, non-biological parent.[71] Indeed, the judicial focus on contractual intent and on the terms of contracted arrangements and the general concern regarding the 'commodification' of children have led one academic to assert that, in the U.S., 'very few courts use the best interest of the child test in cases of surrogacy.'[72]

In California, the case of *Johnson v. Calvert*,[73] together with subsequent statutes and caselaw, are based on a view that the 'gestational surrogate' who is not genetically related to the child falls outside the definition of 'parent.' This approach has been adopted in Ohio, where the Court of Appeals stated that the 'individuals who provide the genes of that child are the natural parents,'[74] and in another case, it was averred that 'the law requires [that those] who provided the child with its genetics . . .

68 (1944) 321 U.S. 158.
69 Ibid at 170.
70 *Doe v. Attorney Gen.*, 487 N.W.2d 484, 487 (Mich. Ct. App. 1990).
71 *Miller-Jenkins v. Miller Jenkins*, 912 A.2d 951, 955 (Vt. 2006).
72 Finkelstein, A., Surrogacy Law and Policy in the U.S., Columbia Law School, (2016), p 22. https://web.law.columbia.edu/sites/default/files/microsites/gender-sexuality/files/columbia_sexuality_and_gender_law_clinic_-_surrogacy_law_and_policy_report_-_june_2016.pdf.
73 851 P. 2D 776 (1993).
74 *J.F. v. D.B*, 848 N.E.2d 873, 879 (Ohio Ct. App. 2007).

must be designated as the legal and natural parents.'[75] Where there is a pre-embryo transfer and approved contract, the intended parents can be named on the original birth certificate, and there is no need for an adoption; in addition, payments for the 'services' of the 'gestational carrier' are considered legal. In New York, the prohibition on surrogacy that followed the *Baby M* case[76] was finally lifted by legislation introduced in 2020, which legalised commercial gestational surrogacy with effect from February 2021.

The scope for exploitation in surrogacy arrangements and the consequent vulnerability of a child's welfare interests were highlighted in a recent case in which a same-sex couple preordered an unborn baby for $8,000 who was duly handed over immediately after birth.[77] The child subsequently suffered serious sexual abuse at the hands of his paedophile parents, undergoing what was described by the U.S. Attorney's Office as 'some of the most heinous acts of exploitation that this Office has ever seen.'[78]

Court orders

There is no equivalent in the U.S. to the array of parental responsibility orders that are statutorily available in the U.K.

PERMANENT LEGAL GUARDIANSHIP

This order, bridging the public/private division in family law, was introduced because:[79]

> [T]he emphasis on legally secure permanent placement is meant to provide the child with psychological stability and a sense of belonging and limit the likelihood of future disruption of the parent-child relationship. . . . [T]raditional adoption does not meet the needs of children in public foster care. Legal options for permanent and legally secure placement should be broad enough to serve the needs of all children in care who are not able to return to their homes of origin.

A permanent legal guardian has custody and control of a child, which includes powers to make decisions concerning that child's care, education, discipline and

75 *Belsito v. Clark*, 644 N.E.3d 760, 762, (Ohio Misc.2d 1994).

76 537 A.2d 1227 (N.J. 1988).

77 See *United States of America v. Mark Jonathan Newton*, United States District Court, 1: 12-CR-0121-SEB-DKL, per Barker J (25 June 2013) 8.

78 Department of Justice, 'Hogsett Announces Charges against Four Men in International Child Exploitation Conspiracy' (press release, 28 June 2013) at www.usdoj.gov/usao/ins.

79 See U.S. Department of Health and Human Services, Adoption 2002: The President's Initiative on Adoption and Foster Care: Guidelines for Public Policy and State Legislation Governing Permanence for Children, 1999.

protection. Both birth parents may retain some ongoing rights of contact and access and responsibility for maintenance. Intended for use by those relatives who may not wish to see a complete severance of ties between child and family, the order is particularly appropriate in relation to older children who object to the displacement of their established relationships with parents and siblings. By 2020, 10% of the children exiting the public care system did so by way of permanent legal guardianship.[80]

OTHER

All states have restraint or personal protection orders for use in a domestic violence context. The availability of such orders makes its own contribution to safe parental care.

Conclusion

There is a rather curious clash of paradigms in the U.S. regarding the private rights of parents in relation to their children. On the one hand, as illustrated by *Troxel*,[81] these rights would seem particularly strong relative to other countries. For example, corporal punishment is permissible in all states; all permit a parent to legally abandon their child in a designated 'safe haven'; 'private' adoptions are legal, and parents may determine the placement of their child for that purpose, and for-profit adoption agencies will provide assistance; and commercial surrogacy, allowing prospective parents to become so through a private financial arrangement with a surrogate or agency, is considered in law to be a contractual matter between the parties and one that does not need state involvement through an adoption process. On the other hand, the state is unusually prescriptive relative to other countries as regards imposing limitations on parental rights. For example, the U.S. persuasively pioneered the nonconsensual adoption of children from the public care system, an approach subsequently followed in the U.K., parts of Australia, and now Ireland, and, most notably, many states have now abolished the right to choose not to be a parent.[82]

Arguably, either way, the fact that the law retains its traditional focus on parental rights must detract from the importance it attaches to the welfare interests of children and perhaps goes some way towards explaining why it has not ratified U.N. CROC, with its firm declaration in support of the paramountcy principle.

80 See AFCARS Report FY, (2019), www.acf.hhs.gov/sites/default/files/documents/cb/afcarsreport28.pdf.

81 *Troxel v. Granville*, 530 U.S. 57 (2000).

82 The federally recognised right for a pregnant woman to choose not to be a parent, established by the USSC rulings in *Roe v. Wade*, 410 U.S. 113, and *Planned Parenthood v. Casey*, 505 U.S. 833, was extinguished by the USSC ruling in *Dobbs v. Jackson Women's Health Organisation*, 597 U.S._2022.

Part III

Canada

5 Policy, principles, legislation and courts

Introduction

Canada is a federated nation of ten provinces and three territories. The governments – federal, provincial, territorial and First Nations – have each established their own separate legislative, administrative, and procedural machinery for addressing issues relating to the welfare interests of children, machinery complicated by bilingualism and bijuralism[1] and the challenges of geography. Family law responsibilities are divided: federal government has jurisdiction over marriage, divorce, and ancillary matters such as custody and maintenance;[2] provinces have jurisdiction over matters related to the separation of married or unmarried couples; and for adoption and child protection, there is some degree of jurisdictional overlap. Moreover, as Québec is Canada's only civil law jurisdiction, and Nunavut is largely populated by the Inuit, both these entities tend to operate in many respects as outliers. It is therefore dangerous to make generalisations and risky to draw comparisons with respect to law and practice in the different Canadian jurisdictions. Just collating and comparing rates of provision for children in out-of-home care across provinces is problematic, and it is almost impossible to identify nationwide trends with any confidence.[3] As recently as May 2022, the U.N. Committee on the Rights of the Child again criticised the absence of any nationwide system for collecting data on children.[4]

That said, this chapter essentially follows the format established in Chapter 2. It begins with the historical development of the policy and principles that form the

1 Established initially by the Québec Act 1774, then by the British North America Act, and now protected by the Constitution Act 1867, s 92(13). This provides for a division of authority that removes 'property and civil rights' from the federal heads of power and reserves them exclusively to the jurisdiction of the provinces. Québec is thereby empowered to exercise property and civil rights in accordance with French civil law while British common law prevails elsewhere.

2 Reserved to federal government by the Constitution Act 1867.

3 The resulting difficulties have been well documented; see, for example, the concern expressed by the U.N. Committee on the Rights of the Child in October 2012, when it drew attention to the continuing difficulties relating to matters such as 'legislation, coordination, [and] data collection' (at para 8).

4 See, further, at https://www.ohchr.org/en/press-releases/2022/05/experts-committee-rights-child-commend-canada-truth-and-reconciliation.

DOI: 10.4324/9781003269564-9

foundations for the law relating to the welfare of children in Canada. In so doing, it differentiates between public family law and its civil and criminal jurisdictions, private family law, and hybrid public/private court orders and proceedings. It considers the beginnings of a recognition in the law of children's welfare interests and rights in each of those contexts. It then outlines the framework of legislation and courts, domestic and international, as it relates to Canadian children.

Policy, principles, legislation and courts

The U.N. CRC, in its 2012 report, expressed its concern 'that the best interests of the child is not widely known.'[5] It urged Canada:

> to strengthen its efforts to ensure that the principle of the best interests of the child is appropriately integrated and consistently applied in all legislative, administrative and judicial proceedings, as well as in all policies, programmes and projects relevant to and with an impact on children.[6]

The following year, UNICEF added to the pressure for a higher priority to be given to the welfare of children in a report that ranked Canada a lowly 17 out of the 29 developed countries surveyed in terms of their response to children in need.[7] This message was repeated more recently in the 2020 recommendation made by the Canadian Bar Association (Child and Youth Law section) in its 'Alternative Report to the UN Committee on the Rights of the Child' that 'Canada and the provinces and territories should include the best interests of the child in all legislation, court decisions and policy decisions affecting children.'[8]

Policy

Formally, public concern for the welfare of children in Canada can probably be dated to the setting up of the Children's Aid Society (CAS) in 1891 in Toronto.[9] Founded in the U.S. in 1853, this organisation focused on the plight of abandoned children and was instrumental in inducing the Canadian government to enact the Prevention of Cruelty to and Better Protection of Children Act 1893. That legislation authorised CAS to establish a network of branches to address the social

5 Ibid, at para 34.

6 Ibid, at para 35.

7 See, UNICEF Child Well-Being Index: Canada Ranked 17th Out Of 29 Wealthy Nations, *Huffington Post*, 10 October 2013, at http://www.huffingtonpost.ca/2013/04/10/unicef-child-well-being-canada_n_3050119.html.

8 See, further, at https://www.cba.org/CMSPages/GetFile.aspx?guid=fdb96dc7-35e0-4b6d-8918-40ba6607582a.

9 Policy relating to the welfare interests of children has more recently been strengthened by the creation of the Prime Minister's Youth Council in July 2016 for youth to consult with the prime minister specifically on policy issues. See, further, Canada, Report of the Prime Minister's Youth Counsel, (2019), at https://www.canada.ca/en/campaign/prime-ministers-youth-council/about/report.html.

problem of abandoned and neglected children and supervise children in the community, and it provided a process whereby the legal guardianship of such children could be transferred to the society.[10] Such services were needed to address the plight of unmarried mothers. In Canada, as in countries such as Ireland, the prevailing socio-religious norms during the early to middle decades of the 20th century were such that many unmarried mothers became victims of exploitive 'nursing homes,' where their babies all too often suffered abnormally high death rates or were illegally sold for private adoption.[11] Evidence testifying to the extent and traumatic effect of the pressures on unmarried women during this period was received by the Standing Senate Committee on Social Affairs and Technology in March 2018.[12]

Public family law policy relating to children: civil jurisdiction

As McLachlin CJ commented in *Gosselin v. Quebec (Attorney General)*,[13] 'age-based distinctions are a common and necessary way of ordering our society.' Unfortunately, however, there is no one agreed age of majority for all purposes of Canadian law. In Alberta, Ontario, Saskatchewan, Manitoba, Québec and Prince Edward Island, the age of majority is 18, and in British Columbia, New Brunswick, Nunavut, Nova Scotia and Newfoundland and Labrador, it is 19. The importance of being able to legally define a 'child' is evident in the range of laws with provisions in which:[14]

> age is employed as the qualification for pursuits that require skill or judgment. Consider the laws regulating voting, driving, drinking, marrying, contracting, will-making, leaving school, being employed, etc. In regulating these matters, all jurisdictions impose disabilities on young people, employing age as a proxy for ability. Such stereotyping is inevitably inaccurate, because individuals mature at different rates.

Nonetheless, in this most basic matter, as in so many other aspects of law and social policy relating to children, there is endemic disparity across the provinces and territories of Canada.

Despite the lack of reliable nationwide data, it would seem that the number of children being transferred from parental to state care has been increasing. Information sheets from the Canadian Child Welfare Research Portal produced estimates of such transfers for the years 1992 until 2007 and for the years 2008 until 2013,

10 In time, CAS became partially funded by local government (in Ontario, not until the 1960s); with its headquarters in Ontario, it is now nationwide, with 49 agencies exercising statutory child protection powers and working to promote the best interests, protection, and well-being of children.

11 See, for example, Cahill, B.L., *The Butterbox Babies*, Fernwood Publishing Co Ltd, (2007).

12 See The Shame is Ours: Forced Adoptions of the Babies of Unmarried Mothers in Post-War Canada, at https://sencanada.ca/en/info-page/parl-42-1/soci-adoption-mandate/.

13 2002 SCC 84, [2002] 4 SCR 429, at para 31.

14 Hogg, P.W., *Constitutional Law of Canada* (5th ed.), (2007), vol 2, at p 668.

ranging from 42,000 in 1992 to 67,000 in 2007. A report from the Child Welfare League of Canada estimated the number of children in care in 2000 to be 76,183.[15]

THE PREVENTION/PROTECTION BALANCE

Canada in the 1960s, along with other more developed nations, experienced the social effects of contraceptive availability, legalised abortion, increased rates of divorce and adoption, the number of single mothers, etc, all of which weakened the traditional role of the marital family and led to a focus on salvaging the welfare interests of the many children affected. The federal Child Welfare Act 1975 was something of a milestone in that it established a baseline for standards of parental care and for the associated grounds of CAS intervention in family life.

Safe havens Canada has no 'safe haven' laws like those in the U.S. that allow parents to anonymously 'safely surrender' their child in a designated 'baby hatch' in a police station, hospital or fire station without fear of prosecution. This has not stopped the introduction of such facilities in Edmonton, Alberta, and in three hospitals, where they are referred to as 'angel cradles.'

FOSTER CARE

In 2022, there were more than 63,000 children in foster care, a higher rate of care admissions than in other developed nations. Moreover, the 2016 national census revealed that although Indigenous children comprised only 7.7% of all Canadian children, they constituted 52% of the foster care population. It has been argued that 'the current state of the Canadian child welfare system exists as a system akin to traditional residential schools due to the disproportionate representation of Indigenous children.[16] (See, further, Chapter 8.)

KINSHIP CARE

Kinship care in Canada owes much to the well-established tradition among the First Nations for children to be cared for by members of their extended family or band.[17] It has recently been noted that a characteristic of adoption from state care takes the form of a child fostered out with a member of their extended family being subsequently adopted by that relative. There would appear to be no available

15 See, further, Canadian Child Welfare Research Portal at https://cwrp.ca/sites/default/files/publications/Children%20in%20out-of-home%20care%20in%20Canada%20in%202019_0.pdf.

16 Newland, E., Indigenous Children in Canada's Foster Care System: Bill C-92 and the Importance of Cultural Identity, *Children's Legal Rights Journal*, (2021): 42(1), at https://lawecommons.luc.edu/clrj/vol42/iss1/5.

17 See, for example, First Nations Child and Family Caring Society of Canada, *Supporting First Nations Adoption*, (2010), at http://www.fncaringsociety.com/sites/default/files/13.FNCFCS-Supporting-First-Nations-Adoption-Dec2010.pdf.

nationwide statistical data on kinship adoption, partially, perhaps, because the overlap with First Nations custom adoption adds to the auditing complexities. (See, further, Chapter 8.)

ADOPTION FROM STATE CARE

In Canada, as in other countries, the state as carer of last resort has probably always taken responsibility for receiving and then placing for adoption the infants that birth parents were unable or unwilling to care for. In practice, this responsibility continues to be borne by CAS and such other adoption agencies as are registered to do so.

The enforced adoption of many Indigenous children which followed the initiative of Margaret Edgar, who launched the Open Door Society in 1959, became known as 'the 60s scoop.' (See, further, Chapter 1.) The relative merits of preserving the bonds of culture and family attachments of such children when weighed against the prospective welfare benefits provided by non-Indigenous adopters were considered in the seminal case *Racine v. Woods*.[18] (See, further, Chapter 8.) The reverberations of that case and the scandal of 'the 60s scoop' continue to overshadow relationships between government authorities and First Nations and to compromise the contemporary use of adoption and other child care services in an Indigenous context.

RESIDENTIAL CARE

State intervention, as in the residential schools scandal, could be abusive (see, further, Chapter 1), but non-interventionism also resulted in abuse: records of child sexual abuse by Catholic Church clergy in community facilities across Canada date back to the 1980s in Newfoundland and continue well into this century. This association between residential facilities and the systemic abuse of children has left a legacy of recrimination that has tainted the contemporary role of residential care for children and young people in Canada. (See also Chapter 8.)

Public family law policy relating to children: criminal jurisdiction

There are strong parallels in the origins and development of the Canadian and U.S. juvenile justice systems. As with its U.S. counterpart, the origins of the Canadian system can be dated to the end of the 19th century with the introduction of industrial schools, which were seen as the answer to the growing problem of juvenile delinquency. Legislation passed in 1864 and taking effect in 1874 established industrial schools as facilities where delinquent and neglected or abandoned children could be sent to receive religious instruction and be taught a trade. The first of these schools – the Qu'Appelle Industrial School, the Battleford Industrial School

18 [1983] 2 SCR 173.

in Saskatchewan, and St. Joseph's School southwest of Calgary – opened in the 1880s. At the beginning of the 20th century, the nation's first juvenile probation officers were appointed in Ottawa in 1906, followed by the Juvenile Delinquents Act 1908. This legislation, providing legal processes separate from those of adults for addressing criminal behaviour, was grounded in a social welfare philosophy which sought to treat rather than punish child offenders. In due course, the 1908 Act was replaced by the Young Offenders Act 1984, which increased the age of criminal responsibility from 7 to 12; switched from a welfare-oriented approach to one of responsibility and accountability; and while focusing more on protection of the public, still recognised that youth have special needs due to their immaturity.

THE WELFARE/JUSTICE BALANCE

The Youth Criminal Justice Act 2003, replacing the 1984 Act, inaugurated the contemporary juvenile justice system. This statute introduced preventative provisions and sought to balance a focus on accountability, through meaningful consequences, with rehabilitation and reintegration. It emphasised out-of-court and noncustodial options for nonviolent youth while also providing custody options for those who committed more serious offences. The Safe Streets and Communities Act 2012 amended the 2003 act to make available firmer measures for the courts to deal with repeat offenders and violent youths found guilty of serious offences.

School shootings While not as frequent nor on the same scale as in the U.S., this phenomenon is not unknown in Canada and occurred most recently in February 2022 in Toronto.[19] In most cases, however, the perpetrator tends to be an adult.

Private family law policy relating to children

Family breakdown can be a precursor to breakdown in parental care, which, in turn, can lead to children being admitted to the public child care system. The Canadian marital family would now seem to be more fragile than formerly.[20]

MATRIMONIAL

Since the introduction of divorce in 1968 followed by a relaxing of the grounds in the Divorce Act 1985,[21] the annual divorce rate in Canada has steadily increased. According to Statistics Canada, from 2001 to 2011, married couples dropped from

19 A 14-year old boy then shot and killed a youth in Scarborough High School. Other school killings perpetrated by children include: 28 April 1999, at W.R. Myers High, Taber, Alberta, involving a 14 year-old perpetrator, and La Loche High School, Saskatchewan, where the killer was 17 years of age. See, further, at https://globalnews.ca/news/8621977/list-canadian-school-shootings/.

20 See, further, Statistics Canada, A Fifty Year Look at Divorces in Canada, 1970–2020, at https://www150.statcan.gc.ca/n1/daily-quotidien/220309/dq220309a-eng.htm.

21 The Divorce Act 1985 is now amended with effect from March 2021.

70.5% to 67.0% of all census families, and then dropped further to 65.8% by 2016. Of considerable significance is the rise in the number of those who choose to remain unmarried: in 1981, unmarried couples accounted for 6.3% of all families in Canada, but by 2016, they accounted for 17.8%.[22] If, as stated by the Canadian Encyclopedia, common-law relationships 'are generally more short-lived and dissolve more frequently than marriages,' then their proportionate increase may well correlate with an increase in breakdowns of parental care, leading to an increased risk of children coming into the public child-care system.

GUARDIANSHIP AND WARDSHIP

The National Children's Alliance of Canada, in its 2000 report, noted that:[23]

> Another emerging option of family-based care is evolving, namely guardianship care. Guardianship care is a status between that of foster care and adoption; guardianship care is granted to a known family member or specified friend, to indicate permanency of care. The province would retain legal guardianship status until the child reaches adulthood.[24]

While a parent is inherently the guardian of their child, guardianship may be awarded by the court to a third party or assigned to such a person by means of a power of attorney. Once appointed, a guardian is vested with parental powers and duties with respect to the named child, which need not necessarily be exercised to the exclusion of a parent.

Wardship is used as a default public order for children for whom all care responsibilities have been transferred by court order from the parent(s) to the state. Being vested with all parental rights, the state is then obliged to further the best interests of a ward, or 'Crown ward,' by arrangements that provide for their care in a family setting. This is achieved by placement either in the public foster care system or in the private realm of adoption. In practice, by far the majority of such children are left to age-out in state care.[25]

ADOPTION

According to the Canadian Encyclopedia, adoption was introduced first in New Brunswick in 1878 in order to save the babies of unmarried mothers from the stigma of 'illegitimacy' by placing them with married couples.[26] The stigma was

22 See https://www150.statcan.gc.ca/n1/pub/11-627-m/11-627-m2017024-eng.htm.

23 See Farris-Manning, C. and Zandstra, M., Children in Care in Canada, op cit, at p 3.

24 Ibid, citing Aitken, G., Extending Options in Permanency Planning, in *Permanency Planning in the Child Welfare System*, Ottawa, Sparrow Lake Alliance: Children in Limbo Task Force, (2002), at p 23.

25 See, further at: https://www.theglobeandmail.com/opinion/editorials/crown-wards-a-group-of-kids-that-are-not-all-right/article577611/.

26 See, further, at: http://www.thecanadianencyclopedia.ca/en/article/adoption/.

real, prompting many unmarried mothers to discreetly retire to maternity homes for their confinement, from which their child might be adopted. Some such homes were engaged in 'trafficking' the babies to the U.S., and one in particular – the Ideal Maternity Home in Nova Scotia which functioned from the late 19202 to the late 1940s – became notorious for engaging in infanticide, burying the infants in butter boxes.[27]

Adoption has long since become established throughout Canada. In general, the adoption statutes do not emphasise the centrality or overriding importance of the welfare interests of the adoptee: in Ontario, for example, the statutory duty is for the court to be no more than satisfied that the order is 'in the child's best interests.'[28]

The U.N. CRC has pointed out that:

> domestic adoption legislation, policy and practice are set by each of the provinces and territories and vary considerably from jurisdiction to jurisdiction and as a result Canada has no national adoption legislation, national standards, national database on children in care or adoption and little known research on adoption outcomes.[29]

It recommended that there should be 'one set of adoption rules across all of Canada that are in line with the Convention and other international rules that protect children's rights.'[30]

INTERCOUNTRY ADOPTION: HISTORICAL

As a receiving country, Canada's experience dates back to the 19th century when, as a former colony of the British Empire, it benefitted from the tens of thousands of children shipped from Britain to be adopted or otherwise taken in by Canadian families. It has been estimated that approximately 100,000 such children aged five years and older were received in Canada between 1826 and 1939.[31] This practice, since renounced by the countries and organisations involved as a mistaken exercise of state power and acknowledged as harrowing for many of the children concerned, stands as a benchmark and a reminder of the potential for state abuse of children's welfare interests. (See, further, Chapter 1.)

27 See Cahill, B.L., *Butterbox Babies*, Fernwood Publishing Co Ltd, (2007).
28 Child and Family Services Act 1990, s 146(1).
29 See the U.N. Committee on the Rights of the Child, 61st session, C/CAN/CO/3–4, October 2012, at para 57.
30 Ibid, at para 27.
31 See, for example, Kohli, M.P., *The Golden Bridge: Young Immigrants to Canada, 1833–1939*, Natural Heritage Press, Toronto, (2003). Also, see Parker, R., *Uprooted: The Shipment of Poor Children to Canada, 1867–1919*, The Policy Press, Bristol, (2008).

FAMILY PLANNING, ABORTION, SURROGACY, IVF, ETC

The Well Women organisation, founded in Canada and since spreading to countries such as the U.K., South Africa and New Zealand, represents the global leadership shown by Canada in relation to the evolution and social acceptance of women's reproductive rights.

Abortion services have been legally available, albeit initially in restricted circumstances, since 1969. In 1988, the Supreme Court of Canada in *R. v. Morgentaler*[32] ruled that the abortion law prohibitions were unconstitutional as they infringed upon a woman's right to 'life, liberty and security of person' in violation of s 7 of the Charter of Rights and Freedoms. As Dickson CJ then explained:

> Forcing a woman, by threat of criminal sanction to carry a foetus to term unless she meets certain criteria unrelated to her own priorities and aspirations, is a profound interference with a woman's body and thus a violation of her security of the person.

Thereafter, Canada became one of a small number of countries without a law restricting abortion. It is now regulated by the Canada Health Act and treated like any other medical procedure in accordance with provincial and medical regulations.[33] The annual abortion rates show a steady decline from 108,844 in 2011 to 85,195 in 2018. As elsewhere, abortion rates, together with improved contraceptives, directly correlate with falling third-party domestic adoptions.

Surrogacy Since the introduction of the Assisted Human Reproduction Act 2004, altruistic surrogacy has been legal in Canada[34] but not in Québec, which does not recognise surrogacy arrangements, whether commercial or altruistic.[35] Some of the related legal ramifications were examined in the 2009 Ontario case of *C (M.A.) v. K. (M.)*,[36] when Cohen J denied an adoption application by a lesbian with respect to her partner's birth child. Finding that the sperm donor father had maintained a close and caring relationship with the six-year-old child since her birth and that the applicant had in place a written agreement addressing the parties' respective roles and rights, Cohen J ruled that the effect of an adoption order would be contrary to the child's best interests as it would undermine her 'sense of place in the world, her confidence in her experience of the world and her understanding of who her family is.'[37] (See, further, Chapter 7.)

32 [1988] 1 SCR 30.

33 However, as Lori Chambers comments, major problems with access to abortion remain (note to author, 16 August 2022).

34 See, further, Snow, D., *Assisted Reproduction Policy in Canada: Framing, Federalism and Failure*, University of Toronto Press, (2018).

35 See *In the Matter of X (Adoption)* 091, 2009 QCCQ 628, [2009] RJQ 445 (Can. Que. Youth Ct.).

36 *M.A.C. v. M.K.*, 2009 ONCJ 18 (Can. Ont. Ct. J.). A full account of this case can be found in Bala, N. and Ashbourne, C., 'The Widening Concept of Parent in Canada' op cit, at pp 13–14.

37 Ibid, at para 64.

Principles

In Canada, as in the U.S. and other developed nations, it is the nexus of principles that protect the private life of the family and its members from unwarranted state intrusion which constitute the core of family law and determine the role to be played in that law by the principle of the welfare of the child.

Paramountcy principle

The SCC in *Young v. Young*[38] referred to the best interests of the child as a child's 'positive right to the best possible arrangements in the circumstances.' There is no mention of the paramountcy principle in the Child Protection Act 1998. The 2019 changes to federal family laws maintain the best interests of the child as the only consideration for parenting decisions under the Divorce Act and include various measures to promote those interests. While these changes do not mention the paramountcy principle, they do identify welfare as a 'primary consideration' which specifies that a child's safety, security and well-being are the most important factors to consider. A similar provision is included in the family law statutes of Alberta and British Columbia.[39] In Manitoba, however, the paramountcy principle is referenced in the Child and Family Services Act 1985:[40]

> 2(1) The best interests of the child shall be the paramount consideration of the director, an authority, the children's advocate, an agency and a court in all proceedings under this Act affecting a child, other than proceedings to determine whether a child is in need of protection.

Those authorised to apply the paramountcy principle must ensure their decisions comply with what is considered to be the best interests of that particular child; they may find the consent of a parent or the child to a suggested course of action to be perfectly valid but choose to reject this in favour of another option which it considers to better meet the best interests test. As McIntyre J once said:

> [I]t must be the aim of the Court . . . to choose the course which will best provide for the healthy growth, development and education of the child so that he will be equipped to face the problems of life as a mature adult.[41]

This view was subsequently endorsed by L'Heureux-Dubé J: '[C]ourts must be directed to create or support the conditions which are most conducive to the

38 [1993] 4 SCR 3 at 10. See, also, *Van de Pierre v. Edwards*, [2001] 2 SCR 1014.
39 See, further, Department of Justice at https://www.justice.gc.ca/eng/rp-pr/fl-lf/famil/c78/03.html#secA.
40 As amended by Bill 41, The Child and Family Services Amendment Act 2022.
41 *King v. Low*, [1985] 1 SCR 87 at p 101.

flourishing of the child.'[42] These judicial comments, together with the broad absence of legislative references to paramountcy, must be taken as indicating that the principle does not play the same role in Canadian family law as it does elsewhere – for example, in that of the U.K.

PARAMOUNTCY: CHILD'S CONSENT

When faced with the dilemma of a conflict between the views of an adolescent child and their parents, the judiciary tend to adopt an approach that tapers the child's and parents' respective capacities to authorise treatment necessitated by the former's medical condition in accordance with the child's age and maturity. This approach has also gained academic recognition: age cutoffs:

> may function as an indicator to shift legal presumptions. Thus, children below the age of consent are presumed to lack capacity unless there is evidence to show otherwise, and those above that age are presumed to have capacity until shown otherwise.[43]

In *J.S.C. v. Wren*,[44] for example, a 16-year-old girl had received medical approval for a therapeutic abortion, but her parents sought an injunction to prevent it because the age of majority was 18. Kerans J concluded that the girl was capable of consenting to the abortion on her own behalf:[45]

> We infer that she did have sufficient intelligence and understanding to make up her own mind and did so. At her age and level of understanding, the law is that she is to be permitted to do so. . . . Parental rights (and obligations) clearly do exist and they do not wholly disappear until the age of majority. The modern law, however, is that the courts will exercise increasing restraint in that regard as a child grows to and through adolescence.

Similarly, *In Re A.Y.*[46] concerned a 15-year-old Jehovah's Witness who had cancer and required blood transfusions as well as chemotherapy. The court found both that the child was mature and that it was not in his best interests to impose treatment. Wells J noted that the treatment was less than 40% likely to be effective, was not essential, and was contrary to the mature adolescent's wishes. (See, also, *Van Mol*,

42 *Young v. Young*, op cit, at p 65.

43 See Berg, J., et al., in *Informed Consent: Legal Theory and Clinical Practice* (2nd ed.), Oxford University Press, (2001).

44 (1986), 76 A.R. 115 (C.A.).

45 Ibid, at paras 16 and 13. See, also, *Van Mol (Guardian ad Litem of) v. Ashmore*, 1999 BCCA 6, 168 D.L.R. (4th) 637.

46 (1993), 111 Nfld. & P.E.I.R. 91 (Nfld. S.C.). See, also, *Region 2 Hospital Corp. v. Walker* (1994), 150 N.B.R. (2d) 366 (C.A.).

later in this chapter.) In contrast, the court in *Dueck (Re)*[47] found that the treatment refusal of a 13-year-old boy had been unduly influenced by his controlling father, rendering his refusal involuntary, thus permitting the court to authorise the required chemotherapy and surgery. Again, in *Alberta (Director of Child Welfare) v. H. (B.)*,[48] a 16-year-old girl with acute myeloid leukaemia and her parents, all Jehovah's Witnesses, refused to consent to her receiving urgent life-saving treatment involving blood products. The hospital and physicians would not treat the girl given her refusal as they were of the view that she was a mature adolescent, capable of making an informed decision and, therefore, entitled to refuse treatment.[49] Jordan J found that the girl was not mature enough to make the decision to die, concluding that 'intelligence, thoughtfulness, exemplary behaviour and notable academic achievement are not sufficient when the magnitude of the decision faced by a 16-year-old involves a certain risk of death'|; his decision was upheld on appeal.[50] (See, further, later in this chapter.)

APPLICATION TO ADOPTION AND OTHER MATTERS

In the aforementioned *C. (M.A.) v. K. (M.)*,[51] the adoption application by a lesbian couple – the custodial parents and primary caregivers of the child – was contested by the biological father, a sperm donor and actively involved parent. In recognition of the importance of a caring birth parent to the ongoing welfare interests of the child, the court refused to dispense with the need for his consent and rejected the adoption application.

Principle of parental rights

As Rand J put it in *Hepton v. Maat*:[52]

> *[P]rima facie* the natural parents are entitled to custody unless by reason of some act, condition or circumstance affecting them it is evident that the welfare of the child requires that that fundamental natural relation be severed.

While a parent by fault or default may breach a statutory duty owed to their child and thereby lose custody, in some cases, an exercise of parental rights that is

47 (1999), 171 D.L.R. (4th) 761 (Sask. Q.B.).
48 2002 ABPC 39, [2002] 11 W.W.R. 752.
49 See *Malette v. Shulman* (1990), 72 O.R. (2d) 417 (C.A.), at p 424, where the court found that 'the doctrine of informed consent is plainly intended to ensure the freedom of individuals to make choices concerning their medical care. For this freedom to be meaningful, people must have the right to make choices that accord with their own values regardless of how unwise or foolish those choices may appear to others.'
50 Ibid, at p 761. See also *Hôpital Ste-Justine v. Giron*, 2002 CanLII 34269 (Que. Sup. Ct.); *U. (C.) (Next friend of) v. Alberta (Director of Child Welfare)*, 2003 ABCA 66, 13 Alta. L.R. (4th) 1.
51 2009 ONCJ 18 (CanLII).
52 [1957) SCR 606.

compliant with statutory law may also compromise or violate a child's welfare interests and at least raise questions as to the parent's fitness to continue custody. The Criminal Code provides at least two such sets of circumstances: s 268(3), which 'allows for parents and medical practitioners to undertake nonconsensual, cosmetic surgeries on intersex infants,' and s 43, which permits parental chastisement. Both practices have been condemned by many professional bodies.[53]

PARENTAL RESPONSIBILITY AND CORPORAL PUNISHMENT

The Criminal Code, s 43, permitting the use of reasonable force by parents and teachers to discipline a child or pupil, was examined by the SCC in *Canadian Foundation for Children, Youth and the Law v. Canada (Attorney General)*[54] (the 'spanking case'). The court, in a majority decision, found that fundamental justice did not require that laws affecting children be in their best interests: the welfare interests of a child was not a principle of fundamental justice. It determined that such disciplinary measures did not constitute cruel and unusual treatment or punishment, nor did they violate ss 7, 12 and 15(1) of the charter, but it did prohibit the use of corporal punishment in schools. It ruled that the force used must not be severe, and it must be intended for educative or corrective purposes, relating to restraining, controlling or expressing disapproval of the actual behaviour of a child capable of benefitting from the correction. The court warned that:[55]

> Corporal punishment using objects, such as rulers or belts, is physically and emotionally harmful. Corporal punishment which involves slaps or blows to the head is harmful. These types of punishment, we may conclude, will not be reasonable.

Binnie J, dissenting, offered the alternative and decidedly more persuasive view:

> To deny protection against physical force to children at the hands of their parents and teachers is not only disrespectful of a child's dignity but turns the child, for the purpose of the Criminal Code, into a second class citizen. Such marginalization is destructive of dignity from any perspective, including that of a child. Protection of physical integrity against the use of unlawful force is a fundamental value that is applicable to all.

53 See, for example, the Canadian Bar Association recommendation that government amends the Criminal Code to postpone genital normalising surgeries on children until the child can meaningfully participate in the decision, except where there is immediate risk to the child's health and medical treatment cannot be delayed (May 2019). Also see the repeated objections by the U.N. CRC to corporal punishment (from 2003 to 2022).

54 [2004] 1 SCR 76, 2004 SCC 4.

55 Ibid, at para 37.

The U.N. CRC has repeatedly expressed its concern on this matter:[56]

> The Committee recommends that the State party adopt legislation to remove the existing authorization of the use of 'reasonable force' in disciplining children and explicitly prohibit all forms of violence against children, however light, within the family, in schools and in other institutions where children may be placed.

It did so most recently in May 2022.[57]

SHARING PARENTAL RESPONSIBILITIES

In the absence of court orders, neither parent has exclusive responsibility for their child, and such responsibility as they hold jointly will steadily diminish as that child matures through adolescence. However, judicial intervention may well result in a rebalancing or abridging of parental responsibilities. So, for example, in *Young v. Young*,[58] the noncustodial parent – a Jehovah's Witness – protested that his right to develop the children's religious beliefs was being obstructed by their mother. The SCC took the view that the welfare of the child was the overriding principle, and therefore, the authority of the custodial parent to make decisions relating to religious activities must be secured in order to protect the children from any harmful stress. The same approach was evident in *B. (R.) v. Children's Aid Society of Metropolitan Toronto*[59] and in *A.C. v. Manitoba Director of Child and Family Services*,[60] when, in both cases, the SCC gave greater weight to the welfare interests of a child than to the freedom of religion rights of Jehovah's Witness parents. It may be that the latter are a special case in that the rigidity of their beliefs adds a layer of control to their *locus standi* as parents, which can be readily recognised as having the potential to compromise the welfare interests of their children.

Consanguinity principle

Consanguinity is now treated by the Canadian judiciary as simply one factor among the many that may be relevant to a child's best interest when determining custody disputes. The courts have for some time been clear that there can be no preferencing a birth parent's claim to custody over all other considerations that may constitute a child's welfare.[61]

56 See, further, at https://endcorporalpunishment.org/human-rights-law/crc/session-034-2003/.
57 See, further, at https://www.ohchr.org/en/press-releases/2022/05/experts-committee-rights-child-commend-canada-truth-and-reconciliation.
58 [1993] 4 SCR 3.
59 [1994] SCJ No 24.
60 [2009] SCJ No 30.
61 See, for example, *King v. Low*, (1985) CanLII 59 (SCC).

NO PRESUMPTION FAVOURING CONSANGUINITY

Justice Martin, on behalf of the SCC in *B.J.T. v. J.D.*,[62] when awarding custody to the maternal grandmother rather than to the child's birth father, placed the blood-tie considerations into perspective with the following advice:

> [J]udges are not obliged to treat biology as a tie-breaker when two prospective custodial parents are otherwise equal. Placing too great an emphasis on a biological tie may lead some decision makers to give effect to the biological parent's claim over the child's best interests and parental preferences should not usurp the focus on the child's interests.

She added:

> [A] child's bond is a consideration that should prevail over the 'empty formula' of a biological tie. A biological connection is no guarantee against harm to a child and a child can be equally attached to persons who are not their biological parents and those persons can be equally capable of meeting the child's needs.

This ruling has important implications, given that many children are now parented in foster care and LGBT families where there is often no genetic link between parent and child. (See, further, Chapter 6.)

Proportionality principle

The 'Oakes test,' established by the SCC in *R. v. Oakes*,[63] determines when an infringement of a charter right is reasonable and justifiable. Firstly, it requires the purpose of the infringing law to be of sufficient importance to warrant overriding a constitutionally protected right or freedom. Secondly, if that is the case, then there must be a 'proportionality test' to establish that the means chosen are reasonable and demonstrably justified: the law must be rationally connected to the objective, the law must impair the right no more than is necessary to accomplish the objective, and the law must not have a disproportionately severe effect on the rights infringed.

The Oakes test must now be viewed in the light of the *Doré* framework,[64] which is used when an administrative agency is involved (e.g. in *Loyola*[65]). As Guy puts it, in *Doré*, the SCC held that administrative discretionary decisions implicating a charter right 'should be reviewed using a values-based, administrative law

62 2022 SCC 24.
63 [1986] 1 SCR 103.
64 *Doré v. Barreau du Québec*, 2012 SCC 12.
65 *Loyola High School v. Québec (Attorney General)*, 2015 SCC 12.

approach focused on proportionality, one that asks whether the decision-maker has properly balanced the relevant Charter values and statutory objectives at issue.'[66]

Abella J noted the importance of the proportionality principle in *Manitoba* when she argued that her interpretation of the 'best interests test' in s 25(8) of the Child and Family Services Act:

> enables adolescents to participate meaningfully in medical treatment decisions in accordance with their maturity, creating a sliding scale of decision-making autonomy . . . [which] reflects a proportionate response to the goal of protecting vulnerable young people from harm, while respecting the individuality and autonomy of those who are sufficiently mature to make a particular treatment decision.[67]

Liberty principle

The right to life, liberty, and security of the person is embedded in and protected by the Charter of Fundamental Rights and Freedoms. As La Forest J observed, '[I]n a free and democratic society, the individual must be left room for personal autonomy to live his or her own life and to make decisions that are of fundamental personal importance.'[68] The SCC, in *New Brunswick (Minister of Health) v. G. (J.)*,[69] found that this principle mandates legal representation for a parent in child protection proceedings, to be provided by the state if the parent is 'indigent.' It held that a parent's 'security of the person' – the parent's relationship to the child – is threatened by state action in child welfare proceedings, and, accordingly, the 'principles of fundamental justice' may be invoked to give the court jurisdiction to order such state funding for legal representation.

In *A.C. v. Manitoba*, the SCC noted the importance the judiciary have attached to this principle:[70] Wilson J, in *Morgentaler*, stated that '[liberty], properly construed, grants the individual a degree of autonomy in making decisions of fundamental personal importance'[71]; in *Blencoe*, ' "liberty" is engaged where state compulsions or prohibitions affect important and fundamental life choices'[72]; in *Godbout*, '[T]he right to liberty . . . protects within its ambit the right to an irreducible sphere of personal autonomy wherein individuals may make inherently private choices free

66 See Guy, T.R., Opening the Doré to Proportionality: Discretionary Administrative Decisions and the Charter, LLM thesis, University of Toronto, (2015), p 1, at https://tspace.library.utoronto.ca/bitstream/1807/69099/3/Guy_Trevor_R_201503_LLM_thesis.pdf.

67 Ibid, at para 115.

68 *B. (R.) v. Children's Aid Society of Metropolitan Toronto*, 1995 CanLII 115 (SCC), [1995] 1 SCR 315, at para 80.

69 [1999] 3 SCR 46.

70 *A.C. v. Manitoba (Director of Child and Family Services)*, op cit, at para 100.

71 *R. v. Morgentaler*, [1988] 1 SCR 30, at p 166.

72 *Blencoe v. British Columbia (Human Rights Commission)*, 2000 SCC 44, [2000] 2 SCR 307, at para 49.

from state interference.[73] Sopinka J in *Rodriguez*, for the majority, confirmed that the concept of security of the person encompasses 'a notion of personal autonomy involving, at the very least, control over one's bodily integrity free from state interference and freedom from state-imposed psychological and emotional stress,'[74] while McLachlin J, in dissent, explained:

> Security of the person has an element of personal autonomy, protecting the dignity and privacy of individuals with respect to decisions concerning their own body. It is part of the persona and dignity of the human being that he or she have the autonomy to decide what is best for his or her body.[75]

As the SCC caselaw illustrates, however, a parent may run the risk of losing the protection of s 7 if their particular level of child care breaches statutory child protection standards. So, in *Winnipeg Child and Family Services v. K.L.W.*,[76] the SCC held that state intervention to remove a newborn baby from maternal care without prior court authorisation in a nonemergency situation did not violate the mother's s 7 rights. The court found that, given the mother's history of having her children removed by the authorities on several occasions due to her intoxication, it was not unreasonable that her one-day-old baby should have been peremptorily taken into care: the principles of fundamental justice applicable in the child protection context did not require prior judicial authorisation in such 'nonemergency' situations. As the dissenting Binnie J noted in *Manitoba*, 'the s 7 liberty interest is engaged when the state steps in to prohibit (or compel) fundamental life choices that "[e]veryone" is otherwise free to pursue (or to decline to pursue).'[77]

The application of the liberty principle in the context of 'mature minors' was considered by the British Columbia Court of Appeal in *Van Mol (Guardian ad Litem of) v. Ashmore*:[78]

> Once the required capacity to consent has been achieved by the young person reaching sufficient maturity, intelligence and capability of understanding, the discussions about the nature of the treatment, its gravity, the material risks and any special or unusual risks, and the decisions about undergoing treatment, and about the form of the treatment, must all take place with *and be made by* the young person whose bodily integrity is to be invaded and whose life and health will be affected by the outcome.

73 *Godbout v. Longueuil (City)*, [1997] 3 SCR 844, at para 66.

74 *Rodriguez v. British Columbia (Attorney General)*, [1993] 3 SCR 519, at pp 587–588.

75 Ibid, at 618.

76 2000 SCC 48.

77 *A.C. v. Manitoba (Director of Child and Family Services)*, op cit, at para 217. See also *Young v. Young* [1993] 4 SCR 3.

78 1999 BCCA 6, 168 D.L.R. (4th) 637, at para 75.

The court then concluded that a young person with capacity was entitled to *make* the treatment decision, not just to have 'input' into a judge's consideration of what the latter believed to be the young person's best interests. Whether this rationale would transfer to circumstances in which the young person's judgement was found to be unduly influenced – most obviously by their or their parents' beliefs as Jehovah's Witnesses – is, perhaps, a different matter. Whether the rationale would survive a gravity test requiring the young person to show that they fully appreciate the consequences when the decision is one of life or death is again open to question.

Legal system: legislation, courts, welfare/rights and representation

Canada, being like its neighbour a federation of jurisdictions, is similarly without a national system of legislation and courts dedicated to the law relating to children.

Legislative framework

The Constitution, particularly s 7 of the charter, as interpreted by the SCC, together with the provisions of international treaties, conventions and protocols and some key federal statutes, help induce a degree of nationwide uniformity in law and practice. That said, each and every province and territory independently legislates and applies the law relating to children, much of which is quite dated. This has been a matter of concern to the U.N. CRC:

> given the State party's federal system and dualist legal system, the absence of such overall national legislation has resulted in fragmentation and inconsistencies in the implementation of child rights across the State party, with children in similar situations being subject to disparities in the fulfilment of their rights depending on the province or territory which they reside in.[79]

INTERNATIONAL LAW

Canada ratified the International Covenant on Economic, Social, and Cultural Rights in 1976, the U.N. Convention on the Rights of the Child (U.N. CROC) in 1991 (and has ratified the first two of the three optional protocols), the Hague Convention on International Adoption in 1997 with effect throughout the provinces and territories in 2006, and the Palermo protocol on trafficking in 2000.[80] Ratification or accession has also been completed in relation to the International Convention on the Elimination of All Forms of Racial Discrimination (1970); the International Covenant on Economic, Social and Cultural Rights (1976); and the Convention on the Elimination of All Forms of Discrimination against Women (CEDAW) (1981).

79 Committee on the Rights of the Child, 61st Session (2012): CRC/C/CAN/CO/3-4, at para 10.
80 This protocol to prevent, suppress and punish trafficking in persons, especially women and children, is intended to reinforce the U.N. Convention against Transnational Organized Crime. Its relevance, for present purpose, lies in the importance it places on preventing child trafficking.

Neither at federal level nor at the provincial and territorial level has the U.N. CROC or its first and second protocols been incorporated into domestic law, and the third optional protocol – to promote better monitoring and resolution of violations of children's rights – has yet to be ratified. Canada adopted the United Nations Declaration on the Rights of Indigenous Peoples (UNDRIP) in 2016 but has declined to incorporate it into domestic law, although in 2019, British Columbia became the first Canadian jurisdiction to enact UNDRIP.[81]

DOMESTIC LAW: THE CONSTITUTION AND FEDERAL LEGISLATION

The Constitution of Canada consists of the Constitution Act 1982, together with its predecessor the Constitution Act 1867 (formerly the British North America Act 1867) and all other statutes and orders referred to in the schedule and any amendments.

The Canadian Constitution, like its U.S. counterpart, is a product of the common law. As a result, it, too, has a proven capacity to respond to changing social circumstances. So, for example, the court in *Re Vancouver Regional Free Net Association and Minister of National Revenue*[82] found that free community access to the internet in the 20th century could, by analogy, be viewed as a contemporary public utility equivalent to the free public access to 'highways' permitted by an early 17th-century statute.[83] Again, in *Reference Re Same Sex Marriage*,[84] the SCC found that the meaning of marriage was not frozen in time, in accordance with its definition under s 91(26) of the Constitution Act 1867, but must be allowed to evolve with Canadian society, which was now represented by a plurality of groups. This elasticity has enabled the Constitution to be very relevant to contemporary social developments affecting the family and the welfare interests of children. (See also Chapters 2 and 9.)

Canadian Charter of Rights and Freedoms

An integral part of the Constitution Act 1982, the Canadian Charter of Rights and Freedom, is of central importance.

Section 2(a) states that everyone has the right to enjoy the fundamental freedoms of conscience and religion. However, as Iacobucci and Major JJ observed in *B. (R.) v. Children's Aid Society of Metropolitan Toronto*:[85]

> Just as there are limits to the ambit of freedom of expression (e.g. s 2(b) does not protect violent acts[86]), so are there limits to the scope of s 2(*a*), especially

81 Declaration on the Rights of Indigenous Peoples Act, SBC 2019, c 44.

82 (1996) 137 DLR (4th) 206 Federal Court of Appeal. Also see *Everywoman's Health Centre Society v. Canada*, [1991] 2 C.T.C. 320, 92 D.T.C. 6001 (F.C.A.)

83 See the Preamble to the Statute of Charitable Uses 1601. Also see *Vancouver Society of Immigrant and Visible Minority Women v. M.N.R.*, [1999] 1 SCR 10.

84 [2004] 3 SCR 698.

85 [1995] 1 SCR 315, at para 226.

86 Ibid, citing: *R. v. Zundel*, 1992 CanLII 75 (SCC), [1992] 2 SCR 731, at pp 753 and 801; *R. v. Keegstra*, 1990 CanLII 24 (SCC), [1990] 3 SCR 697, at pp 732 and 830.

> so when this provision is called upon to protect activity that threatens the physical or psychological well-being of others.

Section 7 states that everyone has the right to life, liberty, and security of the person and the right not to be deprived thereof except in accordance with the principles of fundamental justice. However, as the SCC found in *Manitoba*:

> [Section] 7 was enacted for the purpose of ensuring human dignity and individual control, so long as it harms no one else. . . . [T]he liberty or autonomy right is not absolute, even for adults, nor does it trump all other values. Limits on personal autonomy that advance a genuine state interest do not violate s 7 if they are shown to be based on rational, rather than arbitrary grounds.[87]

Section 15 states that every individual is equal before and under the law and has the right to the equal protection and benefit of the law without discrimination and, in particular, without discrimination based on race, national or ethnic origin, colour, religion, sex, age or mental or physical disability.

Section 27 declares, 'This Charter shall be interpreted in a manner consistent with the preservation and enhancement of the multicultural heritage of Canadians.' It is seen as stating a core principle of Canadian policy, an assurance of cultural pluralism that includes and respects the First Nations.

An Act Respecting First Nations, Inuit and Métis Children, Youth and Families 2020 This legislation affirms the rights of First Nations, Inuit and Métis peoples to exercise jurisdiction over child and family services; establishes national principles such as the best interests of the child, cultural continuity and substantive equality; contributes to the implementation of the United Nations Declaration on the Rights of Indigenous Peoples; and provides an opportunity for Indigenous peoples to choose their own solutions for their children and families.

Child and Family Services Act 2017 This Ontario statute strongly resembles the Child and Family Services Acts of other Canadian jurisdictions such as British Columbia, Manitoba and Nova Scotia.

Civil Marriage Act 2005 Marriage was redefined by this federal Act as 'the lawful union of two persons to the exclusion of all others.' It also amended the Divorce Act 1985 to change its corresponding meaning of 'spouse' to mean 'either of two persons who are married to each other.'

87 *A.C. v. Manitoba (Director of Child and Family Services)*, op cit, at p 618 and [136–38]. Also see *Ciarlariello v. Schacter*, [1993] 2 SCR 119, per Cory J, at p 135 and Reference re ss. 193 and 195.1(1)(c) of the Criminal Code (Man.), [1990] 1 SCR 1123, at p 1177: 'Section 7 is . . . implicated when the state restricts individuals' security of the person by interfering with, or removing from them, control over their physical or mental integrity.'

Youth Criminal Justice Act 2003 This federal legislation, governs the criminal activities of children aged 12 to 17. Its basic principles, as stated in s 3(1), are to reinforce respect for societal values; encourage the repair of harm done; be meaningful to the offender; respect gender, ethnic, cultural, and linguistic differences; and respond to the needs of Aboriginal young persons and young persons with special requirements.[88]

Child Protection Act 1998 The legislative intent of this federal statute, amended most recently in 2014, is to protect and promote the rights and welfare interests of all children, including those from Indigenous communities, and to protect children from all forms of violence, abuse, neglect, exploitation and discrimination, with a focus on preventative services and family strengthening.

The Canadian Multiculturalism Act 1988 This statute gives official recognition to multiculturalism as a fundamental characteristic of Canadian society and requires federal institutions to take this into account when exercising their functions. As stated in *Ishaq v. Canada (Citizenship and Immigration)*,[89] the Multiculturalism Act requires federal officials to (c) promote policies, programs and practices that enhance the understanding of and respect for the diversity of the members of Canadian society; . . . (f) generally, carry on their activities in a manner that is sensitive and responsive to the multicultural reality of Canada.[90]

Child and Family Services Act 1988 Replaced by the Child Protection Act 1998.

Divorce Act 1985 This federal statute was amended in 2020 by Bill C-78, with effect from March 2021, to include the requirement that when considering the best interest factors in the act, 'the court shall give primary consideration to the child's physical, emotional and psychological safety, security and well-being' (s 16(2)). While the grounds remain the same, it has introduced changes in terminology, substituting 'parenting arrangements' for 'custody' and 'access.' It also, finally, mentions violence as a factor to consider as a contraindicator to access.

The Criminal Code Introduced in 1892 by the Parliament of Canada in accordance with s 91(27) of the Constitution Act 1867, this federal statute defines and makes provision for dealing with most criminal offences. It includes legislation such as the Young Offenders Act 1981, which raised the minimum age of criminal responsibility to 12 years, and the Youth Criminal Justice Act 2002. The Criminal Code includes forms of child abuse and is administered by the Department of Justice.

88 See, further, at https://www.justice.gc.ca/eng/csj-sjc/just/11.html.
89 [2015] 4 FCR 297, 2015 FC 156.
90 Ibid, at para 63.

OTHER RELEVANT LEGISLATION

The Canadian Human Rights Act 1985 improved and extended the largely ineffective Canadian Bill of Rights 1960. Section 3(1) broadened the law to ensure equal opportunity for individuals, to expressly prohibit discrimination on a federal basis (replicated at province and territory levels), and to prohibit discrimination on grounds that include religion and sexual orientation. The Criminal Law Amendment Acts 1968–69 and 2001 introduced major changes to the Criminal Code including, respectively, more permissive provisions to govern homosexuality and abortion and measures to better protect children from sexual exploitation.

Courts and regulatory framework

Canada accepts the jurisdiction of the International Criminal Court and, indeed, was largely responsible for establishing it. Unlike the U.S., it also accepts the International Court of Justice, and both accept the Universal Periodic Review process, which provides an international peer monitoring forum for the ongoing review of national progress in addressing human rights concerns, including those relating to religion and belief. The United Nations Human Rights Committee (U.N. HRC) monitors implementation of the International Covenant on Civil and Political Rights in Canada and produces reports advising the federal government as to changes it might make to law, policy and practice that would improve national compliance with covenant principles. Its brief includes child welfare matters. So far, Canada has participated in three review cycles – 2009, 2013 and 2018.

FEDERAL COURTS AND REGULATORY BODIES

The domestic hierarchy of regulatory tribunals and courts with a right of appeal ultimately to a Supreme Court is replicated in each province and territory and presided over by the Supreme Court of Canada (SCC).

The Supreme Court of Canada (SCC)
This final court of appeal has a federal jurisdiction enabling it to adjudicate on and formulate governing principles in relation to cases drawn from all areas of law, including those relating to children. States and territories each have their own judicial and regulatory systems.

The Canadian Human Rights Commission (CHRC) The Canadian Human Rights Commission, an independent body established at the federal level, was created to administer the Canadian Human Rights Act 1977.

The Canadian Human Rights Tribunal Established under the Canadian Human Rights Act 1977, the jurisdiction of this tribunal is restricted to federally regulated activities, and thus, most human rights claims come before the provincial tribunals. It is independent of the Canadian Human Rights Commission, which refers cases to it for adjudication under the Act.

SPECIALIST COURT SYSTEM

As in the U.S., there is no national system of specialist courts to adjudicate matters affecting the welfare interests of children.

Juvenile courts Following the introduction of the federal Juvenile Delinquents Act 1908, these courts – in some places known as Youth Justice Courts – were established over time in each province and territory by means of jurisdiction-specific legislation, rather than by federal mandate. Two years earlier, in 1906, Canada's first juvenile probation officer had been appointed in Ottawa with the brief of 'reforming the children in their homes and, if possible, the home itself.'

Section 3(1)(d) of the federal Youth Criminal Justice Act 2003 states the rights of young persons appearing before the court. These include the right to be heard and to participate in the course of proceedings. Section 25(1) states the important principle that a young person who is detained by the police for any reason must be informed at once of their right to advice and representation by counsel and be given the opportunity to avail themselves of consultation with counsel before any proceedings are commenced. Legal aid is to be provided, where necessary, to ensure the right can be given effect.

Family courts There are no family courts as such in Canada, at least not as this construct is known in the U.K., despite the Law Reform Commission's recommendation in 1976 that they be established; some cities, however, have instituted a type of family court. However, increasingly, court management techniques provide for the same judge to preside over all hearings relating to a particular child. Moreover, child protection cases and the criminal trial of the parent(s) often run concurrently. These small steps highlight the need for a more holistic, nationwide family court approach.

Regulatory bodies The Charter of Rights and Freedoms – specifically s 15, which prohibits discrimination on the basis of age – together with the Human Rights Act 1977 provides authority and an agenda for the Canadian Human Rights Commission (CHRC) to intervene where it has grounds to believe that children may be suffering from inequality or discriminatory treatment. The work of this federal body is complemented by that of similar EHRC bodies at provincial and territorial levels, though at all levels, the brief of such bodies for children's welfare interests is marginal.

OFFICE OF THE CHILDREN'S LAWYER

As was said in *Ontario (Children's Lawyer) v. Ontario (Information and Privacy Commissioner)*,[91] 'the Children's Lawyer not only represents the child's interests; she provides a safe, effective way for the child's voice to be heard.'[92] The court com-

91 2018 ONCA 559.
92 Ibid, at para 70.

mented on the unique role of the children's lawyer, describing it as 'fundamental to the proper functioning of the legal system.'[93] It linked the role of the children's lawyer to the best interests of the child, who is entitled to heightened protections within the law, and to the importance of the relationship between children and their lawyers to the administration of justice.[94]

CHILDREN'S OMBUDSMAN/CHILD ADVOCATE

Some provinces, such as New Brunswick, have combined this office with that of ombudsman.

Canada has yet to establish an independent national human rights institution with a mandate to protect and promote the rights of children and youth at the federal level, although most provinces and territories have children's advocates or representatives with such a mandate. The Canadian Bar Association (CBA) has pointed out that:[95]

> Federal areas of jurisdiction affecting children – such as immigration, youth criminal justice, child welfare funding, health and education services for Indigenous children on-reserve, divorce law, taxation and federal social benefits – fall between jurisdictional cracks for children, and could be more effectively addressed by a National Commissioner. This institution could also provide the response and engagement necessary to address the rights and interests of Indigenous children across Canada, in keeping with the spirit of reconciliation and the requirements of UNDRIP.

The CBA also note:

> [I]n three sets of Concluding Observations from 1995, 2003, and 2012, the UN Committee on the Rights of the Child reiterated the pressing need for Canada to establish an independent, federal, human rights institution to protect, promote and monitor the implementation of children's rights.[96]

The committee repeated its concern in June 2022.[97]

93 Ibid, at paras 46 and 53.

94 Ibid, at para 56. As reported in the Canadian Bar Association (Child and Youth Law Section)'s 'Alternative Report to the UN Committee on the Rights of the Child,' (2020), op cit, at p 33. However, as Lori Chambers comments, '[T]he conservative government in Ontario recently eliminated this office and the work is now (in theory, but not really in practice) handled by the Ombudsman' (note to author, 16 August 2022).

95 Ibid, at p 5.

96 Ibid, at p 7.

97 See, further, at https://www.ohchr.org/en/press-releases/2022/05/experts-committee-rights-child-commend-canada-truth-and-reconciliation.

SPECIAL RAPPORTEUR

In 1991, the Special Rapporteur on the Sale and Sexual Exploitation of Children reported on this issue as it relates to Canada.[98] More recently, in May 2022, the U.N. Special Rapporteur on the Rights of Indigenous people announced that he is planning a Canadian trip to examine the 'overall human-rights situation' of Indigenous people in light of the discoveries of possible unmarked graves near former residential schools.

Representation for children

Representation is particularly important when there is a potential conflict of interest between the child and their parent or other party.[99] However, as children do not normally have party status in family law or child protection proceedings, they do not automatically qualify for legal representation or, indeed, for the legal aid often necessary to pay for it.[100] However, as has been pointed out, 'in a number of provinces (Alberta, Ontario and Québec) lawyers are commonly appointed to represent the interests of children in child protection case, and at least in some cases may advocate for the outcome desired by the child.'[101]

While the court may order representation for a child in public proceedings (child protection), it is less likely to do so in private proceedings (matrimonial). The report *Meaningful Change for Family Justice: Beyond Wise Words* states that 'the majority of family cases involve children, who are vulnerable, usually unrepresented non-parties who seldom participate directly in the process.'[102]

In the previously mentioned *C. (M.A.) v. K. (M.)*,[103] Justice Cohen appointed counsel for a five-year-old child who was the subject of an adoption application on the basis that the child was too young to have informed views but that representation could protect the child's best interests by identifying broader issues than those raised by the parties themselves. In Ontario, legislative amendments in 2006 to the Child and Family Services Act 1990 now permit a child to have legal representation at any stage in adoption proceedings, and where the court determines that legal representation is desirable, it may authorise the children's lawyer to represent

98 See, further, at https://digitallibrary.un.org/record/225725?ln=en.

99 See *New Brunswick (Minister of Health and Community Services) v. G.(J.)*, [1999] 3 SCR 46.

100 Note that 'in some jurisdictions, such as British Columbia, the government gives no funding for legal representation for children and has actively opposed this prospect,' as reported in the Canadian Bar Association (Child and Youth Law Section)'s 'Alternative Report to the U.N. Committee on the Rights of the Child, (2020), op cit, at p 33.

101 Department of Justice, *Concurrent Legal Proceedings in Cases of Family Violence: The Child Protection Perspective*, citing Bala, Birnbaum, and Bertrand, 'Controversy about the Role of Children's Lawyers: Advocate or Best Interests Guardian? Comparing Attitudes & Practices in Alberta & Ontario – Two Provinces with Different Policies' (accepted for October 2013), *Family Court Review*. See, further, at https://www.justice.gc.ca/eng/rp-pr/fl-lf/famil/fv-vf/p5.html#fn64-rf.

102 Family Justice Working Group, *Meaningful Change for Family Justice: Beyond Wise Words*, Ottawa, (2013), at 16.

103 2008 ONCJ 212.

the child. In contrast, the court in *J.E.S.D. v. Y.E.P.*[104] took a narrow approach to children's participatory rights, including with respect to legal representation for a 16-year-old girl, though the same court in *A.B. v. C.D.*[105] fully supported a 14-year-old trans boy's ability to bring and defend a family law proceeding with his own lawyer of choice. Such inconsistency without explanatory reasoning reflects a breadth of discretionary judicial interpretation of welfare interests at variance with Article 12 of U.N. CROC.

THE CHILD IN COURT

The U.N. Committee on the Rights of the Child, in its 2012 report, expressed concern that inadequate mechanisms were available 'to ensure the implementation of the right of the child to be heard' as required under U.N. CROC, Article 12. It specifically recommended that 'the views of the child be a requirement for all official decision-making processes that relate to children . . . and that children be given the right to be heard when decisions are being made that will affect them' including custody, child welfare, criminal justice, immigration and the environment; that Canada create complaints mechanisms for children in case their right to be heard is violated with regard to judicial and administrative proceedings; and that children have access to an appeals procedure.[106]

The right of children to be heard in decisions taken on their proposed adoption is provided in some provincial legislation, such as that of Prince Edward Island and Alberta. The right to be heard in relation to accessing transitioning therapy was upheld in *K. (N.) v. H. (A.)*,[107] which concerned a parental dispute as to whether or not J.K., their 11-year-old child, should engage in such therapy. Justice Skolrood, in a strong decision, unequivocally cognisant of the child's welfare/rights on a matter of such importance for his future welfare, was firmly of the view that 'these issues cannot be properly considered without J.K.'s direct participation, nor would it be fair to J.K. for the court to attempt to do so.'[108] He also noted that 'the overriding consideration in making that determination is the best interests of the child.'[109]

CONSENT OF CHILD

The issue of the necessity for an underage child's consent to a decision affecting their welfare is something that has frequently exercised the Canadian judiciary, who have responded with some equivocation.

104 2018 BCCA 40.
105 2020 BCCA 11.
106 See the U.N. Committee on the Rights of the Child, 61st session, C/CAN/CO/3-4, October 2012, at paras 36 and 37.
107 2016 BCSC 744.
108 Ibid, at para 40.
109 Ibid, at para 44.

In relation to a child's adoption, every province and territory requires the consent of the child concerned if they're above a certain age, usually 12. However, there is currently considerable statutory variation regarding this requirement. In Ontario, the consent of a child aged 7 years or older must be obtained, but the court is merely required 'where it is practical to do so to hear the child,'[110] and 'a child 12 years of age or more who is the subject of an application under this section is entitled to receive notice of the application and to be present at the hearing.'[111] In British Columbia, the consent of every child aged 12 or more will be sought in all adoption proceedings including stepparent and kinship applications. In Manitoba, the presumptive age at which minors are entitled to be heard by the court on matters affecting themselves is 16.[112]

Unsurprisingly, the issue often arises in relation to underage Jehovah's Witnesses requiring urgent medical treatment. Before 1996, the judicial approach tended to favour respecting the decision of parent and child to withhold their consent to treatment. This was the case in *Re L.D.K.*[113] concerning a 12-year-old girl suffering from acute myeloid leukaemia when she and her parents, all devote Jehovah's Witnesses, refused their consent to chemotherapy as it would necessitate blood transfusions. Similarly in *Re A.Y.*,[114] the Newfoundland Supreme Court found it unnecessary to interfere with the consent of a 15-year-old boy suffering from terminal cancer and refusing a transfusion on religious grounds. However, from 1996, the judicial approach changed to question whether an adolescent had the maturity to fully appreciate the consequences of withholding their consent to life-saving treatment. Court intervention was deemed necessary to authorise treatment, for example, in *H. (T.) v. Children's Aid Society of Metropolitan Toronto*,[115] when a 13-year-old girl with aplastic anaemia and her mother, both Jehovah's Witnesses, refused to consent to any treatment involving blood products. In *H. (P.) v. Eastern Regional Integrated Health Authority*,[116] Justice LeBlanc considered whether the court had authority to order a 16-year-old child to undergo treatment where the child had capacity to refuse. He determined that the girl did not have the required capacity but held that even if she had, he would have ordered treatment pursuant to the court's *parens patriae* jurisdiction as her decision still had to be compatible with a judicial determination of what was construed to be in her best interests. Such circumstances often give rise to wardship applications. (See, further, Chapter 7.)

The SCC examined the consent issue somewhat exhaustively in *A.C. v. Manitoba (Director of Child and Family Services)*,[117] which concerned a child aged 14 years

110 Child and Family Services Act 1990, s 152(3).

111 Ibid, s 153(5). Subsequently amended in 2006 to entitle such a child to 'participate in the proceeding as if he or she were a party.'

112 See *Manitoba (Director of Child and Family Services) v. A.C.* (2007), 212 Man.R. (2d) 163.

113 (1985), 48 R.F.L. (2d) 164 (Ont. Prov. Ct. (Fam. Div.).

114 (1993), 111 Nfld. & P.E.I.R. 91.

115 (1996), 138 D.L.R. (4th) 144 (Ont. Ct. (Gen. Div.)).

116 2010 NLTD 34.

117 2009 SCC 30, [2009] 2 S.C.R. 181.

and 10 months, a devout Jehovah's Witness, who was hospitalised with Crohn's disease. Some months before her admission, she had completed an advance medical directive with written instructions that she was not to be given blood transfusions under any circumstances. She did so with full knowledge that such a transfusion was necessary if she were to avoid severe health consequences and was wholly supported in that decision by her parents. Assessments by three clinical psychiatrists concluded that she understood the issues and their consequences. The relevant legislation – ss 25(8) and (9) of the Child and Family Services Act – stated that, for a child under 16, the court could authorise treatment if it considered this to be in the child's best interests; for a child aged 16 and over, no medical treatment could be ordered without the child's consent unless the court was satisfied that the child lacked the ability to understand the relevant information or the consequences of a treatment decision. The court at first instance ordered that C receive blood transfusions, having concluded that when a child is under 16, there are no legislated restrictions of authority on the court's ability to order medical treatment in the child's 'best interests.' The Court of Appeal concluded that the legislation ousts the common-law principles relating to 'mature minors' and instead empowered the court to make treatment decisions for those under 16, with or without capacity, based on a best interests test. A child's wishes and capacity are relevant to the analysis, but not determinative. The subsequent appeal to the SCC was on the grounds that the relevant legislative provision was unconstitutional because it unjustifiably infringed C's rights under ss 2(a), 7, and 15 of the Canadian Charter of Rights and Freedoms.

As Abella J for the SCC explained:[118]

> The application of an objective 'best interests' standard to infants and very young children is uncontroversial. Mature adolescents, on the other hand, have strong claims to autonomy, but these claims exist in tension with a protective duty on the part of the state that is also justified.

She went on to say that the provision:

> strikes a constitutional balance between what the law has consistently seen as an individual's fundamental right to autonomous decision making in connection with his or her body, and the law's equally persistent attempts to protect vulnerable children from harm. . . . Mature adolescents have strong claims to autonomy, but these claims exist in tension with a protective duty on the part of the state that is justified by the difficulty of defining and identifying 'maturity.' . . . [I]t is the ineffability inherent in the concept of 'maturity' that justifies the state's retaining an overarching power to determine whether allowing the child to exercise his or her autonomy in a given situation actually accords with his or her best interest.[119]

118 Ibid, at para 82.

119 Ibid, at para 86. Note that Binnie J, dissenting, was of the view that a mature minor – who understands the medical condition and the consequences of refusing treatment – should have the right to so refuse, whether or not a judge considers such refusal to be in the young person's best interests,

Furthermore:

> the best interests standard must be interpreted in a way that is not arbitrary (to avoid violating s 7 of the Charter); not discriminatory on the basis of age (to avoid a s 15 violation); and not contrary to a child's right to freedom of religion protected by s 2(a).[120]

She went on to acknowledge that in order to promote the objective of according weight to the choices of adolescents in a manner reflective of their evolving maturity:

> paternalism should always be kept to a minimum and carefully justified. . . . The difficulty lies in establishing a formula which authorises paternalistic interventions to protect adolescents from making life-threatening mistakes, but restrains autocratic and arbitrary adult restrictions on their potential for autonomy.[121]

As she put it:

> [I]nterpreting the best interests standard so that a young person is afforded a degree of bodily autonomy and integrity commensurate with his or her maturity navigates the tension between an adolescent's increasing entitlement to autonomy as he or she matures and society's interest in ensuring that young people who are vulnerable are protected from harm.[122]

Or, more succinctly: '[T]he "best interests" standard operates as a sliding scale of scrutiny, with the adolescent's views becoming increasingly determinative depending on his or her ability to exercise mature, independent judgment.'[123]

In a majority ruling, the SCC explained the conditions for a valid consent in that context, but arguably with more general application, as follows:[124]

> [A] judge should take into account the nature, purpose and utility of the recommended medical treatment and its risks and benefits; the adolescent's intellectual capacity and the degree of sophistication to understand the information relevant to making the decision and to appreciate the potential consequences; the stability of the adolescent's views and whether they are a true reflection of his or her core values and beliefs; the potential impact of the adolescent's lifestyle, family relationships and broader social affiliations

120 Ibid, at para 97.
121 Ibid, at para 105, quoting Fortin, J., *Children's Rights and the Developing Law* (2nd ed.), London, LexisNexis, (2003) at pp 26–27.
122 Ibid, at para 108.
123 Ibid, at 22.
124 Ibid, at [96].

> on his or her ability to exercise independent judgment; the existence of any emotional or psychiatric vulnerabilities and the impact of the adolescent's illness on his or her decision-making ability. Any relevant information from adults who know the adolescent may also factor into the assessment.

The court seemed clear, on principle, that the ability of adolescents to make treatment decisions 'is ultimately calibrated in accordance with maturity, not age.'[125] As was then accurately noted:

> [T]his reluctance to interpret the 'mature minor' doctrine as demanding automatic judicial deference to the young person's medical treatment decisions where doing so will put the adolescent's life or health in grave danger seems to stem from the difficulty of determining with any certainty whether a given adolescent is, in fact, sufficiently mature to make a particular decision.[126]

This judicial interpretation of the 'best interests' test as affording a young person 'a degree of bodily autonomy and integrity commensurate with his or her ability to exercise mature, independent judgment' is arguably a bit suspect. The exposition seems to lead to the evidently satisfactory conclusion that it 'respects the right of mature adolescents to participate meaningfully in decisions relating to their medical treatment.' However, there is no indication that any set of circumstances might exist which could instead lead to respect for the right of such a mature adolescent to give or withhold an autonomous and valid legal consent.[127] In practice, it would seem that when faced with an issue of real gravity and urgency, the courts, in balancing the expressed wishes of a mature adolescent against what it considers to be the child's best interests, will lean towards the latter.[128]

Conclusion

Disparate information systems across provinces and territories, coupled with the absence of any systematised collection or coordination of data at the federal level, make it as difficult to build a coherent overall picture of the law governing children's welfare/rights in Canada as it must be to plan national policy, monitor practice or formulate legislation in relation to such matters. Nonetheless, the publications of domestic bodies such as the Department of Justice and the Canadian Bar Association (Child and Youth Law Section) and international bodies such as UNICEF and the U.N. Committee on the Rights of the Child, together with those of the many academics referenced in this chapter, make it possible to draw certain tentative conclusions.

125 Ibid, at [111].
126 Ibid, at para 70.
127 *A.C. v. Manitoba (Director of Child and Family Services)*, 2009, op cit, at [108].
128 See, for example, *A.M. v. C.H.*, 2019 ONCA 939.

In terms of principles, it would seem that vestiges of the traditional meaning and role ascribed to parental rights in the common law continue to be quite prominent, with a resulting adverse effect on the relative standing of the welfare principle. Evidence for this can be seen, for example, in a continuance of the parental right to physically chastise their children and in the caselaw illustrations of instances in which the consent of parents, rather than that of the child concerned, is required in decision-making regarding the latter's welfare. Indeed, the need for a child's consent is absent in many relevant legal proceedings, as is any mandatory requirement that their interests be represented in private family law proceedings. Moreover, the absence of any mention of the paramountcy principle in federal legislation such as the Child Protection Act 1998, the Divorce Act 1985, or its 2019 amendments is also indicative of a general reticence to establish the welfare interests of a child as the matter of paramount importance in all issues affecting their well-being.

Clearly, there is a need for leadership from the federal government to establish the paramountcy principle as a benchmark in child welfare policy, integrate it into a coherent policy, and ensure that it is then infused throughout family law.

6 The welfare principle in contemporary practice

Public family law, civil and criminal jurisdictions

Introduction

Canada has an unusually high number of children admitted to the state public child care system – 9.2 per 1,000, compared to 6.9 in the U.S. This, together with the overrepresentation of Indigenous children in both the child welfare and criminal justice systems, provides a stark measure of failed preventative state intervention and evidence of a reliance instead on containing the effects of social dysfunction rather than on a willingness to promote the welfare of children.[1]

This chapter considers children's welfare interests and rights in the context of public family law, civil and criminal: essentially, care and protection and juvenile justice. It is mainly concerned with identifying and analysing key cases in order to examine and evaluate how and why public family law as it relates to children has evolved as it has and to identify any distinctive characteristics in its current functioning in Canada.

The welfare principle in contemporary practice: public family law, civil jurisdiction

The federal Department of Health and Human Services in Canada, unlike its U.S. counterpart, does not have jurisdiction to maintain oversight of child welfare service provision by provinces and territories, nor does it have any authority or capacity to provide them with funding. However, in recognition of this deficit, the federal government in 1988 launched the ongoing Family Violence Initiative (FVI), which is led by the Public Health Agency of Canada and brings together multiple departments to prevent and address family violence, including child maltreatment. The Child Maltreatment Surveillance and Research Working Group is mandated to provide advice to the FVI regarding national child maltreatment surveillance and research while the Canadian Incidence Study of Reported Child Abuse and Neglect (CIS) provided the first national child maltreatment study. The CIS has completed reports in 1998, 2003, 2008 and 2018–19. This multi-department project would seem to be, in part, a mapping exercise designed

1 See, further, https://quintechildrenshomes.com/foster-care-statistics-in-canada/.

DOI: 10.4324/9781003269564-10

to estimate the nature and extent of national child welfare needs; identify the related framework of legislation and agencies at province and territorial levels; and explore the possibilities for national coordination of data, resources and service providers.[2]

Prevention

Responsibility for preventative service provision rests on the provinces and territories (except for the First Nations provision, which is largely federally funded), and each gives effect to its duties through its own child welfare legislation, which mandates the consensual and coercive intervention of child welfare officers who are usually employed by the national network of children's aid societies or provincial agencies such as Child Protection Services or Child and Family Services. It has been noted by some that the intervention of these agencies is focused more on the threshold of child protection than on children and families in need, which might account for the relatively high numbers of admissions to state care.[3]

State duties to support families in need

The UNICEF report in 2013, ranking Canada 17th out of the 29 developed countries surveyed in terms of their response to children in need, would seem to have prompted government awareness that more resources must be channelled towards disadvantaged communities.[4]

SERVICE PROVISION

Children's aid societies (which function under different names in some provinces) are the main national providers of preventative services to vulnerable families through their early intervention counselling services and parenting programmes, often offered in partnership with other community agencies. The Public Health Agency of Canada provides, or supports other community-based agencies to provide, a range of services for families with young children on a nationwide basis. For more than two decades, it and its provincial and territorial partners have been involved in child maltreatment surveillance and have collaborated on data collection, analysis and interpretation.

2 See, further, www.canada.ca/en/public-health/services/publications/health-risks-safety/provincial-territorial-child-protection-legislation-policy-2018.html.

3 See, for example, Gilbert, R., Kemp, A., Thoburn, J., Sidebotham, P., Radford, L. Glaser, D., and Macmillan, H. L., Recognizing and responding to child maltreatment, *The Lancet*, (2009): *373*(9658), 167–180; Fallon, B., Trocmé, N., Fluke, J., Van Wert, M., MacLaurin, B., Sinha, V., Hélie, S., and Turcotte, D., Responding to child maltreatment in Canada: Context for international comparison, *Advances in Mental Health*, (2012): 11(1), 76–96; and Gough, P., Shlonsky, A., and Dudding, P., An overview of the child welfare systems in Canada, *International Journal of Child Health and Human Development*, (2009): 2(3), 357–372.

4 See UNICEF Child Well-Being Index: Canada Ranked 17th out of 29 Wealthy Nations, *Huffington Post*, 10 October 2013, www.huffingtonpost.ca/2013/04/10/unicef-child-well-being-canada_n_3050119.html.

JORDAN'S PRINCIPLE

This is a child-first principle aimed at ensuring 'First Nations children can access public services ordinarily available to other Canadian children without experiencing any service denials, delays or disruptions related to their First Nations status.'[5] (See, further, at Chapter 8.)

State intervention: consensual

Child welfare services at province and territory levels tend to be structured, staffed, and resourced more to respond to child abuse and neglect than for consensual intervention to prevent such situations arising.

SPECIFIC SUPPORT SERVICES

Respite care may be authorised by temporary care agreements (in which children are placed in short-term foster care with the written agreement of the parents); voluntary agreements (in which the parents agree that while the child will remain in their care, they will meet certain conditions, such as substance abuse treatment or parenting courses); or kinship placements (in which children are placed with family members). Accessing such services and coping with the associated lengthy time delays are acknowledged to be issues for Canadian families in need and may be a consequence of poor interagency collaboration and a weak sense of collective responsibility among the professionals involved. There would seem to be some truth in the comment that 'Canada needs to improve its service delivery that supports the children and families in need, therefore diverse and readily available services are required in order to bring significant changes to the current child-protection system.'[6] However, in the course of its latest report to the U.N. CRC, mention was made of some improvements in this respect, which included the creation of the Canada Child Benefit to provide support to low-income families, the establishment of an early learning and child-care framework across Canada, and investments in education and other services for Indigenous children.[7]

Children with disabilities It has been pointed out that:[8]

> The service response to children and youth with disabilities, youth with complex behavioural and mental health problems, and youth transitioning out of care, is often not sufficient to meet their needs. The system has been designed with security concerns at the forefront, but the developmental needs of children and youth are not well integrated, nor are they understood by many.

5 See, further, https://fncaringsociety. com/jordans-principle.

6 Ivan, G., Child Protection in Canada and England: A Comparative Analysis, *Journal of Politics and Law*, (2021): 14(2), 100–113, at p 109.

7 See, further, U.N. Human Rights Committee, press release (18 May 2022), www.ohchr.org/en/press-releases/2022/05/experts-committee-rights-child-commend-canada-truth-and-reconciliation.

8 Gough, P., Shlonsky, A., and Dudding, P., An overview of the child welfare systems in Canada, *International Journal of Child Health and Human Development*, op cit, at p 367.

Protection

In addition to the federal statute – the Child Protection Act 1998 – each province and territory has its own act (usually titled as a variant of 'Child and Family Services'), the most recent being the Child, Youth and Family Services Act 2017 in Ontario.[9] Consequently, there is no uniform nationwide interpretation of what constitutes 'abuse' or 'neglect.' Furthermore, there seems to be much truth in the observation that:

> Canadian child protection systems as they are currently structured are funded to respond to reports of child maltreatment, or risk of maltreatment, but are generally not well funded to take action in areas of social service that would prevent maltreatment from happening in the first place.[10]

As mentioned earlier, the paramountcy principle is broadly excluded from statutes governing decision-making in relation to a child in need of protection. The federal statute restricts itself to the mandatory requirement that courts make an order in the 'best interests' of a child which, in s 2, it states is to be interpreted with reference to the following considerations:

(a) the safety of the child;
(b) the capacity of a parent to properly discharge parental obligations;
(c) the physical, mental, and emotional needs of the child and the appropriate care or treatment to meet those needs;
(d) the physical, mental, and emotional level of development of the child;
(e) the views of the child, where appropriate;
(f) a secure place for the child and the development of a positive relationship as a member of a family;
(g) the love, affection, and ties between the child and persons who have had custody of the child;
(h) the love, affection, and ties between the child and other persons in the life of the child;
(i) the cultural, racial, linguistic, and religious heritage of the child;
(j) if the child is aboriginal, the importance of preserving the cultural identity of the child;
(k) the capacity of persons other than a parent to exercise custody rights and duties respecting a child;
(l) the continuity of care for the child and the possible effect of disruption of that care on the child; and
(m) the difference in the concept of time and the developmental capacity of a child.

9 This legislation is said to 'more meaningfully espouse child rights principles than other legislation in Canada, per Canadian Bar Association, Alternate Report' op cit, at p 26.

10 Gough, P., Shlonsky, A., and Dudding, P., An overview of the child welfare systems in Canada, *International Journal of Child Health and Human Development*, 2(3), 357–372, at p 357.

The 2017 Ontario statute suggests that the 'best interests' test be interpreted 'as an evolutionary compendium of considerations that give increased strength to increased maturity.'[11] Interestingly and exceptionally, Part II of the 2017 Act has sections headed 'Rights of Children Receiving Services' and 'Rights of Children in Care,' which state and address the elements of children's meaningful participation in decision-making processes. It includes the following:

S 3. Every child and young person receiving services under the Act has the following rights:

(a) to express their own views freely and safely about matters that affect them;
(b) to be engaged through an honest and respectful dialogue about how and why decisions affecting them are made and to have their views given due weight, in accordance with their age and maturity;
(c) to be consulted on the nature of the services provided or to be provided to them, to participate in decisions about the services provided or to be provided to them, and to be advised of the decisions made with respect to those services;
(d) to raise concerns or recommend changes with respect to the services provided or to be provided to them without interference or fear of coercion, discrimination, or reprisal and to receive a response to their concerns or recommended changes; and
(e) to be informed, in language suitable to their understanding, of their rights.

This declaratory approach is in keeping with the wording and spirit of U.N. CROC, Article 12, and illustrates Ontario's singular endeavour to give statutory effect to children's rights rather than solely to their welfare and, to that extent, is not representative of other provincial statutes.

As the SCC noted in *Manitoba*, '[T]he overarching goal of statutes such as the Child and Family Services Act is to protect children from harm,'[12] but under this legislation, 'the distinction between promoting autonomy and protecting welfare is presumed to collapse at age 16, subject to evidence to the contrary,'[13] as the legislation acknowledges in s 25(9) that mature minors who are 16 and over are presumed to have sufficient capacity to make their own decisions.[14]

State intervention: coercive

The Child Protection Act 1998, as amended in 2014, remains the only relevant federal statute. In s 9, it provides a long list of factors indicating when a child might be

11 *A.C. v. Manitoba (Director of Child and Family Services)*, (2009), op cit, at para 113.

12 Ibid, citing *Winnipeg Child and Family Services v. K.L.W.*, 2000 SCC 48, [2000] 2 SCR 519, at para 15; *B. (R.) v. Children's Aid Society of Metropolitan Toronto*, [1995] 1 S.C.R. 315, at p 382; and *Syl Apps Secure Treatment Centre v. B.D.*, 2007 SCC 38, [2007] 3 SCR 83, at para 2.

13 *A.C. v. Manitoba*, op cit, per Arbella J, at para 111.

14 The same presumption is to be found in the Mental Health Act, s 2, and in the Health Care Directives Act, s 4(2).

defined as being in need of protection. Each province and territory has modelled its own statute on the 1998 Act, declaring the particular child protection and neglect grounds justifying state intervention and stating the upper age at which a child's needs will cease to justify such intervention. The latter varies from a maximum of 16 (e.g. Newfoundland and Labrador) to 19 (e.g. British Columbia and New Brunswick).[15] Any such intervention must be Charter compliant. The Canadian Incidence Study of Reported Child Abuse and Neglect is the only source of nationally aggregated information on investigated child maltreatment; the most recent report, for the years 2018–19, was published in 2021.[16] Of particular note is the finding that the rate of child maltreatment investigations in Canada in 2019 was higher than those reported in previous years but similar to Australian and American studies.

MANDATORY REPORTING

The legal duty to report instances of child abuse or neglect or reasonable suspicions thereof is to be found in s 10 of the 1998 federal statute and in all provincial and territorial child protection legislation. Some statutes provide for penalties only for failure to report by certain professionals; others provide for penalties for any individual who fails to report, and in a few jurisdictions, there is no penalty for failing to report abuse or neglect. All provide immunity from prosecution for those who, in good faith, report actual or suspected maltreatment of a child.

Care proceedings

Justice Sheilagh O'Connell has noted that:[17]

> The primary focus of a child protection case is the protection and wellbeing of the children involved. The best interests of the children are considered paramount.

In practice, however, statute law does not confer a paramount weighting on best interests, and child neglect, rather than child abuse, is the main ground for statutory care proceedings in Canada.[18]

15 See, further, www.canada.ca/en/public-health/services/publications/health-risks-safety/provincial-territorial-child-protection-legislation-policy-2018.html.

16 See, further, https://cwrp.ca/publications/denouncing-continued-overrepresentation-first-nations-children-canadian-child-welfare.

17 *Children's Aid Society Region of Halton v. O.(J.)*, 2013 ONCJ 191, 2013 O.J. 1691, at para 29.

18 Trocmé, N., Fallon B., and MacLaurin B., Canadian incidence study of reported child abuse and neglect – 2003: Major findings, Minister of Public Works and Government Services, Canada, (2005). See, further, https://doi.org/10.1016/j.chiabu.2003.07.003.

CARE PLAN

Perhaps the nearest Canadian equivalent to a U.K. care plan is the Answer and Plan of Care form parents are required to fill out in response to the child protection concerns of a children's aid society (CAS). Essentially, this is a parental statement to the court outlining how the parents propose to care for their child. It might, for example, state that the child will be the subject of a care order and be placed by CAS in a foster home for a period, after which the care order might be replaced by a supervision order.

EMERGENCY PROTECTION ORDER

Unlike the equivalent situation in England and Wales, intervention in family matters by a statutorily empowered social worker on child protection grounds does not require the prior authorisation of a court or justice of the peace (British Columbia being an exception). Under s 23 of the 1998 Act, a child found to be at immediate risk of harm may be peremptorily removed from the family – 'child apprehension' is the term used – and taken, under s 25, to a place of safety. Another differentiating feature of child protection in the two countries is the lack of a collaborative ethos, backed up by interagency protocols, that mandates the sharing of information and the coordination of professional and agency involvement in child protection work.

CARE ORDER/GUARDIANSHIP

An investigation into a report of child abuse or neglect will be conducted by the statutorily designated child welfare agency, usually a Children's Aid Society (CAS) or Child and Family Services. If it concludes that there is evidence to substantiate the report, it will then consider whether a voluntary agreement with the parents is feasible.

If so, then, under s 18 of the 1998 Act, such an agreement – including a care plan – is drawn up, and temporary custody and guardianship of the child are vested in the agency director for a time-limited period. However, under s 20:

> [W]here the Director determines after an assessment or an investigation that the parent of a child is unable or unwilling to provide for a child and presents no alternative plan, or the plan for the child is not acceptable to the Director, the parent may make an agreement with the Director for the permanent surrender to the Director of the custody and guardianship of the child.

Under s 21, all parental rights are then terminated.

If not, and the director determines that the child is in need of protection, under s 29, the matter is brought before the court in a disposition hearing for an order for either (a) supervision, (b) temporary custody and guardianship followed by supervision, (c) temporary custody and guardianship or (d) permanent custody and guardianship. There is no Canadian equivalent to the menu of discrete, clearly defined orders available in the U.K. courts. Under s 41, the temporary custody and guardianship orders are subject to specific time limits. A notable feature of the 1998 act is the s 13(3) requirement that:

> where a child is 12 years old or more, a plan of care shall not be effective unless: (a) the plan of care has been explained to the child in a manner appropriate to the child; and (b) the Director has considered the views of the child.

SUPERVISION ORDER

Under s 38(2) of the 1998 act, at the conclusion of a disposition hearing, the court can issue a supervision order, which may include the following terms:

(a)(1) a requirement that during a period of supervision, the director shall be permitted to see the child on a regular basis, independent of a parent;
(a)(2) a requirement that appointments with the director during a period of supervision be scheduled in a manner consistent with the plan of care submitted by the director;
(b) directions to allow the director to provide child protection services to the child or for the benefit of the child;
(c) directions respecting the place of residence of the child and the persons residing with the child;
(d) directions respecting contact with the child by any person;
(e) requirements respecting assessment, treatment, or services to be obtained by a parent; and
(f) such other terms as the court may consider appropriate in the circumstances.

State care

The Canadian child-care population is relatively large,[19] and within it, Indigenous children are disproportionately represented. (See, further, Chapter 4.)[20] Entry into public care occurs when 'the children concerned are receiving a level of parenting care that is below the minimum standard tolerated in our community.'[21] In 2013,

19 In 2001, 1.1% of Canadian children were in care, compared with 0.07% in Germany (in 2004), 0.17% in Japan (in 2005), 0.55% in England (in 2005), 0.66% in the United States (in 2005), and 1.2% in France (in 2003). See, further, Thoburn J., Globalisation and child welfare: Some lessons from a cross-national study of children in out-of-home care, Vol. 228, *School of Social Work and Psychosocial Studies*, University of East Anglia, (2007).

20 See, further, https://fncaringsociety.com/.

21 See *Sask. Minister of Social Services v. E.(S.)*, [1992] 5 WWR 289 (Sask. QB).

there were an estimated 62,428 children in out-of-home care across Canada,[22] and 'the number of children in care in Canada is increasing every year.'[23]

The U.N. Committee on the Rights of the Child has been 'deeply concerned at the high number of children in alternative care and at the frequent removal of children from their families as a first resort in cases of neglect or financial hardship.'[24]

Foster care: partnership, rehabilitation and concurrent planning

At the turn of the century, the National Children's Alliance of Canada drew attention to the fact that:[25]

> Historically, permanency planning alternatives consisted of family reunification or adoption. More recently, models for permanency have expanded beyond these extremes on the permanency continuum. Options such as Kinship Care, Customary Care, Guardianship Care, Open Adoption and subsidised adoption are more recent alternatives being utilised, or explored, which have the capacity to provide consistency and offer permanence for children.[26]

Abella J in *Manitoba* seemed aware that choice from such a range of options should not be limited to judicial or administrative decision-making but that it also provided an opportunity for adolescents in state care to have some say as to their preference when she commented that 'it is inherently arbitrary to deprive an adolescent under the age of 16 of the opportunity to demonstrate sufficient maturity when he or she is under the care of the state.' She was of the view 'that the 'best interests' test, properly interpreted, provides that a young person is entitled to a degree of decisional autonomy commensurate with his or her maturity.'[27]

FOSTER CARE

The majority of children placed in foster care are aged between 6 and 18, many are one of a group of siblings, and most have some degree of health or social care needs. Under s 45 of the Child Protection Act 1998, any such child, the subject of agreement or an order for permanent custody and guardianship, will remain in the

22 Jones, A., Sinha, V. and Trocmé, *Children And Youth In Out-Of-Home Care In The Canadian Provinces*, Canadian CW Research, (2015).

23 See Farris-Manning, C. and Zandstra, M., Children in Care in Canada: A Summary of Current Issues and Trends with Recommendations for Future Research, *Child Welfare League of Canada,* (2000), www.nationalchildrensalliance.com/nca/pubs/2003/Children_in_Care_March_2003.pdf.

24 See the U.N. Committee on the Rights of the Child, 61st session, C/CAN/CO/3–4, October 2012, at para 55.

25 Ibid, at p 13.

26 Ibid, citing Crosson-Tower, C., *Exploring Child Welfare: A Practice Perspective* (2nd ed.), Allyn & Bacon, Massachusetts, 2001, at p 331, and Aitken, G., Extending Options in Permanency Planning in the Child Welfare System, op cit, at pp 23–24.

27 *A.C. v. Manitoba*, op cit, at para 114.

care of the director until they reach the age of 18 years, are adopted or marry, or the agreement or order is terminated.

As of 2021, there were some 63,000 children in the Canadian public care system and living either in approved foster homes, kinship placements, group homes or larger residential centres. On average, a child in Canadian foster care experiences five changes of placement, which erode opportunities for psychological bonding and are clearly detrimental to their welfare.

Some of the problems associated with foster care and social work management of placements were revealed in the so-called 'Easter Bunny case,'[28] which concerned state-approved Christian foster parents and the two children placed with them who were removed after a couple of months because the foster parents rejected the Children's Aid Society of Hamilton's instructions regarding the Easter Bunny. The monitoring social worker, having concerns regarding the possibly restrictive effect of the couple's religious values, had advised them that it was part of their duty as foster parents to teach the girls about the Easter Bunny because she considered this to be part of Canadian culture. The couple responded with an assurance that while they intended to play hide-and-seek games with chocolate eggs and other games at Easter, they were not prepared to make any reference to the girls about such a mythical entity as the Easter Bunny, unless the girls made specific enquiries. The children were promptly removed from their care, and the couple's status as foster parents was cancelled. Subsequently, the couple's objection to being so treated was upheld by the Ontario Supreme Court, which found that the agency had violated their Charter right to freedoms of conscience, religion and expression.

Wards of the state This term – or 'Crown wards' – refers to those children in the public care system for whom all parental rights and responsibilities have been vested in the state.[29] As has been noted:[30]

> A Crown Wardship Order[31] is the most profound order that a court can make. To take someone's children from them is a power that a judge must exercise only with the highest degree of caution, and only on the basis of compelling evidence, and only after a careful examination of possible alternative remedies.

Mostly, these are older children, aged five years or more, or have special needs such as belonging to sibling groups, suffering from health issues or having behavioural or learning difficulties. A most important legal feature of this status is that carries a presumption against access, and the onus to rebut that presumption lies

28 *Derek and Frances Baars v. Hamilton Children's Aid Society*, 2018 ONSC 1487.

29 See the Child and Family Services Act 1990, s 65.2(1)(c).

30 *Children's Aid Society of Toronto v. EU*, 2014 ONCJ 299 (CanLII), per Justice Sherr, at para 116, citing *Catholic Children's Aid Society of Hamilton-Wentworth v. G. (J)*, (1997) 23 R.F.L. 4th 79 (SCJ-Family Branch).

31 Note that, in Ontario, the term 'extended society care' is now substituted for 'Crown Wardship.'

with the person seeking access.[32] It has been estimated that more than 20,000 children across Canada are permanent wards of the state, of whom only about 1,200 are adopted annually.[33]

It would seem that once a wardship order is made, there is no obligation to prove the child is adoptable or to identify a prospective adoptive family.[34] In many cases, court-ordered access for birth family members is perceived as presenting an insurmountable legal obstacle to achieving adoption, despite the fact that post-adoption contact arrangements are now quite common.

Kinship placements Census figures reveal a 26% increase in children being cared for by grandparents between 2001 and 2011, from 35,090 to 44,095. In addition, the number of Canadian children placed in informal kinship care following a maltreatment investigation increased by over 50% between 1998 and 2008, from 0.93 per 1,000 children to 1.45.[35]

Kinship placements are often preferred placements for child welfare agencies, which can generate controversy, as was the case in *Nova Scotia (Community Services) v. TG*,[36] when a foster parent, hoping to adopt a child placed with them, challenged the social welfare agency's preference for a kinship placement. In finding no evidence of bias, Fichaud JA – in a prescient observation – warned that claims of bias by foster parents could be used by them to generate delay in order to strengthen a child's attachment and enhance their claim to be best positioned to advance a child's best interests.

Partnership and rehabilitation Caselaw indicates that the courts are well aware of the risks that foster care arrangements present for the birth parent/child relationship.[37] L'Heureux-Dube J has warned that '[s]ince the best interests of the child are presumed to lie with the parent, the child's psychological integrity and well-being may be seriously affected by the interference with the parent-child relationship'[38] and further noted that '[u]nnecessary disruptions of the [parent-child] bond' can cause 'significant trauma to both the parent and child.'[39] The Court of Appeal in *C (G) v. Catholic Children's Aid Society of Hamilton-Wentworth*[40] found that the foster parents' rights had been 'carefully circumscribed' in order to 'prevent the foster

32 See *Children's Aid Society of Toronto v. D.P.*, 2005 CanLII 34560 (ON CA), [2005] O.J. No. 4075 (Ont. C.A.).
33 See, further, www.cyc-net.org/profession/readarounds/ra-papp.html.
34 See *CAS Niagara v. J.C.*, 2007 Canlii 8919 Div.Ct.
35 Public Health Agency of Canada, (2010). Canadian incidence study of reported child abuse and neglect 2008: Major findings. Ottawa, ON: Public Health Agency of Canada.
36 2012 NSCA 43, at paras 42, 105, 109.
37 See, further, Wiegers, W., Child Placement and the Legal Claims of Foster Caregivers, *University of British Columbia Law Review*, (2019), www.thefreelibrary.com/CHILD+PLACEMENT+AND+THE+LEGAL+CLAIMS+OF+FOSTER+CAREGIVERS.-a0597913025.
38 *NB v. G(J)*, [1999] 3 SCR 46, at para 76.
39 *Winnipeg Child and Family Services v. KLW*, 2000 SCC 48, at para 72.
40 (1998), 161 DLR (4th) 466, 40 OR (3d) 334 (CA), at para 24.

parents from potentially acquiring an advantageous position to that of the natural parents.' The SCC, in *Catholic CAS of Metropolitan Toronto v. M(C)*,[41] emphasised that the emotional well-being of the child was of 'utmost importance,' and the finding of whether a child needed protection was not to focus exclusively on the ability or deficiencies of the parent but could also be based on the likelihood of adverse consequences for the child due to their separation from a foster family that had been caring for the child on a long-term basis. (See also Chapter 7.)

Nonetheless, Canadian courts give serious consideration to the question of whether the home circumstances of a child in care have improved sufficiently to warrant the return of the child to parental care instead of proceeding towards possible adoption.[42] As Justice Sherr stated, in the aforementioned *Children's Aid Society of Toronto v. EU*, any such prospect of the child being returned:

> must arise from something more than a heartfelt expression of a parent's desire to resume care of the child. . . . [T]hey must face some better prospects than what existed at the time of the society's removal of the child from their care and have developed some new ability as a parent.[43]

It may well be that this approach is dependent to some degree on whether the initial parental failure had its roots in neglect or abuse. In the latter instance, as it was trenchantly put in *Children's Aid Society of Ottawa-Carleton v. H. (L.)*,[44] there was a need for separation from the child's original parent or parents so that the child could 'rage against them.'

In *Nova Scotia (Community Services) v. T.H.*,[45] a family court judge had placed two children (aged eight and ten) in permanent care, subject to them remaining in their current foster placement. His order included access for the parents and conditions designed to prevent the agency from seeking adoptive placements, suggesting a possible future return to the mother. On appeal, the judge was overruled as he had no authority to impose such conditions on a permanent care order: in applying the best interests test, he was not entitled to prevent the statutory authority from determining for itself the most appropriate placement once the order was made, and this could include an adoption placement.

Generally, in Crown wardship cases, the courts will explore whether the parent has been given an opportunity to parent. Where the statutory agency frustrates contact with the parent and offers no services, this consideration must come into the equation.[46] The agency also has a duty to reassess its position as circumstances

41 [1994] 2 SCR 165, at para 40.

42 See *Children's Aid Society of Kingston v. F.R.*, (1975), 23 R.F.L. 391 (Ont. Prov. Ct. – F.D.).

43 Op cit, at para 118.

44 1994 CanLII 5236 (ON CJ).

45 2010 NSCA 63 (CanLII).

46 See *Children and Family Services for York Region v. A.W. and M.M.*, [2003] O.J. no. 996 (Sup. Ct.); *CCAS v. P.A.M.* [1998] O.J. No. 3766 (OCJ); *CAS of the United Counties of Stormount, Dundas and Glengarry v. C.K.*, [2001] O.J. No. 128 (Sup. Ct.).

warrant over time.[47] In functional terms, the parental right of access determines rehabilitation: parental access to a child in public care – usually a Crown ward – will be managed at the discretion of the statutory agency in accordance with whether or not this is demonstrably furthering the welfare interests of the child concerned. It must not cut back access in preparation for a possible success in its Crown wardship application, allowing the agency to then argue that a 'limited relationship' exists between child and parent.[48] The court will not merely 'rubber stamp' decisions previously made by the agency.[49]

Justice Susan Himel, in *Children's Aid Society v. E.L.*,[50] was of the view that in order to give effect to the statutory (child protection) scheme, and recognising that stability and continuity for children is desirable, it was appropriate to impose a threshold test of material change in circumstances. The test was not whether the parents have seen the light and intend to change but whether they have, in fact, changed and are now able to give the child the care that is in their best interests. There should be no experimentation with a child's life. Giving the parents another chance necessitates the child having one less chance;[51] it must be demonstrated that the parents are able to parent the child without endangering his or her safety.[52]

Termination of parental rights A child removed from their birth family because of abuse, neglect, or abandonment is first placed in foster care or a group home, under the authority of a care order, until social workers can either help the birth family to the point where reunification is achieved, or it becomes clear that this is not possible, and court proceedings are duly initiated to terminate parental rights. The court may then make the child a Crown ward on the grounds that reunification with the birth family has proven unsuccessful or inappropriate. The status of Crown ward means that all parental rights with respect to the child so designated have been permanently removed, and consequently, the consent of birth parents for the adoption of that child is not legally required. Nonconsensual adoption of children in care refers, in practice, to the adoption of some of the many thousands of Crown wards in foster care. When a child has such status, the Crown (Province) has the rights and responsibilities of a parent and, in that capacity, can declare the child eligible for adoption, but the process can take months or years. According to the May 2002 'Report Card on Adoption' by the Adoption Council of Canada, there

47 See *Children's Aid Society of the Niagara Region v. D. (W.)*, 2004 CanLII 66347 (ON S.C.), (2004), 1 R.F.L. (6th) 84 (Ont. S.C.J.); *Children's Aid Society of the Niagara Region v. B. (C.)*, [2005] O.J. No. 3878 (Ont. S.C.J.); *Children and Family Services of York Region v. E. (P.)*, [2003] O.J. No. 4884 (Ont. S.C.J.); and *Children's Aid Society of London and Middlesex v. S. (E.V.F.)*, 2004 CanLII 34346 (ON S.C.), (2004), 1 R.F.L. (6th) 68 (Ont. S.C.J.).

48 See *Catholic Children's Aid Society of Metropolitan Toronto v. Pier Angelii M.*, (1998) CanLII 14476 (ON C.J.).

49 See *Children's Aid Society of Hamilton v. E.O.*, 2009 CanLII 72087 (ON S.C.).

50 [2003] O.J. No. 3281 (O.S.C).

51 See *Children's Aid Society of Winnipeg (City) v. R.*, (1980), 19 R.F.L. (2d) 232 (Man.C.A.).

52 See *Children's Aid Society of Brockville, Leeds and Grenville v. C.*, [2001] 2001CarswellOnt 1504.

were then over 66,000 Canadian children in foster care (93 per 10,000 aged 0–18), of whom about 22,000 were Crown wards, but fewer than 1,700 were adopted annually across the country – 2.5% less than in the U.K. and U.S.[53] By July 2014, there were approximately 30,000 children and young persons with the legal status of Crown wards in foster care who were thus available for adoption.[54]

Once issued, a wardship order triggers the paramountcy principle, which grants the state full discretion to take such steps as may be necessary to promote the welfare interests of the child. Paradoxically, however, wardship in a Canadian context would seem more likely to obstruct than facilitate adoptions from care. This is in large part due to a judicial practice of issuing a parental access order with respect to a ward, though this is only permissible where there are grounds to believe that a meaningful relationship exists between parent and child that is beneficial to the latter. As Justice Perkins explained in *CAS of Toronto v. T.L.*:[55]

> If a Crown wardship order is to be made and a party has sought an access order, determine whether the relationship between the child and the person who would have access is both meaningful and beneficial to the child (Section 59(2.1)(a)). If not both meaningful and beneficial, dismiss the claim for access. If so, go to the next step.
>
> Determine whether the access would impair the child's future opportunities for adoption (Section 59(2.1)(b)). If so, dismiss the claim for access. If not, go to the next step.
>
> Determine whether an access order is in the child's best interests. If not, dismiss the claim for access. If so, make an access order containing the terms and conditions that are in the child's best interests (Section 58).

It might be noted that this approach would seem to be based on a presumption that post-adoption birth parent access is, per se, not conducive to furthering the adoptee's welfare interests, which, as practice elsewhere indicates, is not necessarily the case. On the other hand, it might more simply reflect the fact that, as Lori Chambers suggests, ' "open adoption" is not fully recognised in Canadian law.'[56]

Concurrent placements The practice of placing children, the custody and guardianship of whom has been judicially assigned to the director of social welfare services, with foster parents who are dual approved as foster carers and adopters is well established in Canada. Indeed, as more foster parents claim the right to adopt children placed with them, concern has been expressed about a 'foster care

53 See Ross, E., Adoption Issues and Ideas' in *Transitions*, Vanier Institute of the Family, Vol 31, Issue 2, (2001).

54 See Eggertson, L., president of the Adoption Council of Canada, http://canadaheartgallery.ca.

55 [2010] O.J. No. 942.

56 Note to author: 16 August 2022.

scoop.'[57] This is particularly contentious in relation to Indigenous children, who are disproportionately represented in foster care and, of necessity, may be placed with non-Indigenous foster parents. (See, further, Chapter 8.)

Residential care

Currently, this form of provision includes out-of-home placement in a facility such as a group home or treatment centre. It is provided for emotionally disturbed children, young offenders, and others who are experiencing problems, including behavioural and adjustment issues, and cannot function in a family setting. The National Children's Alliance of Canada reported a considerable increase in recourse to such facilities at the turn of the century due to overcrowded foster care placements.[58]

SECURE ACCOMMODATION

A growing reason for committal to secure accommodation is to enforce treatment for drug-addicted youths. The objectives of such 'secure care' are stabilisation and detoxification for those deemed to be at immediate risk of serious physical or psychological harm. By 2021, secure care legislation had been enacted in Alberta, Saskatchewan, Manitoba, Ontario, Québec, New Brunswick and Nova Scotia. Whether enforced care and mandatory treatment promotes the welfare interests of those subjected to it has been questioned, but, of course, it's impossible to know what the consequences of nonintervention would have been.

Adoption

As was emphasised in *CAS Peel v. W.O., R.S.B., H.B. and S.B.*,[59] the benefits of adoption are considerable: it creates an exclusive and binding legal relationship, provides a permanent home, grants rights of inheritance and devolution of property, and removes any possibility of third-party interference, and there is no risk of future court action. While it is not possible to establish accurate aggregated numbers of adoptions nationwide, let alone differentiate the related trends, the following account from 2007 may be broadly representative.[60]

Each year for the past five years, approximately 1,600 children were adopted into families in Ontario through one of these three services (public child care, intercountry and private domestic). The largest number – more than 800 a year – are

57 See Sinclair, R., Adoption: Canada' in Ned, J.D. and Frost, C.J., (eds), *Contemporary Issues in Child Welfare: American Indian and Canadian Aboriginal Contexts*, Vernon, BC, JC Charlton Publishing Ltd, (2017), at p 165.

58 See, for example, Saskatchewan Children's Advocate, A Breach of Trust: An Investigation into Foster Care Overcrowding in the Saskatoon Service Centre, (2009).

59 [2002] O.J. No. 1099 (OCJ).

60 See, Forever Families: Ontario's Adoption System, www.children.gov.on.ca/htdocs/English/infertility/report/foreverfamilies.aspx.

public adoptions, followed by about 650 intercountry adoptions and 150 private domestic adoptions.

DOMESTIC VOLUNTARY ADOPTION

The findings of the last nationwide adoption survey were published in 1993.[61] This reported that the number of domestic adoptions had dropped by almost 50% between 1981 and 1990, from 5,376 to 2,836. The biggest drop was in the number adoptions from the care system. During that time, private adoptions remained steady at about 1,000 a year but increased from 17% to 40% of total adoptions. By 2001, of the estimated 4,118 adoptions, 2,243 or 54% were domestic.[62]

ADOPTION FROM PUBLIC CARE

In recent years, domestic adoptions have steadily grown in number largely due to ICA becoming more difficult; more assertive policies to increase adoptions from state care; and the fact that from the early years of this century, adoptions by same-sex couples have become legalised in every province and territory. The latter development has clearly benefitted the welfare interests of the many children who would otherwise have remained in the care system.

Unaccompanied migrant minors

'Canada lacks a clear policy framework consistent with the best interests of unaccompanied minors seeking asylum,'[63] of whom there were some 2,000 to 4,000 in Canada in 2016. This assertion by the CBA has been attested to by the CRC in each of its Concluding Observations to Canada (1995, 2003 and 2012), when it expressed a specific and significant concern that Canada had not appropriately applied the best interests of the child principle in all immigration and asylum processes. It's not a new problem. A century ago, the Empire Settlement Act 1922 provided for the passage of unaccompanied juveniles 14 to 17 years of age to Canada, but the practice had to be abandoned in 1925 following three child suicides.[64] More recently, Human Rights Watch and other groups have also raised objections regarding the detention of immigrant children and families with children.[65] Justification for the concerns of such bodies would seem well supported by recent practice and related caselaw, despite Canada having ratified the United Nations Convention on the Rights of the Child, which states that 'the best interests of the child' are always

61 See Sobol, M., and Daly, K., *Adoption in Canada*, (1994).
62 See U.N. Department of Economic and Social Affairs, *Child Adoption: Trends and Policies*, (2009), at p 69.
63 The Canadian Bar Association (Child and Youth Law Section), 'Alternative Report to the U.N. Committee on the Rights of the Child, (2020), op cit, at p 21.
64 See *the Canadian Encyclopedia*, www.thecanadianencyclopedia.ca/en/article/child-migration-to-canada.
65 See also the *Canada 2016 Human Rights Report* at www.state.gov/documents/organization/265782.pdf.

a primary consideration, and despite the Immigration and Refugee Protection Act 2001 affirming that the best interests of children in detention must be taken into account. Instead, children wait for lengthy periods to reunite with Canadian resident parents, are often denied visiting rights with them, and are not permitted to 'sponsor' the immigration of parents who remain in their country of origin, and the best interests of the child principle does not apply to any prospect of family reunification in Canada for such unaccompanied migrant minors. The welfare interests and rights of unaccompanied minors are routinely represented by a 'designated representative' rather than by a lawyer.

In *Legault v. Canada (Minister of Citizenship and Immigration)*,[66] the best interest of the child was found to be an 'important factor' that must be given 'substantial weight' in the decision of whether to remove a parent from Canada. The following year, the Federal Court of Appeal ruled[67] that a best interests determination requires the decision-maker to take into account the views of the child in accordance with their age and maturity and that a child's own views about their circumstances are to be considered, as required by Article 12 of U.N. CROC. It held that the immigration officer had erred in failing to take account of the 15-year-old child's strong preference to continue to live in Canada with her mother, who faced deportation, rather than with her father, who was a citizen and not facing deportation.

In *Canadian Doctors for Refugee Care v. Canada*,[68] the Federal Court found that cuts to the Interim Federal Health Program for refugees and refugee children violated their Charter rights. It stated: '[T]he United Nations Committee on the Rights of the Child has provided guidance on how the "best interests" principle is to be applied, noting that the child's right to health is central in assessing a child's best interests.'[69] A year later, in *Kanthasamy v. Canada (Minister of Citizenship and Immigration)*,[70] the SCC emphasised the centrality of the best interests of the child principle to humanitarian and compassionate considerations in applications for permanent residence and noted the need to consider the best interests of a child who is 'directly affected' as a 'singularly significant focus and perspective.' If the child's interests are not 'well-defined' and examined 'with a great deal of attention,' the decision by the immigration authorities may be found to be unreasonable.[71] That same year, the SCC also ruled in *M.M. v. U.S.A.*[72] that a mother should be extradited to the U.S. notwithstanding a finding that it was required under U.N.

66 [2002] 4 F.C. 358 (C.A.).

67 *Hawthorne v. Canada (Minister of Citizenship and Immigration)*, [2003] 2 F.C. 555 (CA).

68 2014 FC 651.

69 Ibid, at paras 11–12.

70 2015 SCC 61. Also see *Baker v. Canada (Minister of Citizenship and Immigration)*, [1999] 2 S.C.R. 817, in which L'Heureux-Dubé J held that 'the decision-maker should consider children's best interests as an important factor, give them substantial weight, and be alert, alive and sensitive to them,' at para 75.

71 *Kanthasamy v. Canada*, at para 39.

72 2015 SCC 62.

CROC and other instruments to consider the best interests of any children who may be adversely affected by decisions regarding their future.[73]

Following the decision in *B.B. v. Canada (Citizenship and Immigration)*,[74] the Immigration and Refugee Protection Regulations were amended in 2019 to include a requirement that consideration be given to the best interests of a child directly affected by an immigration detention or release decision. A new section was added to affirm the principle, in s 60 of the Act, that a minor child should be detained only as a measure of last resort, and it outlined a nonexhaustive list of factors to consider when determining the best interests of the child.

TRAFFICKING

Canada has been identified as a source, destination, and transit country for victims of human trafficking, including children, for the purposes of sexual exploitation and labour.[75] There is good reason to believe that Indigenous women and girls have been disproportionality affected by trafficking – as well as other forms of abuse – over recent decades.[76] A report funded by the Department of Justice which explored the practice of customary adoption gave rise to concerns that links may exist between the practice and the possible trafficking of Inuit women, girls and children. The evidence, largely anecdotal, suggests that some Inuit in the north may be buying and selling their babies and children and that children are being 'prostituted out by a parent, family member, or domestic partner.'[77]

Canada has legislated to combat human trafficking both domestically and transnationally in the Criminal Code, s 279, and in the Immigration and Refugee Protection Act 2002, s 118.

The welfare principle in contemporary practice: public family law, criminal jurisdiction

The preamble to the Youth Criminal Justice Act 2003 specifically references U.N. CROC and declares that Canadian society should have a youth criminal justice system that provides for 'rehabilitation and reintegration.' Section 3(1)(b) adds the requirement that the criminal justice system as it relates to children must be 'based on the principle of diminished moral blameworthiness or culpability.'

73 Ibid, at paras 146–147.

74 2016 FC 1423 (CanLII).

75 See the International Bureau for Children's Rights, Child Trafficking in Canada, www.ibcr.org/en/projets/la-traite-des-enfants-au-canada-2/.

76 See Sethi, A., Domestic Sex Trafficking of Aboriginal Girls in Canada: Issues and Implications, *First Peoples Child & Family Review*, (2007): 3(3), 57–71. Also see Native Women's Association of Canada, Trafficking of Indigenous Women and Girls in Canada, 2018, www.ourcommons.ca/Content/Committee/421/JUST/Brief/BR10002955/br-external/NativeWomensAssociationOfCanada-e.pdf.

77 See Roos, H., The Service and Capacity Review for Victims of Sexual Exploitation and Human Trafficking in Nunavut, Ottawa, (2014). See, further, http://news.nationalpost.com/2014/01/30/start-waking-up-report-warns-of-inuit-child-selling-cites-anecdotal-evidence-of-abuse-trafficking/.

The system

Statistics Canada reports that for the period 2020–21, the annual average daily count of youths in custody decreased by more than one-quarter (-27%), the largest decline in almost two decades, possibly related to COVID-imposed restrictions on movement.[78] Nonetheless, the system has been found to be deficient and Indigenous children to be overrepresented in it.[79] In June 2022, the U.N. CRC expressed concern about juveniles being put on trial and sentenced as adults. It advised that juveniles should have access to juvenile justice at both the trial and sentencing stages.

Children who pose a threat to the welfare of self or others

The Youth Criminal Justice Act 2003, which replaced the Young Offenders Act, provides the legal framework for interventionist measures with respect to those aged between 12 and 17 who commit or are suspected of committing criminal offences. This legislation operates in tandem with the Criminal Code, which makes sexual abuse and physical abuse of children federal crimes, and the arrest and detention provisions in s 10 of the Charter of Rights and Freedoms 1981.[80]

AGE OF CRIMINAL RESPONSIBILITY

A child becomes criminally liable for their actions in Canada, under s 13 of the Criminal Code, at 12 years of age. This use of an age-specific cutoff point has attracted judicial criticism. As Abella J remarked in *Manitoba*, '[A] rigid statutory distinction that completely ignored the actual decision-making capabilities of children under a certain age would fail to reflect the realities of childhood and child development.'[81] McLachlin CJ, perhaps endorsing this view, added, '[I]n the youth criminal law context, it is recognised as a principle of fundamental justice that young persons must generally be treated differently from adults by virtue of their 'reduced maturity and moral capacity.'[82]

PREVENTION

The 2003 act introduced a new emphasis on prevention. Prevention programmes now focus on encouraging and supporting local community initiatives that, for example, help youths learn new social skills and channel their energies into positive activities; ensure that youths are educated and trained for constructive careers that contribute to their communities; ensure that youths receive good nutrition,

78 See, further, https://www150.statcan.gc.ca/n1/daily-quotidien/220420/dq220420c-eng.htm.
79 See, further, www.justice.gc.ca/eng/rp-pr/jr/jf-pf/2019/may01.html.
80 See, further, www.justice.gc.ca/eng/csj-sjc/rfc-dlc/ccrf-ccdl/check/art10.html.
81 *A.C. v. Manitoba (Director of Child and Family Services)*, 2009, op cit, at para 116.
82 Ibid, at para 145, citing *R. v. D.B.*, 2008 SCC 25, [2008] 2 SCR 3, at para 47 per Abella J.

housing, and health care; and protect children from physical, emotional and sexual abuse. Much crime-prevention work is led or coordinated by Public Safety Canada. Since 2008, this agency has focused most of its efforts on developing knowledge of effective practices in relation to early risk factors among at-risk children and youth, youth gangs, recidivism among high-risk groups, and prevention in Aboriginal communities.[83]

Juvenile court

As explained by the Department of Justice, 'the purpose of youth sentences is to hold young people accountable by imposing sanctions that have meaningful consequences for them and that promote their rehabilitation and reintegration into society, thereby contributing to the long-term protection of the public.' The department maintains that proportionality is a key principle in a sentencing context: 'a sentence must be proportionate to the seriousness of the offence and the degree of responsibility of the young person.'[84]

ROLE OF THE WELFARE PRINCIPLE

Although there is no explicit reference in the 2003 Act to this principle, its role is evident in the declared purpose of the system, the range of disposal options it provides, and the procedural safeguards that protect a youth from improper questioning.[85]

Arguably, however, the welfare principle is infringed – if not violated – by provisions that grant judicial discretion to impose adult sentences on youths found guilty of serious offences if they were 14 years of age or older when the crime was committed. Further, the overlap between the child welfare and juvenile justice systems, substantiated by recent research,[86] suggests that the welfare principle functions, to some extent, in a negative role: many drawn into the first system progress into the second.

A further indication of its role can be seen in the strategic part played by the Youth Justice Committees, established under s 18(1) of the 2003 Act, to mediate between the offender, the victim and the needs and resources of the local community. These are operational in a number of provinces and territories and aim

83 See Public Safety Canada, Results of Crime Prevention Programs for 12 to 17 Year Olds, www.publicsafety.gc.ca/cnt/rsrcs/pblctns/rslts-crm-prvntn-12-17/index-en.aspx.

84 See, further, www.justice.gc.ca/eng/cj-jp/yj-jj/tools-outils/sheets-feuillets/syp-dpaa.html.

85 See *R. v. L.T.H.*, [2008] 2 S.C.R. 739, 2008 SCC 49.

86 See Nickel, N.C., Turnbull, L., Wall-Wieler, E., Au, W., Ekuma, O., MacWilliam, L., Enns, J.E., Lee, J.B., McCullough, S., Burchill, C., and Brownell, M., Overlap between child protection services and the youth justice system: protocol for a retrospective population-based cohort study using linked administrative data in Manitoba, Canada, *BMJ Open* 2020, https://bmjopen.bmj.com/content/10/7/e034895.

to 'strike the right balance between accountability and community intervention.'[87] The requirement, under s 25 of the Act, to advise an arrested young person of their rights 'to retain and instruct counsel without delay' and to be represented at any hearing provides further evidence of welfare/rights considerations.

COMMUNITY SENTENCES

The 2003 Act provides for the exercise of discretion by police officers, authorising the issue of a warning, a police caution or a charge in circumstances in which the offence is minor, the offender remorseful and prepared to make reparation, and such a response is indicated by welfare considerations. If the youth agrees, the police can also refer the youth to a programme under s 7 or, if the police decide to refer the case to the courts, the Crown can choose to issue a Crown caution. It also provides a further level of nonprosecutorial measures, known as extrajudicial sanctions, which may be indicated by the seriousness of the offence, the nature and number of previous offences committed by the young person, or any other aggravating circumstances. These are listed under s 42 and may take the form of deferred custody and supervision; a community service order; restitution to the victim and/or participation in nonresidential training programmes; a fine and reprimand; or a probation order, which is the option most frequently used. Importantly, a community disposal option is dependent on the young person giving informed consent; they must know about the sanction, must be given the right to counsel, must be given an opportunity to consult with counsel, and must consent to the use of the sanction. Under s 35 of the Act, in addition to any order that it is authorised to make, 'a youth justice court may, at any stage of proceedings against a young person, refer the young person to a child welfare agency for assessment to determine whether the young person is in need of child welfare services.'

CUSTODIAL SENTENCES

Under s 39 of the Act, a custodial sentence is restricted to those who have committed acts of violence, are repeat offenders, or have committed an indictable offence for which an adult would be liable to two or more years of imprisonment or one with aggravating features. When considering whether to sentence a young person to serve a period of time in a youth custody facility, 'a judge must first consider all available options other than custody that are reasonable in the circumstances, paying particular attention to the circumstances of aboriginal young persons.'[88] Sta-

87 See Youth Justice Committees of Ontario. 'Fact Sheets,' www.justice.gc.ca/eng/cj-jp/yj-jj/tools-outils/sheets-feuillets/commi-comit.html.

88 Department of Justice, op cit.

tistics Canada report that for the period 2020–21, there were about 10,100 youth admissions to correctional services, 42% fewer than the year before: youth admissions to custody (-45%) and to community supervision (-41%).[89]

The U.N. CRC was advised in May 2022 that the relevant legislation had been amended to prohibit children from being held in adult detention centres. Children are now only held in adult detention centres in pretrial detention in exceptional circumstances if no juvenile detention centres are accessible in the region or if the child's safety has been threatened in a juvenile detention centre.[90]

Solitary confinement The 2003 Act declares the purpose of youth justice to be the rehabilitation of child offenders.[91] Arguably, solitary confinement is contrary to that purpose, may also be contrary to ss 9 and 15 of the Charter, and may at least be restricted by s 85(2) of the 2003 Act. Nonetheless, its use in youth custodial facilities is well established, even if currently decreasing.[92] In 2017, the College of Family Physicians of Canada (CFPC) released a statement which supports the ending of solitary confinement in Canadian correctional facilities, including the abolition of its use in youth facilities.[93]

Conclusion

Although the circumstances of Indigenous children are particularly bad, the statistics show that far more non-Indigenous children are to be found in the Canadian public child welfare system than in that of other developed nations. While this may, in part, be due to a low state investment in preventative measures, it results in many children left in 'legal limbo' as Crown wards without any 'parent.' Again, in contrast to other developed nations, all Canadian children remain legally unprotected from parental chastisement. Moreover, the law would seem very equivocal in relation to when a child may exercise their right to consent – or withdraw consent – on issues affecting their welfare interests, and similarly, it is unclear as to when those interests may be legally treated as a matter of paramount importance. It's hard not to conclude that the safeguarding and promotion of the welfare interests of all Canadian children would be greatly assisted by the federal appointment of an independent children's ombudsman.

89 Op cit.

90 See, further, at www.ohchr.org/en/press-releases/2022/05/experts-committee-rights-child-commend-canada-truth-and-reconciliation.

91 *R v. CCN*, 2018 ABPC 148 (CanLII).

92 See, for example, Alberta's Ombudsman's 2021 report 'Youth in Segregation,' www.ombudsman.ab.ca/wp-content/uploads/2021/03/Alberta-Ombudsman-Youth-in-Segregation-Own-Motion_FINAL.docx.pdf.

93 See, further, www.cfpc.ca/CFPC/media/Resources/Prison-Health/Solitary-Confinement_EN_Prison-Health.pdf.

7 The welfare principle in contemporary practice

Private family law and hybrid proceedings

Introduction

There is a general lack of national coherence in the laws relating to children in Canada. As a consequence, the principle of the welfare interests of a child is poorly integrated; its role and weighting varies across proceedings and across provinces and territories. Federal legislation and rulings of the SCC have brought some patchy consistency but only in relation to matters such as care arrangements in a divorce context. Ad hoc judicial reliance on wardship, which introduces the paramountcy principle to resolve urgent and/or complex issues, adds further to the prevailing uncertainty regarding the welfare/rights of Canadian children.

This chapter follows the structure established in Chapter 4. It is largely concerned with examining children's welfare interests and rights in a private family law context: mainly at times of family breakdown, guardianship and adoption. It then considers how such welfare/rights are increasingly crosscutting both sectors through the use of hybrid public/private court orders and statutory proceedings. The greater part of this chapter is concerned with identifying and analysing key cases in order to examine and evaluate how and why the law relating to children has evolved as it has in Canada.

The welfare principle in contemporary practice: private family law

The Charter of Fundamental Rights and Freedoms entrenches constitutional recognition for what might be traditionally viewed as parental rights and affords their exercise a guarantee of protection from unwarranted state interference.[1] In particular, s 7 provides that everyone has the right to life, liberty, and security of the person and the right not to be deprived thereof except in accordance with the principles of fundamental justice.

1 *B. (R.) v. Children's Aid Society of Metropolitan Toronto*, [1995] 1 SCR 315, 122 D.L.R. (4th) 1 and *Canadian Foundation for Children, Youth and the Law v. Canada (Attorney General)*, [2004] 1 SCR 76, 2004 SCC 4.

DOI: 10.4324/9781003269564-11

Children and reconstituted families

Traditional family forms, like traditional parental rights, are giving way to new constructs in all developed nations. Parental responsibilities are now frequently exercised in serial parenting arrangements, often shared between birth parents and others, within a wide range of reconfigured family forms.

'Society is continuously changing and family structures are changing along with it. This must be recognized as a reality and not as a detriment to the best interests of the child.' So Fowler J stated in *C.C. (Re),*[2] when judicial notice was taken of the fact that a family could comprise three legal parents (two fathers and one mother), based on the throuple's sexual relationship; both men being declared fathers. The judge commented that 'I can find nothing to disparage that relationship from the best interests of the child's point of view.'[3] While there is, indeed, no evidence to question that judgment, it does tend to raise the question as to what – from a child's best interests point of view – might be defined as non-viable parenting parameters.

Matrimonial

Contemporary family life in Canada might perhaps appear more stable than formerly, with a divorce rate that has decreased from 12.7 per 1,000 in 1991 to 7.5 per 1,000 in 2019 and fallen further to 5.6 per 1,000 in 2020. However, this gives a false impression; the marriage rate has also been falling as an accelerating number of adults are choosing cohabitation and therefore escaping 'capture' by marriage and divorce statistics. The 2016 census showed that 21.3% of all couples over all age groups were in common-law relationships: more than triple the number reported in 1981, which was 6.3%. For decades, lone-parent families have accounted for an increasing share of families with children, increasing from 17.8% to 19.2% over the period from 2001 to 2016.

DIVORCE, NULLITY, JUDICIAL SEPARATION AND RELOCATION

The Divorce Act 1985, as revised in 1986 and last amended in 2019, with effect from 2021, states that divorce must be based on a breakdown of marriage, which can be established with proof that the parties have been living apart for at least one year immediately before the divorce proceedings or have committed adultery, or one has treated the other with physical or mental cruelty. While s 16(8) of this statute made the best interests of the child the only consideration in determining custody arrangements nationwide, it offered minimal direction on how the test should be applied. Amendments to the Act, which took effect in 2021, now list factors that a court must consider when determining best interests, including several directed at family violence. They require the child's views and preferences to be specifically

2 2018 NLSC 71. Following on from *A v. B,* 2007 ONCA 2, 83 OR (3d) 56 I when Ontario recognised a three-parent family.

3 Ibid, at para34.

considered 'giving due weight to the child's age and maturity, unless they cannot be ascertained.'

This federal legislation – dealing with parties who are, or used to be, married to each other – operates in tandem with provincial legislation dealing with all parents, whether married or not.

The welfare checklist Among the recent changes introduced to the Divorce Act 1985 is a degree of specificity in relation to interpreting 'the best interests' of a child. Because this is federal legislation, in every province and territory, the courts will now have to take into account the same considerations when making parenting arrangements following divorce. In making a decision about a child, it must, under s 16(1), apply only the 'best interests' test and be guided, under s 16(3), by a list of 11 specific factors that include the child's views and preferences, any court action or order relevant to the child's safety and well-being, and any history of family violence. When considering these and other factors, the court must, under s 16(2), give priority to the child's physical, emotional and psychological safety, security and well-being. While this amendment repositions a child's best interests to centre stage in divorce proceedings with added specificity, it does not mention the paramountcy principle, nor does it otherwise add any additional weighting to those interests.

Relocation The law governing child relocation is largely to be found in the amended Divorce Act 1985, s 16(9). The principles applicable to disputes concerning child-care arrangements following the relocation of a parent with direct care responsibility remain basically as initially established in *Gordon v. Goertz*,[4] though with some refinements. The court then set out a two-stage inquiry for determining whether to vary a parenting order and permit a custodial parent to relocate with the child: first, the party seeking a variation must show a material change in the child's circumstances; second, the judge must determine what order reflects the child's best interests in the new circumstances. Subsequent refinements were largely codified in the 2019 amendments to the Divorce Act and now require courts to determine whether relocation is in the best interests of the child, having regard to the child's physical, emotional and psychological safety, security, and well-being. As explained in *Barendregt v. Grebliunas*,[5] the court must consider all factors related to the circumstances of the child, which may include the child's views and preferences; the history of caregiving; any incidents of family violence; or a child's cultural, linguistic, religious and spiritual upbringing and heritage. A court shall also consider each parent's willingness to support the development and maintenance of the child's relationship with the other parent and give effect to the principle that a child should have as much time with each parent as is consistent with the best

4 [1996] 2 SCR 27.
5 2022 SCC 22.

interests of the child. How the outcome of an application would affect either party's relocation plans should not be considered.

In that case, the SCC reinstated the ruling of the court at first instance, which had allocated custody to the relocating mother as there was a significant risk that the bitter relationship between the parents would affect the children if they stayed with their father in what had been the family home. The majority said there was no good reason for the Court of Appeal to admit new evidence and change the decision of the judge at first instance. In such cases, the question is 'whether relocation is in the best interests of the child, having regard to child's physical, emotional and psychological safety, security and well-being.'

COURT ORDERS

Until the recent amendments to the Divorce Act 1985 took effect, the court orders available consisted in the main of 'custody' and 'access,' the traditional duo. It should not be forgotten, however, that court orders for ensuring maintenance for the caring parent have also always played a crucial role in safeguarding the best interests of a child.[6]

Parenting arrangements Now the parenting arrangements made after a divorce or separation make reference to 'decision-making responsibility,' 'parenting time' and 'contact.'

'Decision-making responsibility' refers to the more important parenting choices – matters such as a child's health, education, language and religion. They may be vested exclusively in one parent or be shared jointly. A spouse with decision-making responsibility has the right to ask for and get information about their children's health, education and well-being.

'Parenting time' refers to the time a spouse spends with a child and permits them to make day-to-day decisions (including emergency decisions) while with them. That spouse also has the right to ask for and get information about their children's health, education and well-being.

'Contact' refers to the time that someone who isn't a spouse – a relative, perhaps – might have with a child. Such a person does not have the right to make day-to-day decisions about a child or to get information about the child's health, education and well-being. Under s 16.5 (1), a court may, on application by a person other than a spouse, make an order providing for contact between that person and a child of the marriage.

Some of the complexities involved in determining parenting arrangements were illustrated in the recent slew of court cases – a mix of public and private proceedings – that finally concluded with the SCC ruling in *B.J.T. v. J.D.*[7] This case

6 Federal legislation such as the Family Orders and Agreements Enforcement Assistance Act 1985 and the Garnishment, Attachment and Pension Diversion Act 1985 being particularly important.

7 2022 SCC 24.

concerned a custody contest between a noncustodial birth father and a maternal grandmother with respect to a child for whom the grandmother had shared care responsibility during the first four years of the child's life. Proceedings had originated in a court decision in 2018 that W.D. (born in October 2013) was in need of protection due to his mother's mental health issues. Until that court hearing, he had been cared for by his mother, who had separated from her husband while pregnant shortly after their marriage, and the maternal grandmother. The court then directed that the grandmother should have parental status. In the process of notifying parties, the father was contacted, which was when he first knew of the existence of his son, and he promptly commenced custody proceedings, which were contested by the grandmother. Legal proceedings were interrupted by the director of child protection removing the child from a summer camp – without a court order – and placing him in foster care. Some four weeks later, in January 2018, a court found the child to be in need of protection, and for the next 20 months, he remained in care, despite several court hearings and adjournments. He was removed from foster care, placed with his father where he remained, all contact with the grandmother being severed.

Notwithstanding that the child had a closer biological tie to his father in Alberta, who was 'more or less' equally able to care for his son but was unwilling to support and foster the child's relationship with his grandmother, mother and older half brother, the SCC overturned the Court of Appeal's decision and awarded custody to the grandmother. Sheilah Martin J, for the SCC explained:

> The most important consideration in a child custody case is the best interests of the child. . . . The same standard applies in custody cases involving child protection, unless there is legislation to the contrary. . . . In this case, the Supreme Court found no error in the hearing judge's assessment of the best interests of the child. The hearing judge based her analysis on an extensive review of the evidence, and was not compelled to decide in favour of the father simply due to a closer biological tie.

Arguably, this ruling is in keeping with an established history of the judiciary awarding custody to the 'primary caregiver,' most usually been presumed to be in a child's best interests, and is memorable for the good sense of Justice Martin's observation that 'Children should be afforded the comfort of knowing, with some degree of certainty, where they will live and with whom.'[8]

This approach to custody matters is also applicable in access disputes, as was illustrated almost 30 years ago in *Young v. Young*,[9] when the court ruled that the accessing Jehovah's Witness parent was prohibited from indoctrinating the children during his visits. It found that the 'best interests test' applied, but this should not focus on harm, though the presence or absence of harm could be an important factor.

8 Ibid.
9 [1993] 4 SCR 3.

The need to ensure that the test was satisfied justified imposing restrictions on the father's right of access. Moreover, as was subsequently emphasised in *Gordon v. Goertz*,[10] the 'test' does not imply the existence of a formula to be systematically applied in all circumstances: instead, it must viewed as fact sensitive and applied to fit the particular circumstances of the child concerned.

Guardianship

A guardian is a person legally designated to be responsible for the care and upbringing of a named child. Both birth parents are inherently joint guardians of their child and, unless a court orders otherwise, will continue to be so after their divorce or separation.

COURT APPOINTMENT

A guardianship appointment is most usually obtained by application to the court – mainly under the authority provided by a province's Family Act – which may then issue a guardianship order. Alternatively, a child's parent may make a testamentary appointment with respect to their child to take effect after their death but subject to that appointment being confirmed by the court. Once appointed, a guardian undertakes full decision-making responsibility for the child, is vested with responsibility for parenting time, and may determine any contact arrangements in favour of third parties.

Adoption

There is a lack of nationwide coherence in the approach to matters of adoption law and policy. While all provinces and territories can be said to share a more or less similar policy towards adoption from the public care system, stepparent and kinship adoption, private adoption agencies and intercountry adoption, they differ on matters such as post-adoption support and access to identifying information. They all, however, require an adoption order to be conditional on the consent of the child concerned above a certain age; in most jurisdictions, that age is 12. They also provide grounds for the necessity of that consent to be dispensed with.[11] While in some, the statutory law is quite modern, in others, it is not. All in all, the government would seem to employ a light touch when regulating private adoption and private agencies.

A requirement that the welfare of the child be accorded paramount importance when determining an adoption application is not evident in the legislation of the provinces and territories. Nor is there any statutory requirement to take into account the likely effect of an adoption order on the welfare of the child throughout

10 1996 CanLII 191 (SCC), [1996] 2 SCR 27.

11 *C. (A.) v. A. (V.), 2012 ONCJ 7.*

childhood and none to consider, as in the U.K., its lifelong implications for the child concerned. Private adoptions involving the direct placement of a child by their parent or placement by an adoption agency acting on a for-profit or not-for-profit basis are legally permissible. Interestingly, in the Northwest Territories, the adoption legislation requires the child's views and preferences to be considered before a placement decision is made. In British Columbia, where the prospective adoptee is between 7 and 12 years of age, an authorised person must meet the child, determine whether they understand what adoption means, and report to the court on any views the child might have on the proposed adoption.

ADOPTERS

Domestic adoptions by stepparents, close relatives or other kinship applicants would seem to be decreasing in Canada.

Stepparent adoption A United Nations report in 2009 estimated that of the approximately 2,243 domestic adoptions in 2001, 527 or 12.8% were by stepparents or other relatives.[12] It draws attention to 'the sizeable numbers of adoptions by step-parent or other relatives, ranging between 300 and 600 annually.' The SCC seemed to consider, in *Williams v. Hillier et al.*,[13] that the welfare principle was of doubtful relevance in this context when it came to the conclusion that a stepparent adoption was not subject to the paramountcy principle.

A large proportion of stepparent adoptions involve older children, and some of these can prove contentious. That was the case in *Gill v. Gill*,[14] when the court was faced with the dilemma of balancing the right of a 7-year-old boy to develop a relationship with his birth father – who had become a complete stranger to the child with whom he now wished to establish access – against the disruption this would cause to established family life, in which the boy had formed a close attachment to his mother's new husband. Again, in *C. (A.) v. A. (V.)*,[15] the court was concerned with a stepfather applicant who wished to dispense with the consent of his 12-year-old stepson on the basis that the child did not know that he was not his biological father and that learning this information would cause the child emotional harm. It found that to establish risk of emotional harm that would justify dispensing with the consent of a child, an applicant must provide evidence from an expert witness skilled in making that assessment: for example, a psychiatrist or psychologist.

Cultural/religious affinity Preserving and promoting the multicultural nature of Canadian society, as recognised in s 27 of the Charter and by the Multiculturalism

12 See U.N. Department of Economic and Social Affairs/Population Division, Child Adoption: Trends and Policies, *United Nations*, New York, (2009), at p 199.

13 [1980] 2 SCR 368.

14 1994 CanLII 2644 (BC SC).

15 2012 ONCJ 7.

Act, is central to contemporary public policy. Following recognition of the inherent right to self-determination of First Nations people and their exclusive jurisdiction over child welfare matters, several provinces have introduced explicit adoption legislation reflecting a concern for the appropriate placement of First Nations children and the importance of preserving their cultural identity and unique status.[16]

The North American Council on Adoptable Children (NACAC), representing more than 400 Canadian and American child advocacy organisations, was of the view that:[17]

> Children in need of adoption have a right to be placed into a family that reflects their ethnic or cultural heritage. Children should not have their adoptions denied or significantly delayed, however, when adoptive parents of other ethnic or cultural groups are available.

The SCC, in *Van de Perre v. Edwards*,[18] cautioned against an ideological application of this view when it declared that 'even in adoption cases where it might play a more important role, race is not a determinative factor and its importance will greatly depend on the facts.'[19]

POST-ADOPTION CONTACT, INFORMATION DISCLOSURE AND STATE SUPPORT SERVICES

Generally, in most provinces and territories, adoption and a contact order permitting ongoing access to the adoptee for birth family members are viewed in law as being mutually exclusive. However, in Ontario, the courts have found that the existence of a contact order in favour of birth family members does not of itself prevent adoption where such an arrangement is clearly for the child's benefit.[20] Also, it has been held that although a court cannot order post-adoption access to an adopted child for a birth parent or a member of a birth parent's family, this does not prevent it from doing so to provide such access for a sibling of that child.[21] A distinction – based squarely on the welfare interests of the child – can be made between a person's access to the child and a child's access to a person.[22]

There is no consistent Canadian approach towards information disclosure: although most provinces and territories now provide an adult adoptee with the right to access identifying information, some do not. Ontario, for example, operates

16 See McDade, K., International Adoption in Canada: Public Policy Issues, *Institute for Research on Public Policy*, April 1991.

17 See, further, www.nacac.org.

18 [2001] 2 SCR 1014.

19 Ibid, at para 39.

20 *Durham Children's Aid Society v. R.S.*, [2010] O.J. No. 1134.

21 See *CAS Niagara and J.C.*, 2007 CanLII 8919 Div.Ct. Also, see A.G. (Re), 2009 CanLII 34991 (On S.C).

22 See *CAS of Oxford County v. Christine M., Terry M., and Grant B.*, 1999 Carswell Ont 4812 (OCJ).

a system (the Voluntary Disclosure Registry) to facilitate voluntary disclosure, where adult adoptees and birth parents can indicate a mutual desire for contact.[23] Mostly, the principle of access is conditioned by the right to file vetoes with the Vital Statistics Agency prohibiting the release of any birth registration or adoption order information. The U.N. CRC pointed out in its 2012 report that the necessary information is not always readily available and recommended that 'information about the date and place of their birth and their birth-parents is available to adopted children.'[24] This deficiency has not been helped by the SCC ruling that there is no constitutional right to know one's past by obtaining information on your own past from your sperm donor. In *Ontario v. Marchand*,[25] the court ruled the right 'to know one's past' was not to a principle of fundamental justice within s 7 of the Charter.[26]

The costs of adopting from care are borne by the state, and post-adoption support is generally provided. (See, further, later in this chapter.) Private domestic and intercountry adopters, on the other hand, are largely left unsupported by the state. Provincially licensed adoption organisations provide a variety of pre- and post-adoption services on a for-profit basis to prospective adoptive parents and/or to birth parents.[27]

INTERCOUNTRY ADOPTION: CONTEMPORARY

Recourse to intercountry adoption became a phenomenon in the 1990s. In recent years, Canada's experience as a receiving nation has been of a drop in annual intercountry adoptions: in 2017, there were only 712, down from 903 in 2015 and 1,366 in 2012. Prospective adopters in Canada have also been seriously impacted by the decision of some sending countries to abruptly terminate long-standing bilateral adoption arrangements. The Russian government enacted legislation in July 2013 prohibiting the adoption of children by same-sex couples and single people from countries that recognise same-sex marriage, regardless of the actual sexual orientation of applicants, which has been a particularly serious setback.

Difficulties with Immigration Canada have been experienced by many Canadian couples who, having successfully completed adoption procedures in a 'sending' country – most notably Pakistan[28] – can find themselves facing months or even years of bureaucratic negotiations before bringing back or returning to the

23 See Chambers, L., *A Legal History of Adoption in Ontario, 1921–2015*, University of Toronto Press/Osgoode Society Press, (2016).

24 Para 27(b).

25 (2006), 81 O.R. (3d) 172.

26 See also *Canadian Foundation for Children*, at paras 8–11; *R. v. Malmo-Levine*, [2003] 3 SCR 571 at para 113); and *Cheskes v. Ontario (Attorney General)*, (2007), 288 D.L.R. (4th) 449 at para 116 (Ont. SCJ).

27 The organisation Adopting in Canada provides a list of such agencies: www.canadaadopts.com/canada/resources_priagencies.shtml.

28 See, Johnson, G., on behalf of Citizenship and Immigration Canada. See, further, www.thestar.com/news/canada/2013/08/05/canadas_ban_on_pakistani_adoptions_baffles_parents_clerics.html.

orphanage the child they thought they had successfully adopted.[29] Again, this illustrates how state intervention can be detrimental to the welfare interests of children, even if attributable to difficulties in implementing the Hague Convention.[30]

Surrogacy

Only surrogacy of an 'altruistic' nature – not for profit – is legal in Canada and is regulated by the federal Assisted Human Reproduction Act. Along with other ART procedures, surrogacy is largely a matter for private family law, but there is also a hybrid public/private dimension. (See, further, later in this chapter.)

The Uniform Child Status Act 2010 defines a 'surrogate' as a person who gives birth to a child as a result of assisted reproduction if, at the time of the child's conception, she intended to relinquish that child to (a) the person whose human reproductive material was used in the assisted reproduction or whose human reproductive material was used to create the embryo used in the assisted reproduction or (b) the person referred to in (a) and the person married to or in a common-law partnership with that person. This has not stopped each province and territory from issuing its own legislation, 'British Columbia being the most permissive and Québec – where all surrogacy contracts are regarded as invalid – the most restrictive.'

SURROGATE, CHILD AND THE COMMISSIONING PARENTS

Surrogacy can give rise to complicated issues, particularly in a same-sex context, regarding how best to legally safeguard the projected best interests of the child. This occurred, for example, in the 2007 Alberta case of *H. (D.W.) v. R. (D.J.)*,[31] when the court needed to examine the history of care relationships and determine issues of custody and access on the basis of whether the evidence demonstrated that a nonbiological parent had 'stood in the place of a parent.' Again, in the 2009 Ontario case of *C (M.A.) v. K. (M.)*,[32] when Cohen J denied an adoption application by a lesbian with respect to her partner's birth child. Finding that the sperm donor father had sustained a close and caring relationship with the six-year-old child since her birth and that the applicant had in place a written agreement addressing the parties' respective roles and rights, Cohen J ruled that the effect of an adoption order would be contrary to the child's best interests as it would undermine her 'sense of place in the world, her confidence in her experience of the world and her understanding of who her family is.'[33]

29 See, further, https://globalnews.ca/news/4641266/ontario-couple-return-daughter-to-nigerian-orphanage/.

30 See Hague Convention, Articles 23–25.

31 2007, ABCA 57 (Can. Alta. C.A.).

32 *M.A.C. v. M.K.*, 2009 ONCJ 18 (Can. Ont. Ct. J.). A full account of this case can be found in Bala, N. and Ashbourne, C., The Widening Concept of Parent in Canada, op cit, at pp 13–14.

33 Ibid, at para 64.

When a child is old enough to do so, they may wish to seek identifying information equivalent to that legally available to an adopted person. In *Pratten v. Attorney General (BC)*,[34] such a challenge to the right of sperm donor anonymity was unsuccessful. However, as Lori Chambers comments, 'While *Pratten* is still the leading decision in this area, access to DNA services is rendering the law unenforceable.'[35]

Abduction

As noted by L'Heureux-Dube J, in *R. v. Chartrand*,[36] 'each year, in Canada, hundreds of children are abducted by strangers from playgrounds, parks, school yards and streets,' though in fact, in 80% of abduction cases, the abductor is a parent.

The abduction of children is as problematic for Canadian courts as it is for those elsewhere.[37] It is a offence under s 281 of the Criminal Code (although not all unauthorised parental removals of children are necessarily criminal) and centres on the 'unlawful' taking of a child,[38] which may occur and remain within Canada. The offence also tends to give rise to issues governed by a province's Family Law legislation, though in such instances, the Hague Convention takes priority.[39] Most often, it involves taking a child outside the jurisdiction and usually falls to be settled under the terms of the Hague Convention on the Civil Aspects of Child Abduction, signed by Canada in 1983.

The Convention, Article 11, requires judicial authorities to 'act expeditiously in proceedings for the return of children,'[40] which, as the CBA comment with some justification, means that 'the best interests of individual children in Hague proceedings are often sacrificed to the collective good of deterring child abduction.'[41] That concern comes from the fact that although Article 11 was never intended to operate as a custody determinant, but rather is a preliminary order designed to restore the status quo within the family that existed before the wrongful removal or retention, in practical terms, the return of the child has tended to have that effect by identifying the abducting parent as culpable and the other as more responsible and law abiding. The trouble is that, quite often, a return to the status quo means a return to a family situation dominated by a violent male from whom the abducting parent had fled seeking safety for herself and her child. The role of violence is often a

34 2012 BCCA 480, reversing 2011 BCSC 656.

35 Note to author (21 April 2020).

36 [1994] 2 SCR 864.

37 The first national statistics on missing children were released in 1987, when more than 57,000 cases were reported. In 2019, there were 40,425 accounts of missing children. See, further, www.rcmp-grc.gc.ca/en/gazette/just-the-facts-missing-and-abducted-children.

38 *R. v. Chartrand*, op cit.

39 See, for example, *Hewstan v. Hewstan*, 2001 BCSC 368.

40 *R. v. Jordan*, 2016 SCC 27.

41 The Canadian Bar Association (Child and Youth Law Section), 'Alternative Report to the UN Committee on the Rights of the Child,' 2020, op cit, at p 28.

factor in such cases as is the right of a fearful parent in such a situation – placing appropriate priority on the child's welfare – to take their child to a place of safety.

RETURNING AN ABDUCTED CHILD

The SCC, in *Office of the Children's Lawyer v. Balev*,[42] departed from established Canadian caselaw which had interpreted the Hague term 'habitual residence' by focusing on parental intention. Instead, the court approached the issue of returning the child to their place of habitual residence by seeking to 'determine the focal point of the child's life . . . immediately prior to the removal or detention'[43] by looking at the 'entirety of the child's situation' with no one factor being determinative.[44] This approach, while conforming more with orthodox international Hague caselaw, diverges from that adopted in the U.S.

Proportionality In theory, the law relating to child abduction (ss 181–183 of the Criminal Code and Articles 3 and 5 of the Hague Convention) interprets the offence as one of strict liability, and the legislative intent is to ensure, as far as is practicable, a uniform application of the law. This should leave little scope for considerations of proportionality. In practice, this is largely the case, although, to some extent, this principle would appear to have been in play in the *Balev* case.

Child's wishes In *Balev*, when considering the child's objections to being returned, the court endorsed a 'straight-forward' assessment of the child's age, maturity and objections but then held that even if those elements were established, the application judge had discretion on whether to order the child returned, considering:

> the nature and strength of the child's objections, the extent to which they are 'authentically her own' or the product of the influence of the abducting parent, the extent to which they coincide or are at odds with other considerations which are relevant to her welfare, as well as the general Convention considerations.

As CBA commented, this approach was one that 'could undermine the due weight accorded to the objections of a child of sufficient age and maturity, a concern which has been borne out in subsequent decisions.'[45] It adds that 'objections to return expressed by children are often given less than due weight in the judicial exercise of

42 2018 SCC 16, at para 34.
43 Ibid at para 43.
44 Ibid, at paras 44 and 47.
45 The Canadian Bar Association (Child and Youth Law Section), 'Alternative Report to the UN Committee on the Rights of the Child,' 2020, op cit, at p 27 citing *Andegiorgis v. Giorgis*, 2018 ONCJ 965, at paras 65–68, 76; *Cormier v. Borsk*, 2019 ONCJ 889, at paras 42, 48, 50; *Children's Aid Society of Toronto v. P.B.*, 2019 ONCJ 683, at para 56(1).

discretion even when sufficient age and maturity are established, which minimizes children's effective participation.'[46]

The welfare principle in contemporary practice: public/private family law

Section 7 of the charter would seem to extend constitutional protection to the liberty of 'the person' – which could be interpreted as including family life – from any state intervention that does not derive from 'principles of fundamental justice,' and the SCC has ruled that the welfare principle cannot be so defined.[47] This may constrain application of the principle that the welfare interests of a child should be singled out as being a matter of paramount importance and justifying automatic state intervention in certain types of family matters, which, in turn, may restrict the range of hybrid public/private family law proceedings.

Public/private family law

As noted by McLachlin CJ, in *Gosselin*, it must be recognised that 'age-based distinctions are a common and necessary way of ordering our society.'[48] The distinction has long been evident in determining when a young person can marry, vote, drive, consent to sexual intercourse and sell property. While it remains critical to criminal proceedings, care and protection, and much of private family law, it is now becoming increasingly relevant to hybrid proceedings that transect the traditional public/private divide.

Public service matters

The national poverty threshold impacts child welfare: more socially disadvantaged families find it correspondingly more difficult to satisfy basic needs and have less time, energy and other resources to invest in child care. The significant levels of poverty in Canada, inadequately addressed by public service provision, are arguably causing corresponding levels of parental neglect, which, in turn, results in the responsibility for the care of many children being transferred from birth families to the state.

The first National Advisory Council on Poverty, released in 2020,[49] indicates that the level of poverty in some disadvantaged Canadian communities is indeed significant – more so among Indigenous people – and there is currently a need for

46 Ibid, at p 28, citing multiple sources in support of that view.

47 *Canadian Foundation for Children, Youth and the Law v. Canada (Attorney General)*, [2004] 1 SCR 76, 2004 SCC 4.

48 *Gosselin v. Quebec (Attorney General)*, op cit, at para 31.

49 See *Opportunity for All – Canada's First Poverty Reduction Strategy*, www.canada.ca/en/employment-social-development/programs/poverty-reduction/national-advisory-council/reports/2020-annual.html.

targeted state funding to improve the ability of public services to reduce its effects. It estimates that one in nine Canadians are living in poverty and identifies children as being among the groups worst affected. The U.N. Committee on the Rights of the Child has recently expressed its concern about the welfare of children in Canada, citing structural discrimination against Indigenous and Black children, 'especially with regard to their access to education, health and adequate standards of living.'[50] (See, further, Chapter 8.)

EMPLOYMENT

In Canada as in Ireland, industrialisation and manufacturing, with their attendant factory working conditions, came a good deal later than in the U.K. and the U.S. Canada, like Ireland, continued to be largely an agricultural society well into the 20th century, meaning that while children may well have been exploited when it came to seasonal planting, the harvesting of crops, caring for livestock, etc, they were largely spared the long, harsh, unhealthy and dangerous working conditions endured by their U.K. and U.S. counterparts.

Terms and conditions of employment are matters regulated at the provincial level, and, as with other such matters, each province does so differently. Only employment in public service–type industries – banks, railways, shipping, postal services, etc – is standardised and federally regulated. The federal Canada Labour Standards Regulations 2013, as amended and as largely replicated throughout the provinces, state that persons under 17 years of age may be employed provided that they are not required by provincial law to attend school, the work is not likely to endanger their health or safety, they are not required to work underground in a mine or in employment prohibited for young workers, and they are not required to work between 11 p.m. on one day and 6 a.m. on the following day. These rules protect the welfare interests of working children by defining the nature of work, the number of hours and when they can be worked (not during school or overnight), and the age boundaries for classifying young workers and by specifying the employer's supervision requirements.

HEALTH

In the 2020 publication of *World's Apart: Canadian Companion to UNICEF Report Card 16*,[51] it is noted that:

> [O]ver the past decade, Canada has fallen from 10th to 30th place among 38 affluent countries for childhood well-being. . . . [I]t ranks lowest in child

50 See, further, www.ohchr.org/en/press-releases/2022/06/un-child-rights-committee-issues-findings-cambodia-canada-chile-croatia-cuba.

51 Worlds Apart: Canadian Companion to UNICEF Report Card 16, *Worlds of influence: Understanding what shapes child well-being in rich countries*, (2020), at https://oneyouth.unicef.ca/sites/default/files/2020-09/UNICEF%20RC16%20Canadian%20Companion%20EN_Web.pdf.

> survival (including teen suicide and child mortality), health (including immunisation and unhealthy weight) and children's overall life satisfaction. . . . Canada is among a handful of rich countries with the best conditions for growing up, but the poorest outcomes for children.[52]

This has been a sustained trend. Compared with other wealthy nations, Canada has consistently performed poorly with regard to infant mortality rates;[53] in 2008, Canada was ranked 20th of 30 among Organisation for Economic Co-operation and Development (OECD) nations in child poverty rates.[54] Unquestionably, this statistical picture of the health and welfare of Canadian children is distorted by the particularly adverse circumstances of Indigenous children.

Overall, it would seem that these poor health indicators are largely the result of sustained low levels of public health service provision, which, in turn, reveal that it's the role played by the social determinants of health that can make all the difference to the prospects for Canadian children.

EDUCATION

In Canada, with its long history of state-funded denominational schooling,[55] the judiciary have had an equally lengthy experience of policing the boundaries between religious influence and the welfare interests of children.

For example, there have been a number of school prayer cases in which the mandatory recitation of Christian prayers was found to discriminate against non-Christian pupils. In *Zylberberg v. Sudbury Board of Education (Director)*[100] and *Russow v. BC (AG)*,[101] the judiciary established that the compulsory recitation of the Lord's Prayer – to the exclusion of prayers from any other religion – constitutes an impermissible infringement of religious freedom. School curriculum content has also been controversial. The SCC in *Chamberlain*[56] considered the refusal of the Surrey School Board to approve three controversial books depicting same-sex parented families, which had been promoted as supplementary learning resources as teaching aids in the family life education curriculum. The court found that 'children cannot learn unless they are exposed to views that differ from those they are taught at home' and held that board members, by refusing to permit the use of such books, were imposing their own religious values and seeking to deny children an important learning opportunity. In *SL v. Commission scolaire des Chênes*,[57] the

52 Ibid, at pp 2 and 4.

53 Wilkins R, Berthelot J-M, and Ng E. Trends in mortality by neighbourhood income in urban Canada from 1971 to 1996. *Health Reports (Stats Can)* 2002; 13(Suppl): 1–28.

54 Organisation for Economic Co-operation and Development, *Growing Unequal? Income Distribution and Poverty in OECD Countries,* Paris, (2008).

55 See, for example, *Adler v. Ontario*, [1996] SCR 609.

56 *Chamberlain v. Surrey School Board District 36*, (2002), 221 D.L.R. (4th) 156 (SCC), at para 19. Also see *Hall v. Powers*, 2002.

57 [2012] 1 SCR 235.

SCC dismissed the appeal of Catholic parents who requested exemption for their children from the mandatory Program on Ethics and Religious Freedom (ERC) course because its content was considered incompatible with their family beliefs and added that 'the early exposure of children to realities that differ from those in their immediate family environment is a fact of life in society.' These judicial views are interesting and would seem to rebut the ICCPR presumption – Canada being a signatory state – that the parental right should trump that of the state when it comes to religious teaching.[58] Instead, the judiciary seem to be asserting the interests of pupils to be educated about, and in accordance with, the values of their multicultural society. That this approach does not extend to licensing one religion to use education to proselytise was evident in *Erazo v. Dufferin-Peel Catholic District School Board.*[59] The court then held that non-Catholic children could be exempted from retreats and Catholic mass in a state-funded Catholic school as 'no Catholic school system that is required by law to admit non-Catholic students should have the right to require such participation from their students.'[60]

State-funded denominational schooling has also given rise to expressions of concern from the U.N. Human Rights Committee. In 1999, the committee condemned Canada – particularly Ontario – for exclusively funding Catholic schools in violation of Article 26 of the ICCPR, and it did so again in 2005 when it published its concluding observations regarding Canada's fifth periodic report and observed that Canada had failed to 'adopt steps in order to eliminate discrimination on the basis of religion in the funding of schools in Ontario.' In July 2015, the committee repeated its concern regarding the persistence of religiously discriminating grounds for funding and accessing public schools.[61]

The committee also had concerns regarding children's participative rights in schools. For example, in its concluding observations in 2012, the committee called on Canada to ensure that children have the right to participate in meaningful ways in their schools, families and communities.[62] It further recommended that the views of children be ascertained for all state decision-making relating to their welfare interests, including custody, child welfare, criminal justice, immigration and the environment; that Canada create complaints mechanisms for children in case their right to be heard is violated with regard to judicial and administrative proceedings; and that children have access to an appeals procedure.

It might also be noted that in May 2022, the Permanent Representative of Canada to the United Nations Office at Geneva, advised the U.N. CRC that Canada

58 ICCPR, Article 2 of Protocol 1.

59 2014 ONSC 2072. See also *Sorgini v. Simcoe Muskoka Catholic District School Board*, 2017 HRTO 471.

60 *Erazo*, op cit, at para 27.

61 See U.N. International Covenant on Civil and Political Rights, 'Concluding Observations on the Sixth Periodic Report of Canada,' http://tbinternet.ohchr.org/_layouts/treaty bodyexternal/SessionDetails1.aspx?SessionID=899&Lang=en#sthash.XzzyC1Bz.dpuf.

62 Committee on the Rights of the Child, Concluding Observations on the Combined Third and Fourth Periodic Report of Canada, adopted by the Committee at its 61st session (17 September–5 October 2012), CRC/C/CAN/CO/3-4, at paras 36–37.

had taken concrete actions to improve the lives of children and to further advance children's rights. These included such preventative measures as the establishment of an early-learning and child-care framework across Canada and investments in education and other services for Indigenous children.

Legal proceedings

The traditional public/private boundaries of family law are becoming as fudged in Canada as elsewhere in the developed nations with much the same set of proceedings belonging wholly to neither camp but having attributes of both.

ADOPTION FROM PUBLIC CARE

Nonconsensual adoptions place a priority on preserving the psychological bonds between child and foster parent where a proposed return to birth parents can be shown to present risks for the welfare interests of the child. This is particularly evident when the judiciary are faced with choosing between securing a better future for the child and respecting the rights of abusing or neglectful parents. One such case was *Children's Aid Society of Toronto v. EU*,[63] in which the central issue was whether or not the court should make an access order in favour of the parents of a child in care who had been made a ward and who the society planned should be adopted by her caregivers (friends of the parents). The court found that granting the application would obstruct a planned adoption application from the foster parents. However, the latter – out of respect for the child's wishes – chose to make a contact agreement, and the adoption went ahead.

The policy of adoption from state care has the support of the Adoption Council of Canada, which recommends that adoption and other permanency options be considered for children in care and advocates the use of subsidised adoption for those with complex health and/or social needs. However, the 2014 Canadian Foster Care Adoption Attitudes Survey drew attention to a serious obstacle to adoption from state care in Canada.[64]

There is no Canada-wide system that tracks the number of children who are waiting to be adopted from foster care. Data is available province by province but is not systematically collected or ranked for the country as a whole.

It should, perhaps, be added that this problem is often replicated within provinces, territories and in the First Nations with seemingly little coordination of policy, data and professional resources within those jurisdictions, let alone between them.

Post-adoption support Varying levels of state support are available post-adoption. Indeed, in some states, such as Alberta, all families who adopt a child from public

63 2014 ONCJ 299 (CanLII).
64 Ibid, at p 36.

care receive a monthly subsidy, regardless of the child's needs. While British Columbia, for example, has a post-adoption assistance programme that provides financial support restricted to those children placed by a statutory agency who are designated as having special needs.

WARDSHIP

As La Forest J pointed out in *B. (R.)*, 'the common law has long recognized the power of the state to intervene to protect children whose lives are in jeopardy and to promote their well-being, basing such intervention on its *parens patriae* jurisdiction.'[65] In Canada, the status of 'Crown ward' signifies and institutionalises the singular importance attached to wardship in the context of public child welfare matters.

Urgency or a lacuna in the relevant legislative framework provides the most usual justification for initiating wardship proceedings. For example, in *Beson v. Director of Child Welfare (NFLD)*,[66] the SCC found that the *parens patriae* jurisdiction of wardship could have been exercised to fill a legislative gap, and this would have allowed the paramountcy principle to determine subsequent decision-making in relation to a four-year-old boy peremptorily removed from his probationary adoption placement.[67] The urgency prompting recourse to wardship, often arising in a context where the consent required for treatment is being withheld due to religious convictions, does not always result in the child being made a ward. As mentioned earlier, wardship applications were refused in *Re L.D.K.*[68] with respect to a 12-year-old girl suffering from acute myeloid leukaemia because 'the emotional trauma [the child] would experience' in forced treatment would outweigh the anticipated benefits as:

> this child's life is equally in danger whichever path is taken, whether she is left here [in hospital] and subjected to this treatment or she is allowed to leave and be treated according to the wishes and beliefs of herself and her parents.[69]

Similarly, in *Re A.Y.*,[70] the Newfoundland Supreme Court found that an application with respect to a 15-year-old boy suffering from terminal cancer and refusing a transfusion on religious grounds was unnecessary as he was not 'a child in need of protection' because the blood transfusion was not considered essential. Indeed,

65 *B. (R.) v. Children's Aid Society of Metropolitan Toronto*, 1995 CanLII 115 (SCC), [1995] 1 SCR 315, at para 88, citing, for example, *Hepton et al. v. Maat et al.*, [1957] SCR 606 and *E. (Mrs.) v. Eve*, [1986] 2 SCR 388.

66 [1982] 2 SCR 716.

67 Citing *A. v. Liverpool City Council and another*, [1981] 2 All E.R. 385.

68 (1985), 48 R.F.L. (2d) 164 (Ont. Prov. Ct. (Fam. Div.).

69 Ibid, at pp 169–170.

70 (1993), 111 Nfld. & P.E.I.R. 91.

in the aforementioned *B. (R.)* case, the SCC found wardship to be unnecessary as the provisions of the Ontario child welfare statute were sufficient to allow the court to order that a blood transfusion be given to a baby against the parent's religious convictions because 'a parent's freedom of religion does not include the imposition upon the child of religious practices which threaten the safety, health or life of the child.'[71] However, in *H. (T.) v. Children's Aid Society of Metropolitan Toronto*,[72] a 13-year-old girl with aplastic anaemia and her mother, both Jehovah's Witnesses, refused to consent to any treatment involving blood products. The two treating physicians, as well as a child psychiatrist, testified that the girl lacked the maturity to judge the foreseeable consequences of her decision. She was found not 'capable of expression of refusal of consent,' was made a temporary ward of the state because of the urgent circumstances, and the paramountcy principle of wardship was then applied to authorise the required treatment.[73]

Most often, the rationale in *B. (R.)* prevails, and wardship applications do not succeed because, as McLachlin CJ noted in *Manitoba*, the statutory provision 'ousts the common law regarding mature minors'[74] and blocks the possibility of recourse to wardship. He was then certain that the Child and Family Services Act provided 'a complete statutory scheme' which 'displaces the existing common law regarding medical decision-making by "mature minors."'[75] Although, as she went on to explain, in order to 'resolve the dilemma between adolescent autonomy and the state's interest in ensuring child welfare, the CFSA allows courts to authorize necessary treatment under certain conditions' by utilising the wardship jurisdiction.

COMMERCIAL SURROGACY

The Assisted Human Reproduction Act 2004 in effect prohibits and criminalises commercial surrogacy in Canada: a surrogate mother may only be reimbursed for surrogacy/pregnancy-related expenses. This does not, of course, prevent Canadians from entering into commercial surrogacy arrangements elsewhere, and in increasing numbers, they are doing so. Nor has it stopped many non-Canadians from availing themselves of the services provided by surrogacy clinics in Canada: indeed, this country is often the preferred destination for those engaging in international surrogacy tourism, due to the standards of clinical health care and related costs; the commissioning 'parent(s)' then make arrangements for payment to be lodged outside the jurisdiction. Both avenues make commercial surrogacy a hybrid private/public family law proceeding in Canada.

For Canadians utilising overseas commercial surrogacy services, the Uniform Child Status Act 2010 is significant as, where there is no genetic link between the

71 *B. (R.)* op cit, at para 225.

72 (1996), 138 D.L.R. (4th) 144 (Ont. Ct. (Gen. Div.).

73 See, further, Sneiderman, B., Irvine, J.C. and Osborne, P.H., *Canadian Medical Law*, chapter 20, The Mature Minor Patient and the Refusal of Treatment, (2003), at p 465.

74 *A.C. v. Manitoba (Director of Child and Family Services)*, (2009), op cit, at para 126.

75 Ibid, at para 123.

commissioning parents and the child or where no adoption order has been granted to them in the child's country of origin, it may obstruct the child's entry into Canada, which, clearly, would seriously compromise his or her welfare interests.[76]

Court orders

Only a very limited range of statutory orders available to the Canadian judiciary have a cross-public/private family law application.

PERMANENT LEGAL GUARDIANSHIP

The welfare of children found by the court to have been abused or neglected by parents has, for the past century and more, been transferred to the Children's Aid Society by means of legal guardianship orders.

RESTRAINING ORDER

Under s 44 of the Child Protection Act, the court may issue a restraining order preventing a named person from having contact or communication with a particular child or mandating that such contact be subject to conditions.

Conclusion

In June 2022, the U.N. Committee on the Rights of the Child released a report expressing serious concerns about the welfare of children in Canada, particularly those who are Indigenous.[77] This is important because of the evidence, alluded to earlier, that poverty, combined with low levels of public service provision, which anyway are often not very accessible in remote areas, can tip the balance, making a vulnerable family unit into a noncoping one, prone to experiencing parental neglect and perhaps leading to family breakdown. As the statistics convincingly illustrate, poverty-related parental incapacity has an inordinate impact on Indigenous communities, resulting in their children being overrepresented in the child welfare and juvenile justice systems, as well as in custody, guardianship and adoption proceedings. When that occurs, issues regarding the preservation of a child's cultural identity can become a primary legal component of their welfare interests.

Although determining what constitutes those welfare interests and the weight given to them in general varies considerably, it has to be noted that the Divorce Act 1985, as amended in 2019 with effect from 2021, now offers an appropriate federal model for provinces and territories to apply when making such a determination. That legislation makes the 'best interests' test (s 16(1)) mandatory, and

76 See, further, www.cic.gc.ca/English/resources/manuals/bulletins/2012/ob381.asp.

77 See, further, www.ohchr.org/en/press-releases/2022/06/un-child-rights-committee-issues-findings-cambodia-canada-chile-croatia-cuba.

when interpreting it with respect to a child's particular circumstances, it requires the court to be guided by a welfare checklist list of 11 specific factors (s 16(3)), including the child's views, and to give priority to the child's physical, emotional and psychological safety, security and well-being (s 16(2)). This template, if adjusted to include and define the circumstances in which the paramountcy principle would have a role, might provide an appropriate template with more general applicability.

Part IV

The Indigenous children of North America

8 The Indigenous children of North America

Introduction

The following working definition of 'Indigenous communities, peoples and nations' has been suggested by Martinez Cobo:[1]

> Indigenous communities, peoples and nations are those which having a historical continuity with pre-invasion and pre-colonial societies that developed on their territories, consider themselves distinct from other sectors of the societies now prevailing on those territories, or parts of them. They form at present non-dominant sectors of society and are determined to preserve, develop and transmit to future generations their ancestral territories, and their ethnic identity as the basis of their continued existence as peoples, in accordance with their own cultural patterns, social institutions and legal system.

Some modern Western nations include within their borders such distinct Indigenous communities, each established over many centuries and sustained in accordance with traditional customs that have survived relatively intact into the 21st century. This is the case, for example, with Indigenous people in Canada and the U.S. These distinct cultural communities are, to varying degrees, coherent entities founded on rules, traditions, and beliefs governing relations within and between families and applying to the functioning of their social system as a whole. They differ from their Westernised hosts in many ways, not least in the respective sets of laws and customs that govern the family. In particular, the welfare of children, which offers a revealing insight into the life of any culture, indicates the nature of differences in the value systems that now separate modern Western society from its Indigenous counterpart.

This chapter examines the distinctive characteristics of the law relating to children in the Indigenous communities of Canada and the U.S. Its purpose is to identify the differences between the functions of Indigenous and non-Indigenous legal systems and to consider their significance for the welfare/rights of children in terms

1 Cobo, M., Study of the Problem of Discrimination Against Indigenous Populations, UN Doc. E/CN.4/Sub.2/1986/7, at paras. 379–82.

DOI: 10.4324/9781003269564-13

of law, policy and practice. As both systems now operate within the larger frame of reference provided by an ever-growing body of international law, the chapter begins by outlining and considering the bearing of such law on the culture, family life and welfare of the child in Indigenous communities. It then proceeds by examining, in turn, the contemporary role of the welfare principle in the law relating to children in the First Nations/Inuit of Canada and then in relation to the American Indians and Alaskan Native (AI/AN) of the U.S.

Indigenous people and international law

The law relating to Indigenous children not only operates in tandem with national statutory laws but also falls to be measured, and increasingly so, against the provisions of international law. The First Nations and the American Indians, the subjects of this chapter, are Indigenous citizens of Canada and the U.S., respectively. For them, as for their counterparts in other nations, the U.N. Declaration on the Rights of Indigenous Peoples (UNDRIP) and the U.N. Convention on the Rights of the Child (U.N. CROC) form the main axis of internationally recognised protective rights for the welfare/rights of their children, but other international laws are also relevant, as are bodies such as the Inter-American Court of Human Rights (IACtHR), which, since 2001, has expanded the range of rights to include the spiritual and cultural relationship of Indigenous Peoples to their traditional lands.

Need for international protection

The vulnerability of Indigenous communities has long been evident. Exposed initially to the predatory activities of colonial entrepreneurs taking their lands for forestry, mining and farming – which continues[2] – and then to the progressive attrition caused by the incidental impact of disease, lifestyle and lack of socio-economic opportunities, they have become endangered in all their traditional homelands. Their customs and way of life, their cultural heritage, their language and the space occupied by their ancestors for millennia have, over the past few generations, been rapidly shrinking. This is broadly apparent all along the interface between Indigenous and non-Indigenous communities but is perhaps most starkly evident in family matters.

International protection: generic provisions

The provisions of U.N. Conventions and the principles forged through human rights jurisprudence apply, at least in theory, not just to the more affluent in modern developed nations but equally to their fellow citizens in Indigenous communities who live alongside them, often in third-world conditions. One such U.N. initiative

2 See, for example, Tull, D.L., China's Engagement in Africa: Scope, Significance and Consequences, in *Journal of Modern African Studies*, 44(3), Cambridge University Press, Cambridge, 2006, at pp 459–479.

was the Children's Rights and Business Principles: Good Practices per Principle (U.N. Global Compact, 2012–15), which provides a set of principles to guide companies on the full range of actions they can take in the workplace, marketplace and community to respect and support children's rights.

In addition, an overlay of Indigenous-specific provisions which seek to identify and address their particular agenda of needs is being gradually superimposed in recognition of the inherent vulnerabilities common to such communities.

THE INTERNATIONAL LABOUR ORGANISATION'S CONVENTION (ILO)

This convention focuses on the global issue of labour exploitation. In that context, its introduction of the Worst Forms of Child Labour Convention (No. 182) has implications for the welfare of children in general, including Indigenous children, as does the ILO Convention 138 on the Minimum Age for Admission to Employment, which aims to ensure that children do not leave school to start working too young by setting the age at which children can be employed or work.

THE HAGUE CONVENTION ON PROTECTION OF CHILDREN AND COOPERATION IN RESPECT OF INTERCOUNTRY ADOPTION 1993

The Hague Convention, which entered into force on 1 May 1995, has now been ratified by some 101 contracting states, including the U.S. and Canada.[3] Its preamble declares that 'each State should take, as a matter of priority, appropriate measures to enable the child to remain in the care of his or her family of origin.'

THE INTERNATIONAL COVENANT ON CIVIL AND POLITICAL RIGHTS (ICCPR) 1966

This multilateral treaty was adopted by the United Nations General Assembly on 16 December 1966 and came into force on 23 March 1976. It commits its parties to respect the civil and political rights of individuals, including children: Articles 1, 24, 26 and 27 are particularly relevant. As of 2018, the Covenant had been ratified by 172 countries; the U.S. and Canada[4] are both parties. It now includes first and second optional protocols.

THE U.N. CONVENTION ON THE RIGHTS OF THE CHILD (U.N. CROC) 1989

This Convention, which acquired the force of law on 2 September 1990, has now been ratified by 194 countries, including Canada. Its preamble refers to 'the importance of the traditions and cultural values of each people for the protection and harmonious development of the child.'[5] The following articles are particularly relevant:

3 Australia signed and ratified on 25 September 1998. Canada signed on 12 April 1994 and ratified on 19 December 1996. New Zealand ratified on 18 October 1998.

4 Ratified 19 May 1976.

5 See also Articles 5, 20 (particularly 20.3), and 30.

Article 2 Nondiscrimination. Requires the state to take all appropriate measures to ensure that a child is protected against all forms of discrimination or punishment on the basis of the status, activities, expressed opinions or beliefs of the child's parents, legal guardians or family members. It provides for overlapping sources of discrimination.

Article 3 Best Interests of the Child. Requires the state in all actions concerning children, whether undertaken by public or private social welfare institutions, courts of law, administrative authorities or legislative bodies, to treat the best interests of the child as a primary consideration.

Article 4 Economic, Social, and Cultural Rights. Requires the state to provide for the cultural and collective rights of the individual Indigenous child.

Article 6 Life, Survival, and Development. Requires the state to ensure the survival and development of the child.

Article 7 Identity. Requires the state to ensure a child has the right to know and be cared for by their parents.

Article 12 Participation. Requires the state to ensure the right of a child to participate and express their views in all matters affecting the child.

Article 18 Upbringing by Parents. Requires the state to ensure the right of parents to have the primary responsibility for the upbringing and development of the child, to provide appropriate assistance to parents in the performance of their child-rearing responsibilities, and to ensure the best interests of the child will be their basic concern.

Article 20 Culturally Congruent Placements. Requires the state, when considering a foster or adoption placement, to have due regard to the desirability of continuity in a child's upbringing and to the child's ethnic, religious, cultural and linguistic background.

Article 21 Adoption. Requires the state to ensure that the best interests of the child shall be the paramount consideration in adoption.

Article 30 Minority Culture. Requires the state to ensure that a child who is Indigenous shall not be denied the right, in community with other members of their group, to enjoy their own culture, to profess and practise their own religion, and to use their own language.

THE INTERNATIONAL COVENANT ON ECONOMIC, SOCIAL AND CULTURAL RIGHTS (ICESCR) 1966

This multilateral treaty was adopted by the United Nations General Assembly on 16 December 1966 and came into force from 3 January 1976. It commits its parties to working towards the granting of economic, social and cultural rights to the non-self-governing and trust territories and individuals, including labour rights and the right to health, education and an adequate standard of living. Articles 2, 10, 14 and 15 are particularly relevant. As of 2018, 166 countries had ratified the Covenant, including Canada.[6]

THE INTERNATIONAL CONVENTION ON THE ELIMINATION OF ALL FORMS OF RACIAL DISCRIMINATION (ICERD) 1965

This United Nations Convention commits its members to the elimination of racial discrimination and the promotion of understanding among all races. It was adopted and opened for signature by the United Nations General Assembly on 21 December 1965 and entered into force on 4 January 1969. As of April 2018, it had 88 signatories and 182 parties. Articles 2 and 5 are particularly relevant. Its impact on national legislation can be seen in the implementation of legislation outlawing racial discrimination by the state, in the workplace, and in the provision of services such as housing and education, including the Canadian Bill of Rights 1960, followed by the Canadian Human Rights Act 1985.

Article 1 is of particular importance for present purposes. This defines 'racial discrimination' as follows:

> [A]ny distinction, exclusion, restriction or preference based on race, colour, descent, or national or ethnic origin which has the purpose or effect of nullifying or impairing the recognition, enjoyment or exercise, on an equal footing, of human rights and fundamental freedoms in the political, economic, social, cultural or any other field of public life.

This definition does not distinguish between discrimination based on ethnicity and race but specifically covers discrimination on the basis of caste and other forms of inherited status. Whether a particular action or policy discriminates is judged by its effects, as determined by whether that action has an unjustifiable disparate impact on a group distinguished by race, colour, descent or national or ethnic origin.

THE UNIVERSAL DECLARATION OF HUMAN RIGHTS (UDHR) 1948

This Declaration, as ratified by the General Assembly of the United Nations in 1948, together with its two Optional Protocols,[7] constitutes the International Bill of Human Rights. It attained the status of international law in 1976. The U.S. and Canada are among the countries to have ratified it, and both have subsequently introduced domestic human rights legislation.

6 Ratified 19 May 1976.

7 The International Covenant on Economic, Social and Cultural Rights and the International Covenant on Civil and Political Rights.

International provisions specific to Indigenous people

That there is a growing body of international provisions relating specifically to the needs of Indigenous people is largely due to work progressed under the auspices of the United Nations. Again, to date, there is little evidence of transformative action taken on these provisions.

THE U.N. PERMANENT FORUM ON INDIGENOUS ISSUES

This is an advisory body to the Economic and Social Council with a mandate to discuss Indigenous issues related to economic and social development, culture, the environment, education, health and human rights. It has its origins in the Working Group on Indigenous Populations, established by the Council in 1982 to develop a set of minimum standards that would protect Indigenous peoples.

In the First Decade of the World's Indigenous People (1995–2004), the Permanent Forum was established, together with the Special Rapporteur on the rights of Indigenous peoples. During the Second Decade of the World's Indigenous Peoples (2005–2015), the Expert Mechanism on the rights of Indigenous Peoples was created.

The adoption of the United Nations Declaration on the Rights of Indigenous Peoples by the General Assembly in 2007 marked a significant milestone in the relationship between the U.N. and the world's Indigenous peoples.[8]

THE UNITED NATIONS DECLARATION ON THE RIGHTS OF INDIGENOUS PEOPLES (UNDRIP)

On 13 September 2007, after some 25 years of negotiations, this Declaration was eventually adopted by the General Assembly. While 143 nations were able to endorse the declaration, only the four CANZUS nations – Australia, the U.S., New Zealand and Canada, the largest and most developed of those with an Indigenous population to protect – voted against it. The Declaration comprehensively addresses issues such as collective rights, cultural rights, and identity, in addition to rights to education, health, employment, land and language, among others. It emphasises the right of Indigenous people to maintain and strengthen their own institutions, cultures and traditions and to pursue their development in accordance with their aspirations and needs. Arguably, many of the rights asserted in the Declaration have attained the status of customary international law due to the emerging international consensus on the right of Indigenous peoples to their traditional

8 At the 11th session of the Working Group 2005–06, the chairperson, Mr Luis-Enrique Chavez (Peru), prepared a compilation of proposals submitted and discussed during the 10th session, which formed the basis of negotiation. The declaration, adopted by the U.N. Human Rights Council in June 2006, is the exact version proposed by Chairperson Chavez.

lands.[9] Provisions with particular relevance for family life and the rights/welfare of children include the following:

Article 7 Indigenous peoples have the collective right to live in freedom, peace, and security as distinct peoples and shall not be subjected to any act of genocide or any other act of violence, including forcibly removing children of the group to another group.

Article 8 Indigenous peoples and individuals have the right not to be subjected to forced assimilation or destruction of their culture.

Article 20 Indigenous peoples have the right to maintain and develop their political, economic and social systems or institutions; to be secure in the enjoyment of their own means of subsistence and development; and to engage freely in all their traditional and other economic activities.

Article 34 Indigenous peoples have the right to promote, develop and maintain their institutional structures and their distinctive customs, spirituality, traditions, procedures, practices, and, in cases where they exist, juridical systems or customs, in accordance with international human rights standards.

OTHER

Of note are the U.N. Guiding Principles on Internal Displacement 1998, which specify that 'states are under a particular obligation to protect against the displacement of Indigenous peoples, minorities, peasants, pastoralists and other groups with a special dependency on and attachment to their lands.' Also of relevance is the HRC's General Comment on Freedom of Movement, which refers to the 'close and enduring connections between a person and a country, connections which may be stronger than those of nationality.'[10] Again, the ILO Convention concerning Indigenous and Tribal Peoples in Independent Countries 1989 (No. 169) is significant.

International law and central principles

Although as yet without the force of law, this Declaration, together with the processes and participants that brought it to fruition, serves to prepare the ground for the next stage in a continuum that is leading, perhaps, towards an international agreement on the terms on which Indigenous and non-Indigenous people may cohabit with mutual respect for differences in cultural legacy, current laws and

9 See, *Mayagna (Sumo) Awas Tingni Community. v. Nicaragua*, Judgment, Inter-A. Ct. H.R. (ser. C) No. 79, para 140(d).

10 Human Rights Committee, General Comment 27, Art. 12, U.N. Doc. CCPR/C/21/Rev.1/Add.9 (1999).

aspirations. Even at this stage, however, certain principles have emerged to form a fulcrum on which to balance the respective rights of both sets of people.

SOVEREIGNTY

For all peoples everywhere, this principle has been pivotal: it is fundamental to the laws governing nation states, and it underpins international law. Aligning or realigning national borders so as to better fit the communities that have chosen to live there is an ongoing process everywhere – currently including the Ukrainians, the Kurds and the Palestinians – and can only be resolved when boundaries are recognised, verified and firmly established in law by the parties concerned.

The external exercise of determining national boundaries is mirrored internally by a similar process between Indigenous communities and the dominant non-Indigenous population. The principle of tribal sovereignty has been of central importance to the American Indians and to the Alaska Natives in their struggle and negotiations with state authorities. It has featured in many treaties. Their success in asserting this principle can be seen in the infrastructure of tribal governance with its own laws, courts, health, welfare and policing authorities, which are recognised and respected – to varying degrees – by their non-Indigenous counterparts.

So, for example, in *Worcester v. Georgia*,[11] Justice Marshall found that:

> Indian nations have always been recognised as 'distinct, independent, political communities' and are, as such, qualified to exercise powers of self-government, not by virtue of any delegation of powers from the Federal Government, but by reason of their original tribal sovereignty.[12]

The extent to which Indigenous people can truly be held to have been vested with sufficient authority to independently manage their own affairs is contentious. One area in which their autonomy has always been repeatedly contested is in the very basic matter of the upbringing of their children. If tribal laws have to give way to state law on such a matter, this must give rise to questions about the reality of tribal sovereignty. (See, further, Chapter 1.)

CULTURAL INTEGRITY

Distinguishing and maintaining a respectful differential between the cultures of Indigenous and non-Indigenous sectors of the national population have very largely failed throughout North America. Historically, the principle was treated with derision by the non-Indigenous and its erosion stoically accepted by those who had nurtured it and prized it as conferring a unique identity on each tribe for countless

11 31 U.S. 515.

12 Cited by Daes, E.-I., A., Indigenous Peoples Permanent Sovereignty Over Natural Resources, paper presented at the National Native Title Conference, Adelaide, (3 June 2004).

generations. The devastating consequences of early state intervention in tribal matters has left only remnants of what had once been an holistic, integrated way of life with a pronounced spiritual dimension. Now the emblematic significance of tribal cultural heritage has acquired political salience and is assured of respect by some, but, arguably, when it comes to issues affecting the welfare of a child, preserving the cultural integrity of the links between child and tribe is not always prioritised.

Canada

In the words of Justice Mactavish, '[N]o one can seriously dispute that Canada's First Nations people are amongst the most disadvantaged and marginalised members of our society.'[13] Any doubts on this matter were laid to rest by the findings of the Canadian Human Rights Tribunal's nine-year-long hearing on allegations that the federal government of Canada provided child welfare services to First Nations children and families on reserve that were flawed, inequitable and discriminatory. On 26 January 2016, the tribunal ruled in favour of the plaintiffs,[14] finding that First Nations children were being discriminated against: specifically, that the on-reserve child welfare system received up to 38% less funding than elsewhere. It concluded that the federal government's arbitrary funding formula failed to consider 'the actual service needs of First Nations children and families' and created 'incentives to remove children from their homes and communities,' and, consequently, 'too many children living in First Nations communities are being taken from their families and placed in care.'

Indigenous communities and the welfare of the child

In 1867, the confederation process initiated under the British North American Act made 'Indians and Lands reserved for Indians' a federal responsibility within the new Dominion of Canada. This process included treaties with the Indigenous peoples and resulted in amendments to the Indian Act which made all Indigenous children wards of the federal government. Their customary laws are nationally recognised and find constitutional protection under both the 1876 act and the Constitution Act 1982, s 35. Constitutional jurisdiction for Indigenous children in Canada generally rests with the federal government, but provincial jurisdiction frequently overlaps, and this creates uncertainty about which level of government has responsibility. Funding for Indigenous children varies depending on whether they live on or off reserve and whether or not they have tribal status under the Indian Act 1876.[15]

13 See *Canada (Human Rights Commission) v. Canada (Attorney General)*, 2012 FC 445, at para 334.

14 *First Nations Child and Family Caring Society of Canada et al. v. Attorney General of Canada (for the Minister of Indian and Northern Affairs Canada)*, 2016 CHRT 16.

15 An Act to amend and consolidate the laws respecting Indians, S.C. 1876, c 18, amended to make attendance compulsory.

Definitions

The last national census in 2016 estimated the Indigenous population as totalling 1,673,785 people, or 4.9% of all Canadians: 977,230 First Nations people; 587,545 Métis; and 65,025 Inuit. This disparate population of some 600 distinct self-governing entities or bands is mostly concentrated in the provinces of Ontario, British Columbia, Alberta and Manitoba, but Indigenous people can be found across Canada.

FIRST NATIONS

Children of the First Nations are those entitled to be registered as 'Indians' and are accorded that status under the Indian Act. They may live on or off reserves. Eligibility for status for children has evolved since the Indian Act was first amended in 1951 but has been plagued by imposed definitions of identity and, specifically, by gender discrimination.[16]

INUIT

The Inuit are the Indigenous people of Nunavut, a newly created territory of some two million square kilometres occupying almost one-fifth of the land mass of Canada with a population at the time of the census of a mere 38,780, of whom 84% were Inuit living in 28 villages. The Inuit are considered 'Indians' for the purpose of the Constitution Act, s 91(24).

MÉTIS

Métis children are defined for the purposes of s 35 of the charter according to self-identification, ancestral connection and community acceptance. Prior to the ruling in *Daniels*[17] (see, further, later in this chapter), the Métis and nonstatus Indians were not classified as 'Indians' under s 91(24) of the Constitution of Canada. Thereafter, a change in classification of the Métis people and nonstatus Indians allowed all Indigenous peoples to be defined as 'Indians' under the Constitution.

INDIGENOUS COURTS

This is a culturally appropriate dispute resolution forum that is inclusive, respectful and designed by Indigenous people. As there are many diverse Indigenous peoples in Canada, each Indigenous court reflects the local Indigenous culture and is therefore unique.[18] Indigenous courts form part of the provincial court system and are given equal weight, respect and enforcement powers as provincial courts. The

16 *McIvor v. Canada (Registrar of Indian and Northern Affairs)*, 2009 BCCA 153 and *Descheneaux v. Canada (Procureur General)*, 2015 QCCS 3555.

17 *Daniels v. Canada (Indian Affairs and Northern Development)*, [2016] S.C.R. 425 (Can.).

18 See, further, at http://scow-archive.libraries.coop/library/documents/Aboriginal_Courts_Fact_Sheet.pdf.

matters over which such a court has jurisdiction depend on the outcome of negotiations in each province, but usually, their jurisdiction will include family law.

Background

In keeping with the experience of Indigenous people elsewhere, the history of those in Canada also records abuse suffered at the hands of the non-Indigenous population.[19] Government policies of assimilation and integration were often strategically directed towards children. This has been well documented, including the intergenerational effects of removing children from their ancestral homes, families and communities that originated with the residential school experiences and continued with adoption and with the child protection laws that followed. (See, further, Chapter 1.)[20]

It has been rightly asserted that 'many experts in Canadian child welfare now point to the residential school period as the beginning of an intergenerational cycle of neglect and abuse.'[21] This was acknowledged in *Brown v. Canada (Attorney General)*[22] when, following eight years of proceedings initiated on behalf of survivors of the '60s scoop,' the court found in favour of the plaintiffs, determining that Canada had breached a common-law duty of care to take steps to prevent Indigenous children who were placed in the care of non-Indigenous foster or adoptive parents from losing their cultural identity. The effects of this abusive use of residential schools and adoption were not just felt by the children, families and communities impacted by the trauma at that time, but have been singled out as the root cause of the current overrepresentation of Indigenous children across all indices of social disadvantage because, as Wiegers puts it, they 'displaced traditional parenting practices and exposed children to cultural loss and high rates of abuse.'[23]

CHILD PROTECTION AND CULTURAL IDENTITY

State intervention into tribal affairs on child protection grounds in the latter half of the 20th century most often led to Indigenous children being placed outside their family and community due to the lack of approved Indigenous foster parents.

19 See, for example, the Royal Commission on Aboriginal Peoples, Looking Forward, Looking Back, Ottawa, 1996.

20 See Stolen Generations, a local Aboriginal nonprofit group, which in 2002 began a project dealing with the adoption process affecting Aboriginal people across Canada. The project was funded by the Aboriginal Healing Foundation and sponsored by the Ma Mawi WI Chi Itata Centre Inc.

21 See Saskatchewan Child Welfare Review Panel Report, For the Good of Our Children and Youth: A New Vision, a New Direction, at p 18. See, further, at http://saskchildwelfarereview.ca/CWR-panel-report.pdf. In 2008, the Canadian prime minister acknowledged and apologised for the injustice caused to children, their families and the Indian communities by Indian Residential Schools. See, further, at http://pm.gc.ca/eng/news/2008/06/11/prime-minister-harper-offers-full-apology-behalf-canadians-indian-residential.

22 2017 ONSC 251.

23 Wiegers, W., 'Child Placement and the Legal Claims of Foster Caregivers,' *University of British Columbia Law Review*, 2019, at https://www.thefreelibrary.com/CHILD+PLACEMENT+AND+THE+LEGAL+CLAIMS+OF+FOSTER+CAREGIVERS.-a0597913025.

While this practice perpetuated the corrosive dynamic established in the residential schooling and enforced adoption eras, it was, ironically, justified by the welfare of the child. (See, further, later in this chapter.)

Evolving policy, principles and law

As the Truth and Reconciliation Commission pointed out:[24]

> Child protection, education, health, criminal justice, cultural identity, family, economic and social conditions for Indigenous children are very different than they are for non-Indigenous children, and the practice of law across many of these areas calls for an understanding of these issues.

Policy

Between 1991 and 2019, four separate commissions of inquiry addressed, from a number of different perspectives, the legacy of the treatment of Indigenous peoples: the Royal Commission on Aboriginal Peoples, the Truth and Reconciliation Commission of Canada ('Truth and Reconciliation Commission'), the Public Inquiry Commission on Relations between Indigenous Peoples and Certain Public Services in Québec: Listening, Reconciliation and Progress ('Viens Commission') and the National Inquiry into Missing and Murdered Indigenous Women and Girls.[25] The Royal Commission, which submitted its report in 1996, indicated that the central theme of its recommendations was that Indigenous peoples must have room to exercise their autonomy and structure their own solutions. This would clearly have implications for that area of family and community life which had suffered most from traumatic state intervention – the care and protection of their children.

In its 2015 report, the Truth and Reconciliation Commission set out a series of measures for reducing the overrepresentation of Indigenous children in child welfare systems. The Viens Commission concluded in 2019 that systemic discrimination existed against First Nations, and a youth protection system that placed Indigenous children with non-Indigenous foster families was inappropriate. That same year, the National Inquiry into Missing and Murdered Indigenous Women and Girls made several recommendations also aimed at placing the design and implementation of culturally appropriate child and family services in the hands of Indigenous peoples as part of the exercise of their right to self-determination.

24 See Truth and Reconciliation Commission of Canada, 2015, Recommendation 27, at https://web.archive.org/web/20200513112354/https://trc.ca/index-main.html.

25 In September 2016, in response to the 2015 report by the Inter-American Commission on Human Rights into the murders and disappearances of Indigenous women and girls, the Canadian government launched a two-year national inquiry, which issued its report *Reclaiming Power and Place* in 2019.

Principles

While the Indian Act and the charter sought to establish certain Indigenous-specific principles, it was really not until the publication of this series of government-funded enquiries, accompanied by international pressure for government initiatives to address the findings, that momentum gathered for new legislation. The resulting Act Respecting First Nations, Inuit and Métis Children, Youth and Families 2020 has established a principled platform from which structural changes may be launched, giving the Indigenous communities more autonomy in the management of their affairs, perhaps especially as regards services and legal proceedings relating to the welfare of their children. In the meantime, family law principles in general are applied through statute law, which makes little allowance for Indigenous children, though the principle of consanguinity will have greater salience in an Indigenous context. (See, further, Chapter 3.)

Jordan's Principle

Essentially, this principle was formulated to eliminate service inequities and delays in provision for First Nations children. It established a procedure to bridge the jurisdictional gap between federal and provincial governments regarding the payment of services for Indigenous children.[26] Approved by parliament in 2007 and subsequently judicially recognised,[27] it is a child-first principle for resolving jurisdictional disputes within and between federal and provincial/territorial governments. It holds that when a First Nations child requires services that are available to all other children, the government of first contact must pay for and provide that service and then seek reimbursement from another government, if appropriate. The legislative intent is to ensure that jurisdictional disputes between levels of government do not prevent First Nations children from promptly getting the services to which they are entitled. However, as CBA argue, 'Canada has ineffectively and narrowly implemented the principle and denied children services in violation of the best interests of the child.'[28] In *Pictou Landing*, the federal court stated: 'Jordan's principle is not to be narrowly interpreted.'[29] It was government failure to interpret and apply Jordan's principle to mitigate service inequities for Indigenous children that ultimately led to federal legislation in 2019 and 2021, though this did not deter the CBA from recommending in 2020 that 'Canada should comply with Jordan's principle to ensure Indigenous

26 See, further, the Jordan's Principle Working Group, Without denial, delay, or disruption: Ensuring First Nation children's access to equitable services through Jordan's principle, (2015), at https://www.afn.ca/uploads/files/jordans_principle-report.pdf.

27 *First Nations Child and Family Caring Society of Canada and the Assembly of First Nations v. Attorney General of Canada*, 2016 CHRT 2.

28 The Canadian Bar Association (Child and Youth Law section) 'Alternative Report to the U.N. Committee on the Rights of the Child,' 2020, op cit, at p 23.

29 *Pictou Landing Band Council & Maurina Beadle v. Attorney General of Canada*, 2013 FC 342, at para 83.

children's access to necessary services is not delayed due to jurisdictional disputes,'[30] nor did it stop the U.N. CRC, in its May 2022 report, from raising questions regarding the application of the principle to support services for First Nations children.[31]

Equity of service provision

The aforementioned decision in *Daniels*[32] was a landmark ruling that established a state duty to rebalance provision for Indigenous children. It began in 2007 when the First Nations Child and Family Caring Society of Canada and the AFN filed a human rights complaint charging the Canadian government with 'systematically providing less funding for child welfare services to on-reserve First Nations children than is provided for children who are off-reserve.' Finally, in 2012, the court for judicial review ruled that 'failure to ensure comparable funding for on- and off-reserve services can be considered racial or ethnic discrimination,' which ended a lengthy appeals process.

In 2019, as a consequence of the *Daniels* decision and the accompanying media-generated public concern, Bill C-92 – An Act Respecting First Nations, Inuit and Métis Children, Youth and Families – became law, with effect from January 2020. This legislation was developed by governments at the federal and provincial levels working in conjunction with Indigenous groups to design strategies that would enable Indigenous children and youth to maintain their connections with their families, communities and culture. It shifted the focus of child and family services to preventing the removal of children from their families and communities.[33]

Bill C-92 recognises the right of Indigenous people to self-governance of their child welfare systems, with resources provided by the federal government. This, however, is subject to the proviso that Indigenous groups first enter into 'coordination agreements' with the government of the province in which they are located. The legislation also embeds a significant caveat: s 23 states that the best interests of the child override any Indigenous law. There are concerns that this clause may be judicially deployed to, in effect, continue the policy the bill was intended to redress: that it will justify placements of Indigenous children in need of care and protection with non-Indigenous foster carers, thereby paving the way for their adoption. In substance and legislative intent, Bill C-92 is somewhat similar to the U.S. Indian Child Welfare Act 1978.

Respect for cultural identity

Politically and judicially, this has become a moral imperative to be recognised and taken fully into account whenever issues arise regarding the care, protection and custody of Indigenous children. (See, further, later in this chapter.)

30 See, further, at https://www.cba.org/CMSPages/GetFile.aspx?guid=fdb96dc7-35e0-4b6d-8918-40ba6607582a.

31 See, further, at https://www.ohchr.org/en/press-releases/2022/06/un-child-rights-committee-issues-findings-cambodia-canada-chile-croatia-cuba.

32 *Daniels v. Canada (Indian Affairs and Northern Development)*, op cit.

33 See, further, Minsky, C., Recent Changes to Indigenous Child Welfare in Canada, *Children's Legal Rights Journal*, (2021): 41(1), 79–83 at https://lawecommons.luc.edu/clrj/vol41/iss1/10.

Law

The relevant domestic law, dating from the Royal Proclamation 1763, which established a baseline of colonial respect for the First Nations, consists of the federal constitutional and statutory framework, the Indigenous-specific statutes and Indigenous treaties and traditional laws, together with the laws of provinces and territories. All must be read and applied in conjunction with the international law as outlined previously.

Domestic legal framework

In the main, the body of contemporary domestic law relating to Indigenous communities and the welfare of their children is the same as for the non-Indigenous. (See, further, Chapter 5.) It does, however, provide some intersecting and special protections for Indigenous children in all Canadian provinces and territories.

THE CONSTITUTION

The Constitution Act 1982, s 91(24), gives the federal government 'exclusive Legislative Authority' over 'Indians and the Lands reserved for the Indians' on and outside reserves. In practice, this jurisdiction is not absolute, and certain subjects overlap with provincial jurisdiction, creating uncertainty about which level of government has jurisdiction over Indigenous children (e.g. federal government generally pays for services for those residing on reserve while provinces pay for services off reserve, but disputes arise in relation to the latter). The Jordan principle was formulated to address this issue.

Provincial legislation, such as child protection statutes, requires Aboriginal culture, identity and heritage to be considered as part of the best interests of the child test.

CANADIAN CHARTER OF RIGHTS AND FREEDOMS 1982

Section 7 This states that 'everyone has the right to life, liberty and security of the person and the right not to be deprived thereof except in accordance with the principles of fundamental justice.'

Section 25 This guarantees that certain Charter rights and freedoms shall not be construed so as to abrogate or derogate from any Indigenous, treaty, or other rights or freedoms that pertain to the Indigenous peoples of Canada including:

(a) any rights or freedoms that have been recognized by the Royal Proclamation of 7 October 1763; and
(b) any rights or freedoms that now exist by way of land claims agreements or may be so acquired.

Section 35 This declares, 'The existing aboriginal and treaty rights of the aboriginal peoples of Canada are hereby recognized and affirmed.'

'Indigenous' refers to First Nations people, Métis and the Inuit. An Indigenous right is a practice, custom, or tradition integral to the distinctive culture of the Indigenous group claiming the right which has continuity with their traditional practices, customs and traditions.

THE INDIAN ACT 1985

This statute applies to First Nations children living on reserves in Canada and authorises the federal government to regulate and administer the day-to-day lives of registered Indians and reserve communities in matters that include governance, land use, health care and education. It was used to authorise the attendance of First Nation children at residential schools and to prohibit the practice of Indigenous ceremonies and rituals. It functions in conjunction with some local agreements, such as the Inuvialuit Final Agreement and the Yukon First Nation Final Agreements. Among its many amendments was Bill C-31 which sought to eliminate discriminatory provisions and ensure compliance with the Charter.

AN ACT RESPECTING FIRST NATIONS, INUIT AND MÉTIS CHILDREN, YOUTH AND FAMILIES 2020[34]

This formative piece of legislation, which gives effect to the provisions of Bill C-92, became law in January 2020. It affirms the rights of First Nations, Inuit and Métis to exercise jurisdiction over child and family services, establishes national principles such as the best interests of the child, cultural continuity and substantive equality; contributes to the implementation of the United Nations Declaration on the Rights of Indigenous Peoples; and provides an opportunity for Indigenous people to choose their own solutions for their children and families. It was followed in July 2020 by the signing of a protocol to establish a new structure to support discussions on the implementation of that Act by the Assembly of First Nations and the government of Canada.

This new legislation is intended to address the overrepresentation of Indigenous children in the child welfare system and maintain the connections between such children and their families, communities and cultural identity. It does so by creating national standards for child and family services for Indigenous people that provide better protection for those connections than has been available through provincial laws, and it establishes a process for recognition and implementation of Indigenous jurisdiction over child and family services. This is authorised by recognising Indigenous peoples' inherent right of self-government over the care of their children and providing for a process of negotiation with Crown governments to coordinate Indigenous, federal and provincial laws on child and family services.

In April 2022, the Act was referred to the Supreme Court of Canada to determine whether all its provisions were constitutionally compliant: specifically, whether

34 Bill C-92.

provisions giving Indigenous peoples the right to self-government and jurisdiction over child and family services granted Indigenous laws the force of federal law and made them paramount over provincial laws.

The legal system and Indigenous children

As the Department of Justice recently declared 'supporting culturally appropriate, Indigenous-led and community-based justice services is key to making the systemic change Canadians know is necessary.'[35] For this to happen, however, considerable changes need to be made to the Youth Criminal Justice Act 2003. The legislative intent underpinning the Act respecting First Nations, Inuit and Métis Children, Youth and Families 2020 is to address the overrepresentation of Indigenous children and youth in the child welfare system and keep children connected to their families, communities, and culture/national identity. Pending the SCC determination of the act's constitutionality, the legal system will continue to make little differentiation between Indigenous and non-Indigenous children in trouble with the law. (See, further, Chapter 5.)

CONSENT: CAPACITY TO MAKE OR CONTRIBUTE TO DECISIONS

The SCC has rejected age-based restrictions on children's competence – whether Indigenous or otherwise – in favour of every child's 'right to demon-strate mature medical decisional capacity' and to have a voice in medical decisions.[36] The court then strongly expressed the view that:

> [W]e should be reluctant to force [minors] to bow to the will of adults . . . who may . . . know little better than the minor, or who have their own interests . . . at heart, or who may be vindicating their own values.

This approach was, to some extent, followed in *Hamilton Health Sciences Corp. v. D.H.*,[37] which concerned an 11-year-old Indigenous girl who withdrew her consent for the proposed continuation of her chemotherapy and instead wished to avail herself of traditional medicines. Her choice of treatment options was challenged by the hospital administrator on the basis that she was not capable of making an

35 See Addressing the overrepresentation of Indigenous peoples in the criminal justice system in British Columbia, (25 May 2022), at https://www.canada.ca/en/department-justice/news/2022/05/addressing-the-overrepresentation-of-indigenous-peoples-in-the-criminal-justice-system-in-british-columbia.html.

36 See, *A.C. v. Manitoba*, [2009] 2 S.C.R. 181, 184 (Can.) (interpreting a statutory age limit as establishing a presumption of incompetence, given children's right to have their views be given due weight); see also Aria Laskin et al., Beyond Autonomy? A Transnational Comparison of End-of-Life Decision Making by Mature Minors, 18 Mich. St. U. J. Med. & L. 139, 141, 143–44 (2014) (noting Canadian law recognises a child's right to be involved in decisions regarding their own end-of-life care).

37 2014 ONCJ 603; 2015 ONCJ 229.

informed decision and was in need of protection. The court's agreement that the child lacked capacity was itself unsurprising, given her age and the gravity of the decision, but interestingly, it found that the mother's right, as substitute decision-maker, to choose traditional medicine was constitutionally protected by s 35 of the charter, and the child was not in need of protection in the exercise of this right. In effect, the court accepted the child's decision by proxy. In an addendum, the court indicated that 'recognition and implementation of the right to use traditional medicines must remain consistent with the principle that the best interests of the child remain paramount.'

The welfare principle in contemporary practice: public family law, civil jurisdiction

Some provinces have enacted legislation and established policies for Indigenous child welfare agencies to provide services for families on reserves under provincial law (e.g. Ontario: Child and Family Services Act 1984). They depend on federal funding which, following the introduction of the 2020 legislation, will be more generally available for such purposes and may transform service provision for Indigenous children.

State intervention: consensual

Unquestionably, consensual state intervention in Indigenous family affairs may be viewed at best as unsuccessful. Arguably, given the findings made by the National Inquiry into Missing and Murdered Indigenous Women and Girls,[38] state dereliction of its duty of care to Indigenous communities has been on such a scale and for such duration as to approach criminal negligence.

The consequences of state intervention have done little to improve the well-being of Indigenous children. As recently as April 2022, the Native Women's Association of Canada protested that:[39]

> Indigenous children face significantly worse outcomes than non-Indigenous children in Canada. They experience disproportionate poverty rates, domestic violence rates, food insecurity lower education attainment, health conditions and systemic discrimination. Indigenous children inherit intergenerational harms from Canada's colonial legacy, including Indian Residential Schools, 60s scoop and membership exclusion laws.

38 In September 2016, in response to the 2015 report by the Inter-American Commission on Human Rights into the murders and disappearances of Indigenous women and girls, the Canadian government launched a two-year national inquiry.

39 U.N. Committee on the Rights of the Child – Canada's Joint 5th/6th Periodic Review: Alternative Report, at https://www.nwac.ca/assets-knowledge-centre/NWAC-UN-CRC-Submission-Canada-5-6th-periodic-review.pdf.

State duties to support families and children in need

There has been a history of poor coordination between federal and provincial governments in relation to funding for Indigenous communities.

The Indian Act 1985, s 88, makes provision for child welfare services to be delivered in accordance with provincial and territorial legislation. Consequently, each province and territory does so differently. Child welfare services for on-reserve tribes are funded through Aboriginal Affairs and Northern Development Canada and subject to the regulations in the First Nations Child and Family Services section of the National Social Program Manual.

Results from the 2011 National Household Survey show that 38% of Indigenous children in Canada live in poverty, compared to 7% for other children.

PREVENTATIVE INTERVENTION

The preventative and support services for Indigenous children are grossly underfunded,[40] which leads to their being overrepresented in the statutory child care and protection framework.[41] That this can also lead to infanticide was alluded to by Silk in the opening lines of 'Adoption Among the Inuit,' when she observes that:[42]

> In the North American Arctic, infants are sometimes abandoned or killed at birth by their parents. However, some infanticidal events are forestalled when unwanted infants are adopted and raised to adulthood by other members of their communities. In such cases, adoption provides an explicit alternative to infanticide.

By going on to refer to 'the functional linkage between infanticide and adoption in the Arctic,' she draws attention to the possible consequences of an absence of the family planning methods and family support services available in non-Indigenous communities. The lack of adequate preventative measures has been a repeated concern of the U.N. CRC, which, in its May 2022 report, also expressed concern about high numbers of unregistered births, particularly in areas with a high number of Indigenous people.

SERVICE PROVISION

In *First Nations Child and Family Caring Society of Canada and the Assembly of First Nations v. Attorney General of Canada*,[43] the CHRT found that First Nations children were not receiving the same amount of funding as other children for social

40 See *Canada (Human Rights Commission) v. Canada (Attorney General)*, 2012 FC 445, which concerned a complaint, lodged five years earlier by the First Nations Child and Family Caring Society, alleging that chronic underfunding of child welfare services was a violation of their human rights.

41 See Statistics Canada report 'Aboriginal Peoples in Canada: First Nations People, Metis and Inuit,' (2016), at https://www150.statcan.gc.ca/n1/en/subjects/indigenous_peoples/indigenous_children?

42 See, Silk, J., Adoption Among the Inuit, *American Anthropological Association*, (1987): 15(3), 320–330 at p 320.

43 2016 CHRT 2, [2016] 2 C.N.L.R. 270.

services intended to support vulnerable families and maintain family unity. This funding deficit resulted in First Nations children being prematurely and disproportionately removed from their homes and placed in care in violation of the best interests of the child. The CHRT decision stated: '[T]he best interest of the child is a paramount principle in the provision of [child welfare or child and family] services and is a principle recognised in international and Canadian law.'[44] The CHRT affirmed that:[45]

> In the best interest of the child, all First Nations children and families living on-reserve should have an opportunity . . . equal with other individuals to make for themselves the lives that they are able and wish to have and to have their needs accommodated, consistent with their duties and obligations as members of society.

The tribunal concluded by ordering the federal government to: (a) cease its discriminatory practices regarding child and family services, (b) reform the FNCFS programme and the 1965 agreement, (c) cease applying a narrow definition of Jordan's principle, and (d) take immediate measures to implement the full meaning and scope of that principle.

Subsequently the CBA, arguing in support of the CHRT, added that:[46]

> Despite the aim of Jordan's Principle to facilitate the equitable provision of services to Indigenous children, there have been denials, delays and disruptions of services to these children, creating a crisis for Indigenous health care and other services. There must be better coordination in legislation, judicial decisions and administration across the country, as well as meaningful consultation with Indigenous lawmakers.

These developments served to generate the momentum leading to Bill C-92 and the Act respecting First Nations, Inuit and Métis Children, Youth and Families 2020, which promises to transform state support for Indigenous families.

State intervention: coercive

Constitutional arrangements have long established that while responsibility for 'Indians' is a federal matter, child care and protection for Indigenous as for non-Indigenous children are assigned to provincial authorities. The SCC confirmed this nearly 50 years ago when it ruled that, notwithstanding the ambit of federal jurisdiction, provincial authorities had the power and the responsibility to intervene on a tribal reservation when there was reason to believe that there

44 Ibid, at para 3.
45 Ibid, at para 482.
46 CBS at p 24.

was a risk to the welfare of a child.[47] However, increasingly, provincial authorities will generally defer to tribal courts on minor issues affecting children on reservations.

COURT ORDERS

The care and protection orders and consequent 'out-of-home' options for Indigenous children have been the same as for their non-Indigenous counterparts (see, further, Chapter 6), though the 2020 legislation may bring changes in the future. Custody or guardianship orders are variously described across the provinces: for example, as interim and extended society care orders in Ontario and as temporary and continuing custody orders in British Columbia. Children may be placed in foster care at any point in this process: in the immediate wake of the apprehension of a child; in the course of court proceedings; or thereafter, when a child is in permanent or extended care.

State care

As has been noted:[48]

> The situation of Indigenous children in Canada may be the greatest problem confronting the child welfare system. Although Indigenous people constitute 7.7 per cent Canada's overall population, the 2016 census by Statistics Canada shows that 52.2 per cent of all children in the care of the state are Indigenous.

Nationally, the number of Indigenous children in the care system rose by 71.5% from 1996 to 2001. The 2016 National Household Survey indicated that those aged 0–14 years were placed in foster care at 13.1 times the rate of others.[49] When making such placements, there is a statutory requirement that kinship ties and the cultural identity of the children should be preserved and that Indigenous people should be involved in planning and delivering services to children and families in ways that are sensitive to the cultural, racial and religious heritage of the families receiving them. Placements should be made with members of the extended family or within Indigenous communities. However, given the shortage of Indigenous foster parents, children are often not so placed.

47 *Natural Parents v. Superintendent of Child Welfare*, (1976), 60 D.L.R.

48 See the *Canadian Encyclopedia* at https://www.thecanadianencyclopedia.ca/en/article/child-welfare.

49 See Fallon, B., Lefebvre, R., Trocmé, N., et al., Denouncing the Continued Overrepresentation of First Nations Children in Canadian Child Welfare, (2019) at https://cwrp.ca/sites/default/files/publications/FNCIS-2019%20-%20Denouncing%20the%20Continued%20Overrepresentation%20of%20First%20Nations%20Children%20in%20Canadian%20Child%20Welfare%20-%20Final_1%20%282%29.pdf.

Foster care: partnership, rehabilitation and concurrent planning

As might be expected, the tensions which normally accompany state management of relationships between a child in foster care, their birth parents, and the foster parents are a good deal more acute when the child is Indigenous, and the foster parents are not.

FOSTER CARE

It is reported that most Indigenous children in foster care50 are admitted on grounds of neglect.51 This suggests that there is a low threshold for admission to state care, which catches more Indigenous children simply because they are in poorer families and, in practice, operates to identify and 'rescue' those in need of protection from the effects of poverty rather than from parental abuse or wilfulness.

PARENT/CHILD RELATIONSHIP

The SCC has recognised the fundamental interest that both parent and child have in preserving their relationship and in the duty of the authorities to be facilitative.[52] It is an approach with widespread judicial support. Lamer CJ in *New Brunswick (Minister of Health and Community Services) v. G (J)*,[53] for example, warns that 'as an individual's status as a parent is often fundamental to personal identity, the stigma and distress resulting from a loss of parental status is a particularly serious consequence of the state's conduct.'[54] Further, 'since the best interests of the child are presumed to lie with the parent, the child's psychological integrity and well-being may be seriously affected by the interference with the parent-child relationship.'[55] In *Winnipeg Child and Family Services v. KLW*, L'Heureux-Dube J, noted that 'unnecessary disruptions of the [parent-child] bond' can cause 'significant trauma to both the parent and child,'[56] while Arbour J identified a child's interest both in 'being protected from harm and . . . in a continuing parental relationship.'[57] In accordance with the Charter, s 7, both parent and child have a right not to be deprived of such rights except in accordance with principles of fundamental justice. (See, further, later in this chapter and also Chapter 3.)

50 See Wiegers, W., 'Child Placement and the Legal Claims of Foster Caregivers,' *University of British Columbia Law Review*, (2019).

51 See Wray, M. and Sinha, V., Foster Care Disparity for Aboriginal Children in 2011, Centre for Research on Children and Families (2015), at cwrp.ca/sites/default/files/publications/en/165e.pdf. Also see Fallon, B., et al., Ontario Incidence Study of Reported Child Abuse and Neglect – 2013: Major Findings, (2015) at cwrp.ca/sites/default/files/publications/en/ois-2013_final.pdf.

52 See *B(R) v. Children's Aid Society of Metropolitan Toronto*, [1995] 1 SCR 315 at para 83.

53 [1999] 3 SCR 46.

54 Ibid, at para 61.

55 Ibid, at para 76.

56 2000 SCC 48, at para 72.

57 Ibid, at para 15.

The welfare principle in contemporary practice: public family law, criminal jurisdiction

'Indigenous youth are overrepresented at all stages of the criminal justice system,' as the Department of Justice acknowledge.[58] In 2017–18, while representing 8% of the Canadian population, Indigenous youth accounted for 48% of admissions to custody in the nine reporting jurisdictions (excluding Nova Scotia, Québec, Alberta, and Yukon), as opposed to 37% in 2014–15. Male Indigenous youth accounted for 47% of male youth admissions to custody, and female Indigenous youth accounted for 60% of admissions. In January 2021, the federal government committed to developing, in consultation and cooperation with provinces, territories, and Indigenous partners, an 'Indigenous Justice Strategy' to address systemic racism, inequities and the overrepresentation of Indigenous people in the justice system. In that context, it was acknowledged that 'Indigenous youth who need help often find themselves caught between the child welfare and criminal justice systems.'[59]

The system

This system is governed primarily by the Youth Criminal Justice Act 2003, as amended in 2012, and applies to youths between the ages of 12 and 18 years of age who are alleged to have committed an offence. While the 2003 act expressly provides that Indigenous children and band councils be given distinct consideration when applying Canadian law, the law is nonetheless the same as that applied to non-Indigenous children. (See, further, Chapter 5.) The output of this system is such that, according to the Council of Provincial and Child Advocates, (2010), 'for Aboriginal children and youth in Canada, there is a greater likelihood of involvement in the criminal justice system, including detention in a youth custody facility, than there is for a high school graduation.'[60]

Following the introduction of the 2020 legislation, there has been growing support for an Indigenous-controlled court system based on Indigenous culture.[61]

Children who pose a threat to the welfare of self or others

The incidence of violent attacks by and upon Indigenous youth is considerably greater than its prevalence among the non-Indigenous. In 2004, Public Safety Canada estimated that 9,815 youths aged 12 to 17 were accused (charged or otherwise)

58 See Department of Justice, Indigenous Youth Roundtables, at https://www.justice.gc.ca/eng/cj-jp/yj-jj/tools-outils/iyr-trja.html#ftnref1.

59 The Hon David Lametti, Minister of Justice and Attorney General of Canada, News Release, Department of Justice (2 March 2021).

60 Canadian Council of Provincial and Child Advocates, Aboriginal Children and Youth in Canada: Canada Must Do Better, pp 1–14, at p 6, (23 June 23 2010). See, further: http://www.cccya.ca/images/english/pdf/aboriginal_children_youth_advocates_position_paper_2010.pdf.

61 Reinforced by research projects such as the National Indigenous Courtworkers: Indigenous Youth-Centered Justice Project (at Ryerson University), launched in 2021, which aims to improve outcomes for Indigenous youth who are involved in both the child welfare and youth criminal justice systems.

of a criminal offence on a reserve. This rate (24,391 per 100,000) was more than three times higher than the average for the rest of Canada (7,023). In 2008, of the Indigenous youths in the 15-to-24 age group, 425 of every 1,000 were victims of violent incidents (excluding spousal violence) while the corresponding rate for their non-Indigenous counterparts was 268 per 1,000.[62]

PREVENTION

Among the 'Declaration of Principles' in the Youth Criminal Justice Act 2003 is that of supporting crime prevention by referring young persons to programmes or agencies in the community to address the circumstances underlying their offending behaviour. The stated objectives of this Act are preventing crime by addressing the circumstances underlying a young person's offending behaviour; rehabilitation of young persons who commit offences and facilitating their reintegration into society; and ensuring that a young person is subject to meaningful consequences for their offences, in order to promote the long-term protection of the public.

However, since inception of the youth criminal justice system, the number of Indigenous youth within custodial facilities has remained the same or increased while the population of white youth has drastically decreased. Clearly, the preventative goal of the 2003 Act is not having much success with respect to Indigenous youth.

Tribal/state youth court

As Asmi points out, the failure of the criminal justice system to mitigate Indigenous overrepresentation is unmistakable: 'despite a reduction in overall youth incarceration rates by 33 percent since 2012/2013, the proportion of Aboriginal youth admitted to correctional services has increased from 21 percent in 2006/7 to 37 percent in 2016/2017.'[63]

ROLE OF THE WELFARE PRINCIPLE

Arguably, the introduction of s 718.2(e) to the Criminal Code – following the *Royal Commission on Aboriginal Peoples* report[64] – requiring the judiciary to pay 'particular attention to the circumstances of Indigenous offenders' was intended to have an ameliorative or welfare function by prompting decisions favouring noncustodial options, where possible, when sentencing Indigenous offenders.

62 See, further, at https://www.publicsafety.gc.ca/cnt/rsrcs/pblctns/ststclsnpsht-yth/index-en.aspx?wbdisable=true.

63 See Asmi, S., Indigenous Youth Restorative Justice: Addressing Over Representation in the Canadian Criminal Justice System, Samuel Centre for Social Connectedness, (2019), citing Statistics Canada, *Adult and Youth Correctional Statistics in Canada, 2016/2017,* at https://www.socialconnectedness.org/wp-content/uploads/2019/10/Indigenous-Youth-Restorative-Justice.pdf.

64 Hurley, M.C. and Wherrett, J., *The Royal Commission on Aboriginal Peoples*, (1999), at https://publications.gc.ca/Collection-R/LoPBdP/EB/prb9924-e.htm/.

SENTENCING

The principles declared in the 2003 Act indicate that diversionary methods rather than custody are to be the preferred response of the youth justice system to offenders, but the evidence suggests that although this is having some success with other offenders, it is not benefitting Indigenous youth. Public Safety Canada report that while Indigenous youth represented only 6% of all youth in the 2006 general population, in 2008–09, they represented 27% of youth remanded, 36% of youth admitted to sentenced custody, and 24% of youth admitted to probation.[65]

Some have attributed the overrepresentation of Indigenous youth in the criminal justice system to the fact that implementation of the diversionary option is left to the discretion of police and prosecutors, which may leave room for discriminatory attitudes to choose a custodial sentence rather than a diversionary option.[66] Others maintain that such discretionary bias is just one symptom of a more fundamental problem: systemic racism, a legacy from the era of colonialism.[67] Note that restorative justice principles[68] are meant to have a particular applicability to Indigenous people precisely because they are so disproportionately represented in custodial facilities.[69]

The welfare principle in contemporary practice: private family law

The statutory laws governing marriage, divorce and separation are equally applicable to Indigenous and non-Indigenous Canadians. (See, further, Chapter 7.) While marriage and divorce are still conducted in accordance with customary practice among some tribes, both ceremonies must also meet the formal requirements of statutory law and regulations if they are to be legally binding.

Matrimonial

In Canada, it has been long recognised that Indigenous women, whether First Nation, Métis, or Inuit, are disproportionately affected by gender-based and intimate partner violence. Although the divorce rate in the Indigenous communities is the lowest in the country, this may be due to lack of female empowerment. Consequently, the suggested amendments in Bill C-78 to the Divorce Act – which received Royal assent in 2019 – emphasise the need to ensure greater protection for Indigenous women and

65 Public Safety Canada, op cit, citing Calverley, D., Cotter, A., & Halla, E., Youth custody and community services in Canada – 2008/2009, *Juristat* 30(1). Ottawa, (2010), ON: Statistics Canada.

66 See Corrado, R.R., Kuehn, S. and Margaritescu, I., Policy Issues Regarding the Overrepresentation of Incarcerated Aboriginal Young Offenders in a Canadian Context, *Youth Justice*, (2014), at https://journals.sagepub.com/doi/abs/10.1177/1473225413520361.

67 See, among others, Luo, D., The Overrepresentation of Indigenous Youth in the Criminal Justice System; Exposing a Problematic Reality of Imprisoned Marginalized Groups in Canada, *The Society: Sociology & Criminology Undergraduate Review*, pp 69–74, at https://jps.library.utoronto.ca.

68 See, Asmi, S., (2019), op cit.

69 *R. v. Gladue*, 1999 CanLII 679 (SCC), [1999] 1 S.C.R. 688, 133 C.C.C. (3d) 385).

children and specifically to require the court in divorce proceedings to take into account any family violence and, in particular, its impact on the child, its impact on the child's relationship with each spouse, and the capacity of any person who engaged in family violence to prioritise the best interests of the child and to meet the needs of the child. It includes a non-exhaustive checklist of criteria to be applied to determine what, in the particular circumstances, constitutes the welfare interests of the child.

CUSTODY

The court may make an order granting a parent sole or joint custody: in the former instance, it may also grant the noncustodial parent a defined right of access. Alternatively, a family member such as a grandparent, stepparent, aunt or uncle may apply to the court to be granted custody. Any determination of custody or access will be made on the basis of the best interests of the child, one prominent aspect of which will be the child's right to maintain their cultural identity and connections with their tribe and its heritage.

Guardianship

This private family order is most often utilised as an alternative to adoption in the context of long-term kinship and stepparent care arrangements. It can result from a private agreement or court order assigning guardianship responsibilities for a named child to a named person and is equally applicable to Indigenous and non-Indigenous children. (See, further, Chapter 3.)

Adoption

Customary adoption is specifically recognised under both the Indian Act and the Aboriginal Custom Adoption Recognition Act 1994. In its most basic form, it simply rests on an agreement, usually verbal, whereby one family gives a child to another, to be raised by the latter. Evidence of an adoption properly executed by Indigenous custom would normally include the consents of the natural and adopting parents, the child's voluntary placement with the adopting parents, the adopting parents' Indigenous heritage or entitlement to rely on Indigenous custom, and the presence of a rationale for Indigenous custom adoption.[70] The reasons for such an adoption, as noted by Morrow J in *Re Deborah*,[71] generally conform to a recognisable pattern:[72]

> Looking back over the more than 200 cases that I have heard to date there is no doubt in my mind that these reasons are always there and are all based on good sense: the mother had to go to hospital and could not look after the

70 See *Re: Tagornak Adoption Petition*, [1984] 1 C.N.L.R. 185 (N.W.T.S.C.).
71 [1972] 5 WWR 203 (sub nom. *Re Tucktoo and Kitchooalik*) 28 DLR (3d) 483 (NWTCA).
72 Ibid, at p 198.

> child; this is the third or fourth child in a row and my wife cannot look after it; this is a twin and my wife cannot look after two of the same age; we have lots and the grandmother is lonely and wants this one to look after.

Private adoptions are regulated by the Adoption Act 1998 to safeguard the interests of all parties and to ensure the protection and well-being of the child. A private adoption occurs when the child to be adopted is not the subject of a care order and can be arranged directly by the birth parent(s) and adopting parent(s), as long as the requirements of the 1998 Act and the regulations have been met.

WELFARE INTERESTS

Should issues arise and a customary adoption come before the court – which seldom happens – then it will be subject to the standards prescribed by statutory law. So, for example, *In the Matter of X*,[73] the Court of Québec (Youth Division) found that in customary adoptions, the best interests of the child should remain the paramount consideration, and therefore the state authorities could intervene to remove an adopted Indigenous child from their alcoholic Inuit adopter and place them in foster care. More generally, customary adoptions would seem to be congruent with welfare interests in some important respects: the child generally knows they have been adopted, they know their birth parent(s), the openness of such adoption enables the Indigenous child to maintain access to their birth family members and community, and the transparency avoids any future difficulties with information access. This practice allows for relationships to develop between the adopted child and members of the birth family throughout the child's life. Indeed, the original purpose was for the adopted child to return to the birth family in the event of the death of their adoptive parents. Customary adoption has the important advantage of preserving the integrity of the child's cultural identity. (See, further, later in this chapter.)

The welfare principle in contemporary practice: public/private family law

The distinction between public and private family law is perhaps less clear cut in Indigenous than in other communities.

Public service matters

Endemic poverty has had a crippling intergenerational impact on many Indigenous tribes, families and the welfare of their children. Results from the 2011 National Household Survey show that 38% of Indigenous children in Canada live in poverty, compared to 7% of other children, and it is reported that those in state care

73 [2006] R.J.Q. 2513.

are mostly admitted on grounds of neglect rather than wilful parental behaviour.[74] There are unmistakable social determinants of health standards in Indigenous communities. Moreover, Human Rights Watch has drawn attention to the fact that:[75]

> The water supplied to many First Nations communities on lands known as reserves is contaminated, hard to access, or at risk due to faulty treatment systems. The poor water and sanitation conditions have a disparate and negative impact on at-risk populations, including children.

It further notes the persistent government failure to address the health consequences of decades-old mercury contamination on First Nation land.

In short, the national framework of public service provision has disproportionately failed Indigenous children relative to others.

Legal proceedings

The public/private intersect is much the same in proceedings such as care and protection, custody, guardianship, restraining orders, etc. (See, further, Chapter 3.) Clearly, the 2020 legislation has paved the way for future structural changes that will result in some legal proceedings becoming adapted to better fit Indigenous culture, but in the meantime, the main area of procedural difference and associated cultural contention is in the use of adoption.

ADOPTION FROM STATE CARE OR 'DEPARTMENTAL ADOPTION'

Departmental adoption of a child in state care, whether consensual or coercive, is wholly governed by the legislative procedures, regulations, standards and policies established by the Adoption Act 1998. (See, further, Chapter 7.)

In practice, most departmental adoptions – whether or not they involve Indigenous children – result from foster carers transitioning to adopters and receiving financial support to do so. However, where the child is Indigenous and the applicants are not, such adoptions can be contentious. So, for example, in *Nova Scotia (Community Services) v. TG*,[76] a foster parent sought to adopt an Indigenous child and argued that the director's preference for a kinship placement constituted bias. Fichaud JA found that the legislature was entitled to prioritise criteria relevant to a child's best interests. He took the view that prioritising 'racial compatibility and sibling cohesion' was evidence not of bias but rather of adherence to law as expressed in the act. In *RP v. Alberta (Director of Child, Youth and Family*

74 See, Wray, M. and Sinha, V., Foster Care Disparity for Aboriginal Children in 2011, Centre for Research on Children and Families, (2015), at cwrp.ca/sites/default/files/publications/en/165e.pdf.

75 See, further, Human Rights Watch, at https://www.hrw.org/world-report/2021/country-chapters/canada.

76 2012 NSCA 43.

Enhancement),[77] the panel had disapproved of the director's decision to remove a four-year-old child who had been placed at birth in a foster-to-adopt home and then made subject to a permanent guardianship order. According to the Court of Appeal, the act required a consideration of all factors, and the director had wrongly prioritised maximum contact with the child's Indigenous grandmother, who had care of her two siblings, above or at the expense of other factors, such as the desirability of preserving the child's bond with 'the only family she has ever known.' The appeal panel's finding that the child would suffer 'severe trauma, grief and loss' if her attachment to the foster parents was disrupted elevated their claim over that of the grandmother, particularly where the 'child's ancestry is only one-quarter Cree' and where the foster family identified as an Indigenous family.[78] Bielby JA believed that the relationship with the child's Cree family and culture could be developed and sustained through access rights granted to the grandmother in the adoption order. Granting access to the foster caregivers, however, was not expressly considered by the Court of Appeal as an option. When the director failed to reconsider his position, a Queen's Bench judge subsequently found that this failure or refusal presented an 'uncontemplated' situation, which allowed the court to rely on its *parens patriae* jurisdiction and issue an adoption order favouring the foster parents.

Cultural identity and welfare The departmental adoption of an Indigenous child by non-Indigenous adopters is generally held to be incompatible with such a child's welfare. However, applying the 'best interest test' to prioritise continuity of care over culture or ancestral connections was endorsed many years ago by the SCC in its landmark *Racine* decision.[79]

State intervention in all Indigenous communities must, to some degree, compromise their cultural integrity. Indeed, the U.N. Committee on the Rights of the Child has expressed its concern 'that vulnerable children, including Aboriginal . . . children, who are greatly over represented in the child welfare system often lose their connections to their families, community, and culture due to lack of education on their culture and heritage.'[80] When such placements are made, there is a requirement that kinship ties and the cultural identity of the children should be preserved; that Indigenous people should be involved in planning and delivering services to their children and families; and that the community should be involved in planning and providing services in ways that are sensitive to the cultural, racial and religious heritage of the families receiving them.

The issue of cultural identity was considered by the SCC In *Natural Parents v. Superintendent of Child Welfare et al.*[81] The SCC was concerned with a nonconsensual adoption application from non-Indigenous foster parents with respect to an

77 2015 ABC A 171.

78 Ibid, at paras 69, 97, 75, and 95, respectively.

79 *Racine v. Woods*, [1983] 2 SCR 173.

80 See the U.N. Committee on the Rights of the Child, 61st session, C/CAN/CO/3–4, October 2012, at paras 42 and 43.

81 [1976] 2 S.C.R. 751.

Indigenous child removed from abusing or neglecting parents and placed in their care by state authorities. The court at first instance had refused the application on the grounds that there was an inconsistency between state adoption legislation and the Indian Act, which would result in the child losing their Indigenous status if adopted, and this was precisely what the Indian Act sought to prevent. The British Columbia Court of Appeal accepted the inconsistency but found that, as the adoption legislation was subordinate to the Indian Act, its provisions would generally apply subject only to any restriction resulting from noncompliance with particular provisions of the latter. Consequently, the adoption could go ahead, and the child's Indigenous status would survive his adoption by the non-Indigenous couple. The SCC upheld the Court of Appeal decision, reaffirming that the Adoption Act, rather than imposing restrictions on Indigenous people, makes it possible for Indigenous children to have the same right to be adopted as all other children. Subsequently, in *Racine v. Woods*,[82] the SCC, in what came to be viewed as a benchmark decision for weighing the relative significance of cultural matters, concluded that the welfare interests of the child strongly suggested that an opportunity for bonding/attachment provided by placing an Indigenous child in a non-Indigenous family home outweighed any possible long-term loss to the child's cultural identity. Thereafter, although open to criticism on the basis that a higher value was placed on the individualistic nature of the best interests of the child than on the collective interests of First Nations,[83] that decision was often deployed as justification for non-Indigenous placements. In retrospect it perhaps stands as an indicator of a significant disconnect between two different mindsets.

More recently, in *Re R.T.*,[84] the Saskatchewan Court of Queen's Bench (Family Law Division) found that adoption and 'the ability of children to maintain their culture' were not mutually exclusive concepts and ruled that children could be placed for adoption with non-Indigenous families because, in the circumstances, that was in their best interests. This approach has attracted the criticism that it may not be compatible with the long-term best interests of the children concerned.[85]

WARDSHIP

In *Beson v. Director of Child Welfare (Nfld)*,[86] the failure to investigate and substantiate allegations of abuse before removing a child from his pre-adoptive parents constituted a denial of procedural fairness. The Supreme Court also noted that the adoption statute in question did not allow for an appeal to an adoption appeal board

82 [1983] 2 S.C.R. 173.

83 See Kline, M., *Child Welfare Law: Best Interests of the Child Ideology and First Nations*, 30 Osgoode Hall LJ, (1992), at pp 375 and 396.

84 (2004), 259 Sask. R. 122.

85 See Rae, L., Inuit Child Welfare and Family Support: Policies, Programs and Strategies, the National Aboriginal Health Organisation, Ottawa, Ontario, (2011), at p 7. Further, at http://www.naho.ca/documents/it/2012_ICWFS-Policies-Programs-Strategies-Summary.pdf.

86 [1982] 2 SCR 716, 142 DLR (3d) 20.

by the applicants and identified this omission as a gap or deficiency that allowed the court to make such an order under its *parens patriae* jurisdiction.[87]

The United States of America

The federal Indian Child Welfare Act (ICWA) 1978 is often referred to as the 'gold standard' for state engagement with the Indigenous tribes, families, and children that comprise the AI/AN population of the U.S. Yet, more than 40 years later, the constitutionality of the ICWA is being challenged in the USSC[88] by plaintiffs who wish to facilitate the adoption of AI/AN children by non-AI/AN applicants, something the act was specifically designed to prevent. It is a challenge that goes to the heart of what, in the law relating to such children, constitutes their welfare interests.

Indigenous communities and the welfare of the child

The U.S. federal government's claim to recognise the 'sovereignty' of Native American people is, in practice, not quite that simple.[89] On top of the broad rule that matters of family law – including the welfare of children – are constitutionally reserved to the states, there are complex jurisdictional difficulties in differentiating between the *locus standi* of various Indigenous tribes and the rest of the population. In order to have the status of a federally recognised tribe, that entity must be able to prove continuous existence since the beginning of the 20th century[90] and to have been subsequently recognised by government through formal treaties, which largely means the tribes impacted by the Indian Relocation Act 1956. Many tribes have been unable to do so but nonetheless qualify for state recognition. The criteria for such recognition and the resulting ambit of self-governance vary from state to state. Many have done so and, if resident on a reservation, are consequently subject only to federal law and are otherwise self-governing in accordance with their particular tribal laws and treaties; if not resident on a reservation, tribal members are fully subject to state laws. This is further complicated by rules governing Indigenous people which determine who may qualify as a tribal member. However, the Indian Child Welfare Act 1978 does provide a federal umbrella of principles and provisions which facilitates some consistency across the states.

87 Ibid, at 724.

88 In 2021, *Brackeen v. Bernhardt* No. 18–11479 (5th Cir.2019) was appealed to the USSC.

89 Arguably, long since undone by developments such as the decision in *U.S. v. Clapox*, 35F. 575 (1888), which effectively recognised a federal right to intervene in tribal laws and processes, and the Indian Citizenship Act 1924, the effect of which was not so much to confer citizenship upon the AI/AN as to enforce their subjugation to national law.

90 The Indian Appropriations Act 1871 ended recognition of independent Native nations. Thereafter, they were treated as 'domestic dependent nations' subject to applicable federal laws. This law preserved the rights and privileges agreed to under the treaties, including a large degree of tribal sovereignty.

Definitions

According to the U.S. Census Bureau, as of 2020, the American Indian and Alaska Native population comprised some 9.7 million people (up from 5.2 million in 2010, an increase of 86.5% since 2010, to constitute 2.9% of the U.S. population).[91] They are members of 574 federally recognised tribes, whose members speak at least 200 different languages, located in 34 states, less than half of whom are on reservations, the rest living away from tribes in urban and rural settings across the U.S. Family matters, including child protection and family support, are most usually seen as internal issues – aspects of tribal sovereignty – to be addressed by tribal welfare systems and tribal courts. The U.S. Department of the Interior provides services to 1.9 million American Indian and Alaska Natives that include education, social services, law enforcement and administration of tribal courts.[92]

AMERICAN INDIAN/ALASKA NATIVE (AI/AN)

The 574 federally recognised tribes have the right to form their own governments, to enforce laws (both civil and criminal) within their lands, to tax, to establish requirements for membership, to licence and regulate activities, to zone and to exclude persons from tribal territories.

INDIAN

'Indian' means any person who is a member of an Indian tribe or who is an Alaska Native and a member of a regional corporation as defined in s 1606 of Title 43.

INDIAN TRIBE

This means any Indian tribe, band, nation, or other organised group or community of Indians recognised as eligible for the services provided to Indians by the secretary because of their status as Indians, including any Alaska Native village as defined in s 1602(c) of Title 43.

INDIAN CHILD

An 'Indian child' is defined for the purposes of the Indian Child Welfare Act (ICWA) 1978 as an unmarried person under the age of 18 who is a member of or 'is eligible for membership in an Indian tribe and is the biological child of a member of an Indian tribe.' It is left to the tribes to determine a child's Indian status[93] and,

91 See U.S. Census Bureau, at https://www.census.gov/library/stories/2021/08/improved-race-ethnicity-measures-reveal-united-states-population-much-more-multiracial.html.

92 See U.S. Department of the Interior, at https://www.doi.gov/international/what-we-do/tribes.

93 Determined on the basis of the tribe's blood quantum requirement. See, further, Spruhan, P., A Legal History of Blood Quantum in Federal Indian Law to 1935, 51 S.D. L. REV. 1, 4–5 (2006).

if affirmed, to declare to the statutory authorities the right of the relevant tribe to be involved in decisions regarding that child's future. However, an 'Indian tribe' has a restricted meaning: it refers only to those tribes recognised by government through formal treaties, which largely means the tribes impacted by the Indian Relocation Act 1956. Tracing ancestors in smaller Indian bands to establish a child's status can be a lengthy and costly process.

RESERVATION

This means Indian country as defined in s 1151 of Title 18 and any lands not covered under such section, title to which is either held by the United States in trust for the benefit of any Indian tribe or individual or held by any Indian tribe or individual subject to a restriction by the United States against alienation.

INDIAN COUNTRY

This legal term refers to lands over which Indian tribes exercise jurisdiction, including reservation land, dependent Indian communities and trust allotments.

TRIBAL COURT

This means a court with jurisdiction over child custody proceedings which is either a Court of Indian Offenses, a court established and operated under the code or custom of an Indian tribe, or any other administrative body of a tribe which is vested with authority over child custody proceedings.

Background

Recognition of the status of all Indigenous people born in the United States – American Indian/Alaska Native (AI/AN) – as U.S. citizens was not granted until the Indian Citizenship Act 1924. The long history of government policy aimed at containing and assimilating Indigenous people came to an end in the latter half of the 20th century, as the civil rights movement began to address the issues of inequality and discrimination that they had long endured. By then, war, disease, and confinement to reservations had ravaged the once-proud and resilient tribes that had occupied the land and defined its cultural context for countless generations.[94] As in Canada, the experience of residential schools and enforced adoption caused much trauma to the sense of tribal cultural identity and to the psychological welfare of subsequent generations of Indigenous children.

94 See, further, the Bureau of Indian Affairs (BIA), for a history of federal government treaties etc with Indian tribes: https://www.bia.gov/bia.

CHILD PROTECTION AND CULTURAL IDENTITY

Much the same approach that had driven the residential school and forced adoption initiatives was also present – at least until the latter half of the 20th century – in relation to child protection. It would seem that child welfare staff too often interpreted the traditional Indian custom of communal care responsibility for children as evidence of parental neglect and removed children found to be living on the reservation but with distant relatives. Such children were then frequently placed with non-Indigenous foster carers, ostensibly on short-term placements, but many foster parents, in due course, applied to adopt the children placed with them by the child welfare authorities. Needless to say, this served to continue the erosion of Indigenous culture and further their victim status.

Evolving policy, principles and law

Luth argues that 'American Indians/Alaskan Natives (AI/AN) have historically been forcefully integrated into the child welfare system. Their relationship began before a formal child welfare system was established in the United States and continues to the present.'[95] This is perhaps a consequence of the federal government assuming the role of trustee for the well-being of its Indigenous people,[96] as attested to in numerous treaties signed between the United States and tribal nations which included phrases like 'promise of all proper care and protection' in exchange for tribal land and natural resources.[97] That care and protection extended to safeguarding the welfare interests of Indigenous children.

Policy

Before the first child welfare legislation was introduced in 1974, many tribes used the authority of the Indian Civil Rights Act 1968 to establish self-governance rules relating to family matters. This was followed by the Indian Self-Determination and Education Assistance Act 1975, which gave tribes the power to implement programmes created by federal government, such as the Indian Health Services (which

95 Luth, R.J., The Intersection of American Indians/Alaskan Natives and the Child Welfare System: A Review of the Literature, in *McNair Scholars Research Journal*, (2016): 9, Article 8, at p 1. Further at https://commons.emich.edu/cgi/viewcontent.cgi?referer=&httpsredir=1&article=1104&context=mcnair.

96 See *Cherokee Nation v. Georgia* 30 U.S. (5 Peters), 1 (1831).

97 The U.N. HRC has expressed concern regarding the lack of free prior and informed consent of Indigenous people when decisions are taken in relation to issues such as sacred sites and mineral extraction on their lands. See, further, at www.wired.com/2014/03/united-nations-human-rights-committee-considers-report-united-states/.

performed involuntary sterilisation on over 3,000 American Indian women during the 1970s.)[98] It has been claimed that:

> before 1978, approximately 80 percent of Native American families living on reservations lost at least one child to the foster care system, according to data compiled by National Indian Child Welfare Association. Additionally, more than 25 percent of all Native children were removed from their families, with 85 percent receiving placements outside of their tribes or relatives.[99]

Since then, AI/AN children have continued to be grossly overrepresented in foster care.

The Indian Child Welfare Act (ICWA) 1978

The ICWA was the outcome of government concern at federal and state levels regarding the disproportionate representation of Indigenous children in the public care system[100] and by the seemingly inevitable progression to similar overrepresentation in the prison system. Much importance was attached to the dislocation suffered by the many children uprooted from their cultural and familial context to be fostered with non-Indigenous families and to the coherence and integrity of tribal structures that had to bear the shame and loss of their children. The ICWA represented a legislative intent to reset state/Indigenous relationships by reconstructing Indigenous cultural practices, particularly in relation to family matters, while strengthening a sense of connection between the Indigenous child and the Indigenous tribe.[101] Responsibility for Indigenous children residing or domiciled on tribal land and for Indigenous children eligible for tribal membership was to be exclusively vested in the tribes.[102] Should state intervention on grounds of child abuse or neglect result in a court order for the removal of parental rights, the relevant tribal authorities must be immediately notified so that they may consider whether an appropriate tribal placement is available and suitable for the needs of that particular child or the statutory authorities should make alternative arrangements, including a possible non-Indigenous adoption placement. Among the problems that flowed

98 See, U.S. General Accounting Office, Investigations of Allegations Concerning Indian Health Service' (4 November 1976): 4, 19–20, doc. number B166403(5).

99 See, further, at https://www.potawatomi.org/blog/2021/04/06/disproportionate-representation-of-native-americans-in-foster-care-across-united-states/.

100 Congressional hearings in 1977 (25 U.S.C. 1901) revealed a pattern of wholesale state intervention in Indian families and removal of children into state care. The rate of removal was three times greater than that of non-Indian children, and 25–35% of those removed were placed in foster or adoptive placements.

101 See Halverson, K., et al., Culture Loss: American Indian Family Disruption, Urbanization, and the Indian Child Welfare Act, *Child Welfare League America*, (2004): 81(2), at pp 319, 324.

102 H.R. Res. 95–1386, at 9 (1978), as reprinted in 1978 U.S.C.C.A.N. 7530, 7531 (cited in Bual, H., op cit, at p 274).

from this federal initiative was that it was not uniformly interpreted and applied: 12 states enacted different versions of the statute, resulting in different judicial rulings on the same issues across the country. Further, although directing responsibility for managing Indigenous affairs back to the jurisdiction of the tribe, its elders and their chief, the ICWA has to function in tandem with other non-Indigenous-specific legislation. Some parameters of the ICWA jurisdiction were imposed by Public Law 280,[103] which limited tribal authority in certain areas, including child welfare–related proceedings, by recognising that it would operate in subordination to equivalent state legislative provisions. A Model Tribal-State Indian Child Welfare Agreement, drafted by the American Indian Law Centre, was introduced in 1986 to facilitate nationwide consistency when agreements are made between a tribe/tribes and a state department on matters relating to the welfare interests of a child. More recently, the ICWA approach was further developed on a federal basis by the Family First Prevention Services Act 2017, which introduced broad changes to the U.S. foster care system.

The National Indian Child Welfare Association has drawn attention to failings in the implementation of the ICWA. It claims that:

> [T]he most critical issues of noncompliance involve: (1) lack of regular oversight of ICWA implementation; (2) AI/AN children not being identified early in child welfare proceedings; (3) tribes not receiving early and proper notification of child welfare proceedings involving their member children and families; (4) lack of placement homes that reflect the preferences defined within ICWA; (5) limited training and support for state and private agency staff to develop knowledge and skills in implementing ICWA, and (6) inadequate resources for tribal child welfare agencies to participate and support their state and private agency counterparts.[104]

Lee adds '[T]here is no federal administrative body authorized to oversee ICWA implementation and compliance and there is no comprehensive and uniform collection of Indigenous child welfare data to measure the impact of ICWA.'[105]

System failures

State policies aimed at providing supportive intervention in AI/AN affairs would seem to have been constrained by significant failures in administrative systems.

103 (PL 280). (18 U.S.C. § 1162(2012), 28 U.S.C. § 1360 (2012), 25 U.S.C. §§ 1321–1326).

104 See, further, at https://www.nicwa.org/wp-content/uploads/2016/11/Improving-the-Well-being-of-American-Indian-and-Alaska-Native-Children-and-Families.pdf.

105 See Lee, A.A., Oversight and Compliance with the Indian Child Welfare Act of 1978: A Policy Analysis, M.A. thesis in American Indian Studies, UCLA, (2015), p 2 at https://escholarship.org/content/qt3135s6rj/qt3135s6rj_noSplash_89ac74b4b41de6d42bbfecc51a4d14ce.pdf.

FUNDING SERVICE PROVISION

A 1994 report by the Department of Health and Human Services[106] provided a picture of the situation for tribal access to Title IV-E and other federal social service and child welfare funds. The report documented that tribes were then receiving little benefit or funding from federal Social Security Act programmes, specifically from Title IV-E Foster Care and Adoption Assistance, the Title XX Social Services Block Grant, and Title IV-B Child Welfare Services and Family Preservation and Support Services monies. Since the 1990s, tribes and tribal organisations were only able to directly access such federal human service programme funding provided under the Title IV-B Promoting Safe and Stable Families programme and the Temporary Assistance to Needy Families (TANF) block grant.

DATA COLLECTION

The National Child Abuse and Neglect Data System (NCANDS) provides information only on those American Indian/Alaskan Native families and children who are reported to state child protection authorities, whose cases are investigated by state child protective service systems, and who self-identify as American Indian/Alaskan Native. NCANDS does not include American Indian/Alaskan Native children who come to the attention of and are served by tribal social service systems. It is estimated that 40% of all cases of child abuse and neglect among AI/AN children are not reported to the NCANDS.[107]

The Adoption and Foster Care Analysis and Reporting System (AFCARS) provides information only on those American Indian/Alaskan Native children who self-identify as American Indian/Alaskan Native and are placed by state child welfare agencies in foster care. AFCARS data does not include American Indian/Alaskan Native children who receive foster care services from tribal children's programmes. It is estimated that approximately two-thirds of AI/AN children in foster care are placed by state child welfare agencies, and one-third to 40% are placed in foster care by tribal authorities.[108]

These failures in data collection systems must obstruct effective policy-making.

Principles

Only relatively recently and, as in Canada, in response to pressures generated by a series of public enquiries have certain basic principles emerged around which a reframed policy governing state intervention in AI/AN affairs is now formulated.

106 See Office of Inspector General (OIG), Opportunities for Administration for Children and Families to Improve Child Welfare Services and Protections for Native American Children, (August 1994), OEI-01–93–00110, at https://oig.hhs.gov/oei/reports/oei-01–93–00110.pdf.

107 See Earle, K.A. & Cross, A., Child Abuse and Neglect among Indian/Alaska Native Children: An Analysis of Existing Data, Portland, Oregon, National Indian Child Welfare Association, (2001).

108 Earle, K.A., Child Abuse and Neglect: An Examination of American Indian Data, (2000), at http://www.nicwa.org/resources/catalog/research/2000/02.Child_Abuse.pdf.

Tribal sovereignty

This term refers to the right of the AI/AN to self-govern and to take responsibility for the health, safety and welfare of its peoples resident within tribal territory. The U.S. Constitution recognises that tribal nations are sovereign governments.

Such is the extent of tribal sovereignty that there is now a duality in many public-sector procedures. with state and tribal systems functioning in parallel with designated cross-over points. There is recognition, if somewhat uncertain in extent, that there are areas in which the state must respect AI/AN tribal autonomy. Most court proceedings and child protection work are now routinely acknowledged to be tribal responsibility and duly assigned to tribal authorities. Government funding is made available to enable tribal delivery of tribal services to tribal members: for example, in relation to day care for children, the elderly and those with a disability. (See, further, Chapter 1.)

Preference for family-based care

The presumption, in law and in child psychology, that family-based care is the preferred means of safeguarding and promoting the welfare of a child has been firmly established for some decades. Only in very recent years, however, has that presumption prioritised birth-family care over all other alternatives as being best and as warranting legislative endorsement. The Family First legislation, clearly proclaiming as its purpose the prevention of children entering foster-family care, is a landmark statute in that it gives legal recognition to both the importance of parental care and an accompanying parental entitlement to the state support necessary to maintain it.

Establishing family-based care as a principle for guiding policy and practice also signifies an official recognition that residential care, as associated with the residential schools scandal, has been a failure and is no longer an acceptable form of state intervention. This led, inevitably, to an expansion in foster care services, which, in turn, has triggered concern regarding how the statutory foster parent scheme fits with the informal shared-care approach traditionally utilised by AI/AN communities. It would seem that foster care services provided by the child's tribal community is the preferred option: a kinship placement with a relative or tribal member who has a good relationship with the family and is approved as a foster parent is generally the objective; such a placement might be subsequently reinforced by a guardianship order.

Respect for cultural identity

State recognition of AI/AN culture in a child welfare context was not formally established until the introduction of the ICWA in 1978. This legislation instilled respect for cultural identity by provisions that included a requirement that an AI/AN child be placed in foster or adoptive homes that reflect their culture; granting exclusive tribal jurisdiction over custody proceedings concerning an AI/AN child when so requested by the tribe or parent; and requiring state and federal courts to recognise and, if necessary, enforce orders or decrees issued by tribal courts. Since then, the training of staff in state facilities – such as courts, schools, hospitals, clinics, etc – together with the relegation of many state procedures to tribal facilities has done much to embed an awareness of Indigenous culture into the social infrastructure.

The law

Although the U.S. has failed to ratify the U.N. Convention on the Rights of the Child (U.N. CROC), with its unequivocal Article 3 declaration that the best interests of the child must be the primary consideration in all decisions affecting his or her welfare, it has ratified a number of significant international conventions including UNDRIP, ICRED and the ICCPR. (See, further, Chapter 2.)

Domestic legal framework

Excepting the Indian Child Welfare Act 1978 and such other statutes as the Indian Civil Rights Act 1968 and the Indian Self-Determination and Education Assistance Act 1975, there is limited federal legislation specific to AI/AN children and their families. Instead, relevant provisions are mainly subsumed within legislation with a universal application, such as the Adoption Assistance and Child Welfare Act 1980. To a large extent, therefore, AI/AN-related provisions are to be found in national statutes. (See Chapter 2.) As family law matters are constitutionally delegated to the states, other relevant legislation is enacted in different forms by the legislature of each state.

THE CONSTITUTION

As has been stated:[109]

> The United States has a unique political and legal relationship with the federally recognized American Indian and Alaska Native (AI/AN) tribes across the country, as set forth in the Constitution of the United States, treaties, Executive Orders, and court decisions. For centuries, the Federal Government's relationship with these tribes has been guided by a trust responsibility, a long standing commitment on the part of our Government to protect the unique rights and ensure the well-being of our Nation's tribes, while respecting their tribal sovereignty.

All rights guaranteed in the Constitution (see, further, Chapter 2) are available to the AI/AN.

109 See the preamble to Executive Order 13592 at https://obamawhitehouse.archives.gov/the-press-office/2011/12/02/executive-order-13592-improving-american-indian-and-alaska-native-educat.

FOSTERING CONNECTIONS TO SUCCESS AND INCREASING ADOPTIONS ACT 2008

This Act 'enabled federally recognized Indian tribes to directly operate Title IV-E programs for the first time.'[110] Funds were also used to create the National Resource Center for Tribes, and grants were available to develop self-sufficient child welfare agencies. The aim of this act was to improve outcomes for those in foster care and connect children with extended relatives.

THE MULTIETHNIC PLACEMENT ACT 1994 (MEPA)

This addresses the disparity of ethnic groups in the child welfare system and, arguably, conflicts with the ICWA. The ICWA emphasises the importance of the relationship between tribe and child, establishes the principle that the placement of an Indigenous child is a tribal responsibility, and requires decisions taken regarding care arrangements for Indigenous children to respect and protect their cultural identity and their connections with tribal members. On the other hand, while the MEPA focuses on the length of time spent in foster care, it requires decision-makers to respect the equality and nondiscrimination principle by ensuring that the race and ethnicity of non-Indigenous Americans does not in itself prevent their adoption of an Indigenous child.

THE INDIAN CHILD WELFARE ACT 1978 (ICWA)

This statute was the result of government alarm at the numbers of Indigenous children being admitted or committed to state care: prior to the Act, 'over 25% of all Indigenous children were living in foster homes, adoptive homes, and/or boarding schools.'[111] The legislative intent of the ICWA was to protect tribal children and their families by establishing basic federal guidelines for the process of AI/AN child removal, foster care placement, adoption and termination of parental rights while adhering to tribal-specific traditions and values.

INDIAN HEALTH CARE IMPROVEMENT ACT 1976 (IHCIA)

This cornerstone of legal authority for the provision of health care to American Indians and Alaska Natives was critical to modernising and improving the healthcare system for Indigenous people.

INDIAN SELF-DETERMINATION AND EDUCATION ASSISTANCE ACT 1975

Resulting from American Indian activism, the Civil Rights Movement and social programmes of the 1960s, this act recognised the right and need of Native Americans for self-determination.

110 See Children's Bureau, Administration for Children & Families at https://www.acf.hhs.gov/cb/policy-guidance/pi-10–11.

111 Lee, A.A., Oversight and Compliance with the Indian Child Welfare Act of 1978: A Policy Analysis, UCLA, thesis, (2015), p 1, at https://escholarship.org/uc/item/3135s6rj.

THE INDIAN CIVIL RIGHTS ACT 1968

This established the right of self-governing tribes to police the basic fundamental rights – the freedoms of religion, speech, press, peaceful assembly, etc – within their tribes, together with the rights to trial by a jury and freedom from prosecution for unreasonable search and seizure. It comprises Titles II through VII of the Civil Rights Act of 1968, which makes many but not all the guarantees of the U.S. Bill of Rights applicable to the tribes.

THE TRANSFER ACT 1954

The Act states that 'all functions, responsibilities, authorities, and duties . . . relating to the maintenance and operation of hospital and health facilities for Indians, and the conservation of Indian health . . . shall be administered by the Surgeon General of the United States Public Health Service.'

The legal system and Indigenous children

The Indian Child Welfare Act 1978, among other things, recognises in s 1911 the exclusive tribal jurisdiction over AI/AN children resident or domiciled on reservations (except when that jurisdiction is concurrent between the tribe and state); it provides for the transfer of off-reservation court proceedings to tribal courts, absent parental objection or good cause to the contrary; recognises the right of American Indian and Alaska Native tribes to intervene in state court proceedings; and requires state courts to accord full faith and credit to tribal public acts, records and court judgments. If the child does not reside on tribal land but is member of a tribe (or eligible for membership), then all affiliated tribes should be notified, and the tribe has the option to decline the transfer; this 'serving notice' requirement has proven to be difficult in relation to non–federally recognised tribes. If the transfer is accepted and successful (neither parents nor the state prosecutor objects to the transfer) by an affiliated tribal court, the tribe takes over the child's case. If the case is not successfully transferred but the child is still a member or is eligible for tribal membership, then ICWA still applies, regardless of what court processes the case.[112] Where there are issues of concurrent jurisdiction among state courts, the Uniform Child Custody Jurisdiction and Enforcement Act 1997 requires jurisdiction to be conferred on the child's 'home state.'

REPRESENTATION

The Indian Civil Rights Act 1968[113] provides that 'no Indian tribe in exercising powers of self-government shall . . . (8) deny to any person within its jurisdiction the equal protection of its laws or deprive any person of liberty or property without

112 Luth, R.J., The Intersection of American Indians/Alaskan Natives and the Child Welfare System: A Review of the Literature, in *McNair Scholars Research Journal*, (2016): 9, Article 8, at p 91.
113 25 U.S.C. §1302(8).

due process of law.' This provision, in theory, ensures that tribal courts exercise due process. In addition, the ICWA provides that tribal courts should make legal representation available for the parties and for the child, if the latter is not a party to proceedings.[114] The role of such an attorney is to advise the court of the child's wishes and to advocate for the child's protection, safety and well-being.

CONSENT: CAPACITY TO TAKE OR CONTRIBUTE TO DECISIONS

In practice, an AI/AN child is for most purposes – mainly decisions regarding personal health – recognised in statute law as having the capacity to give or withhold consent from 12 years of age. This, it has to be said, seems rather odd given the volume of contentious cases regarding this issue with respect to older non-Indigenous children. (See, further, Chapter 4.)

The welfare principle in contemporary practice: public family law, civil jurisdiction

Prior to the introduction of the ICWA in 1978, state intervention in AI/AN family life was largely on a coercive basis. Little funding was made available, other than small amounts from the Bureau of Indian Affairs, to the more than 500 tribes for the social service funding necessary to keep children out of the public welfare system. Consequently, admissions of AI/AN children to that system had been disproportionately high for many years.

State intervention: consensual

For state intervention to be purposeful and to stand a chance of being effective, it must be predicated on verified factual information. The Adoption and Foster Care Analysis and Reporting System (AFCARS), which provides the data and identifies the trends on which much government policy is based, had been traditionally deficient in the data collated on AI/AN children. This seemed to be remedied in 2016, when an AFCARS Final Rule was published under the Obama administration with over 60 new data elements for AI/AN children, families and their caregivers. However, in 2017, the Trump administration delayed implementation, and when the 2020 version was published, it had retained only ten of the elements in the 2016 version. This attracted the comment that while the retained elements would be useful, they 'will not begin to address the systemic problems that contribute to the racial disparities in foster care.'[115] A court ruling is being sought on this matter as it is alleged that the 2020 Final Rule makes it harder for tribes to vindicate their and their children's rights and to protect their children's well-being.

114 RCW 13.38.110.

115 See Simmons, D., NICWA Director of Government Affairs and Advocacy, at https://www.nicwa.org/latest-news/afcars-data-collection-for-native-children/

State duties to support families and children in need

There have been some studies which have identified the predictive indicators of an AI/AN child being in need of out-of-home care. Carter's findings typify those of many others: 'neglect was the child maltreatment type most associated with the disproportionate placement of American Indian/Alaskan Native children into out-of-home care'; indeed, they were 'four times more likely to be removed from their families because of physical neglect'; also, there is an 'association between the removal of American Indian/Alaskan Native children from their homes and poverty'; and, in conclusion, the fact 'that "basic needs" is such a strong predictor for American Indian/Alaskan Native children to be removed from their homes should give pause to the federal government and child protection services.'[116] Carter also draws attention to what is viewed as being the 'institutional racism that permeates many child welfare agencies' and suggests that this may well be playing a part in the overrepresentation of AI/AN children in the child welfare system.[117]

PREVENTATIVE INTERVENTION

The Indian Child Welfare Act 1978 was introduced with the explicit objective of reducing the disproportionate numbers of AI/AN children, relative to non-Indigenous children, who were entering the public child welfare system and explicitly mandates intensive service provision ('active efforts') for vulnerable families to prevent child abuse and neglect and keep children safely in their homes. Despite that initiative, more than 40 years later, the disproportionate intake persists.

Traditionally and today, a distinguishing feature of family life in Indigenous communities is the degree to which the extended family provides a natural helping network that protects children and participates in their upbringing: the parenting of AI/AN children is regarded as being, to some extent, a shared community responsibility. Reliable state funding enables tribal governments to ensure that services are available to keep children within the tribe, reduce the number of tribal children in foster care, and facilitate the discharge of those in such care. In 1980, Congress enacted the Adoption Assistance and Child Welfare Act, creating Title IV-E of the Social Security Act, providing an entitlement to funding for foster care and adoption assistance services for income-eligible children who are placed by state or public agencies with which the state has an agreement. Access to Title IV-E funding, in order to provide subsidised guardianship for relative caregivers, enabling them to assist or replace failing parental care, was a crucial mechanism for channelling preventative state intervention. However, although some tribes received limited support for child welfare services through the Indian Child Welfare Act and other federal programmes, tribes could not directly access the largest source of federal

116 See, for example, Carter, V., Prediction of Placement into Out-of-Home Care for American Indian/Alaskan Natives Compared to Non-Indians, *Children and Youth Services Review*, 2009, 1–7 at 2 and 5.

117 Ibid, at p 6.

child welfare funding: Title IV-E of the Social Security Act. This resulted in large numbers of AI/AN children under tribal jurisdiction not having the same access to child welfare resources as other children and the consequent disproportionate rate of tribal children being admitted to the public child welfare system.

SERVICE PROVISION

The fact of institutionalised disparity in service provision for AI/AN families and their non-Indigenous counterparts has been well established for some years and was noted in a 2007 Pew Trust report.[118] That report recommended that tribal governments be given direct access to Title IV-E so they would have the flexibility to design services to meet community needs, be more able to support community-based practices, and thereby improve outcomes for AI/AN children. The Family First Act 2018 was, at least in part, a response to the concerns raised in that report. It signalled a significant change in policy – away from managing the exit of children from the public care system towards preventing their entry into it – by a new investment of federal funds to assist states in the provision of a range of family support services. (For type of services see, further, Chapter 2.) In an initiative directed towards strengthening legal protection for parental rights, the Family First Prevention Services Act 2018 has sought to counter the policy direction indicated by the Every Child Deserves a Family Act 2013. With effect from October 2019, federal funds have been made available through Title IV-E reimbursement for preventative services that help children, their parents and/or kinship caregivers avoid the need to have children removed from their homes.

State intervention: coercive

Prior to 1974, there were no formal federal or state policies that dealt with the abuse or neglect of children, whether Indigenous or not. The Child Abuse Prevention and Treatment Act (CAPT) 1974 was the first major federal statute with such a focus, though it did not directly address those issues in an Indigenous context. It required states to create systems for reporting and investigating allegations of neglect in order to receive funding.

COURT ORDERS

Whether issued by a state or tribal court, the range of statutory orders is the same. In the main, these comprise a care order, an order for custody or guardianship, and an order for the termination of parental rights. (See, further, Chapter 2.) There is a standard requirement in state laws that the child be involved in the development of their own care plan, including placement decisions and in any plan for permanency.

118 See Pew Charitable Trust report 'Time for Reform: A Matter of Justice for American Indian and Alaskan Native Children,' (2007), at https://www.pewtrusts.org/-/media/legacy/uploadedfiles/wwwpewtrustsorg/reports/foster_care_reform/nicwareportpdf.pdf.

In public care

Again, regardless of which of the parallel care routes – state or tribal – by which an AI/AN child is admitted, the options are much the same (see, further, Chapter 4), subject to the ICWA mandatory hierarchy of placement choices and the explicit requirement that the professionals involved – from probation service or the child welfare authorities – ensure that members of the child's family and tribe are engaged in formulating the care plan.

Foster care: partnership, rehabilitation and concurrent planning

American Indian children are at least three times more likely to be placed in foster care than children in the general population.[119] It is reported that in Alaska, Indigenous children make up 18% of the child population but 55% of the children in foster care; in South Dakota, the figures are, respectively, 15% and 53%; while in Minnesota, the overrepresentation has increased substantially from 2004 to 2009, as it did in Montana, Nebraska and North Dakota.[120]

FOSTER CARE

The Indian Child Welfare Act 1978 requires the state, when making a foster care placement for an AI/AN child, to protect the cultural identity of that child and their tribal connections. Specifically, s 1915 directs a hierarchical order of foster care placement options for such a child. Priority is always to be given first to a member of a child's immediate family, followed by the extended family, then other members of the child's tribe, and finally, to other Indian families. The ICWA prioritises the best interests of the child and tribe. Section 1921 states that if there is a higher standard of state or federal law that protects the rights of parents or Indian custodians, the higher standard should be applied.

AI/AN placement As Bual points out: 'ICWA is meant to allow the child's tribe the opportunity to choose an appropriate placement for the Indian child when the child's parents no longer have rights to the child, and the child is currently placed within foster care, pre-adoptive or adoptive placements.'[121] The stated adoption placement preferences are much the same as for foster care. In order of priority, they are (a) an extended family member of the child, (b) a member of the child's tribe, and (c) another

119 See Center for the Study of Social Policy, Annie E. Casey Foundation, & Alliance for Racial Equity in Child Welfare, (2011).

120 See Cross, T., Seneca Nation of Indians and founder and executive director of the National Indian Child Welfare Association at https://indiancountrytoday.com/archive/native-americans-expose-the-adoption-era-and-repair-its-devastation.

121 Bual, H., op cit, at p 280.

AI/AN family.[122] However, as Bual goes on to explain, '[C]ourts have implemented the Indian Family Exception Doctrine and the Existing Indian Family Doctrine into custody cases of Indian children as a method to bypass ICWA.'[123] The first rests on the assumption that if the parent with sole care responsibility is not an Indian, then the relinquishment of their child to non-Indian adopters is not depriving them of an Indian upbringing as this was never in the parent's gift.[124] The second refers to situations in which the family from which a child is removed following state intervention on grounds of parental abuse or neglect is one that is not practising an Indian culture. Again, the child is not being deprived of an experience that was never on offer. However, in the second instance, there is an argument that Indian kinship networks should be explored before the authorities default from the ICWA to the statutory adoption process. Both doctrines seem to sidestep the central issue that it is the entitlement of an Indian child to realise their cultural identity that is at stake – separate and distinct from rights of their parents or immediate family – and consequently, the onus rests on the court to satisfy itself that good reasons exist, grounded on the welfare interests of the child, to grant an adoption application foreclosing that possibility.

Where, as in *Mississippi Band of Choctaw Indians v. Holyfield*,[125] both birth parents are resident members of an Indian tribe, then the unmarried mother's subsequent voluntary relinquishment of their children will not be permitted to circumvent the rights of the tribe and children to secure an Indian adoption placement. In the *Matter of Adoption of T.A.W.*,[126] the Indian and non-Indian separated spouses had their parental rights terminated with respect to an Indian child who was recognised as such by the tribe. The state Supreme Court found that the subsequent adoption placement of the child with his stepfather was flawed as the ICWA required that 'active efforts be undertaken to remedy and rehabilitate the parents of Indian children before their parental rights may be terminated.'[127] Again, the legal focus was on the child: the court recognised that when parental rights are being terminated with respect to an Indian child, the issue is not whether the parent losing the rights is an Indian or non-Indian parent but that the child is Indian and entitled to the provisions and services outlined by the ICWA. Arguably, while the focus was indeed on the child, it was less concerned with their immediate welfare interests, attachments, etc – and more with the political/cultural interests the child represented.

Non-AI/AN placement Such placements arise either because the birth parent(s) choose to place or to have a child placed outside tribal care arrangements or because child protection issues require an Indigenous child to be taken into public care and placed in a foster home. The numbers of such children entering the public

122 As explained by the National Indian Child Welfare Association. See, further, at https://www.nicwa.org/wp-content/uploads/2016/11/Improving-the-Well-being-of-American-Indian-and-Alaska-Native-Children-and-Families.pdf.

123 Ibid.

124 *In the Matter of the Adoption of Baby Boy L*, 231 Kan. 199, 643 P.2d 168, 175 (1982).

125 490 U.S. 30, 38 (1989).

126 186 Wash.2d 828, 834 (2016).

127 Ibid.

care system, coupled with the severe lack of state-approved Indigenous foster parents, results in many Indigenous children being reared by non-Indigenous foster parents, some of whom, in time, lodge adoption applications.[128]

Adoptive Couple v. Baby Girl[129] concerned a baby girl, voluntarily relinquished for adoption by her non-Indigenous unmarried mother who was separated from the father, and duly placed by an adoption agency with a non-Indigenous couple whose adoption application was contested by the child's noncustodial father, a registered member of the Cherokee Nation. The latter then filed a notice of intervention, stating that Baby Girl was an 'Indian Child' as defined under the ICWA. The family court's ruling, rejecting the adoption application and granting custody to the biological father, was endorsed by the state Supreme Court. On reaching the USSC, however, this decision was overturned as the court found, in a 5–4 vote, that a noncustodial parent cannot invoke the ICWA to block an adoption voluntarily and lawfully initiated by a non-Indigenous parent. The USSC held that the ICWA was designed to stop the unwarranted removals of Indigenous children from Indigenous families 'due to the cultural insensitivity and bias of social workers and state courts.' It found that under §1915(a) of the ICWA, the non-Indigenous couple is not prevented from adopting the child when there are no preferred individuals or entities (the Indian tribe) formally seeking to adopt the child.[130] In this case, however, the court reasoned that because the Indigenous father never had either legal or physical custody and had previously relinquished his parental rights, the ICWA's goal of preventing the breakup of Indigenous families did not apply; had he claimed the right to undertake parental care himself, the outcome might well have been different. Moreover, the ICWA's preference for placing an Indigenous child with family, other members of the tribe, or other Indigenous families did not apply in this case because no other parties beside the adoptive parents had come forward to adopt Baby Girl. The girl was returned to her adoptive parents.

Brackeen v. Bernhardt[131] originated in 2017 with an application from white foster parents to adopt the two-year-old Indigenous boy placed in their care. The child's biological parents, registered members of the Navajo and Cherokee Nations, contested the application, arguing that the matter was governed by ICWA and, moreover, that the Navajo Nation had identified an Indigenous family placement in New Mexico. In October 2018, Judge Reed O'Conner ruled for the federal court that the ICWA was unconstitutional. He found that:

> ICWA's racial classification applies to potential Indian children [who are eligible for tribal citizenship] including those who will never be members of their ancestral tribe, those who will ultimately be placed with non-tribal family members, and those who will be adopted by members of other tribes.

128 For example, in Utah, at any one time, there are approximately 100 AI/AN children in foster care, but as of 2016, the state had fewer than 15 state-licensed AI/AN foster homes.

129 570 U.S. 637 (2013).

130 Ibid, at 2558.

131 No. 18–11479 (5th Cir. 2019).

The law, he concluded, was a 'race-based statute' that treats Native children differently. The applicants were given permission to proceed with the adoption. The plaintiffs in this case – sent on remand to the U.S. Fifth Circuit Court of Appeals – included several families interested in adopting Indigenous children and a non-Indigenous biological parent who wanted her Indigenous child to be adopted by a non-Indigenous family and argued that ICWA is race based and violates the Equal Protection Clause of the U.S. Constitution. The defendants, including several tribal nations, counter that 'Indian' is a political rather than a racial designation. This case – now scheduled to be heard by the USSC – will focus on the constitutionality of the ICWA and would seem to be crystallising issues relating to the welfare interests of the child in the complex nexus of issues now entangled at the interface of Indian sovereignty and federal legislation.

When authorising a non-AI/AN placement, the court must inform the Indigenous child – or ensure that information is available to them in the future – about the 'tribal affiliation, if any, of the individual's biological parents and provide such other information as may be necessary to protect any rights flowing from the individual's tribal relationship.'[132] There is some evidence from a 2017 research project that Indigenous children adopted away from their tribe, families and culture are more likely than other adopted children to struggle with drug abuse, alcohol addiction, suicide, self-harm and other mental health issues.[133]

PARENT/CHILD RELATIONSHIP

Once placed, the relationship between foster carer(s) and child naturally develops and may grow to compromise any prospect of rehabilitating the child with their birth parent(s). Use of the resulting bonding and attachment to justify retention of a child in their foster family because removal would jeopardise their welfare interests is, as Bual alleges, often a 'long-term, calculated legal strategy' – known to U.K. social workers as concurrent planning' – and one which works to the detriment of birth parents, whether Indigenous or not.[134] In this way, a foster care placement may become an adoption placement by default. However, ICWA was intended to counter any such argument and, notably, in *In re Alexandria P*,[135] it did. This was an instance in which, after protracted legal proceedings, the court enforced ICWA principles and directed that the child be removed from foster parents who had cared for her for some years and become adoption applicants and be placed instead with members of her extended tribal family.

132 25 U.S.C. § 1917 (1988).

133 See Landers, A, et al., American Indian and White Adoptees: Are There Mental Health Differences? at http://www.ucdenver.edu/academics/colleges/PublicHealth/research/centers/CAIANH/journal/Documents/Volume%2024/24%282%29_Landers_ai_and_white_adoptees_54.pdf.

134 Bual, H., Native American Rights & Adoption by Non-Indian Families: The Manipulation and Distortion of Public Opinion to Overthrow ICWA, *American Indian Law Journal*: (2018): 6(2), 271–294, at p 287, https://digitalcommons.law.seattleu.edu/ailj/vol6/iss2/6.

135 204 Cal.Rptr.3d 617, 621–22 (2016). See, also, *Matter of Custody of L.M.S.*, 187 Wash.2d 567, 578 (2017).

The welfare principle in contemporary practice: public family law, criminal jurisdiction

The ICWA specifically excludes criminal juvenile delinquency proceedings from the jurisdiction of the tribal courts, but it otherwise applies to state juvenile courts with respect to children for whom there has been a termination or surrender of parental rights, and either the child or one of the parents is associated with a federally recognised Native American Indian tribe. The U.S. Government Accountability Office released a report in 2018 that revealed an overall decline in AI/AN youth involvement in justice systems between 2010 and 2016 but their overrepresentation in some states and underrepresentation in others.[136]

The system

Crimes committed on Indigenous land can fall under the jurisdiction of the federal, state, or tribal justice systems,[137] depending on the location of the crime, the type of crime, the status of the perpetrator, and the status of the victim. Moreover, juveniles may be transferred out of any of these jurisdictions and into the adult justice system. This complex arrangement determines which justice system will handle the processing of tribal youth accused of criminal activity. In practice, however, most juvenile cases are handled in state courts[138] and come within the purview of the Office of Juvenile Justice and Delinquency Prevention.[139]

Children who pose a threat to the welfare of self or others

While the violent crime rate for U.S. youth has steadily declined over the past few years, the rate of violent juvenile crime in tribal communities continues to grow. The violent crime rate among AI/AN youth is twice the U.S. national rate. Tribal communities are also afflicted by high rates of domestic violence, child abuse and neglect, alcohol use, and gang involvement. They are overrepresented in arrests for alcohol, drug offences and absconding. Some are involved in murder, including mass school shootings.[140]

136 See, further, Policy Research Centre, *American Indian and Alaska Native Youth in the Juvenile Justice System: A Guide to the Data* (updated in 2020), at https://www.ncai.org/policy-research-center/research-data/prc-publications/NCAI_Policy_Research_Center_AIAN_Juvenile_Justice_Data_FINAL_1_2020.pdf.

137 See Dorgan, et al., Attorney General's Advisory Committee on American Indian and Alaska Native Children Exposed to Violence, *Ending Violence So Children Can Thrive*, (2014) and Adams et al., *Tribal Youth in the Federal Justice System*, the Urban Institute, (2011).

138 See Hockenberry, S. and Charles Puzzanchera, C., *Juvenile Court Statistics 2011*. Pittsburgh: National Center for Juvenile Justice, (2014).

139 See, further, at: https//ojjdp.ojp.gov.

140 In 2005, at Red Lake High School, Minnesota, a 16-year-old pupil shot and killed ten people, including himself.

PREVENTION

As of 2010, there were approximately 2.1 million AI/AN youths,[141] and compared to the general youth population, they suffered disproportionately – then and now – from adverse conditions such as poverty, poor health, exposure to alcohol and substance abuse, and family violence. These disadvantages leave them disproportionately likely to become victims: of violence, alcoholism, mental health issues including suicide, and diabetes. As mentioned earlier, they also receive a disproportionately low level of public service provision, which means that tribal authorities do not have the resources, staff or infrastructure to implement effective preventative strategies. Inadequate resources for juvenile justice have long been a challenge for tribal communities, resulting in insufficient training of law enforcement and other justice personnel and a shortage of programmes to combat juvenile delinquency through appropriate prevention, intervention and sanction activities. The Coalition for Juvenile Justice reports that preventative intervention measures have focused on 'responding to trauma and exposure to violence, better addressing substance abuse issues and mental health needs, addressing family needs and offering more diversion programmes and youth leadership development opportunities.'[142] The Defending Childhood Policy Initiative, a federal grant-awarding programme run by the Office of Juvenile Justice and Delinquency Prevention, is designed to increase the capacity of tribes to enhance their juvenile justice and related child service systems, such as child welfare and education, and to improve the lives of tribal youth exposed to violence.

Tribal/state juvenile court

Some but not all ICWA provisions apply to all juvenile delinquency cases: s 602, so applies but neither it nor s 300 (dependency) nor s 601 (status offences: e.g. underage consumption of alcohol) apply to AI/AN juveniles in all circumstances. They have no application, for example, where the child and family are affiliated with a tribe that is not federally recognised; in a juvenile delinquency case where child's conduct would be a crime if committed by an adult; and where the child does not currently qualify for tribal membership, but the child and family are Native American and part of the tribal community. Nevertheless, even in non-ICWA cases where the tribe is not federally recognised, tribal representatives should be notified, and there is court discretion to facilitate their involvement. The ICWA requirements with regard to formal legal processes such as serving notice, making active efforts to locate and engage the tribe, involvement of qualified expert-witness testimony, and heightened evidentiary standards apply only when a child is either in foster

141 U.S. Census, 2010, at https://www.census.gov/prod/cen2010/briefs/c2010br-10.pdf.

142 See Coalition for Juvenile Justice, American Indian/Alaskan Native Youth & Status Offense Disparities: A Call for Tribal Initiatives, Coordination and Federal Funding, p 1, and further at https://www.juvjustice.org/sites/default/files/resource-files/SOS%20Tribal%20Brief%20FINAL.pdf and https://www.juvjustice.org/sites/default/files/resource-files/SOS%20Tribal%20Brief%20FINAL.pdf.

care or at risk of entering it and either a hearing is pending to terminate parental rights; the child is in foster care or in an adoptive or pre-adoptive placement, due to abuse or neglect in the child's home; or only status offences are involved and not conduct which would be criminal if the child were over the age of 18.

From the outset, the court, county welfare department, and probation department have an affirmative and continuing duty to inquire whether a child for whom a petition under s 300, 601, or 602 may be or has been filed is or may be an Indigenous child, and, if so, the court must remind the probation department and/or the child welfare authorities of their duty to ensure the child's right to maintain tribal, family, and cultural connections, and they must contact and facilitate the involvement of tribal representatives in the proceedings.

ROLE OF THE WELFARE PRINCIPLE

While reference is made in the ICWA and relevant state laws to the importance of safeguarding 'the best interests of the child,' for all practical purposes, the welfare principle is interpreted and applied as meaning primarily the child's cultural heritage and connections with their tribe. The indications are that legislators are now leaning towards introducing provisions requiring the judiciary to be mindful of the overrepresentation of Indigenous children in the justice system and, by giving more consideration to welfare factors, avoid noncustodial options whenever possible.

SENTENCING

The Indian Civil Rights Act 1968, s 1302(7), restricts tribal courts to a sentencing tariff capped at one year in custody and a fine of not more than $5,000, though they may impose several such custodial sentences to run consecutively.[143] In practice:[144]

> American Indian and Alaska Native (AI/AN) young people are almost twice as likely to be petitioned to state court for skipping school, violating liquor laws, and engaging in other behaviors that are only illegal because of their age (often known as status offenses). Once involved with the state court system, they are less likely to be placed on probation and experience higher rates of detention and residential placements.

Not only are AI/AN youth disproportionately represented in the juvenile justice system (with one 2008 study finding that tribal youth comprise 60% of the juvenile justice population), but they are also often held in long-term facilities far away from their tribal lands.[145]

143 *Alaska v. Native Village of Venetic* 522 U.S. 520 (1998).

144 See Coalition for Juvenile Justice, op cit, at p 1.

145 See, further, at https//youth.gov/youth-topics/american-indian-alaska-native-youth/juvenile-justice.

The welfare principle in contemporary practice: private family law

The legislative intent underpinning the ICWA was to protect the best interests of Indigenous children and to promote the stability and security of Indigenous tribes and families. It explicitly gave tribes the right to intervene in any state court child welfare proceeding relating to the custody of a Native American child; the case may then be transferred to the tribal court.

Matrimonial

In recent decades, most Indigenous persons have moved out of their tribal reservations to live in urban settings and can no longer rely on traditional forms of support from family, extended family and other members of their tribe. Consequently, the rates of family breakdown, separation and divorce are increasing, with more cases of contested custody arrangements coming before tribal and state courts.[146] Native Americans are now at the highest statistical risk of experiencing divorce, with 44% of men and 45% of women ultimately ending one or more marriages.[147] Such family fragility clearly presents a correspondingly higher risk for the welfare interests of Native American children.[148]

Court orders

Divorce proceedings and parental custody disputes for AI/AN, as for all other citizens, are governed by the Uniform Marriage and Divorce Act 1970, as amended, and are matters reserved for the state courts. In effect, this means that the latter determines most issues relating to the welfare of AI/AN children. Indeed, state courts are specifically excluded by the ICWA from having any jurisdiction over proceedings for divorce where there are no children involved or where neither parent qualifies for custody. Those proceedings, together with guardianship, adoption, and foster care proceedings; proceedings for termination of parental rights; and those concerning minor juvenile offences – and the associated court orders – all lie within the jurisdiction of the tribal courts. Notice must be served on the relevant tribe of any custody dispute involving their Indian child, and the tribe can oversee placement, make specific requests, or take jurisdiction of the case if necessary.

146 See Palimaru, A.I., Brown, R.A., Arvizu-Sanchez, V. et al., Risk and Resilience Among Families in Urban AI/AN Communities: the Role of Young Adults, in *Journal of Racial and Ethnic Health Disparities* (2022), at https://doi.org/10.1007/s40615-022-01240-7.

147 See American Community Survey, 2014 data, at https://www.washingtonpost.com/news/wonk/wp/2016/04/06/who-gets-divorced-in-america-in-7-charts/.

148 See, for example, Limb, G.E. and Shafer, K., American Indian Fragile Families and the Marriage Initiative: A Replication Study, *Advances in Social Work*, (2019): 19(1), 201–216.

CUSTODY

Under the ICWA, s 1911:[149]

> An Indian tribe shall have jurisdiction exclusive as to any State over any child custody proceeding involving an Indian child who resides or is domiciled within the reservation of such tribe, except where such jurisdiction is otherwise vested in the State by existing Federal law. Where an Indian child is a ward of a tribal court, the Indian tribe shall retain exclusive jurisdiction, notwithstanding the residence or domicile of the child.

So only tribal courts can hear cases involving custody of Indigenous children who live on reservations, but if they live off reservation, then the state courts may do so, though only after notifying tribal authorities and giving them time to consider possible involvement in the proceedings.

GUARDIANSHIP

A guardianship application must be supported by clear and convincing evidence, including expert testimony that the child's placement with their Indigenous family is likely to result in serious emotional or physical damage to the child. The 'clear and convincing' standard is a higher standard than required in most child custody proceeding and is intended to provide a greater level of protection for Indigenous families and, most of all, for their children.

Permanent legal guardianship was introduced because:[150]

> [T]he emphasis on legally secure permanent placement is meant to provide the child with psychological stability and a sense of belonging and limit the likelihood of future disruption of the parent-child relationship. . . . [T]raditional adoption does not meet the needs of children in public foster care. Legal options for permanent and legally secure placement should be broad enough to serve the needs of all children in care who are not able to return to their homes of origin.

Legal guardianship, accompanied by welfare payments, was recommended in 2009 by the Pew Trust as a mechanism for facilitating the exit of AI/AN children from the public child welfare system and into the care of a relative.[151]

149 U.S. Code Annotated, Title 25, Indians, Chapter 21. Indian Child Welfare (Res & Annos): 1911(a); RCW 13.38.060.

150 See Department of Health and Human Services, Adoption 2002: The President's Initiative on Adoption and Foster Care; Guidelines for Public Policy and State Legislation Governing Permanence for Children, 1999.

151 Pew Report, 'Time for Reform' op cit.

CONSERVATORSHIP

A conservator is responsible for managing the finances and property of a child, whether Indigenous or not, and their appointment may be necessary when such a child inherits or otherwise acquires assets such as money or property. This court appointment is made in response to a petition showing why such asset management is necessary. The conservator has a limited role and, while responsible for a child's assets, is not responsible for their welfare.

Adoption

Each state has its own adoption statutes and other ancillary legislative provisions. For the country as a whole, it is largely the Family First Prevention Services Act 2018 and the Adoption and Safe Families Act 1997, in conjunction with the amended Adoption Assistance and Child Welfare Act 1980[152] and certain other important statutes, which together form the contemporary legislative framework for adoption.[153] This framework is supplemented by the provisions of international conventions and by the Intercountry Adoption Act 2000.

CUSTOMARY ADOPTION

As has been pointed out 'tribal customary adoption is the transfer of custody of a child to adoptive parents without terminating the rights of the birth parents.'[154] As no legal rights are transferred, such an arrangement is a purely internal tribal matter; the national courts have no jurisdiction and no cause for involvement unless issues arise regarding matters such as health and safety factors in the placement, child trafficking, or subsequent allegations of child abuse/neglect. Arrangements made are left dependent on the continuing goodwill of the parties involved and on the mediation of tribal authorities, but legal enforcement has been problematic. The primary hallmarks of customary adoption are the birth parent(s) retain legal responsibility for their child; custody rights transfer to the adopters; the adoptee retains any inheritance rights in the birth parent(s)' estate; openness, in terms of ongoing contact with the birth family, is assured; full transparency as regards origins information is always accessible; and the adoptee grows up with full knowledge of and participation in their society and culture. Perhaps of greatest consequence is the fact that customary adoption need not be permanent; it can be terminated at any time at the initiative of any of the parties involved.

152 Provided federal funding for state foster care and adoption programmes.

153 Essentially, along with the Constitution, the following U.S. federal statutes are of paramount importance: the Indian Welfare Act (25 U.S.C., Chap 21), the Adoption Assistance and Child Welfare Act 1980 (42 U.S.C., § 620), the Child Abuse Prevention and Treatment and Adoption Reform Act (42 U.S.C., Chap 67), and the CRS-annotated Constitution. The Code of Federated Regulations (45 C.F.R., Part 1356) also plays an important role.

154 See National Child Welfare Resource Center for Tribes at http://www.nrc4tribes.org.

Since 2010, California has granted legal recognition to customary tribal adoptions, allowing such placements to be protected and supported by state law and government agencies. Indigenous children in the state public care system who cannot be safely reunited with their parents may, at the option of their tribe, be eligible for adoption by and through the laws, traditions and customs of the tribe without requiring termination of the parental rights of the child's biological parents.[155] As significant as this is, it has to be added that, a decade later, other states have yet to follow the Californian initiative.

PRIVATE ADOPTION

Unlike in other developed countries, private arrangements continue to account for most U.S. adoptions. The birth parents determine not only – and most obviously – all step-adoptions, but also many direct adoption placements, and they usually also take responsibility for selecting adopters from the portfolio of agency-approved persons. Again, unlike other developed Western nations, the U.S. facilitates a profit motive in adoption law and practice. The 'open market' with its 'survival of the fittest' ethos provides the context for adoption agencies as it does for all organisations competing for the same business in the U.S. As with many other home-grown entrepreneurial enterprises, there are adoption agencies that pursue profit-making opportunities domestically and/or internationally. In the latter context, Cross warns (see also Chapter 3) of possible trafficking permeating current adoption practice:[156]

> Today, with the international adoption industry suffering from tighter restrictions imposed by countries such as Russia and China, pressure to keep up with the demand for children has returned stateside. There is evidence of corrupt adoption practices caused by those whose motive is to prey upon the legitimate desire of childless couples to parent, specifically AI/AN children.

WELFARE INTERESTS

As was explained in *Adoptive Couple v. Baby Girl*,[157] the ICWA was designed to stop the practice of unwarranted removal of Indigenous children from Indigenous families 'due to the cultural insensitivity and bias of social workers and state courts.' This, as Diane Kunz notes, 'has made it extremely difficult for potential adoptive parents to adopt children whose birth parents are members of federally registered Indigenous tribes.'[158] To that extent, coupled with the

155 Assembly Bill 1325 (Cook; Stats. 2009, ch 287).

156 Cross, T. L., The Indian Child Welfare Act: We must still fight for our children, in *Reclaiming Children and Youth*, (2014): 23(2), at p 23.

157 12–399 (2013); 398 S.C. 625, 731 S.E.2d 550 (2012). See 2013 U.S. LEXIS 4916, 2013 WL 3184627.

158 Note to author (30 August 2020).

relative lack of AI/AN foster care and adoptive placements, it may well be that this legislation at times, by restricting the range of possible placements, acts as a constraint on the principle of the welfare interests of the child.[159] In practice, the provisions of the Indian Child Welfare Act often need to be considered in conjunction with those of the Interstate Compact on the Placement of Children. (See, further, Chapter 2.)

The welfare principle in contemporary practice: public/private family law

In the U.S. as in Canada, the line between public and private family law in relation to Indigenous children does not seem to be firmly drawn, but again, it is in relation to adoption from care – departmental adoption – that the intersect is both most obvious and contentious.

Public service matters

Insofar as public services are capable of underpinning a welfare threshold for families and their children in such a competitive, capitalist socio-economic nation, it has conspicuously failed to do so for those in the AI/AN community. For that sector of the population, the poverty rate was 20.3% in 2019, compared with 9.0% of non-Hispanic whites, while in overall unemployment, the respective rates were 7.9% and 3.7%.[160] As the U.S. Department of Health and Human Services notes: '[S]tudies on urban American Indian and Alaska Native populations have documented a frequency of poor health and limited health care options'[161] while researchers have recorded higher rates of substance- and alcohol-use deaths among AI/AN youth than in the general population.[162] Much the same indices of relative social disadvantage can be found in other areas such as education, life expectancy, etc. In short, a large proportion of AI/AN children start life from a lower-than-average welfare threshold, and this continues into and throughout adulthood. While it's impossible to gauge the extent to which a legacy of historical state abuse has contributed to their present level of comparative disadvantage, there can be little doubt that long-term government policies of forced displacement, urban relocation, and enforced assimilation have eroded cultural systems and traditional support networks and contributed significantly to the current welfare deficits of the AI/AN and their children.

159 See, Fanshel, D., *Far From the Reservation: The Transracial Adoption of American Indian Children*, The Scarecrow Press, (1972).

160 See U.S. Department of Health and Human Services at https://minorityhealth.hhs.gov/omh/browse.aspx?lvl=3&lvlid=62.

161 Ibid.

162 Paul, T. M.; Lusk, S. L.; Becton, A. B.; Glade, R., Exploring the Impact of Substance Abuse, Culture, and Trauma on American Indian Adolescents, *Journal of Applied Rehabilitation Counseling*, (2017): 48(1), 31–39.

Legal proceedings

Given the restricted range of legal proceedings, it is to be expected that custody, guardianship and wardship, together with ancillary proceedings for restraining orders and maintenance, would provide the bulk of cross-over public/private family law litigation. (See, further, Chapter 2.) Additionally, parental interstate abduction cases are on the increase, as is the volume of cases concerning unaccompanied migrant children.

ADOPTION FROM PUBLIC CARE OR 'DEPARTMENTAL ADOPTION'

Adoption applications with respect to AI/AN children are frequently made by non-AI/AN foster parents who have had total care responsibility for such a child, placed with them by the state authorities for several years, with whom they have developed strong bonds of reciprocal attachment. Moreover, as the adoption of AI/AN children in state care attracts a state subsidy, there can be a financial incentive for adopters prepared to facilitate the state policy of transferring care responsibility from the public to the private sector. (See, further, Chapter 3.) Despite the cautionary advice that the ICWA is intended to prevent AI/AN adoptions by non-AI/AN applicants, some foster parents, as noted, do eventually lodge such applications, and this gives rise to serious issues centred on whether such an adoption, by compromising the adoptee's cultural identity, thereby adversely impacts their long-term welfare interests. This is the central dilemma in the current case of *Brackeen v. Bernhardt*,[163] which now awaits a decision from the USSC.

CULTURAL IDENTITY AND WELFARE

The ICWA, according to the National Indian Child Welfare Association, 'promotes the best interest of Indian children by keeping them connected to their culture, extended family and community, which are proven protective factors.'[164] There is an argument that by differentiating between the AI/AN and the rest of the U.S. population, the ICWA is granting appropriate recognition to the principle of tribal sovereignty. Some, on the other hand, claim that the ICWA is inherently discriminatory; by overtly preferencing the AI/AN, it breaches the Constitution's equal protection guarantee. These are fundamental issues for the Indigenous people of the U.S., and the verdict to be delivered by the USSC in *Brackeen v. Bernhardt* will have profound implications for the welfare of many of their children.

WARDSHIP

A 'ward of the state' is a child whose care and custody has been legally vested in the state as guardian of last resort. Alternatively, a guardianship order may be made by the court appointing a trusted adult – the guardian – to assume care and

163 No. 18–11479 (5th Cir. 2019).

164 See, further, at https://www.nicwa.org/wp-content/uploads/2018/10/Setting-the-Record-Straight-2018.pdf.

protection responsibilities for a minor – the ward. Both interpretations, being public and private, respectively, are often made with respect to AI/AN children. In fact, the child protection law in the U.S. could be said to have its foundations in the concept of wardship. (See, further, Chapter 2.)

Conclusion

State intervention in the family life of Indigenous people on child welfare grounds has not fared well. The legacy of mistrust resulting from a long period of intergenerational trauma makes it very difficult to now establish a positive working relationship between government and the Indigenous communities such as would enable their children to escape the current levels of poverty and overrepresentation in the criminal and welfare systems and avail themselves of opportunities in education, training and sport – the well-trodden pathways to socio-economic success – as do their non-Indigenous fellow citizens. At the very least, child welfare considerations and equality and nondiscrimination laws make it a matter of some urgency that renewed efforts are made to reduce the number of poor health indicators that convincingly demonstrate just how very disadvantaged the children of Indigenous communities are relative to others.

Practices affecting the welfare of children traditionally and currently used by the First Nations, the Métis and the Inuit in Canada and the American Indian and Alaska Native population in the U.S. are illustrative of the type of practices found among Indigenous communities in other countries. Similar, too, is the nature of their relationship with the state: the pattern of historical colonial abuse and strategies for enforced assimilation, including the use of residential schools and adoption as a means to that end, were replicated elsewhere, and so also has the process of an evolving mutual understanding that has seen the state retreat from its initial attempts to impose its legal system on Indigenous culture and instead to allow the present duality whereby state and Indigenous systems run in tandem, subject to agreed cross-over protocols.

The principles of international law, particularly those concerned with fundamental human rights, apply uniformly across nations and equally to all their citizens, including those in Indigenous communities. It is possible that international law, in conjunction with the legal developments currently pending in both countries, might in the near future quite radically change the status quo as regards the law governing the welfare and rights of Indigenous children.

Part V

Themes of commonality and difference

9 Themes and a comparative jurisdictional analysis

Introduction

This chapter, like its counterpart in *Children & the Law: Shaping the Modern Welfare Principle in the British Isles*, undertakes a comparative analysis of the principle and its role and functions in two jurisdictions: in this case, the U.S. and Canada, as profiled in earlier chapters. It then conducts the same exercise in relation to the Indigenous children of those nations. In both instances, it does so by following the structure of the jurisdiction chapters, trawling through the material they present to identify emerging themes. It focuses on key aspects of the principle, identifying significant differentiating national characteristics and tracing some broad contemporary patterns/trends of commonality and difference.

It begins, therefore, by dealing consecutively with matters of policy and principle, then with legislation and the court system, giving consideration, in the latter instance, to both domestic and international law. It identifies and examines differences in public family law as it relates to the welfare of children in the nations concerned: first in the civil law, then in the criminal law, and then in relation to private family law. It goes on to consider the extent of a convergence in the similar and increasing use of hybrid court orders – applicable across both the public and private sectors of family law – and assesses the significance of this development. Finally, the chapter turns to examine themes of difference and commonality in the law relating to the welfare interests of Indigenous children in the same two countries.

(A) Canada and the United States: the welfare principle in a non-Indigenous context

In each nation, the legislative framework governing the law relating to children and the role and weighting of the welfare principle within that law is, in theory, equally applicable to all children. In practice, the design and application of that law takes little account of the special circumstances of Indigenous children. Increasingly, it seems like a separate body of law is being built to address welfare interests that are perceived to be distinctively different.

DOI: 10.4324/9781003269564-15

Policy, principles and the legal system

It is notable that in the U.S. and Canada, as in the U.K., it was the initiatives taken by voluntary organisations and the pressure of their advocacy that induced the state to introduce the first legislative measures dealing with child cruelty and neglect and the associated responsibilities of parents.

Policy

The *parens patriae* jurisdiction of wardship transferred with colonialism to the U.S. and Canada. In both countries, it would seem to have put in place a basic legal platform for the state's relationship with children as protector of their welfare, and in both, it continues to play a residual role. However, in neither could the hallmark of wardship – the principle that the welfare of the child must be treated as of paramount importance in matters relating to their upbringing – be said to be the guiding light for ensuring the consistent prioritising of welfare considerations in the contemporary law, policy and practice relating to children.

Public family law relating to children: civil jurisdiction

In the U.S. and Canada, as in the U.K., child abuse and the need for a related government policy emerged in the early 1960s, generated by academic studies on the 'battered child syndrome.'[1] Since then, in keeping with trends throughout the developed nations, the statistical data available for Canada and the U.S. show increased numbers of children being removed from parental care and entering the public child welfare system.

THE PREVENTION/PROTECTION BALANCE

By the latter decades of the 20th century, consensual, preventative state intervention to assist vulnerable families had become an established, if weakly resourced, public service in both Canada and the U.S. In tandem with preventative initiatives, the governments of both nations at federal and provincial levels were refining and broadening the child protection grounds for state intervention in family affairs.

Prevention The availability of 'safe havens' is a very contentious issue and one on which there is no consistency among the developed nations.[2] There use is prohibited, for example, in the U.K.[3] but is legally permissible in France, Germany and as many as nine other European countries. It is condemned by the U.N. CRC as contravening a

1 See, for example, Kempe, C.H., Silverman, F.N., Steele, B.F., Droegemueller, W. & Silver, H.K., The Battered Child Syndrome, *Journal of the American Medical Association*, (1962).

2 See, further, at www.theguardian.com/world/2012/jun/10/unitednations-europe-news.

3 See the Offences Against Persons Act 1861, s 27, which makes it a criminal offence to abandon a baby.

child's right, under Article 7, to be known and cared for by their parents.[4] This is one aspect of state preventative intervention for which policy has been and remains different in the U.S. and Canada: while such facilities are available in all states, legally sanctioned, and used to safely deposit many babies every year in the U.S., only very recently have one or two appeared in Canada, and their legal standing is uncertain.

Despite policy initiatives intended to drive forward adoption and kinship care, the statistics in both countries clearly show that a large proportion of children admitted to the public care system remain there, notwithstanding a steady increase in the numbers waiting to be adopted.

Foster care The policy of kinship placements as an alternative to foster care, reinforced by the use of guardianship orders, has been positively developed for some years by public child care agencies in both countries. The attraction of such placements is that they provide for minimal disruption to a child's sense of belonging within the family, class, culture and locality of their birth. One significant point of jurisdictional difference is that in the U.S., fostering services – as with adoption – are largely privatised, adding a for-profit dimension to the public care system in that country.

Adoption from public care The policy emphasis on kinship placements often leads to adoption, with many children being returned through that process to their kinship networks. In general, the policy of encouraging and financially subsidising adoption from state care would seem similar in Canada and the U.S. to that established in the U.K. They all broadly share the same approach towards children in the care system: where feasible, such children are to be given the opportunity to enjoy family life secured through permanence by adoption, even if this has to be pursued on a non-consensual basis by legally dispensing with the need for parental consent.

Residential care The assimilation policy saw generations of Indigenous children in both countries being removed from their families of origin to residential schools, where they were rigorously taught to abandon their Indigenous culture in favour of Westernised cultural norms. This failed experiment in eugenics caused intergenerational trauma for the Indigenous people of both countries and also had the incidental effect of undermining the legitimacy of state residential facilities as a contemporary form of provision for children in the public care system.

Public family law relating to children: criminal jurisdiction

For most of the 19th century, juveniles who committed crimes were treated by the legal system in much the same way as adults. Not until the end of that century did the law and policy towards juvenile offenders in Canada and in the U.S. begin to

4 See United Nations Committee on the Rights of the Child, *Concluding Observations: Czech Republic* (4 August 2011), CRC/C/CZE/CO/3–4, [50].

change. In both countries, the first step was one of statutorily defining a juvenile justice process that was separate from, but still provided cross-over access to, the adult penal system.

THE WELFARE/JUSTICE BALANCE

Initially, in both countries, the judicial approach to juvenile crime was based on the assumption that the state, vested with the ancient *parens patriae* responsibilities and authority of the Crown, had delegated its powers to government agencies which would, in turn, act in the best interests of a child, as a caring parent towards children with deviant behaviour. By the end of the 20th century, this had given way to a common jurisdictional emphasis in juvenile justice on safeguarding the public, blended with a mix of training and rehabilitation measures that have ever since represented the balance struck between welfare and justice considerations in the two systems. A differentiating jurisdictional characteristic had, however, begun to acquire salience in the U.S. as the 'due process' clause in the Constitution was applied to ensure that processes and outcomes of juvenile justice conformed to constitutionally protected standards. Arguably, juvenile court proceedings in the U.S. have since became more adversarial in nature than their Canadian counterparts: requiring all the normal components and safeguards of an adult trial and tending to transfer juveniles into the adult criminal justice system while also adopting a similarly punitive approach when it comes to disposal options.

School shootings This phenomenon occurs in both jurisdictions but is far more prevalent in the U.S., where it would seem to be indicative of some systemic flaw in the development of psychological bonds that in 'normal' families would inhibit any such extreme violence by one child on another. While children killing other children is clearly abhorrent, it is also aberrant. This did not used to happen in the U.S. but has now come to be so common as to be strongly associated with that particular country. When and why it somehow became 'psychologically permissible' there more so than elsewhere[5] is very much a matter that warrants closer study in a book concerned with the welfare of children, but there does not seem to be much relevant research, and word count limitations prevent any meaningful exploration of the subject at this point. Although it clearly impacts child welfare and needs to be noted as a particular feature of juvenile crime in the U.S., it is less clear what its implications are more broadly for the law and policy relating to children in this country and possibly in others in due course.

5 The prevalence of guns is unlikely to be much of a causality factor; ease of access to guns long preceded this phenomenon. Video games may be making a contribution in terms of inuring sensibilities, generating violent fantasies, etc. Possibly the fading of the birth-to-death nuclear family unit, with its inbuilt boundaries, role reciprocity, and taboos, and the increase in more fluid family structures, often containing non–genetically related children, may be playing a part in promoting shallow attachments and disinhibited behaviour. Then there is the growing proclivity for identity issues. The welfare of all children clearly necessitates research into the aberrant behaviour of a few.

Private family law relating to children

Traditionally, the law has presumed that the welfare interests of children were subsumed within and appropriately represented by the rights of their parents; not until that authority had been displaced or good reason shown for such displacement would the welfare interests of the child warrant separate consideration. More recently, in Canada and the U.S. as in other developed countries, this equation has been reversed: child welfare and parental rights are readily (arguably, too readily) seen in legal terms as separate and distinct, with the rights of parents only exercisable subject to the welfare of their children not being unduly infringed.

MATRIMONIAL

The marriage rate in both countries is currently declining, but while divorce in Canada is increasing, it is decreasing in the U.S. However, in both, families have changed: parents are no longer necessarily heterosexual; families often comprise parents and children who are not necessarily genetically related; and overall, the traditional family unit is undergoing fundamental change with profound challenges for the future of family law. It would seem probable that in both, impermanent family structures and serial parenting arrangements are more likely to result in children with attachment issues, and for some, this will manifest itself in behavioural problems that may well lead them into deviant behaviour and into the public child welfare system.

GUARDIANSHIP AND WARDSHIP

These, initially the most private of family law orders, have now, in Canada and the U.S. as in the U.K., become mediatory instruments in both public and private sectors of that law. They essentially blend a mix of state and parental responsibilities with respect to the welfare of a child and would seem to be increasingly used at the initiative of courts, state authorities and parents.

ADOPTION

Again, this traditional and most private of family law orders has broadened in legal usage – in Canada, the U.S., the U.K., and elsewhere – as it adapted to address the social changes affecting the family. These countries have in common the fact that, in recent decades, the main use of adoption has been the opposite of that for which it was initially intended: a birth mother acting jointly with a child's stepfather to legally acquire rather than to relinquish parental responsibility. In relation to domestic adoption, these two countries each have at least one distinctive characteristic: in the U.S., the involvement of for-profit adoption agencies and the parental right to directly place their child are strong indicators of jurisdictional difference; in Canada, the simple lack of a national database on children who are either available for adoption or have been adopted is quite singular.

As abortion and improved contraceptives became more accessible, so the opportunities for domestic adoption were reduced, causing prospective adopters in both countries to turn to intercountry (ICA) sources: the 1970s saw the beginning of an influx of children from Korea. In recent years, older children with significant care needs now make up a much larger share of international adoptees, which is perhaps indicative of ICA becoming more a process for addressing the needs of children than of adopters, but both countries have experienced a sharp drop in ICA as traditional sending countries such as China and Russia impose restrictions on adopter eligibility.

FAMILY PLANNING, ABORTION, SURROGACY, IVF, ETC

Women's reproductive rights were pioneered in the U.S. but in subsequent years have become front and centre of that country's 'culture wars,' which are now a distinctive jurisdictional characteristic. Following the *Dobbs*[6] ruling in 2022 and the consequent prompt introduction of legislation restricting access to abortion in at least 15 states, these wars and the risks for the welfare of some children – sadly unwanted – can only increase. Such matters are a good deal less contentious in Canada. The fact that abortion and other measures are more freely available in that country is now a distinctive differentiating jurisdictional characteristic. This provides or contributes to a planned parenting context in Canada, which, to that extent, affords more accommodation for parental determination of the welfare interests of children than will be available to their U.S. counterparts.

Surrogacy International commercial surrogacy may have displaced adoption as the preferred option for those seeking a baby. Bluntly put, where choice rather than altruism is in play, prospective adopters may simply decide that as surrogacy provides a genetic link, it offers better value. Commercial surrogacy is so well established in Canada as to make that country a top destination resort in international health tourism. While surrogacy in some U.S. states is similarly available, that country's 'culture wars' are inhibiting factors in other states.

Principles

The right to privacy, as constitutionally implied in both countries, confers on entities such as individuals and families the right to be protected from government intrusion.

The paramountcy principle

It seems reasonably clear that in both countries, this principle has a doubtful legal status and functionality – certainly less so than in the U.K. This limits the capacity of judiciary, parent, child, or any others to give unconditional priority to the

6 *Dobbs v. Jackson Women's Health Organization*, No. 19-1392, 597 U.S., (2022).

welfare interests of a child when determining a course of action relating to those interests. In the U.S., more so than in Canada but similarly to Ireland, statute law has been constrained from asserting the paramountcy principle because of the constitutional protection singled out for the rights of parents as reinforced by Supreme Court rulings. In both countries, the laws regulating child welfare–related matters are relegated to states and provinces, resulting in a disparate range of weightings being given to the welfare principle in different contexts, depriving it of any possibility of acquiring a consistent, comprehensive and nationally defined role.

PARAMOUNTCY: CHILD'S CONSENT

In keeping with the traditional legal presumption that responsibility for the welfare interests of a child is a matter that lies within the rights and responsibilities of parents, the latter are generally taken to be vested with the authority to make decisions – certainly medical decisions – on behalf of their child. This approach continues despite a fundamental principle of the U.N. CROC, as elaborated in the General Comments, that an 'adult's judgement of a child's best interests cannot override the obligation to respect all of the child's rights under the U.N. CROC.'[7]

Although, in the U.S., all 50 states have statutes that in certain circumstances allow or require a minor to give their consent to proposed medical treatment, there is stronger evidence of a residual paternalism that restrains the judiciary from unequivocally accepting the decision of an under-16-year-old adolescent. In Canada, the courts seem to operate on the principle that the greater the age and maturity of the child, the lesser the scope for parental determination and vice versa. Nonetheless, in both jurisdictions, it is difficult not to see in the caselaw a definite judicial reluctance to let adolescents under the age of 16 take decisions when this may result in their death; when the decision is in relation to abortion, in the face of parental opposition, the judiciary have less difficulty respecting the adolescent's decision. In effect, the judiciary in both jurisdictions, when dealing with the veracity of a child's consent, perhaps regard the paramountcy principle as a useful default to be deployed to override an adolescent's decision when they disagree with it.

Principle of parental rights

Although family-based care has, for some decades,[8] been judicially recognised as the preferred means of safeguarding and promoting the welfare of a child, only comparatively recently has this warranted legislative endorsement. In both countries, an outright abuse of parental rights that breaches a statutory duty to ensure

7 Committee on the Rights of the Children, General Comment No. 14 (2013) on the right of the child to have his or her best interests taken as a primary consideration (art. 3, para. 1) CRC/C/GC/14, at para 4.

8 See, further, Elster, J., Solomonic Judgments: Against the Best Interest of the Child, 54 *University of Chicago Law Review* 1 (1987).

the welfare interests of children will naturally result in proceedings that may well lead to a loss of custody

PARENTAL RESPONSIBILITY AND CORPORAL PUNISHMENT

The law in both Canada and the U.S. permits a parent to use corporal punishment to chastise their child, subject to the condition that the degree of physical force is 'reasonable.' The retention of this most primitive aspect of parental rights is unusual among developed nations and cannot be said to be compliant with U.N. CROC and the welfare of the child principle.

The consanguinity principle

Judicial reticence to endorse the 'blood link' as a persuasive factor when considering custody disputes is obvious in both Canada and the U.S. However, judicial reluctance is challenged by the clear preference of welfare authorities in both countries – now legislatively endorsed – for kinship foster care placements.

The proportionality principle

This principle, which owes much to judicial explication in many ECtHR rulings and is firmly part of U.K. child-care jurisprudence, is noticeably absent in equivalent USSC rulings. It does, however, attract a good deal of judicial attention in Canada.

The liberty principle

This principle features prominently in the constitutions of both Canada and the U.S., where it affords protection to a parent's relationship with their child when this is threatened by state intervention in child welfare proceedings. In particular, the weighting given to parental rights in U.S. family law is closely linked to the principle of liberty.

The legal system and the public sector: legislation, courts, welfare/rights and representation

The federated structures of both Canada and the U.S. mean that their legal systems are replicated at state and province levels, with considerable legislative differences at those levels, leaving little opportunity for federal government to impose nationwide laws.

Legislative framework

There are some umbrella pieces of federal legislation which, together with the respective constitutions and judicial decisions of their Supreme Courts, bring a degree of commonality to law and practice across all states and provinces.

INTERNATIONAL LAW

With the exception of the U.N. CROC (not yet ratified by the U.S.), both countries are subject to much the same framework of relevant international law.

DOMESTIC LEGISLATION

To a large extent, in matters of family law and child welfare, the states and provinces legislate in accordance with the politics of their constituencies, which means that they can differ markedly from each other. There are real cultural differences within each country – for example, between Québec, Nunavut and British Columbia – as there are between, say, Utah, South Carolina and California, let alone the differences between states and provinces. So domestic child welfare– related legislation within and between both countries can be disparate, incoherent and difficult to compare on a like-for-like basis.

However, the fact that both countries share the same common law heritage and, in particular, have Constitutions that derive from that heritage, should facilitate a degree of similarity in the shaping of their laws relating to children. This assumption has now been shaken somewhat by the USSC decision in *Dobbs* which casts doubt on the continuing value of the common law doctrine of precedent in the U.S.

Courts and regulatory framework

While the national framework of courts and regulatory bodies is much the same in both countries, they differ somewhat in their acceptance of international courts.

INTERNATIONAL JUDICIAL AND REGULATORY BODIES

Canada, unlike the U.S., accepts the jurisdiction of the International Criminal Court and the International Court of Justice. An international regulatory monitoring regime is provided for both countries through the Universal Periodic Review process, which is an important mechanism for analysing, comparing and contrasting national progress in relation to child welfare issues and other matters.

DOMESTIC JUDICIAL AND REGULATORY BODIES

The judicial architecture is much the same in both countries: the hierarchical structure of the state/province courts with attendant regulatory and advisory bodies is very similar, as is the federal court system, which is crowned by a federal Supreme Court that tests, on appeal, decisions of lower courts against provisions of the national Constitution.

FAMILY COURT AND FAMILY PROCEEDINGS

Unlike Canada, several states in the U.S. have introduced family courts. It is open to question, however, whether they are equivalent to the U.K. model, with integrated systems and procedures in designated courts staffed by trained specialist judiciary and other personnel. Tribal courts and legal processes, functioning in tandem with their statutory counterparts, are a characteristic feature of both jurisdictions.

JUVENILE COURT AND CRIMINAL PROCEEDINGS

Both countries have juvenile or youth courts, which were initially established at the beginning of the 20th century and now function with much the same cohort of professional support with respect to similar sets of proceedings. There are jurisdictional differences, however, in the lower-age threshold for offenders, disposal options and the cross-over with the adult legal system.

CHILDREN'S COMMISSIONER/OMBUDSMAN/RAPPORTEUR/CHILD ADVOCATE

The role of such an official is to act as an independent representative of children's interests in contexts such as child protection, rather than as a representative for an individual child. This most usually involves functions of research (identifying significant issues, collating related data, and involving relevant parties) and advocacy (building a case and assertively presenting it to relevant bodies to achieve change in law, policy or practice).

In neither the U.S. nor Canada is there such a national official/body, though both do have some variant in most states/provinces. International rapporteurs with varying briefs for child welfare issues are periodically engaged in both countries.

Representation for children

Clearly, if children are to have access to justice, then they need legal representation. Only then can they get the information needed to understand and effectively engage in proceedings, be informed about all aspects of the process, and be advised as to options and decisions to be taken and their consequences. The federated nature of both countries means that there is no standardised system, rules or cadre of professionals trained in child welfare issues as in the U.K., uniformly applicable in every state/province. Representation is not guaranteed in either country, particularly in private family law proceedings, but is more likely in the U.S., where 'due process' case precedents are rigorously applied.

CHILD IN COURT

The extent to which a child is authorised to participate in proceedings affecting their welfare interests – to have legal or other representation, to give consent to validate decisions taken relating to those interests – and whether their participation is age dependent are matters that determine whether or not the child is being treated as the subject of or a party to those proceedings. There do not appear to be any hard-and-fast rules on the right of a child to be heard on matters affecting their interests in court. It is probable, however, that such judicial willingness to allow child participation in proceedings would be strongest in the U.S.

CONSENT OF CHILD

In some states and provinces, statutory law, subject to age limitations, does declare such a right – usually in relation to the child's proposed adoption – but in most relevant proceedings, no mention is made of any such right. However, the courts in both countries are building a considerable body of jurisprudence on this matter, particularly around the age and maturity of the child relative to the gravity of the decision. Nonetheless, it can be said with some certainty that in both countries, while the consent of a child may not always be strictly necessary in all legal proceedings affecting their interests, the court will be slow to take decisions against the wishes of a discerning child.

The welfare principle in contemporary practice: public family law, civil jurisdiction

Safeguarding the welfare of children is a matter regulated by the provinces and territories in Canada and by the states in the U.S., although federal government has oversight in the latter, aided by some control over funding streams. In both, though more so in the U.S., the constitutional protection given to the privacy of parents and the integrity and independence of the family unit leaves little scope for a separate legal focus on the rights and welfare interests of children. It has to be said that this exercise in comparative analysis is greatly hindered by the lack of a Canadian national database capable of producing reliable and consistently tracked child welfare–related statistics.

Prevention

The best gauge of the success of a nation's preventative child care policies are the crude but telling statistics of the children it fails and who must then be admitted to state care. Applying that measure, the scale of Canada's failure is not just greater than that of the U.S.; it's greater than that of most developed countries.

State duties to support families and children in need

The Trump administration, as part of its pushback on the liberal legal developments of previous years and to further a return to more conservative family values, would seem to have invested a good deal of political and monetary capital in measures designed to shore up 'the family' as traditionally defined. This included targeting new laws and resources on service provision intended to support families and children in need and reduce the level of foster care admissions. These measures also had the effect of increasing federal control over state provision for families in need. In Canada, criticism regarding the relatively low levels of equivalent preventative service provision from international bodies such as the U.N. CRC resulted in the formulation of the Jordan's Principle and other federal initiatives to address the long-running service shortfall to the children in greatest need.

STATE INTERVENTION: CONSENSUAL – SUPPORT SERVICES

Alleviating parental stress, with the aim of avoiding court involvement and preventing the need to consider possible child protection procedures, is most often addressed by services such as counselling, cash grants or an offer of respite care. The national approach to such provision differs in that the U.S. has a well-established framework of federal legislation and funding mechanisms for directly targeting areas of state-identified need which has recently been boosted by the Title IV-E prevention services initiative; in contrast, the Canadian response would appear to be province led, historically without much federal input and resulting in sustained levels of inadequate provision in which service access is problematic. (It is possible that these deficiencies are now being addressed by the federal government.)

Protection

In both Canada and the U.S., there is legislative recognition at federal and state/provincial levels that 'child abuse' may be defined in terms of physical abuse, sexual abuse, emotional abuse or parental neglect, with exposure to domestic violence specifically acknowledged in Canada to be a source of emotional abuse, while 'child neglect' is understood in terms of depriving a child of the 'necessaries of life' or abandonment.

State intervention: coercive

In both countries, as in the U.K. and elsewhere, the publication of *The Battered Child Syndrome* in 1962[9] raised national awareness of child abuse. Again, in both countries, the drive to protect children by removing them from abusive or neglectful parental care would seem to be considerably higher than in the U.K. Mandatory reporting of actual or suspected child abuse or neglect is a statutory requirement throughout both countries, unlike in the U.K.

THE ORDERS

In Canada, as in the U.S., neglect rather than abuse provides the main grounds relied on for the issue of court orders transferring care responsibility from parents to the state. This is significant as it raises the possibility that levels of poverty rather than parental conduct are the primary cause of children being removed from their family homes.

In public care

The Canadian child-care population would appear to be significantly higher, proportionately, than that of the U.S. In both countries, Indigenous children are grossly overrepresented. State care has most often meant routine decision-making by child

9 Kempe, C.H. and Steele, B., *The Battered Child Syndrome*, Chicago University Press, (1962).

welfare officials as to where the child can best be fitted in and a submissive acceptance of that decision by an abused/neglected child. There is no evidence in either country of any awareness that the children concerned might be formally afforded some input regarding their preferred option.

Foster care: partnership, rehabilitation and concurrent planning

In both countries, in common with practice in other developed countries, children who have been failed by parental care are typically placed with foster families following court suspension or termination of their birth parents' rights. In both, some children will be in a temporary foster care placement pending removal to a permanent placement within a statutorily determined time period; some will remain in that foster placement and be adopted by their foster families; others will be matched with approved prospective adopters and transferred by the agency social workers to an agreed adoption placement. The trend towards adoption by foster parents is becoming more pronounced, assisted by state financial subsidies, in both countries.

This trend is deliberately promoted in both countries through the use of 'concurrent placements.' As in England and Wales, this strategy allows state authorities to pursue concurrently both the possibility of family reunification and the alternative of adoption by the foster carers.

PARTNERSHIP AND REHABILITATION

The principle that the state should do all it can to maintain relationships between a child in its care and that child's birth family and work towards reunifying child and family is, in practice, probably violated more often than it's upheld in both countries. Foster care, intended to be a temporary solution, has instead become the ultimate destination for tens of thousands of children in care, the vast majority of whom will not be reunited during childhood with their birth families. Many are shuttled through a series of foster homes; some are adopted by their foster parents. In the U.S., where a high proportion of children are discharged to parental or kinship care, for many this occurs only after they have 'aged out' of the system.

Residential care

The legacy of the abusive residential school regime imposed on Indigenous children in both countries acts as a restraint on its current use as a form of care for all children admitted to the public child welfare system.

SECURE ACCOMMODATION

Children are placed in secure accommodation for a wide range of reasons, including those who have run away from home or from state care as well as those who have committed serious crimes.[10] In both countries, secure accommodation for youths who are judged to be a danger to themselves or to others and require an intensive treatment regime is a growing area of need calling for additional appropriate service provision.

Adoption

Permanency care in a family has for many decades been accepted and promoted as the best option for children in state care following either the voluntary relinquishment of parental rights or the judicial termination of those of failed or abusive parents.

DOMESTIC CONSENSUAL ADOPTION

The state has always had a responsibility to find adopters for children voluntarily relinquished into its care for that purpose. While this particular adoption route has drastically shrunk in scale since the early 1970s, there are always a few babies adopted in this way. In the U.S., commercial as well as nonprofit adoption agencies have come to play a prominent role in such 'private adoptions,' a development which has spread to Canada but not to the same extent.

ADOPTION FROM PUBLIC CARE

In the U.S., as in Canada, the U.K., and elsewhere, the number of children non-consensually adopted from state care annually has been increasing – because more children are entering state care, because it secures permanent family care as the best opportunity for promoting child welfare, and because it is cheaper than state care – to become a prioritsed option for the state with respect to children failed by parental care.

Unaccompanied migrant minors and trafficking

The phenomenon of unaccompanied asylum-seeking children, has become a distinct social issue in recent years in the U.S. and Canada, as in Europe. This phenomenon overlaps with, and may often be used as a source for, the worsening social issue of 'child trafficking,' which is defined in the Palermo Protocol 2000 as recruiting, transporting, harbouring or receiving a child for the purposes of exploitation, such as sexual exploitation or forced labour. While this complex issue is clearly one in which the welfare interests of children are very much at risk – and is deserving of a book dedicated entirely to that subject – there is little political consensus on how best to intervene and protect those interests.

10 See O'Neill, T., *Children in Secure Accommodation*, Jessica Kingsley, (2001).

The welfare principle in contemporary practice: public family law, criminal jurisdiction

The scope for the welfare principle to affect the individualised needs of children in the U.S. juvenile justice system and – though to a lesser extent – that of its Canadian counterpart is more constrained than in other countries by the fact that many juveniles are not wholly subject to that system but instead end up being processed through adult criminal proceedings.

The system

Both the Canadian and the U.S. juvenile justice systems define as being outside their jurisdiction those more than 18 years of age and those accused of grave offences, though there can be wide variation as to how the latter is interpreted at state and provincial levels. In Canada, the disproportionate representation of Indigenous juveniles has been a matter of concern to international bodies, as has the racial disparity – adversely affecting Black Americans – in those admitted to the U.S. system.

Children who pose a threat to the welfare of self or others

The statistical evidence shows a marked reduction in juvenile offenders in both countries in recent years (quite possibly attributable, at least in part, to the COVID-19 pandemic). It also points up the inescapable racial bias in both systems.

AGE OF CRIMINAL RESPONSIBILITY

There is a marked disparity between the two countries in terms of when a child becomes criminally liable for their behaviour: this is fixed nationally in Canada at age 12 while in the U.S., it is mostly age 7 (11 for federal crimes). It does seem extraordinary, in relation to comparable ages in other developed nations, that a higher age of criminal responsibility has not been established on a nationwide basis in the U.S.

PREVENTION

A range of diversionary programmes has been designed to keep youths from becoming involved in the formal justice system and to discourage those who have been involved from recidivism. In many European jurisdictions. such preventative intervention is treated and funded as a form of public service, with specific responsibilities assigned to designated public authorities. In the U.S., however, although there is relevant federal legislation reinforced by funding streams, forms of preventative intervention are left largely to the nonprofit sector rather than the state.

Juvenile court

In both countries, the primary functions of this court would seem to be the protection of the public by holding youths accountable for their criminal behaviour, and to that extent, it is indistinguishable from the purpose of adult courts. However, recent USSC rulings indicate a willingness to differentiate the remit of juvenile and adult courts on the basis that the former should give consideration to the welfare needs of children.

ROLE OF THE WELFARE PRINCIPLE

In the first instance, the role of this principle is evidenced by the extent of the diversionary alternatives available to the authorities instead of a court appearance. In the event of a court hearing being necessary, the relevance of the principle is ultimately demonstrated in the judicially preferred disposal options. It is also evident in the existence of specific provisions governing the sentencing of young offenders, which are separate and distinct from those imposed on adults.

In the U.S., the welfare principle is ostensibly central to the primary objective of the juvenile justice system, which is stated to be the rehabilitation of offenders, but in practice, the objective would seem to be essentially punitive. In Canada, while there is no legislative mention of the principle, its influence can be seen in the role of the youth justice committees and in the more respectful treatment of offenders in court.

COURT ORDERS: COMMUNITY SENTENCES

Community-based measures give tangible effect to welfare considerations, and from that perspective, the greater range of such options in Canada – including 'extrajudicial sanctions' – indicate that its juvenile justice system leans more towards welfare than its U.S. counterpart.

COURT ORDERS: CUSTODIAL SENTENCES

Reliance on custodial rather than community sentences reflects a justice system emphasis on punishment rather than on welfare, which is clearly more the case in the U.S. than in Canada. The fact that in both countries, significant numbers of children end up being incarcerated in adult facilities is a particularly grievous infringement of the welfare principle.

Solitary confinement The generally proclaimed purpose of youth justice is the rehabilitation of offenders. If this is true, then solitary confinement is wholly contrary to furthering that purpose. Nonetheless, it is extensively used with respect to children judged to be in need of a safely structured treatment regime or who may be a risk to themselves or others.

The welfare principle in contemporary practice: private family law

Since at least the closing decades of the 20th century, family law and the courts in Canada and the U.S., as in all developed countries, have been dominated by matrimonial and other proceedings involving care arrangements for children. It is probable that family life is becoming more fluid, transient, and prone to serial parenting arrangements than ever before and is consequently generating an increasing number of situations in which the welfare of children is being compromised.

Children and reconstituted families

A reconstituted or 'blended' family has been defined by the Pew Centre as any household that includes a stepparent, stepsibling, or half sibling.[11] Needless to say, the entailed dislocation and disruption to relationships in such parenting arrangements place a heavy burden on the welfare interests of the children involved.

Matrimonial

In all matrimonial proceedings in Canada and the U.S. in which children are involved, the court will always rule on child custody and child support matters. However, the term 'matrimonial proceedings' is becoming steadily more redundant as the parties in an increasing proportion of court proceedings involving custody or other arrangements concerning the future care of children are unmarried or are not married to each other.

FAMILY BREAKDOWN AND THE WELFARE PRINCIPLE

In Canada, the primary legislation is the Divorce Act 1985, as heavily amended in 2019 with effect from 2021. This federal statute now requires the courts in all provinces to apply the 'best interests of the child' as the only consideration to be taken into account when issuing orders for the future care arrangements for children. It further provides that such 'best interests' are to be determined in accordance with a checklist of 11 factors – with a high degree of specificity, not unlike the U.K. welfare checklist – which require the child's views and preferences to be specifically considered 'giving due weight to the child's age and maturity, unless they cannot be ascertained.' The latter requirement repeats a traditional standard formula, entirely discretionary in application, which fails to import any concrete recognition of a child's rights and retains the subjective clause despite some strong lobbying to have it removed. While the 'best interests test' is necessarily applied in a manner that takes account of the particular child's age, character and circumstances, there is no requirement that it be treated as a matter of paramount importance. It is also clear that, following the introduction of the 2019 amendments, the application of the 'best interests' test as defined in the Divorce Act will be followed – as before the amendments – by the judiciary applying the same interpretation of that test when dealing with custody disputes arising in a nonmatrimonial context.

11 See, further, at www.pewsocialtrends.org/files/2014/11/2014–11–14_remarriage-final.pdf, www.pewresearch.org/fact-tank/2014/12/04/tying-the-knot-again-chances-are-theres-a-bigger-age-gap-than-the-first-time-around/.

In the U.S., the Uniform Marriage and Divorce Act 1970 introduced the requirement that a child's wishes be factored into any determination of his or her best interests in custody decisions; as in Canada, this traditional standard formulaic phrasing left the judiciary with wide discretionary powers to determine what, in any particular set of circumstances, constituted the 'best interests' of the child concerned. In practice, each state has its own legislation dealing with divorce, separation, custody, and associated proceedings in which the 'best interests' test is variously stated, as are the requirements to ascertain and give consideration to the wishes of the child. Unlike Canada, in the U.S., there is no nationwide requirement that this test be interpreted and applied in accordance with a statutorily specified 'welfare checklist.' Significantly, the welfare test does not require the child's consent, nor is there any suggestion that they have any rights in relation to the decision. Again, unlike the equivalent position in Canada, there has been no change to the terminology traditionally used: 'custody,' 'contact,' and 'guardianship' continue to be the focus of proceedings and the resulting court orders, save for the anomaly of 'conservatorship.'

Guardianship

This most ancient of family law orders continues to serve its traditional function, in both Canada and the U.S., of vesting parental responsibility for a child in someone other than the child's parents. When such a person wishes to become a guardian, this must be undertaken through a legal process: generally, a parent will transfer guardianship to a specific person, usually in circumstances in which that parent has a disabling condition – such as opioid addiction or a terminal illness – and wants to plan a legally secure future for their child and does so by means of a sworn affidavit or by court application. Alternatively, where the parent(s) have been found criminally liable for the abuse or neglect of their child, a court may issue a guardianship order in favour of a named responsible person, usually a relative. While the 'best interests' test will almost certainly be applied, this will not be interpreted as giving a child a right to consent or withhold consent to a proposed guardianship, nor does the test imply that the child's welfare interests are treated as being of paramount importance.

Adoption

In Canada, as in the U.S. – but unlike many other countries, such as the U.K. – the law permits private adoptions, either direct parental placements or mediated by a registered nonprofit or for-profit adoption agency, operating on a domestic or intercountry basis. The fact that an estimated 40–50% of annual adoptions are arranged privately is a strong indicator of jurisdictional similarity between Canada and its neighbour. The discretion to permit a commercial component to private placements is a distinctive and long-standing characteristic of the adoption process in the U.S., which, elsewhere, is viewed as contentious. The placement decision is rightly held to be the crucial component in ensuring that an adoption furthers the welfare interests of the child, and for that reason, in other countries, the decision is almost always legally removed from parental discretion and entrusted instead to the professional staff of a government body or a registered independent adoption agency.

ADOPTERS

The U.S. is singular among the developed common-law nations in its approach to potential adopters: restrictive criteria are applied in some states to filter out those deemed to be unsuitable, which in a number of states means excluding applications from the LGBT community.

STEPPARENT ADOPTION

The fact that for many years in both countries, a large proportion of all adoptions have been by stepparents is not unlike the similar trend established in the U.K. Arguably, the welfare interests of a child play, at best, a minimal legal role in such adoptions, which almost always entail the child remaining in the care of a birth parent, in the family home, and within the same extended network of relatives, friends and community facilities.

CULTURAL/RELIGIOUS AFFINITY

Any suggestion that such an affinity between adopters and adoptee is a necessary component of the latter's welfare interests is both statutorily and constitutionally barred from impeding domestic transracial adoptions in Canada as it is in the U.S. and rarely arises in the context of ICA. However, the fact remains that in adoption from the U.S. public welfare system, African American children are consistently underrepresented, which indicates the presence of a racial bias. The reverse issue arises in relation to the adoption of Indigenous children by non-Indigenous applicants, whose right to do so is often challenged on the grounds that such an adoption, by virtue of its lack of racial congruity, deprives the child of their cultural identity and therefore cannot be conducive, in the long term, to promoting their welfare interests.

POST-ADOPTION CONTACT, INFORMATION DISCLOSURE AND STATE SUPPORT SERVICES

Post-adoption contact between adoptee and birth family – now the case in most U.K. adoptions – is not as well established in law and practice in either Canada or the U.S. In both countries, this is legally permissible but is the exception rather than the rule. In the U.S., the possibility of post-adoption contact is compromised by the practice of 'closed' adoption files, and in Canada, it is inhibited by a legislative and judicial approach which is generally not facilitative and is perhaps indicative of a continuing culture of secrecy that has long been associated with adoption. An uncertain level of post-adoption support from public and/or nonprofit organisations is available in both countries. However, in neither do the welfare interests of an adopted child provide any statutory guarantee of pre- or post-adoption access to support services or identifying information.

INTERCOUNTRY ADOPTION

Canada and the U.S. have in common the fact that, in recent years, they have shared the experience of a sharp and sustained drop in annual ICAs. This has been due to several factors, including displacement of ICA by commercial surrogacy, the imposition of new stringent exclusionary criteria by Russia and China, and their ratification of the Hague Convention. It may be, of course, that the precipitous fall in the rate of such adoptions can be interpreted as a measure of the success of Hague in filtering out prospective adoptees whose availability could have been due to fraud and corruption, but whether doing so has added to or subtracted from the welfare interests of those unadopted children is a moot point.

More positively, it has to be acknowledged that the Chinese policy of virtually restricting the use of ICA to children with varying degrees of social or health-care needs – and the willingness of U.S. and Canadian adopters to respond to the challenges involved – has enabled many children from China – and, indeed, from other donor countries that now apply the same policy – to benefit from family life and a level of health care unavailable to them in their countries of origin. Arguably, this can also be seen as an evolving juncture of public/private family law in which the state is outsourcing its public care responsibilities to the private sector.

Surrogacy

In the U.S., unlike Canada, surrogacy is available not just on an altruistic basis but also commercially; therefore, it has a hybrid public/private dimension. (See, further, later in this chapter.)

SURROGATE, CHILD AND THE COMMISSIONING PARENTS

Surrogacy can generate controversy regarding the welfare interests of the children involved. For example, personal identity issues can arise for those born as a result of surrogacy arrangements: issues often complicated by a lack of information on the donor and their genetic background (health, skills/aptitudes, family history, etc).

Abduction

Given the high levels of immigration and emigration in Canada and the U.S., coupled with the volume of interstate and interprovince travel, the incidence of child abduction allegations – or unauthorised removal by a noncustodial parent – has been a particular problem in both countries. Although parental abduction is clearly, at best, a confusing experience for children, generating uncertainty and insecurity, and can be harmful to the welfare of some, stranger abduction is incomparably worse but occurs much less frequently.

RETURNING AN ABDUCTED CHILD

The approach of Canadian authorities to demands for the return of a child abducted – almost always by a parent – from their Canadian home differs from that taken in the U.S. in similar circumstances. Instead of following the U.S. example, with its emphasis on deterring abductions by automatically requiring the prompt return of the child to the place and the person from whom they were abducted, the Canadian judiciary adopt an approach which is perhaps more Hague Convention compliant. The U.S. approach criminalises the abductor and, in effect, determines custody, whereas the Canadian approach, in keeping with Hague, simply seeks to do no more than restore the status quo as it was before the abduction.

Proportionality Judicial interpretation of what constitutes the 'best interests' of an abducted child coupled with the views expressed by an older abducted child have introduced some leeway for a judicial balancing of the interests of the parties concerned and allowed decisions to be reached by applying the principle of proportionality. The *Balev* case[12] in Canada and the *Abbott* case[13] in the U.S. would seem to indicate that this principle is now playing much the same role in the context of child abduction in both countries.

Child's wishes The Hague Convention, Article 13(2), states:

> [T]he judicial or administrative authority may also refuse to order the return of the child if it finds that the child objects to being returned and has attained an age and degree of maturity at which it is appropriate to take account of its view.

While the caselaw shows the judiciary in both countries paying respect to this provision, it also shows that the age at which a child's wishes are to be sought and the weighting then given to them are matters for judicial discretion, which can leave little scope for those wishes to be determinative.

The welfare principle in contemporary practice: public/private family law

Canadian and U.S. caselaw have long established the principle that the liberty and independence of the individual must be protected from any unwarranted state intrusion. However, the increasing number of points at which public law now transects private family law reflects a growing state encroachment on personal liberties.

12 *Office of the Children's Lawyer v. Balev*, 2018 SCC 16.
13 *Abbott v. Abbott*, 130 S.Ct. 1983 (2010).

Public/private family law

The capacity of a *grundnorm* to transcend the context that gave rise to it – allowing it be redefined and broadly repurposed to become a central reference point capable of underpinning a school of jurisprudence – has been explained by Kelsen.[14] The principle of the welfare of the child has clearly attained that status, is steadily extending its reach, and, in so doing, is bridging the traditional divide between private and public family law.

Public service matters

Unquestionably, a society that provides a sufficient platform of public services for all its citizens – health care, housing, education, etc, will, on the 'rising tide floats all boats' principle, thereby also ameliorate child welfare issues. Such a platform will not exist or have that effect in a context of significant poverty when the dynamic is then reversed. In both Canada and the U.S., the wealth disparity between high- and low-income families has reached a level of structural inequality, insufficiently mitigated by public service provision, which must exacerbate child welfare issues. An adequate framework of such services is essential if the parenting capacity of many socially disadvantaged families is to remain adequate: the correlation seems inescapable.

EMPLOYMENT

Human Rights Watch has expressed concern regarding the current health and safety conditions of child employment in the U.S. agricultural industry.[15] It has also drawn attention to the fact that Canada has not taken action to eliminate the overseas practice of employing child labour – at exploitive rates of pay while working long hours in poor workplace conditions – to produce products that feed into the Canadian consumer chain.

HEALTH

The fact that, in 2020, an international body ranked Canada 30th out of 38 affluent countries for childhood well-being would seem a damning indictment of public health and social care provision for children. There would appear to be a strong health and wealth correlation; children in the poorer communities, especially the Indigenous, are the unhealthiest.[16] On this most basic indicator of child welfare, the state is failing the poorest Canadian children. In the U.S., there is

14 See Hans Kelsen, *Pure Theory of Law*, (1934), The Lawbook Exchange, Ltd, 2009.

15 See Human Rights Watch, Fields of Peril: Child Labor in U.S. Agriculture' and 'US: Child Farmworkers Dangerous Lives' at www.hrw.org/news/2010/05/05/us-child-farmworkers-dangerous-lives.

16 See, for example, Raphael D., The health of Canada's children. Part I: Canadian children's health in comparative perspective, *Paediatrics & Child Health*, (2010): 15(1), 23–9.

also cause for concern. The findings of a 2022 report show that there is a significant level of poor mental health among American children.[17] It would seem that the health care of children in the U.S., like so much else, is very much left to market forces. In that country, as in Canada, being governed by social determinants, the health and welfare interests of children are very much tied to parental socio-economic status.

EDUCATION

The relationship between parents, the state and the welfare of children – in the context of education – generates contention in many countries and certainly does so in both Canada and the U.S., where the legacy of residential schools stands as a reminder of how bad those relationships can be. Currently, echoes of clashes generated by religious beliefs and the culture wars now reverberate throughout the classrooms of both countries,[18] though perhaps more so in those of the U.S.

Legal proceedings

In these two countries, with their federated governance structures, where family law and the welfare of children are among the matters that fall to be addressed at state/province level rather than by the federal government, the consequent disparate range of relevant legal proceedings makes a comparative jurisdictional analysis of those proceedings tenable only at a high level of generality.

ADOPTION FROM PUBLIC CARE

While there is considerable variation among the provinces and states, the fact that adoption from care is becoming – and, in some places, has already become – the primary source of adoptees suggests that, in Canada as in the U.S., adoption is now firmly a hybrid public/private family law proceeding. This is heavily supported by state subsidies for the adoption of children from state care and by the recruitment targeting of foster parents who are prepared to adopt. This practice, whereby state responsibilities for neglected and abused children are, in effect, privatised, has been pursued with particular vigour in the U.S., where authorities are incentivised by reinforcement schemes such as federal bonus payments to those who exceed their prescribed quota of annual adoptions.

17 See, Lebrun-Harris, L.A., Ghandour, R.M. and Kogan, M.C., Five-Year Trends in US Children's Health and Well-being, 2016–2020, *JAMA Pediatrics.* 2022; 176(7), https://jamanetwork.com/journals/jamapediatrics/fullarticle/2789946.

18 See, for example, in the U.S., *Peloza v. Capistrano Unified School Dist.*, 37 F. 3d 517 (9th Cir. 1994) and, in Canada, *SL v. Commission scolaire des Chênes*, [2012] 1 SCR 235.

WARDSHIP

In both countries, the powers of wardship are normally sought when statutory procedures are inappropriate or insufficient to cope with complex and/or urgent cases where the welfare interests of a child are at serious risk. Recourse to wardship is frequently made by medical practitioners or concerned others when otherwise caring and competent parents refuse specific treatment for their child on grounds of religious belief; most often, the beliefs are those of Jehovah's Witnesses, and the treatments objected to involve the use of blood products. In both countries, as elsewhere, once a child has been made a ward of court, that court is then empowered to apply the paramountcy principle when making any decision regarding their upbringing: in effect, the court can use that power to override the wishes of all other parties, including the wishes of a ward who is a mature minor, in order to direct that the judicial view prevails.

Additionally, Canada is unique in its use of wardship in that it ascribes that status to an entire class of children: Crown wards are those children in state care for whom all parental rights have been judicially removed by a TPR order, rendering each child available for adoption.

COMMERCIAL SURROGACY

In the U.S., in all but two states, commercial surrogacy is available. This means that normal free market conditions apply, which, in turn, decreases the viability of altruistic surrogacy and leaves this practice functioning in the U.S. largely as a hybrid form of public/private family law. While commercial surrogacy is prohibited in Canada, the fact that – as in Ireland – many couples make commercial surrogacy arrangements overseas and then return home with their child also brings such arrangements into the definition of 'hybrid.' In both countries, this practice inevitably raises thorny questions as to whether it's the welfare interests of a child or the acquisitive interests of childless couples that are being served, though unquestionably, the fact that so much trouble and expense is invested in a 'wanted' child must increase the probability of their welfare being assured.

Court orders

In both countries, in addition to the use of wardship, only a very limited number of court orders meet the definition of 'hybrid.'

GUARDIANSHIP ORDER

Again, in both countries, this ancient order with its origins in private family law has been repurposed to also be available as a public order: a means whereby the state entrusts or is entrusted with physical possession of and day-to-day responsibility for a child deemed by the court to be in need of substitute parental care.

OTHER

In the U.S. and Canada, as in all developed nations, there is a range of orders with a mix of public and private functions. These include orders for maintenance, restraining a parent from unwanted contact, non-molestation, etc., all of which contribute to protecting the welfare interests of children in both countries.

(B) Canada and the United States: the welfare principle in an Indigenous context

The Indigenous inhabitants of the U.S. and Canada are now recognised as full citizens of the countries they have lived in for millennia – such recognition was slow in coming[19] – and on attaining that status, they became wholly subject to national law. Through state/tribal treaties, they also acquired recognition for their tribal laws, customs and practices. Consequently, in both countries, the Indigenous tribes and their members are, to some extent, subject to a dual set of legal systems. Tribal courts and legal processes function, to some extent, in tandem with the national statutory regime as framed by federal and state/province governments; the rules determining the respective jurisdictions of these two systems can be uncertain. In Canada, the span of tribal authority, their courts, and processes is currently being reviewed by the SCC.

Indigenous communities and the welfare of the child

The constitutions of the U.S. and Canada both recognise and provide at least a protective status for Indigenous people, including the welfare of their children, and both delegate most relevant powers for addressing Indigenous issues to the states/provinces, reserving only certain treaty obligations and funding responsibilities to the federal governments. However, in both countries, the web of legal complexities surrounding who qualifies as an Indigenous person, which tribes have formal federal or state/province recognition of that status, and the distinction between on- and off-reservation members makes it difficult to determine in many cases whether state/province, tribe or federal government bears responsibility for matters affecting the welfare of Indigenous children.

Background

As in other countries subject to British colonialism – including but not confined to the so-called CANZUS nations (Canada, Australia, New Zealand and the U.S.) – a policy of cultural defenestration and enforced assimilation of Indigenous people

19 For Indigenous people in the U.S., this was granted on 2 June 1924 under the Indian Citizenship Act 1924. (Though not until 1957 did all Indigenous adults in all states have the right to vote.) The Indigenous people of Canada were granted citizenship on 1 January 1947 under the Canadian Citizenship Act 1947. (Though not until an amendment was passed in 1956 did it become all inclusive, and voting rights for many were denied until the 1970s.)

was rigorously pursued well into the second half of the 20th century. This was reinforced in recent years by an intransigent reluctance to endorse international instruments such as UNDRIP designed to protect those communities.[20]

RESIDENTIAL SCHOOLS AND ADOPTION

The assimilation strategy was pursued in both countries by targeting Indigenous children and applied through the systematic use of residential schools over many generations, with the explicit purpose of stripping children of their cultural identity and replacing it with that of the colonial power. As a late adjunct to policies of residential schooling, Canada and the U.S., in common with other colonial nations in the mid-19th century, resorted to a policy of enforced adoption as part of a strategy to absorb Indigenous children into mainstream Caucasian society. This subject has attracted a good deal of international academic study.[21] As outlined in the relevant jurisdiction-specific chapters, although the policy largely failed, it did cause serious harm, cultural disruption and intergenerational trauma among the Indigenous communities of both countries.

CHILD PROTECTION AND CULTURAL IDENTITY

Given the history of residential schools and adoption being systematically deployed to erode Indigenous culture, it was perhaps unsurprising that in both Canada and the U.S., there would be a suspicion of a carry-over of the same practice into child protection issues. Because of the lack of approved Indigenous foster parents, children removed from their Indigenous parents were often placed with non-Indigenous couples. This phenomenon had the effect of confusing the children involved, compromising their sense of identity, adversely impacting the cultural integrity of the tribes, and adding further to the cycle of tribal intergenerational trauma. There is a considerable body of evidence to suggest that the consequences of repeated exposure to cultural violation can now be seen in the overrepresentation of Indigenous children and adults across all indices of contemporary social disadvantage.

20 The United Nations Declaration on the Rights of Indigenous Peoples (UNDRIP) was adopted by the General Assembly on 13 September 2007, by a majority of 144 states in favour, 4 votes against (Australia, Canada, New Zealand, and the United States). Eventually, the U.S. endorsed in December 2010, with Canada following in September 2021.

21 See, for example: Nichols, R. L., From the Sixties Scoop to Baby Veronica: Transracial Adoption of Indigenous Children in the USA and Canada, in Shackleton, M. (ed.), *International Adoption in North American Literature and Culture: Transnational, Transracial, and Transcultural Narratives*, Helsinki, Palgrave Macmillan, (2017), at 3–26; Jacobs, M., *A Generation Removed: The Fostering & Adoption of Indigenous Children in the Postwar World*, Lincoln: University of Nebraska Press, (2014); Swain, S., 'Homes are Sought for These Children': Locating Adoption within the Australian Stolen Generations Narrative, *American Indian Quarterly*, (2013): 37(1–2), at 203–217; and Newman, E., History of Transracial Adoption: A New Zealand Perspective, *American Indian Quarterly*, (2013): 37(1–2), at 237–257.

Evolving policy, principles and law

The similarity of their historical child abuse experiences – residential schools and forced adoption – perhaps conveys an impression that the national policy, principles and laws of these two countries have evolved similarly. This is not the case. Neither is it the case that their respective evolutionary processes are complete: as of summer 2022, both the U.S. and Canada are engaged with some fundamental issues that will shape the future legal relationships between federal government and the Indigenous people.

Policy

Arguably, it was the civil rights movement in the U.S. that initiated a resurgence of cultural identity among the Indigenous tribes of both the U.S. and Canada from the late 1960s, or, and perhaps more importantly, it triggered a recognition by others of the significance of that identity. Formal recognition of the status of Indigenous people and the responsibilities of government at all levels to respect their rights and ensure their protection began to be demonstrated in the federal legislation of both countries in the late 1970s.

Principles

While more general principles – such as 'proportionality,' 'consanguinity' and 'parental rights' – are undoubtedly relevant, it is those that have particular applicability to the circumstances and experience of Indigenous people and their children that are most salient for present purposes.

Respect for cultural integrity

There is probably no greater issue for Indigenous people everywhere than that they should be allowed to revive, practice and hand down to their children the unique cultural heritage known to their tribe over previous generations. This has been a hard-won battle in Canada and the U.S. in the face of an obdurate state assimilationist policy.[22] It might be added that although there are now claims in both countries – with particular assertiveness in the U.S. – that the tribes have attained recognition of their right to sovereignty, there is little evidence to suggest that an increase in their autonomy has, so far, translated into sovereignty.

Given the civil rights context, it was perhaps inevitable that the principle of respect for the cultural integrity of Indigenous people first found legislative support in the U.S., well before similar initiatives in Canada. The Indian Child Welfare Act (ICWA) 1978 followed the introduction of the Indian Civil Rights Act 1968 and

22 This policy clearly does not square with the claim that the Constitution recognises the tribal nations as sovereign governments (a claim difficult to sustain in the face of evidence such as the Wounded Knee episode, which indicates little federal interest in tribal sovereignty).

the Indian Self-Determination and Education Assistance Act 1975 and was much more significant. With the 1978 Act, the U.S. federal government finally began to address the issues raised 50 years earlier in the Meriam Report.[23] The legislative intent was explicit: it sought to assert a positive legal approach towards the welfare interests of Indian children, protect their cultural identity and reassure all Indigenous people that, henceforth, the cultural affinity between child, parents and tribe would be respected. However, although this legislation restored to tribal governments the power to determine the placement of children, it applied only to federally recognised AI/AN tribes, to the exclusion of state-recognised entities. Nonetheless, the ICWA has ever since been regarded as the 'gold standard' for state engagement with Indigenous tribes.

The 1985 amendments to the Indian Act transformed the latter into what might be viewed as the Canadian federal equivalent of the ICWA. Bill C-31 then sought to eliminate discriminatory provisions and ensure compliance with the charter.

Equity of service provision

A strong argument can be made that the overrepresentation of U.S. and Canadian Indigenous children across all indices of social disadvantage – perhaps particularly in the child welfare and juvenile justice systems – is attributable in good part to their underrepresentation as recipients of government preventative services.

The principle that there should be equity of service provision has been of particular importance to the Canadian Indigenous population, which had protested for many years that federal funding for services was being distributed inequitably, disadvantaging Indigenous children on reservations. This was confirmed by the decision in *Daniels*,[24] which, in turn, led to Bill C-92 – an Act Respecting First Nations, Inuit and Métis Children, Youth and Families – becoming law, with effect from January 2020. This legislation affirmed:

> the right and jurisdiction of Indigenous peoples in relation to child and family services and [set] out principles applicable, on a national level, to the provision of child and family services in relation to Indigenous children, such as the best interests of the child, cultural continuity and substantive equality.

This principle has also had a high salience in the U.S., where lengthy protests from Indigenous communities focused on their inequitable access to federal Title IV funding, which was confirmed in a 1994 report by the Department of Health and Human Services.[25]

23 The Meriam Report, *The Problem of Indian Administration*, (1928), https://narf.org/nill/resources/meriam.html.

24 *Daniels v. Canada (Indian Affairs and Northern Development)*, [2016] S.C.R. 425 (Can.).

25 See Office of Inspector General (OIG), Opportunities for Administration for Children and Families to Improve Child Welfare Services and Protections for Native American Children, (August 1994), OEI-01–93–00110, https://oig.hhs.gov/oei/reports/oei-01–93–00110.pdf.

Law

Although both countries have signed and ratified most international treaties, conventions, etc – including, most importantly for present purposes, UNDRIP – the fact that the U.S. still has not ratified U.N. CROC constitutes a significant point of jurisdictional difference.

Domestically, a complex web of federal Indigenous policy, treaties, and intergovernmental relationships constructed over the centuries, together with state/province laws, form a backdrop to the contemporary body of laws relating to the AI/AN, the First Nation, and other Canadian tribes and to the welfare of their children. Additionally, in both countries, there are constitutional provisions setting out federal responsibilities towards their Indigenous populations.

In Canada, the Act respecting First Nations, Inuit and Métis Children, Youth and Families 2020 promises to establish a new baseline for federal service provision for Indigenous tribes, families and children by ceding control of funding to tribal authorities. This initiative, seemingly recognising tribal sovereignty, is due to be examined by the SCC. That precise issue – whether tribal sovereignty is constitutionally compliant – when determined will also have implications for the corresponding *locus standi* of the AI/AN tribes in the U.S.

The legal system and Indigenous children

Both the U.S. and Canadian legal systems share the troubling distinction of processing a young offender population in which Indigenous children are grossly overrepresented and have been for many years.

REPRESENTATION AND THE CHILD'S CONSENT

In theory, both countries are required to ensure that an Indigenous child – whether appearing before a tribal or state/province court – is represented by an attorney. In addition, a tribal representative or someone 'culturally competent' should be present to safeguard the child's cultural heritage by mediating between the child and court officials, interpreting, and explaining the cultural implications of any matters arising, particularly as regards disposal options. Where a child more than 12 years of age and of sufficient maturity to understand the matter at issue and its significance wishes to give or withhold consent to a decision in relation to that issue, the courts in both countries will at least take their views into account but will reserve to themselves the final responsibility for determining what they consider to be in the child's best interests.

The welfare principle in contemporary practice: public family law, civil jurisdiction

In both countries, the Indigenous and non-Indigenous communities and their respective child welfare agencies are essentially bound by the same state/provincial laws.

State intervention: consensual

The aforementioned shared jurisdictional characteristic of the overrepresentation of Indigenous children in child welfare and juvenile justice systems is clear testimony to a common jurisdictional failure to address the causes of neglect and the criminal behaviour of Indigenous children, which, in turn, points to a lack of effective preventative services.

State duties to support families and children in need

Indigenous children are often chronically disadvantaged. In part, this may be attributable to jurisdictional slippage in responsibility for funding the necessary services: in both countries, long-standing problems have obstructed tribal access to federal funding.

PREVENTATIVE INTERVENTION

Given the research findings,[26] it might have been anticipated that an investment of more resources would be channelled in the direction suggested by the predictive indicators of out-of-home care – poverty, lack of basic needs, etc – with the objective of relieving pressure and preventing the necessity for admission to the child welfare system. In fact, neither those findings nor the explicit preventative legislative principles (such as those found in Jordan's Principle and the ICWA) have increased effective service provision or reduced the overrepresentation of Indigenous children in the welfare and justice systems of either country.

State intervention: coercive

Coercive state intervention in family affairs on grounds of child neglect or abuse is governed by statute and is equally applicable to Indigenous and all other children. In practice, that intervention may be conducted by tribal authorities and be determined by a hearing before a tribal or state/province court (in the case of an off-the-reservation child).

State care

Again, regardless of which of the parallel care routes – state/province or tribal – to which an Indigenous child is admitted, the disposal options are much the same and subject to the mandatory hierarchy of placement choices and the explicit requirement that the professionals involved – from probation service or the child welfare

26 See, for example, in the U.S., Carter, V., Prediction of Placement into Out-of-Home Care for American Indian/Alaskan Natives Compared to Non-Indians, *Children and Youth Services Review*, 2009, and Pew Charitable Trust report 'Time for Reform: A Matter of Justice for American Indian and Alaskan Native Children, 2007; in Canada, Fallon, B., Lefebvre, R., Trocmé, N., et al., Denouncing the Continued Overrepresentation of First Nations Children in Canadian Child Welfare, (2019), op cit.

authorities – ensure that members of the child's family and tribe are engaged in formulating the care plan.

Foster care: partnership, rehabilitation and concurrent planning

The cultural dissonance between the Indigenous and non-Indigenous communities is particularly acute at times of family disruption. Tribal coherence, whereby members are bound by mutual ties of loyalty and belonging, is fundamentally threatened when state authorities or their tribal counterparts pursue invasive inquiries and remove a child from the tribe into state foster care.

FOSTER CARE

In both Canada and the U.S., there are clear statutory directives requiring that when an Indigenous child requires out-of-home care, preference in order of priority should be given to foster care with birth family, a relative or another tribal member. Nonetheless, in both, the shortage of Indigenous foster carers results in children often being placed with non-Indigenous foster parents, often located far from the birth family and other tribal connections. Once placed, every effort must be made to maintain the child's relationships with birth family members, tribe and culture.

PARENT/CHILD RELATIONSHIP

Maintaining the bonds of attachment between a child in foster care and members of their family of origin is clearly more difficult when that child is from an Indigenous community: the shortage of Indigenous foster parents, the distances involved, and quite often the poverty constraints affecting the child's family and community all present real obstacles. The legal obligation requiring child welfare authorities to work towards rehabilitating the child into safe parental care is the same in both countries.

The welfare principle in contemporary practice: public family law, criminal jurisdiction

The fact that in the U.S., as in Canada, Indigenous children are overrepresented in the respective justice systems is probably the single strongest shared jurisdictional characteristic of the law as it relates to offending Indigenous children. The situation is likely to be considerably worse than the statistics indicate because of the significant numbers of youths transferred from the juvenile to the adult systems. Any such transfer would seem to violate the protection owed to children and constitute a breach of the welfare principle.

The system

The authorities and academics of both countries are in agreement that the present system is failing Indigenous youth. In both, there is a distinct policy underway to develop restorative justice as a possible strategy for addressing the common overrepresentation problem. They both are also focusing on exploring ways of transferring more of the administration and adjudication of justice issues from the present system into tribal control. This would seem to be at a more advanced stage in Canada, thanks to the Indigenous justice programme launched in 1996.

Children who pose a threat to the welfare of self or others

Canada and the U.S. are faced with rising violent crimes committed by and upon Indigenous youth. In the U.S., while the violent youth crime rate has steadily declined over the past few years, that committed in tribal communities continues to grow. In Canada, the number of violent crime victims among Indigenous youth is twice that among the non-Indigenous.

PREVENTION

The rates of violent crime, linked inevitably to the overrepresentation of Indigenous children in systems of child welfare and justice, clearly reflect the failure of state/province authorities to implement effective strategies capable of preventing those children from offending. Both countries have recently embarked on initiatives that support crime prevention by referring young persons to community-based programmes and agencies that specialise in diversionary activities and therapeutic interventions.

Tribal/state juvenile court

The authorities in both countries have openly admitted that existing preventative strategies are not working, that the overrepresentation of Indigenous youth in the justice system is a serious indictment of governmental failure to address their needs, and that consequently, a new approach must be devised. The common jurisdictional answer would seem to be to vest more responsibility in the tribal authorities, enabling them to implement culturally appropriate preventative programmes, police a range of antisocial and criminal behaviour, adjudicate on breaches of the law in tribal courts, and impose noncustodial penalties, all of which is in keeping with the 'tribal sovereignty' dictum, but this has yet to be tested for constitutional compatibility.

ROLE OF THE WELFARE PRINCIPLE

It would seem that the legislature and judiciary in both countries have, in recent years, pretty much consistently viewed the welfare of the child very narrowly – as synonymous with preserving the cultural integrity of that child's tribe – and protecting the child's welfare as meaning ensuring ongoing connectivity between child and tribe.

SENTENCING

Despite the existence of government policy and legislative provisions in both countries that facilitate noncustodial options, the end result is a consistent judicial reliance on custody for Indigenous youth. It may be the case that Indigenous children, more so than their non-Indigenous counterparts, get caught up in the welfare and justice systems earlier and more repeatedly for minor antisocial activity, which gives them a record sheet that prejudices the judiciary towards custodial options as alternatives have failed. Alternatively, as Canadian research findings indicate,[27] it may be that the output of the youth justice system simply reflects the systemic racism channelling more Indigenous children into that system. Again, in both countries, a policy is now emerging of giving tribal authorities more responsibility for developing culturally appropriate, noncustodial options that may more effectively engage Indigenous youth and address recidivism.

The welfare principle in contemporary practice: private family law

Extended family and community networks, a strong characteristic of tribal societies, have traditionally played a significant role in providing support to vulnerable family units and preventing family breakdown. In both the U.S. and Canada, this is less often the case than formerly as the majority of Indigenous families are now living off reservation and in urban settings where they have become more prone than others to unemployment, crime and lifestyle health issues associated with substance abuse, obesity, etc.

Matrimonial

Rates of divorce and separation among AI/AN couples are higher than in the rest of the U.S. population. In Canada, while the respective rates are lower, this may be due to the levels of violence and intimidation endured by Indigenous women.[28] Consequently, the Bill C-78 amendments to the Canadian Divorce Act require the court in divorce proceedings to take into account any family violence, in particular its impact on the welfare of a child, and to ensure protection for the Indigenous women and children involved. While marriage and divorce ceremonies may be conducted in both countries in accordance with customary practice, if they are to be formally recognised in law, they must also meet statutory and regulatory requirements.

27 See, among others, Luo, D., The Overrepresentation of Indigenous Youth in the Criminal Justice System; Exposing a Problematic Reality of Imprisoned Marginalized Groups in Canada, *The Society: Sociology & Criminology Undergraduate Review*, 69–74, https://jps.library.utoronto.ca.

28 See, for example, the report by the Inter-American Commission on Human Rights (IACHR), *Missing and Murdered Indigenous Women in British Columbia, Canada* (2014), www.oas.org/en/iachr/reports/pdfs/indigenous-women-bc-canada-en.pdf.

Custody and guardianship are the main court orders available with respect to Indigenous U.S. and Canadian children who become the subjects of parental divorce proceedings in either tribal or state courts. The grounds for granting these orders and the responsibilities they vest in those to whom they are granted are the same as for non-Indigenous applicants.

Custody

Custody issues in both countries generate the greatest political and legal contention when one of the parents of the child concerned is not a tribal member. Again, in both countries, responsibility for determining custody issues will fall to the tribal courts for couples living on reservation and to state/province courts for those who are not or when the custodial parent is non-Indigenous, though this may be challenged by tribal authorities, who may at least assign a tribal member to assist the court and advise on cultural matters. When the child concerned is defined as Indigenous, then the court will take into account the proposed arrangements to protect their cultural identity as constituting an important aspect of the best interests test.

Guardianship

Most tribes in the U.S. as in Canada have a tribal code in which there will be a provision vesting jurisdiction in the tribal court for all guardianship petitions with respect to a tribal child.

In both countries, a permanent legal guardian has custody and control of a child, which includes powers to make decisions concerning their care, education, discipline and protection. Both birth parents may retain some ongoing rights of contact and access and responsibility for maintenance. This order is intended for use by those relatives who may not wish to see a complete severance of ties between child and family and is particularly appropriate in relation to older children who object to established relationships with parents and siblings being displaced. The courts in both countries are having more frequent recourse to this order in circumstances where previously, an adoption order might have been sought because it is less permanent and absolutist and affords greater scope for preserving an Indigenous child's cultural identity.

Adoption

For Indigenous people, there are three types of adoptions: customary, private and departmental. Although these parallel systems are in place, customary adoption has traditionally dominated and is integral to the family life of all Indigenous communities. Departmental adoption, as the name suggests, is one conducted in accordance with statutory law, in which all stages of the process are subject to regulatory controls and to independent professional assessment and monitoring, and is finalised in a court hearing where the welfare interests of the child will determine whether an adoption order will be made. (See, further, Chapters 4 and 7.)

Customary adoption

This arrangement for the care of a child, made between the birth parent(s) and the adoptive parent(s), who are usually relatives or members of the same community, has long been practised among the Indigenous people in the U.S., Canada, and elsewhere. (See, further, Chapter 8.)

While customary adoptions have gained legal recognition in most states/provinces, they have been known to give rise to difficulties, usually in relation to inheritance claims, particularly where land is involved. From the perspective of the welfare of the child, customary adoption offers complete transparency, not just between the two families but among the tribe as a whole. This reduces the probability of identity issues for the adopted child, and it also means that if welfare issues become apparent, support from tribal members will be readily available, and the adoption can be terminated promptly if necessary.

Private adoption

This form of adoption, common to the tribal communities of both countries, usually refers to the personal and direct placing of a child for adoption by their parents, most usually the mother. It can also refer to the involvement of private or commercial agencies, a particular characteristic of the U.S. adoption process, in arranging adoption placements. Either way, the placement is authorised by the birth parent(s). The profit motive associated with private adoptions can add to the contention when the adoption being arranged is that of an Indigenous child by a non-Indigenous couple. As with many other home-grown entrepreneurial enterprises, there are adoption agencies that pursue profit-making opportunities domestically and/or internationally: opportunities driven by the needs of prospective adopters and birth parents.

WELFARE INTERESTS

From a Western professional perspective, both customary and private adoptions can be problematic.

Customary adoption is viewed and treated as essentially a family or tribal affair; the best interests of the child concerned fall to be determined entirely by the parties, with or without advice from tribal representatives. It does not provide for any objective professional assessment or guidance, does not require any form of 'home-study report,' and is not conditional on prior judicial scrutiny or on the issuing of a court order, and there is no requirement that either the commissioner or the registrar be satisfied before officially recognising or registering an adoption – respectively – as to its merits in terms of satisfying the welfare test. Moreover, the time lapse between placement of the child and registration of his or her adoption can take up to six years, which can leave a child in limbo in terms of official identity papers and determining who is legally responsible as the child's legal guardian.[29]

29 Source: Peter Dudding, Director, Nunavut Department of Family Services (2014). See, further, www.nunatsiaqonline.ca/stories/article/65674inuit_orgs_renew_discussion_on_custom_adoption.

Private adoption in practice takes the form of either a direct placement made by a birth mother – perhaps acting through an intermediary such as a priest or doctor – or an indirect placement with parental authority but placement made by an adoption agency. The first is problematic from the welfare of the child perspective as there is no professional involvement: no eligibility or suitability criteria applied to assess the parties and the appropriateness of the placement; no follow-up assessment to determine whether the placement has proven satisfactory or support services are required; and no guarantee of future disclosure to the adoptee of origins information. The second is also problematic from the same perspective as it raises questions as to whether a placement is really serving the best interests of the child or the needs of birth parent(s) and the prospective adopters. The possibility of a profit motive being a factor in agency placement choice also gives rise to concerns.

The welfare principle in contemporary practice: public/private family law

In Indigenous tribal communities, the public/private distinction, so well guarded and endlessly contentious in modern Westernised society, is a good deal less important. Customary adoption, for example, has never been regarded as a secretive, preciously private matter with associated anonymity and taboos for the parties involved but has been more of a transparent and open negotiation shared with the community. This is also the case with most family rites of passage: birth, marriage, divorce, illness, death – they are all occasions for sharing, for the collective involvement of the tribe in ceremonial processes.

Public service matters

The welfare interests of Indigenous children are naturally closely linked to the well-being of their parents and communities. Given that the latter have long experienced systemic and persistent levels of poverty, it is to be expected that this would be reflected in more Indigenous than non-Indigenous children falling through the statutory welfare threshold. The gross overrepresentation of Indigenous children in the national child welfare and youth justice systems of both countries testifies to the disproportionate burden of poverty borne by their families.[30] It might have been anticipated that this would have attracted benign state intervention, providing public services to ameliorate the effects of poverty, targeted towards the Indigenous communities and proportionately greater than elsewhere. In fact, there has been a history of abusive state intervention, making a bad situation worse, replaced in more recent times by an inequitable distribution of government funding in both

30 In relation to the different circumstances of Indigenous and non-Indigenous children, Lori Chambers comments, 'We really have apartheid in regard to the well-being of children' (note to author, 16 August 2022).

countries, disadvantaging Indigenous communities, which has added to the latter's mistrust of state intervention.

Similar evidence of failure to benefit from public service provision and of inadequate or inappropriate delivery of services can be found in the relevant statistics for education (school attendance, early leaving, qualifications obtained, etc) and health (infant mortality rates, dental hygiene, incidences of childhood diseases, etc) in both countries.

Legal proceedings

Needless to say, statutory legal proceedings apply equally to Indigenous and non-Indigenous sectors of the population. For both sectors in both countries, the public/private intersect is most noticeable in proceedings for adoption, custody, access, guardianship and wardship, together with ancillary proceedings for restraining orders and maintenance.

ADOPTION FROM PUBLIC CARE OR 'DEPARTMENTAL ADOPTION'

Departmental adoptions occur either on a consensual basis, following voluntary parental relinquishment, or on a compulsory basis, following permanent care and custody of the child being vested in the director of social services. In both countries, as in all modern developed Western societies, the former and most traditional form of adoption, whereby the state as 'carer of last resort' receives a child from the parent(s) who are unable or unwilling to undertake care responsibility and places them into the custody of approved prospective adopters, is in steep decline. The latter form of departmental adoption – involving a child compulsorily removed from abusive or neglectful parents and judicially 'freed' for adoption – is increasing in a number of countries, including the U.S. and Canada, accompanied by a financial incentive for those adopters prepared to facilitate the state policy of transferring care responsibility from the public to the private sector.

A common jurisdictional feature of departmental adoption in both countries is the number of adoption applications made by non-Indigenous foster parents with respect to Indigenous children – the subject of statutory care orders – for whom they have had exclusive care responsibility for several years and with whom strong bonds of mutual attachment have developed. In both countries, there are political and legal constraints against such adoptions, but in both, they still occur, despite considerable contention regarding whether they are in the long-term best interests of the children concerned.

Cultural identity and welfare In the U.S. and Canada, any adoption in which non-Indigenous applicants propose to adopt an Indigenous child, satisfying the 'best interests of the child' test requires that consideration be given to the cultural identity and heritage of the child; their cultural, racial and religious background must be taken into account. Having taken these into account, whether a holistic view of the welfare interests of the child indicates that all other welfare-related factors outweigh culture-specific factors and justify an adoption must, most probably, turn on the facts presented in each individual case, like all other decisions taken to protect and promote the welfare interests of a child. There can be little room in such decisions for ideology, stereotyping or discrimination.

WARDSHIP

In the concept, jurisdiction, and evolution of wardship can, perhaps, be seen the foundations of the law relating to the welfare of children in both the U.S. and Canada as in many other common-law countries. This would seem to hold true for private family law, the civil and criminal sectors of public family law, the growing range of public/private intersects. Despite many legislative attempts to rein in the ambit of wardship and restrict the opportunities to access it, the judiciary have always found ways of bringing it back into play. It has proven to be an indispensable default mechanism for dealing with complex child-care issues and a useful platform for teasing out principles and assigning responsibilities. There is every indication that wardship will continue to play a significant role in the future of family law, providing a bridge between the public and private sectors.

Conclusion

This chapter conducted a comparative jurisdictional analysis of the law relating to children and the role of the welfare principle in that law, as currently applied in the U.S. and in Canada. In both countries, the application of the law is structured to resemble something approaching a dual system – state/province and tribal – with an additional federal layer; therefore, the analysis followed that structure by dealing separately with the law as it relates to the welfare of non-Indigenous and then Indigenous children.

As regards jurisdictional differences in the law relating to the welfare of non-Indigenous Canadian and U.S. children, perhaps the most distinctive difference lies in the number of children in the care of the state – either in foster care or in a custodial facility. The statistical data – the national lack of which is another Canadian characteristic – shows that the flow of Canadian children into the child welfare or justice systems is much greater than in the U.S. and, indeed, is greater than in most other developed nations. An argument could perhaps be made that, given those statistics along with other indicators such as the absence of 'safe havens,' the proportion of Crown wards remaining unadopted, the numbers of child offenders transferred to the adult justice system, and the history of poor levels of federal funding for preventative services, there are systemic flaws in the ability of the Canadian state – at federal and provincial levels – to coordinate adequate provision so as to protect and promote the welfare of the more vulnerable members of its child population. It could also perhaps be argued in this context that another singular jurisdictional characteristic is the state's privatisation of child services in the U.S. From adoption to custodial facilities, a large proportion of such services have, in effect, been outsourced from the public to the private sector. In the latter instance, some of those services are delivered on a for-profit basis, which can undermine a clear focus on the welfare interests of a child.

However, what the two countries have most in common is their poor regard for the welfare of their Indigenous children, the scale of which is greatest in Canada. While the overrepresentation of Indigenous children in the welfare and justice systems has been a common jurisdictional characteristic for some time, it would seem to be worse in Canada. When this is coupled with the record of Indigenous girls missing presumed murdered[31] and the reports, largely anecdotal, of child trafficking among the Inuit of Nunavut, taken together with the international concern expressed about the levels of poverty, there is good reason to consider that the Canadian state is failing in its duty of care towards Indigenous children.

31 See Reclaiming Power and Place: Report of the National Inquiry into Missing and Murdered Indigenous Women and Girls, Canada, 2019, www.loc.gov/item/lcwaN0028038/.

Conclusion

In both the U.S. and Canada, the law applies the principle of the welfare of the child very unevenly in relation to the interests of Indigenous and non-Indigenous children. It is also uneven in a broader sense due to the federal nature of both countries which, very largely, leaves child welfare law to be determined at the state/province level, leading to considerable regional differences in judicial and legislative interpretation. Moreover, the situation is further complicated by poverty: the Indigenous communities are disproportionately affected by poverty, and the evidence indicates a direct correlation between that and the overrepresentation of their children in the child welfare and juvenile justice systems.

The United Nations Convention on the Rights of the Child 1989 (U.N. CROC)

This Convention, signed by both the U.S. and Canada, together with some 194 other nations, is the most relevant, well known, and far reaching of all international treaties.[1] While it has no designated enforcement mechanism, the Convention is represented by the Committee on the Rights of the Child (CRC), which makes recommendations to member states on the basis of reports filed with it under Article 44 for improvements in national law and practice. The Convention declares 42 substantive rights held to be vested in children, and it binds judicial and regulatory bodies to ensure that any decisions they take on matters affecting the upbringing of a child are Convention compliant. However, only those nations that have both signed and ratified the Convention are so bound. The U.S. alone among all the member countries of the United Nations has failed to ratify and is thus not bound by it. Nonetheless, the U.S. is required not to act in a manner at variance with the Convention's purpose. (See, further, Chapter 2.)

It would seem appropriate, as with the previous book, to apply Convention provisions as a convenient audit mechanism for conducting a comparative analysis of the law currently governing the welfare/rights of a child in the U.S. and Canada.

1 Three optional protocols have since been added: Protocol to Prevent, Suppress and Punish Trafficking in Persons, Especially Women and Children; Protocol Against the Smuggling of Migrants by Land, Sea and Air; and Protocol Against the Illicit Manufacturing of and Trafficking in Firearms.

DOI: 10.4324/9781003269564-16

Article 2 – Non-discrimination principle

This directs that all Convention rights apply to children without exception and without discrimination of any kind. Article 2(2) requires that all appropriate measures be taken to ensure that the child is protected against all forms of discrimination or punishment on the basis of the status, activities, expressed opinions or beliefs of the child's parents, legal guardians or family members.

However, if there is one unmistakable finding to emerge from this study, it is that the Indigenous children in both countries are grossly overrepresented in the child welfare and juvenile justice systems. There is a strong likelihood that this is due to systemic discriminatory attitudes towards these children, perhaps a carry-over from an earlier era when institutionalised discrimination resulted in the 'residential homes' and 'enforced adoption' programmes.

State-funded denominational schooling has also provided a context for alleged discrimination in both countries and so must, to some degree, adversely affect the welfare interests of the children concerned. There have been many 'school prayer' cases in both countries, with the courts ruling that mandatory Christian prayers are discriminatory to non-Christian pupils, while the U.N. CRC has expressed concern regarding discriminatory state funding for some Canadian schools.[2]

Article 3 – Best interest of the child is a primary consideration

Article 3 states the most important principle in the Convention. It requires that 'in all actions concerning children, whether undertaken by public or private social welfare institutions, courts of law, administrative authorities or legislative bodies, the best interests of the child shall be the primary consideration,' thereby conferring on a child the right to have their welfare interests so treated across a range of fora. Additionally, the subsequent articles establish the particular rights held to be vested in a child.

In both countries, the record of prolonged, historical, state-mandated child abuse against Indigenous children has caused intergenerational trauma and testifies to the extent to which the state has been in breach of this fundamental U.N. CROC principle. Consequently, the Indigenous communities have become so marginalised and mistrustful of state intervention that service provision initiatives intended to benefit the welfare of their children have had little traction.

PROTECTION

The protective function establishes a baseline for state responsibility in relation to the best interests of a child, but in neither country is it given a paramount weighting. There is an interesting contrast between the protection provisions in the U.S.

2 See U.N. International Covenant on Civil and Political Rights, 'Concluding Observations on the Sixth Periodic Report of Canada,' http://tbinternet.ohchr.org/_layouts/treaty bodyexternal/SessionDetails1.aspx?SessionID=899&Lang=en#sthash.XzzyC1Bz.dpuf.

Family First 2018 legislation and in Ontario's Child, Youth and Family Services Act 2017. The former emphasises family unity and is focused on service provision to that end; the latter would seem to be concerned with disaggregating a child's welfare from collective family interests in addressing the intervention specifically towards the child and in engaging them in determining what form of protection should be provided. At face value, the latter would appear to be much more mindful of rights vested in the child, whereas the former adopts a traditional family support approach.

FACILITIES

Article 3(3) requires state parties to ensure that 'the institutions, services and facilities responsible for the care or protection of children shall conform with the standards established by competent authorities.'

In both countries, the lack of sufficient Indigenous foster parents and adopters is a serious deficit in state capacity to appropriately meet the welfare needs of children for whom it undertakes care responsibility. In Canada, recent research findings have established that the Indigenous communities have for many years been receiving an inequitable share of state funding for protective services. The availability of adoption for children in the public care system is wholly inadequate in both countries, resulting in many children whose parental rights have been removed being consigned to 'legal limbo' and being left to age out of the care system.

Of particular concern is the practice in both jurisdictions of sentencing and incarcerating some juvenile offenders as though they are adults. This must constitute a basic breach of children's welfare/rights and a misuse of facilities.

Articles 7 and 8 – Right of the child to know their identity

Article 7 recognises the right of a child to information relating to their parents as the means of establishing their own identity. In relation to adopted children, this is a powerful legal acknowledgement that they have a right of access to information in the form of agency records, etc that could potentially contribute to consolidating their sense of identity. For many adoptees in the U.S., however, this right is unavailable due to a birth parent's right to veto any disclosure of identifying information. The continuing agency practice of respecting the parental right by maintaining 'closed' adoption files clearly violates Article 7. The CRC has expressed its concern that this is also an issue in Canada.[3]

CULTURAL IDENTITY

The right to a cultural identity – also given explicit recognition under Articles 8, 9, and 11 of the ECHR; Article 27 of the ICCPR; and Article 12 of UNDRIP – specifically recognises the right of minorities to maintain their own culture, language and

3 See Committee on the Rights of the Child, Session 34 (2003) and, for example, the Adoption Information Act 1997 (Nova Scotia).

religion. It is reinforced by Article 20(3), which states that 'due regard shall be paid to the desirability of continuity in a child's upbringing and to the child's ethnic, religious, cultural and linguistic background.'

This right lies at the heart of the intergenerational trauma that has afflicted the Indigenous communities in both countries. Epitomised most recently by the '60s scoop' but with origins deep in assimilation policies, the right to a cultural identity that reflects tribal affiliation gives rise to constant issues in the context of contemporary fostering and adoption services and in the placement of Indigenous children. It also, of course, is a right that conflicts with the practice of intercountry adoption, of which the U.S. has long been a leading exponent. Further, the problem also arises in relation to African American and Asian children taken into care in the U.S. for whom adoption is the care plan. Often, suitable U.S. adopters are unavailable, and such children may find themselves placed for adoption in Canada or Europe, which makes retention of their cultural identity or acquiring an enduring substitute problematic.

Article 9 – Right of the child not to be separated from their parents

Article 9 requires state parties to ensure that a child shall not be separated from their parents against their will, except when competent authorities subject to judicial review determine, in accordance with applicable law and procedures, that such separation is necessary for the child's best interests.

In practice, this right is most severely stress tested when the issue arises as to whether rehabilitation with birth parents should be pursued with respect to a child compulsorily admitted to the public child welfare system. Under the provisions of U.N. CROC, the authorities are required, from point of admission, to work towards returning a child to their family of origin, but for reasons such as lack of resources, hostile birth parents, the distances involved, and a 'play safe' strategy where there are child protection risk factors, it may be that steps towards rehabilitation are not immediately taken. Alternatively, from point of admission, it may be decided to place the child in a concurrent placement. In either case, the passing of time works in favour of the day-to-day carers and against the birth parents. Rehabilitation programmes are resource intensive, often requiring residential placement for parent and child in an intensive assessment/training facility and/or day centre programmes; these are not always available when needed and are more readily availed of in urban environments. Nor can the stability of an initial foster placement be guaranteed. Disruption and drift in care can easily become the default reality.

Nonconsensual adoption is the ultimate derogation from the Article 9 principle.

CONTACT

Article 9(3) requires states parties to 'respect the right of the child who is separated from one or both parents to maintain personal relations and direct contact with both parents.'

While contact arrangements are relatively easily organised when birth parents and foster carers are living in the same urban area, it can be problematic when they're not, which is often the case in Alaska and northern Canada and very likely when the child is Indigenous as there is such a shortage of appropriate foster parents. Traditionally, contact and adoption have been viewed as mutually exclusive, but this is generally no longer the case as current child care practice has moved away from the 'clean break' approach that was a characteristic of earlier adoptions and now strongly favours post-adoption contact with any members of the birth family with whom the adoptee has had a meaningful relationship. As most domestic adoptions are now of older children, there is a corresponding stronger likelihood that they will have formed such relationships. It would seem probable that compatibility with Article 9(3) is more likely in the U.S. than in Canada as practice in the latter is less inclined to accommodate 'openness.'[4] However, given that in both countries stepparent adoptions continue to be popular, and kinship adoptions have now become the preferred option for adoptable children in the public child welfare system, there is accordingly a greater probability of an adopted child retaining post-adoption the relationships that were previously important.

Article 12 – Right of the child to express an opinion in administrative and judicial proceedings

This states that a child has the right to express their opinion freely and to have that opinion taken into account in any matter or procedure affecting them. This is subject to the caveat that the child concerned must be capable of forming their own views. Due weight, in accordance with the age and maturity of the child, must be given to those views.

In the U.S., there has been a long-standing attempt to lend judicial authority in support of this right of a child to address the court, directly and in person, on matters of importance during the course of proceedings, but that minority opinion has never been unequivocally endorsed.[5] Similarly, in Canada, the lack of firm judicial recognition of this right has attracted criticism from the U.N. Committee on the Rights of the Child.[6] In practice, it is probable that the courts in both countries would permit a mature adolescent who wished to personally address the court on a matter of importance to their welfare to do so, but this remains more a matter of judicial discretion than a child's exercise of their right. There is, of course, no guarantee that any weight will be given to the views expressed.

REPRESENTATION IN COURT

The only legally effective form of representation in court is representation by a lawyer with relevant expertise. In neither the U.S. nor Canada is this guaranteed.

4 See, *CAS of Toronto v. T.L.*, [2010] O.J. No. 942.

5 *Wisconsin v. Yoder*, 406 U.S. 205, 241–49 (1972), per Douglas J at pp 244–245.

6 See the U.N. Committee on the Rights of the Child, 61st Session, C/CAN/CO/3–4, October 2012, at paras 36 and 37.

Articles 13 and 14 – Right of the child to self-determination, dignity, respect, non-interference and to make informed decisions

The requirement to ensure that a child has the right to make informed decisions is, in both countries, subject to the view of a judge or regulator that any such decision is compatible with what they consider to be in the best interests of that child. There are very few matters in relation to which a child aged 16 or younger can unilaterally give legally binding consent, sexual relations being one.

CONSENT

In the U.S., the age of consent is not federally determined; it varies from state to state from 16 to 18, and it varies again according to whether the issue arises in a civil or criminal jurisdiction. In both countries, the capacity of a child aged less than 18 to give valid consent to sex or to access contraceptives or abortion is determined by a combination of age and maturity; at 16 years of age or older, there is a presumption of capacity.[7] Many states in the U.S. accept as legally valid the consent of an underage child to medical treatment and the right of a mother of any age to place her child for adoption.

In both the U.S. and Canada, the issue of the circumstances and the age at which a child might exercise a 'right' to take a decision affecting their welfare interests is far from clear. (See, further, Chapter 9.)

Articles 18 and 19 – Primary responsibility for the upbringing of a child rests with the parent(s)

In the U.S., unlike the U.K.,[8] there is a presumptive right of a child to be cared for by their birth parents. This right is constitutionally protected and well established.[9] Indeed:

> [S]o long as a parent adequately cares for his or her children (i.e., is fit), there will normally be no reason for the State to inject itself into the private realm of the family to further question the ability of the parent to make the best decisions concerning the rearing of that parent's child.[10]

In Canada, the Divorce Act 1985, as amended in 2019 with effect from 2021, does not concern itself with parental rights but unequivocally makes the best interests of the child the only consideration in determining custody arrangements nationwide and provides a welfare checklist to aid functionality when applying the best interests test.

7 *Carey v. Population Services International*, 431 U.S. 678 (1977).

8 See, *Re W (A Child)*, [2016] EWCA Civ 793.

9 See, for example, *Troxel v. Granville*, 530 U.S. 57 (2000).

10 Ibid, at pp 68–69.

Article 18 requires state parties to render appropriate assistance to parents and legal guardians to facilitate the upbringing and development of their children. It is reinforced by Article 18(2), which requires the development of appropriate services for the care of children, and by Article 19(2), which adds that such services should include 'effective procedures for the establishment of social programmes to provide necessary support for the child and for those who have the care of the child.' Clearly the Canadian authorities have for some years been in breach of Articles 18 and 19 as regards providing funds and support for Indigenous children.[11] In the U.S., the family support initiatives taken by the Trump administration, on the other hand, would seem to be very much in keeping with the Convention articles.

Article 21 – Adoption shall ensure that the best interests of the child shall be the paramount consideration

While all provincial adoption legislation in Canada makes the granting of an adoption order conditional on this being compatible with the welfare principle, none specify that the principle must be the paramount concern. Similarly, in the U.S. where every state has its own adoption legislation but none make an adoption order conditional, as in the U.K., on satisfying a 'paramountcy of welfare' test applicable on a projected lifetime basis, although the welfare checklist approach is increasingly becoming a feature of adoption law in the U.S. The fact that a large proportion of all adoptions in both countries are made privately – either by direct parental placement or through an intermediary person or agency acting on behalf of a parent – in itself precludes the possibility of the objective professional analysis necessary to achieve an adoption that satisfies the paramountcy test.

Article 25 – Placements must be subject to periodic review

This article requires periodic review of placements of all types, including foster care and residential units, to ensure that no child in state care is overlooked.

It can be safely assumed that all states/provinces have regulatory requirements providing for periodic reviews of foster care, residential care and adoption placements made from the public child welfare system. It is considerably less certain that ongoing reviews would be conducted with respect to private adoption placements, though an initial check would be made on notification of such a placement. Ongoing periodic reviews are a requirement of many intercountry adoption placements, but the failure to meet this requirement has long been a cause of complaint from authorities in placing countries, particularly from Russian, as evidenced in the case of A.*H. and Others v. Russia*:[12]

> [A]ccording to information from the Ministry of Education and Science, over the course of the past three years adoptive parents from the United States had

11 See *Canada (Human Rights Commission) v. Canada (Attorney General)*, 2012 FC 445.
12 Application Nos. 6033/13, 8927/13, 10549/13 and others, (2017), at para 394.

failed to provide reports about the wellbeing of 653 children adopted from Russia in 1,136 instances.

Given the number of disrupted intercountry adoptions and the suffering of the children involved, there can be little doubt that domestic state-authorised periodic reviews are necessary, perhaps particularly, in 'private' adoptions.

Article 27 – Every child is entitled to a reasonable standard of living

States are required to recognise the right of every child to a standard of living adequate for that child's physical, mental, spiritual, moral and social development.

In the U.S., the numbers in need of welfare programmes – including Supplemental Nutrition Assistance Programs or 'food stamps,' Temporary Assistance for Needy Families, and housing assistance – are rising. An estimated 46 million Americans now live below the poverty line, millions of whom are not covered by any of the welfare programmes, with over 9 million children enrolled in programmes for health care benefits. Moreover, government expenditure on welfare programmes is down from 10% of the federal budget to half that in 2018. The Urban Institute estimates that currently, 24 million children use welfare every month, and at 41%, they constitute the biggest percentage of all welfare beneficiaries.

The corresponding situation in Canada is much the same. It has recently been argued that:[13]

> Child poverty in Canada still remains a 'national disgrace.' Recent data show that 1 in 5 children live in poverty. For Indigenous children, the rate is 1 in 2. Children with disabilities are twice as likely to live in households relying on public assistance. 1 in 5 racialized families live in poverty, compared to 1 in 20 non-racialized families. While there have been significant increases in funding for children, such as the Canada Child Benefit, the outcomes for children, as measured by UNICEF indicators of child well-being, have not improved substantively.

The fact that two of the leading developed democratic nations continue to have serious, apparently systemic problems of child poverty, closely linked to high rates of children admitted to child welfare and youth justice systems, is clearly profoundly troubling.

Articles 30 and 31 – Right of a child from a minority group to practise their culture

Following lengthy and exhaustive official enquiries into historical state-sanctioned abusive residential school and enforced adoption policies, which in both countries sought to eradicate Indigenous culture, there is now a shared awareness of the need

13 See Press Release: Canadian Coalition for the Rights of Children, et al. (16 May 2022), https://rightsofchildren.ca/childrens-rights-in-canada/press-release-on-the-eve-of-canadas-appearance-at-the-un-crc/.

to demonstrate respect for cultural identity. Accordingly, they both have in place federal legislation requiring engagement with tribal authorities on matters impacting Indigenous children and their culture. This has led to the present situation, in which there are often parallel social service programmes in states and provinces to ensure a separate and culturally appropriate form of service delivery for Indigenous children. In practice, this has meant recruiting Indigenous foster carers, prospective adopters, teachers, nurses, midwives, etc, though there continues to be a significant shortfall of such culturally appropriate service providers.

Much the same problem exists in relation to the children of other minority groups, particularly African Americans in the U.S.

Article 35 – Prevention of trafficking in children

This would seem to be a significant and worsening issue in the U.S. The National Human Trafficking Hotline statistics show a 25% jump in human trafficking cases from 2017 to 2018. This includes sex and labour trafficking. Of the more than 23,500 runaways reported to the National Center for Missing and Exploited Children[14] in 2018, 1 in 7 were likely victims of child sex trafficking. Moreover, in addition to domestic trafficking, the constant flow of migrants crossing into the U.S. from Mexico includes many unaccompanied minors, some of whom will also be trafficked.

The Trafficking in persons in Canada report for 2020[15] reveals 2,977 reported incidents of trafficking between 2010 and 2020: the vast majority – 96% – being women and girls, of whom one in four were children. As in the U.S., this form of criminal activity is on the increase in Canada.[16]

The fact that the statistics in both countries show a worsening trend can only mean that both are in breach of Article 35.

Article 37 – No child to be subject to degrading treatment or punishment

The use of reasonable force by parents to chastise their child is permissible in Canada under the Criminal Code, s 43 and in the U.S. under the Child Abuse Prevention and Treatment Act 2003 as it is not, in legal terms, defined as degrading treatment or punishment.[17] While there may be some debate as to whether such chastisement can be so construed, and in many other developed nations, it has long since ceased to be debatable, there can be no doubt that the practice in the U.S. of shackling youths when they appear in open court is degrading, is intended to be

14 See, further, www.reunite.org/?links=national-centre-for-missing-and-exploited-children-ncmec.

15 See, further, https://www150.statcan.gc.ca/n1/pub/85–002-x/2022001/article/00010-eng.htm.

16 See, for example, Cotter, A., Trafficking in persons in Canada, 2018, *Juristat,* Statistics Canada Catalogue no. 85–002-X (2020).

17 *Canadian Foundation for Children, Youth and the Law v. Canada (Attorney General)*, [2004] 1 SCR 76, 2004 SCC 4.

so, and is not convention compliant. Similarly, the use of solitary confinement with respect to youths in U.S. and Canadian prisons is open to the same criticism.

Article 40 – Every alleged child offender to be justly treated

There are several different aspects to this principle.

Firstly, just treatment or due process requires legal representation, which necessitates legal aid and assistance for those who cannot otherwise afford the costs involved. In the U.S., although a juvenile accused of an offence has a constitutional right to be advised and represented by an attorney,[18] there is no guarantee that this will happen. In Canada, the Department of Justice, through its legal aid programme, provides funding to the provinces for the delivery of criminal legal aid services to young persons facing criminal proceedings. In practice, most youths charged with an indictable offence will qualify for the legal aid necessary for attorney representation, but most facing a possible summary conviction will not. Consequently, neither country wholly satisfies the Article 40 requirement.

Secondly, and again in both countries, the age of criminal responsibility is set too low to ensure just treatment.

Thirdly, the practice in both countries of transferring some juveniles to be tried in adult courts is clearly not convention compliant, nor, of course, is the U.S. practice of allowing the death sentence to be carried out with respect to offenders who were children when their crime was committed.

Finally, if the welfare interests of children are to be respected, then the court needs to have a menu of different orders to choose from so as to ensure an appropriate match between the disposal option, the needs of a particular child, and the gravity of the offence. While the Canadian youth justice system goes some way towards meeting this requirement, the very limited disposal options available to the U.S. judiciary leaves the system non–convention compliant.

18 *In re Gault*, 387 U.S. 1 (1967).

Selected Bibliography

Books

Adams, D.W., *Education for Extinction: American Indians and the Boarding School Experience, 1875–1928*, University of Kansas, (1995), (reprinted 1997).

Asmi, S., *Indigenous Youth Restorative Justice: Addressing Over Representation in the Canadian Criminal Justice System*, Samuel Centre for Social Connectedness, (2019).

Bainham, A. (ed.), *The International Survey of Family Law* (2000 ed.), Family Law, (2000).

Bala, N., and Ashbourne, C., The widening concept of parent in Canada: Step-parents, same-sex partners, & parents by ART. *American University Journal of Social Policy & the Law*. (2012): 20(3), 525–560.

Bean, P., and Melville, J., *Lost Children of the Empire*, Unwin Hyman, (1989).

Berg, J., et al., *Informed Consent: Legal Theory and Clinical Practice* (2nd ed.), Oxford University Press, (2001).

Berry, M.E., *The Settlement Movement: 1886–1986*, United Neighborhood Centers of America, (1986).

Bremner, R., *Children and Youth in America: A Documentary History*, Harvard University Press, (1970).

Brookfield, T., *History of Adoption and Fostering in Canada*, Oxford University Press, (2015).

Cahill, B.L., *The Butterbox Babies*, Fernwood Publishing Co Ltd, (2007).

Chambers, L., *A Legal History of Adoption in Ontario, 1921–2015*, University of Toronto Press/Osgoode Society Press, (2016).

Cobo, M., Study of the Problem of Discrimination against Indigenous Populations, *UN Doc*. E/CN.4/Sub.2/1986/7, pp. 379–382.

Crosson-Tower, C., *Exploring Child Welfare: A Practice Perspective* (2nd ed.), Allyn & Bacon, (2000).

Fallon, B., Lefebvre, R., Trocmé, N., et al., Denouncing the Continued Over Representation of First Nations Children in Canadian Child Welfare, (2019). https://cwrp.ca/sites/default/files/publications/FNCIS-2019%20-%20Denouncing%20the%20Continued%20Overrepresentation%20of%20First%20Nations%20Children%20in%20Canadian%20Child%20Welfare%20-%20Final_1%20%282%29.pdf.

Fanshel, D., *Far From the Reservation: The Transracial Adoption of American Indian Children*, The Scarecrow Press, (1972).

Fass, P., *Kidnapped: A History of Child Abduction in the United States*, Oxford University Press, (1997).

Faulkner, N., Parental Child Abduction is Child Abuse, (1999). www.prevent-abuse-now.com/unreport.htm.

Finley, L., *Juvenile Justice*, Greenwood Press, (2007).

Fortin, J., *Children's Rights and the Developing Law* (2nd ed.), LexisNexis, (2003).

Gerber, P., and O'Byrne, K. (eds.), *Surrogacy, Law and Human Rights*, Routledge, London and New York, (2016).

Gibbons, J., and Rotabi, K. (eds.), *Intercountry Adoption: Policies, Practices, and Outcomes*, Ashgate, (2012).

Hogg, P.W., *Constitutional Law of Canada* (5th ed.), Thomson Carswell, (2007).

Jones, M.B., *Decline of the American Orphanage 1941–1980*, The University of Chicago Press, (1993).

Joyce, K., *The Child Catchers: Rescue, Trafficking, and the New Gospel of Adoption*, Public Affairs, (2013).

Katz, S.N., McGrath, M., and Howe, R.-A., *Child Neglect Laws in America*, American Bar Association, (1975).

Keefe, P.R., *Empire of Pain*, Picador, (2021).

Kohli, M.P., *The Golden Bridge: Young Immigrants to Canada, 1833–1939*, Natural Heritage Press, (2003).

Miller, J.R., *Shingwauk's Vision: A History of Native Residential Schools*, University of Toronto Press, (1996).

Morris, A., and Giller, H., *Understanding Juvenile Justice*, Croom Helm, (1987).

Myers, J., A short history of child protection in America. *Family Law Quarterly*. (2008): 42(3), pp. 449–463. JSTOR.

Myers, J.E.B., *Child Protection in America: Past, Present and Future*, Oxford University Press, (2006).

Ned, J.D., and Frost, C.J. (eds.), *Contemporary Issues in Child Welfare: American Indian and Canadian Aboriginal Contexts*, JC Charlton Publishing Ltd, (2017).

O'Halloran, K., *The Politics of Adoption* (4th ed.), Springer, (2021).

O'Halloran, K., *The Principle of the Welfare of the Child: A History*, Routledge, (2022).

O'Halloran, K., *The Welfare of the Child: The Principle and the Law*, Arena/Ashgate Publications, (1999).

Parker, R., *Uprooted: The Shipment of Poor Children to Canada, 1867–1919*, The Policy Press, (2008).

Shackleton, M., (ed.), *International Adoption in North American Literature and Culture: Transnational, Transracial, and Transcultural Narratives*, Palgrave Macmillan, (2017).

Smelser, N.J., and Baltes, P.B. (eds.), *International Encyclopedia of the Social and Behavioural Sciences*, Elsevier, (2001).

Sneiderman, B., Irvine, J.C., and Osborne, P.H., *Canadian Medical Law*, Carswell, (2003).

Snow, D., *Assisted Reproduction Policy in Canada: Framing, Federalism and Failure*, University of Toronto Press, (2018).

Sobol, M., and Daly, K., Adoption practice in Canada. *Child Welfare*. (1995): 74(3), pp. 655–677. JSTOR.

Starkey, K.K., and Bunch, L.N., *Health Insurance Coverage in the United States 2020*. www.census.gov/library/publications/2021/demo/p60-274.html.

Tizard, B., *Adoption: A Second Chance*, Open Books, (1977).

Woolford, A., *Colonial Genocide in Indigenous North America*, 1971, Duke University Press, (2014).

Wray, M., and Sinha, V., Foster Care Disparity for Aboriginal Children in 2011, *Centre for Research on Children and Families*, (2015). cwrp.ca/sites/default/files/publications/en/165e.pdf.

Ziblatt, D., *Structuring the State: The Formation of Italy and Germany and the Puzzle of Federalism*, Princeton University Press, (2006).

Zill, N., *Adoption from Foster Care: Aiding Children While Saving Public Money*, The Brookings Institute, May (2011). https://www.brookings.edu/research/adoption-from-foster-care-aiding-children-while-saving-public-money/.

Zimring, F.E., and Tanenhaus, D.S., *Choosing the Future for American Juvenile Justice*, University Press, (2014).

Reports

Aboriginal Justice Implementation Commission, *Report of the Aboriginal Justice Inquiry of Manitoba*, (1999). http://www.ajic.mb.ca/volume.html.

Adams et al., *Tribal Youth in the Federal Justice System*, The Urban Institute, (2011).

Alberta's Ombudsman's 2021 report Youth in Segregation'. www.ombudsman.ab.ca/wp-content/uploads/2021/03/Alberta-Ombudsman-Youth-in-Segregation-Own-Motion_FINAL.docx.pdf.

American Academy of Child and Adolescent Psychiatry (AACAP) (Juvenile Justice Reform Committee, *Solitary Confinement of Juvenile Offender*, April 2012). https://www.aacap.org/aacap/Policy_Statements/2012/Solitary_Confinement_of_Juvenile_Offenders.aspx.

American Community Survey, 2014 data. www.washingtonpost.com/news/wonk/wp/2016/04/06/who-gets-divorced-in-america-in-7-charts/.

Canada, Report of the Prime Minister's Youth Counsel, (2019). https://publications.gc.ca/site/eng/9.865447/publication.html?wbdisable=true.

Canadian Bar Association (Child and Youth Law section) Alternative Report to the UN Committee on the Rights of the Child, (2020). https://www.cba.org/CMSPages/GetFile.aspx?guid=fdb96dc7-35e0-4b6d-8918-40ba6607582a.

Canadian Conference of Catholic Bishops, Ad Hoc Committee on Child Sexual Abuse, *From Pain to Hope*, see further. www.cccb.ca/wp-content/uploads/2017/11/From_Pain_To_Hope.pdf.

Canadian Council of Provincial and Child Advocates, Aboriginal Children and Youth in Canada: Canada Must Do Better'. www.cccya.ca/images/english/pdf/aboriginal_children_youth_advocates_position_paper_2010.pdf.

Canadian Encyclopedia. www.thecanadianencyclopedia.ca/en/article/child-welfare.

Chandra, A., Abma, J., Maza, P., and Bachrach, C., Adoption, Adoption Seeking, and Relinquishment for Adoption in the United States, *National Centre for Health Statistics* (Advance Data No. 306), (1999), pp. 1–16.

Child Welfare Information Gateway, *Adoption Assistance for Children Adopted from Foster Care*, Children's Bureau: Child Welfare Information Gateway, (2020). https://www.childwelfare.gov/pubs/f-subsid/.

Child Welfare Information Gateway, *Finding and Using Postadoption Services, Department of Health and Human Services*, Children's Bureau, (2012).

Child Welfare Information Gateway: How Many Children Were Adopted in 2000 and 2001?' www.childwelfare.gov/pubs/s_adopted/s_adopteda.cfm.

Child Welfare Information Gateway, Partnering With Relatives to Promote Reunification, (2020). www.childwelfare.gov/pubs/factsheets-families-partner-relatives/.

Children in Limbo Task Force, *Permanency Planning in the Child Welfare System*, Sparrow Lake Alliance, (2002).

Coalition for Juvenile Justice, *American Indian/Alaskan Native Youth & Status Offense Disparities: A Call for Tribal Initiatives, Coordination and Federal Funding*. www.juvjustice.org/sites/default/files/resource-files/SOS%20Tribal%20Brief%20FINAL.pdf.

Cobo, M., Study of the Problem of Discrimination Against Indigenous Populations, *UN Doc. E/CN.4/Sub.2/1986/7*. https://digitallibrary.un.org/record/133666?ln=en.

Committee on the Rights of the Child, Concluding observations on the combined third and fourth periodic report of Canada, adopted by the Committee at its 61st session (17 September–5 October 2012). http://docstore.ohchr.org/SelfServices/FilesHandler.ashx?enc=6QkG1d%2FPPRiCAqhKb7yhsh8%2FU426pHwccUxzN5kmnhLtdnrWm1hJzGwfirOtSF7im%2Btj4%2BJ5n5CPlpIDWXA35DpHXskxTdDvCoa0RW9yOJTACORyOJ17Auf%2Bpplgz6CB.

Committee on the Rights of the Child, General Comment No. 10, Children's rights in juvenile justice, *CRC/C/GC/10*, (2007). https://www.refworld.org/docid/4670fca12.html.

Department of Health and Human Services (HHS), *Adoption 2002: The President's Initiative on Adoption and Foster Care; Guidelines for Public Policy and State Legislation Governing Permanence for Children*, (1999). https://www.worldcat.org/title/adoption-2002-the-presidents-initiative-on-adoption-and-foster-care-guidelines-for-public-policy-and-state-legislation-governing-permanence-for-children/oclc/47975299.

Department of Health and Human Services (HHS), Final Rule, *Nondiscrimination in Health Programs and Activities*. www.hhs.gov/sites/default/files/1557-summary-508.pdf.

Department of Justice, *Concurrent Legal Proceedings in Cases of Family Violence: The Child Protection Perspective*, (2022). https://www.justice.gc.ca/eng/rp-pr/fl-lf/famil/fv-vf/index.html.

Department of Justice, Indigenous Youth Roundtables, www.justice.gc.ca/eng/cj-jp/yj-jj/tools-outils/iyr-trja.html#ftnref1.

Donaldson Adoption Institute, *A Changing World: Shaping Best Practices through Understanding of the New Realities of Intercountry Adoption*, New York, (2013).

Dorgan, et al., Attorney General's Advisory Committee on American Indian and Alaska Native Children Exposed to Violence, *Ending Violence So Children Can Thrive*, (2014). https://www.justice.gov/sites/default/files/defendingchildhood/pages/attachments/2015/03/23/ending_violence_so_children_can_thrive.pdf.

Earle, K.A., Child Abuse and Neglect: An Examination of American Indian Data, (2000). www.nicwa.org/resources/catalog/research/2000/02.Child_Abuse.pdf.

Earle, K.A., and Cross, A., *Child Abuse and Neglect among Indian/Alaska Native Children: An Analysis of Existing Data*, National Indian Child Welfare Association, (2001).

Fallon, B., Van Wert, M., Trocmé, N., MacLaurin, B., Sinha, V., Lefebvre, R., Allan, K., Black, T., Lee, B., Rha, W., Smith, C., and Goel, S., Ontario Incidence Study of Reported Child Abuse and Neglect–2013: Major Findings, (2015). cwrp.ca/sites/default/files/publications/en/ois-2013_final.pdf.

Family Justice Working Group, *Meaningful Change for Family Justice: Beyond Wise Words*, Ottawa, (2013).

Heritage Foundation, The Divorce Rate Is Declining but Still High. www.familyfacts.org/charts/120/the-divorce-rate-is-declining-but-still-high.

Hockenberry, S., and Charles Puzzanchera, C., *Juvenile Court Statistics 2011*, National Center for Juvenile Justice, (2014).

Hollinger, J.H., *Adoption Law and Practice* (vol. 1), Matthew Bender/Lexis-Nexis, (2005).

Human Rights Committee, General Comment 27, Art. 12, UN Doc. CCPR/C/21/Rev.1/Add.9 (1999).

Human Rights Watch, Fields of Peril: Child Labor in U.S. Agriculture' and US: Child Farmworkers Dangerous Lives'. www.hrw.org/news/2010/05/05/us-child-farmworkers-dangerous-lives.

Hurley, M.C., and Wherrett, J., *The Royal Commission on Aboriginal Peoples*, (1999). https://publications.gc.ca/Collection-R/LoPBdP/EB/prb9924-e.htm.

Inter-American Commission on Human Rights, *Children and Adolescents in the United States* Adult Criminal Justice System, (2018).

International Bureau for Children's Rights, Child Trafficking in Canada'. www.ibcr.org/en/projets/la-traite-des-enfants-au-canada-2/.

Jones, A., Sinha, V., and Trocmé, *Children and Youth in Out-of-Home Care in the Canadian Provinces*, Canadian CW Research, (2015).

Jordan's Principle Working Group, Without Denial, Delay, or Disruption: Ensuring First Nation children's Access to Equitable Services through Jordan's Principle, (2015), www.afn.ca/uploads/files/jordans_principle-report.pdf.

Kreider, R.M., *Adopted Children and Stepchildren: 2000'* (U.S. Census Bureau, Census 2000 Special Reports, August 2003). https://www.census.gov/library/publications/2003/dec/censr-6rv.html.

Law Commission of Canada, *Restoring Dignity: Responding to Child Abuse in Canadian Institutions*, (2000). https://publications.gc.ca/site/eng/86523/publication.html.

McDade, K., International Adoption in Canada: Public Policy Issues, *Institute for Research on Public Policy*, April 1991.

Meriam Report, *The Problem of Indian Administration*, (1928). https://narf.org/nill/resources/meriam.html.

National Center for Juvenile Justice, *Juvenile Arrest Rates by Offense, Sex, and Race (1980–2011)*, (February 2014). https://ojjdp.ojp.gov/media/document/22926.

National Council on Crime and Delinquency, *Justice for Some: Differential Treatment of Youth of Color in the Justice System*, (2007). https://www.ojp.gov/ncjrs/virtual-library/abstracts/and-justice-some-differential-treatment-youth-color-justice-system.

National Inquiry into Missing and Murdered Indigenous Women and Girls, (2016). https://www.mmiwg-ffada.ca/final-report/.

New York Advisory Committee to the U.S. Commission on Civil Rights, The Solitary Confinement of Youth in New York: A Civil Rights Violation, (December 2014). https://www1.nyc.gov/assets/boc/downloads/pdf/NYSAC%20to%20U.S.%20Commission%20on%20Civil%20Rights.pdf.

Office of Inspector General (OIG), *Opportunities for Administration for Children and Families to Improve Child Welfare Services and Protections for Native American Children*, (August 1994), OEI-01–93–00110. https://oig.hhs.gov/oei/reports/oei-01-93-00110.pdf.

Office of Juvenile Justice and Delinquency Prevention, US Department of Justice, *Statistical Briefing Book*, (December 2012). https://www.ojjdp.gov/ojstatbb/.

Organisation for Economic Co-operation and Development, *Growing Unequal? Income Distribution and Poverty in OECD Countries*, Paris, (2008).

Pew Center, *On The States, One in 100: Behind Bars in America*, (2008). https://www.pewtrusts.org/en/research-and-analysis/reports/2008/02/28/one-in-100-behind-bars-in-america-2008.

Pew Charitable Trust report, Time for Reform: A Matter of Justice for American Indian and Alaskan Native Children, (2007). www.pewtrusts.org/-/media/legacy/uploadedfiles/wwwpewtrustsorg/reports/foster_care_reform/nicwareportpdf.pdf.

Policy Research Centre, *American Indian and Alaska Native Youth in the Juvenile Justice System: A Guide to the Data* (updated in 2020). www.ncai.org/policy-research-center/research-data/prc-publications/NCAI_Policy_Research_Center_AIAN_Juvenile_Justice_Data_FINAL_1_2020.pdf.

Public Health Agency of Canada, Canadian Incidence Study of Reported Child Abuse and Neglect 2008: Major Findings, Public Health Agency of Canada, (2010).

Rae, L., *Inuit Child Welfare and Family Support: Policies, Programs and Strategies*, The National Aboriginal Health Organisation, Ontario, (2011).

Reclaiming Power and Place: The Final Report of the National Inquiry into Missing and Murdered Indigenous Women and Girls, (2019). www.mmiwg-ffada.ca.

Roos, H., *The Service and Capacity Review for Victims of Sexual Exploitation and Human Trafficking in Nunavut*, Ottawa, (2014).

Royal Commission on Aboriginal Peoples, *Looking Forward, Looking Back*, Ottawa, (1996).

Saskatchewan Child Welfare Review Panel Report, For the Good of our Children and Youth: A New Vision, a New Direction. https://cwrp.ca/sites/default/files/publications/en/SK_ChildWelfareReview_panelreport.pdf.

Saskatchewan Children's Advocate, *A Breach of Trust: An Investigation into Foster Care Overcrowding in the Saskatoon Service Centre*, (2009). https://cwrp.ca/publications/breach-trust-investigation-foster-home-overcrowding-saskatoon-service-centre.

Sedlak, A.J., *Survey of Youth in Residential Placement: Conditions of Confinement*, SYRP Report, Westat, (2016). https://www.ojp.gov/pdffiles1/ojjdp/227729.pdf.

Statistics Canada, *A Fifty Year Look at Divorces in Canada, 1970–2020*, (2022). https://www150.statcan.gc.ca/n1/daily-quotidien/220309/dq220309a-eng.htm.

Statistics Canada, *Adult and Youth Correctional Statistics in Canada, 2016/2017*, www.socialconnectedness.org/wp-content/uploads/2019/10/Indigenous-Youth-Restorative-Justice.pdf.

Statistics Canada report Aboriginal Peoples in Canada: First Nations People, Metis and Inuit, (2016). https://www150.statcan.gc.ca/n1/en/subjects/indigenous_peoples/indigenous_children?

Tatara, T., *Characteristics of Children in Substitute and Adoptive Care: A Statistical Summary of the VCIS National Child-Welfare Database*, American Public Welfare Association, (1993).

Trocmé, N., Fallon, B., MacLaurin, B., Daciuk, J., Felstiner, C., Black, T., Tonmyr, L., Blackstock, C., Barter, K., Turcotte, D., and Cloutier, R., *Canadian Incidence Study of Reported Child Abuse and Neglect – 2003: Major Findings, Minister of Public Works and Government Services*, Canada, (2005). https://cwrp.ca/sites/default/files/publications/cis2003.pdf.

Truth and Reconciliation Commission of Canada, Indigenous and Northern Affairs Canada, (2015). www.rcaanc-cirnac.gc.ca/eng/1450124405592/1529106060525#chp2.

Truth and Reconciliation Commission of Canada, The Missing Children Project'. www.rcaanc-cirnac.gc.ca/eng/1524504992259/1557512149981.

U.N. Committee on the Rights of the Child, (Children's Rights in Juvenile Justice, General Comment No. 10, U.N. Doc. CRC/C/GC/10 (April 25, 2007)) UN Committee on the Rights of the Child, 61st session, C/CAN/CO/3–4, October 2012.

U.N. Dept. of Economic and Social Affairs, *Child Adoption: Trends and Policies*, (2009). https://www.un.org/en/development/desa/population/publications/pdf/policy/child-adoption.pdf.

U.N. Dept. of Economic and Social Affairs, *State of the World's Indigenous Peoples: Indigenous Peoples' Access to Health Services,* (2016). https://www.un.org/development/desa/indigenouspeoples/publications/state-of-the-worlds-indigenous-peoples.html.

U.N. Dept. of Economic and Social Affairs/Population Division, *Child Adoption: Trends and Policies*, (2009). https://www.un.org/development/desa/indigenouspeoples/publications/state-of-the-worlds-indigenous-peoples.html.

UNICEF Child Well-Being Index.

U.S. Census Bureau, Income and Poverty in the United States: 2020'. www.census.gov/library/publications/2021/demo/p60-273.html.

U.S. Conference of Catholic Bishops, *The Nature and Scope of the Problem of Sexual Abuse of Minors by Catholic Priests and Deacons in the United States* (the 'John Jay report'), published by the John Jay College of Criminal Justice, (2004).

U.S. Department of Justice, The Crime of Family Abduction'. www.ojp.gov/pdffiles1/ojjdp/229933.pdf.

U.S. General Accounting Office, Investigations of Allegations Concerning Indian Health Service'. (1976): 4(5), 19–20. https://www.gao.gov/assets/hrd-77-3.pdf.

U.S. General Accounting Office, Report to Congressional Requesters, *Juvenile Justice: Juveniles Processed in Criminal Court and Case Dispositions* 1, (1995). https://www.govinfo.gov/content/pkg/GAOREPORTS-GGD-95-170/html/GAOREPORTS-GGD-95-170.htm.

Washington's Department of Social and Health Services (Office of the Children's Ombudsman) report on the Severe Abuse of Adopted Children, (2012). www.dshs.wa.gov/pdf/ca/SevereAbuseofAdoptedChildrenReport2012.pdf.

Wilkins, R., Berthelot, J.M., and Ng, E., Trends in mortality by neighbourhood income in urban Canada from 1971 to 1996. *Health Reports (Stats Can)*. (2002): 13(Suppl), 1–28.

Youth Justice Committees of Ontario, "Fact Sheets". www.justice.gc.ca/eng/cj-jp/yj-jj/tools-outils/sheets-feuillets/commi-comit.html.

Index

Kolibri 360 GmbH
Ferdinand-Jühlke-Straße 7
99095 Erfurt, Deutschland
produktsicherheit@kolibri360.de